WORKING PAPERS
to accompany

FINANCIAL ACCOUNTING
Tools for Business Decision Making
5th Edition

Paul D. Kimmel PhD, CPA
Associate Professor of Accounting
University of Wisconsin--Milwaukee
Milwaukee, Wisconsin

Jerry J. Weygandt PhD, CPA
Arthur Andersen Alumni Professor of Accounting
University of Wisconsin
Madison, Wisconsin

Donald E. Kieso PhD, CPA
KPMG Peat Marwick Emeritus Professor of Accountancy
Northern Illinols Universily
DeKalb, Illinois

Prepared by
Dick D. Wasson M.B.A., C.P.A.
Southwestern College
San Diego State University
University of Phoenix

WILEY
John Wiley & Sons, Inc.

Cover Photo: National Geographic/Superstock

To order books or for customer service call 1-800-CALL-WILEY (225-5945).

ISBN-13 978-0-470-37975-2

Printed in the United States of America

10 9 8 7 6 5 4 3 2 1

Printed and bound by Courier Kendallville, Inc.

CONTENTS

BE1-5

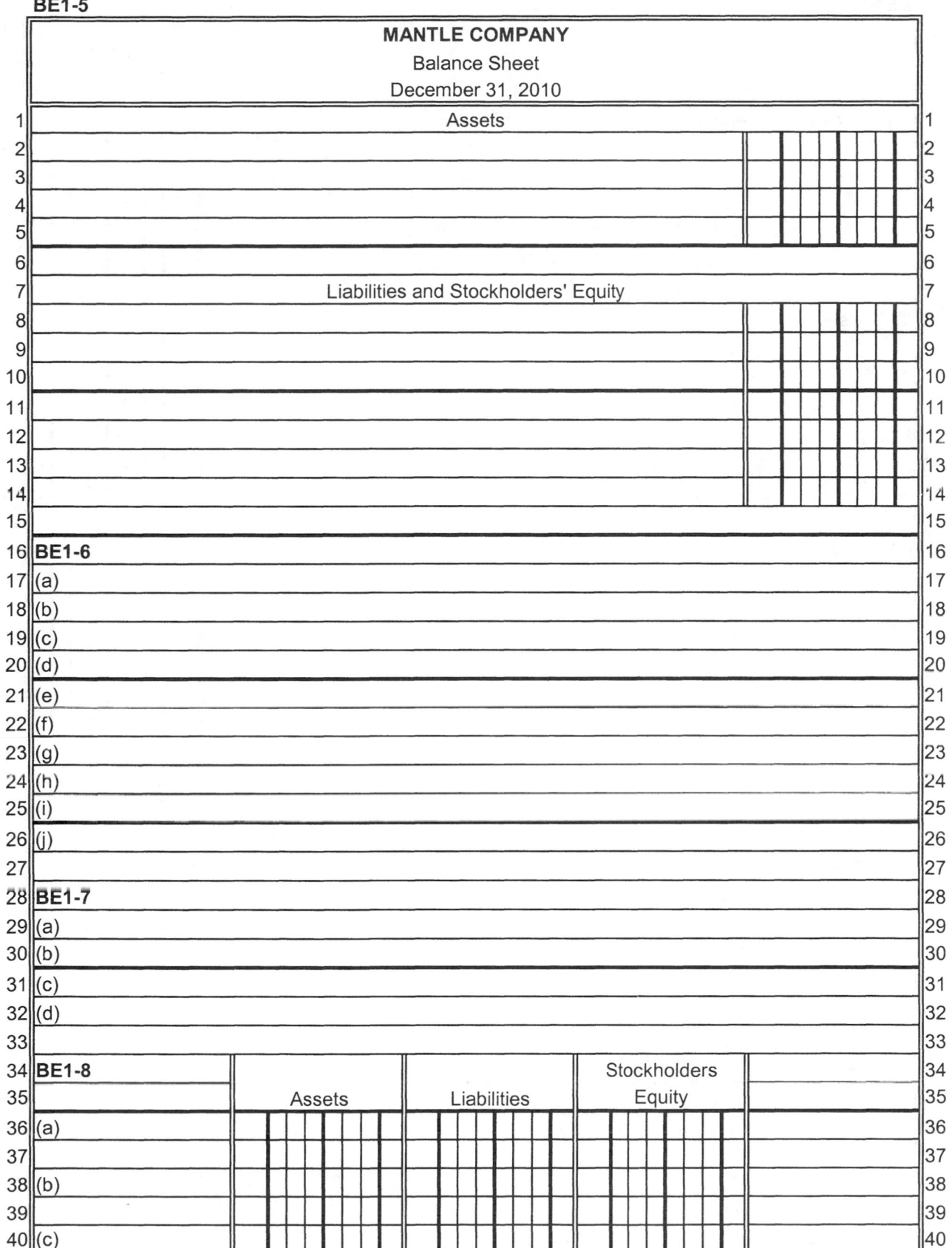

MANTLE COMPANY

Balance Sheet

December 31, 2010

1	Assets	1
2		2
3		3
4		4
5		5
6		6
7	Liabilities and Stockholders' Equity	7
8		8
9		9
10		10
11		11
12		12
13		13
14		14
15		15

BE1-6

(a)

(b)

(c)

(d)

(e)

(f)

(g)

(h)

(i)

(j)

BE1-7

(a)

(b)

(c)

(d)

BE1-8

	Assets	Liabilities	Stockholders Equity	
(a)				
(b)				
(c)				

BE1-9

1	(a) Stockholders' equity:		1
2			2
3			3
4			4
5			5
6			6
7			7
8	(b) Assets:		8
9			9
10			10
11			11
12			12
13			13
14			14
15			15
16	(c) Liabilities:		16
17			17
18			18
19			19
20			20
21			21
22			22
23			23
24			24
25			25
26			26
27			27
28			28
29			29
30			30
31			31
32			32
33			33
34			34
35			35
36			36
37			37
38			38
39			39
40			40

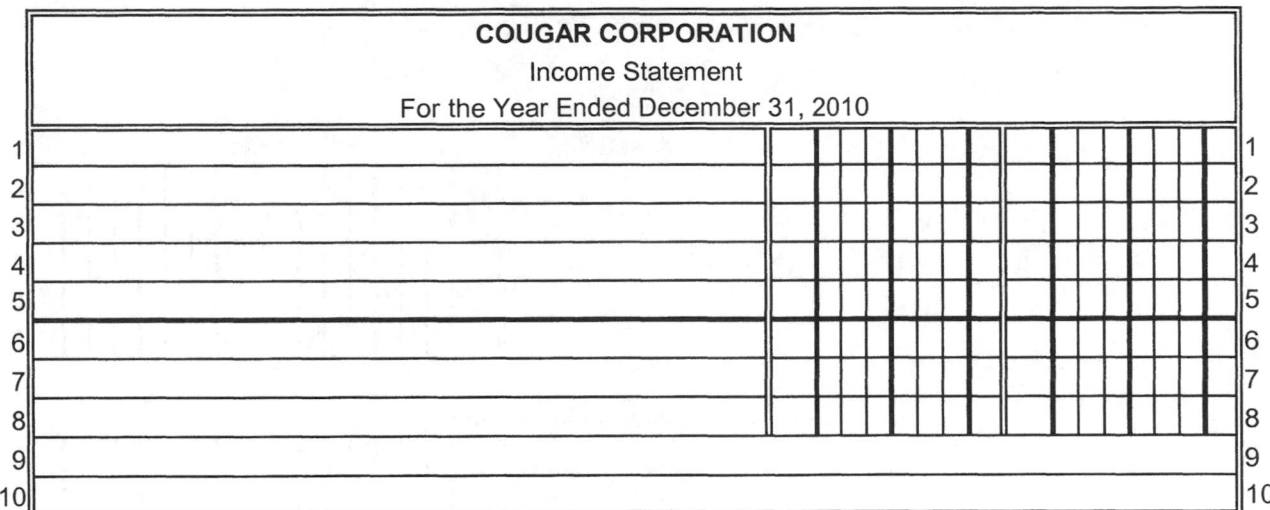

COUGAR CORPORATION

Income Statement

For the Year Ended December 31, 2010

COUGAR CORPORATION

Retained Earnings Statement

For the Year Ended December 31, 2010

	COUGAR CORPORATION				
	Balance Sheet				
	December 31, 2010				
1	Assets					1
2						2
3						3
4						4
5						5
6						6
7						7
8	Liabilities and Stockholders' Equity					8
9						9
10						10
11						11
12						12
13						13
14						14
15						15
16						16
17						17
18						18
19						19
20						20

DENSON CO.

Income Statement

For the Year Ended December 31, 2010

1	Revenues:		1
2			2
3			3
4	Expenses:		4
5			5
6			6
7			7
8			8
9			9
10			10
11			11
12			12
13			13
14			14
15			15

DENSON CO.

Retained Earnings Statement

For the Year Ended December 31, 2010

1		1
2		2
3		3
4		4
5		5
6		6
7		7
8		8
9		9
10		10

(a)

MERCK and CO.
Income Statement
For the Year Ended December 31, 2006
(in millions)

Revenues:		
Expenses:		

MERCK and CO.
Retained Earnings Statement
For the Year Ended December 31, 2006
(in millions)

(b)

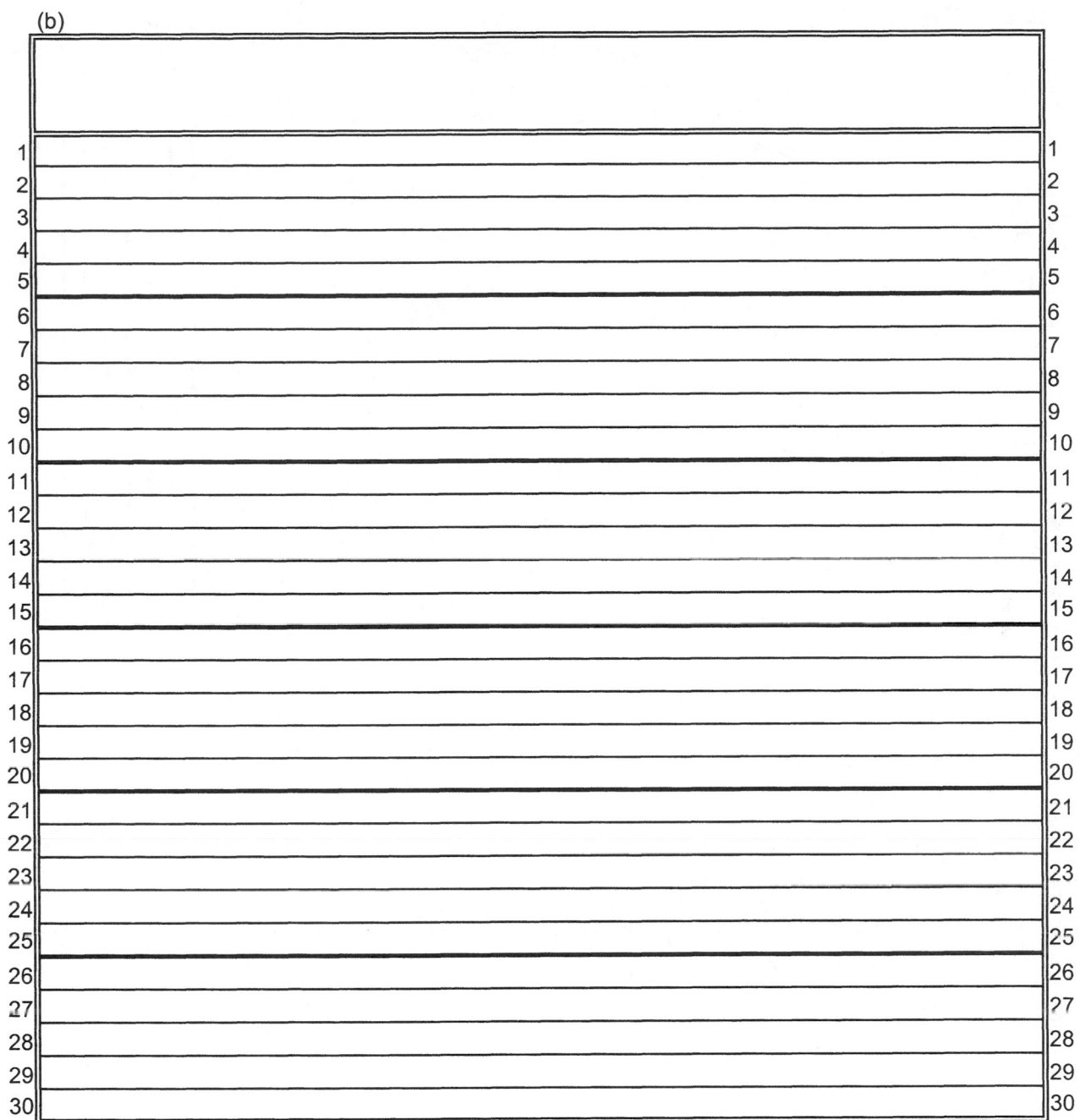

E1-6

WILLINGHAM INC.

Retained Earnings Statement

For the Year Ended December 31, 2010

1		1
2		2
3		3
4		4
5		5
6		6
7		7
8		8
9		9
10	Computation of net income:	10
11		11
12		12
13		13
14		14
15		15

E1-7

1	(a)	1
2		2
3		3
4		4
5		5
6		6
7		7
8		8
9		9
10	(b)	10
11		11
12		12
13		13
14		14
15		15
16		16
17		17
18		18

(a)

1		Cash and short-term investments	1
2		Retained earnings	2
3		Cost of goods sold	3
4		Selling, general and administrative expenses	4
5		Prepaid expenses	5
6		Inventories	6
7		Receivables	7
8		Sales revenue	8
9		Income taxes payable	9
10		Accounts payable	10
11		Franchising revenues	11
12		Interest expense	12
13			13
14			14
15			15

(b)

WAYSIDE INC.

Income Statement

For the Year Ended December 31, 2010

GARRETT, INC.							
Balance Sheet							

	Assets							1
2	Cash	$			5	0	0	0	2
3	Inventory			1	0	0	0	0	3
4	Building			4	5	0	0	0	4
5	Total assets	$		6	0	0	0	0	5
6									6
7	Liabilities and Stockholders' Equity								7
8	Liabilities and Stockholders' Equity								8
9	Accounts payable	$			5	0	0	0	9
10	Stockholders' equity								10
11	Common stock (a)								11
12	Retained earnings (b)								12
13	Total liabilities and stockholders' equity	$		6	0	0	0	0	13
14									14
15									15
16									16
17	Income Statement								17
18	Revenues	$		8	5	0	0	0	18
19	Cost of goods sold (c)								19
20	Administrative expenses			1	0	0	0	0	20
21	Net income (d)								21
22									22
23									23
24	Retained Earnings Statement								24
25	Beginning retained earnings	$		1	0	0	0	0	25
26	Add: Net income (e)								26
27	Less: Dividends				5	0	0	0	27
28	Ending retained earnings	$		2	5	0	0	0	28
29									29
30									30

(a)

(b)

FOREST PARK

Retained Earnings Statement

For the Year Ended December 31, 2010

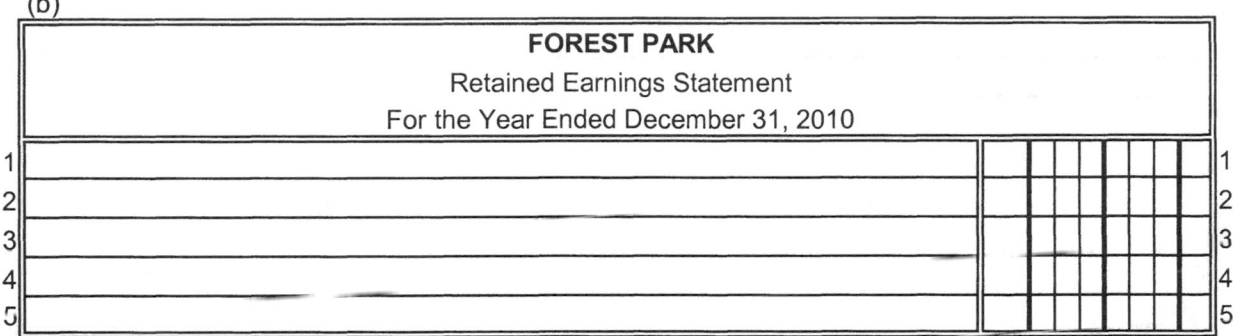

FOREST PARK

Balance Sheet

December 31, 2010

Assets		
Liabilities and Stockholders' Equity		

(c)

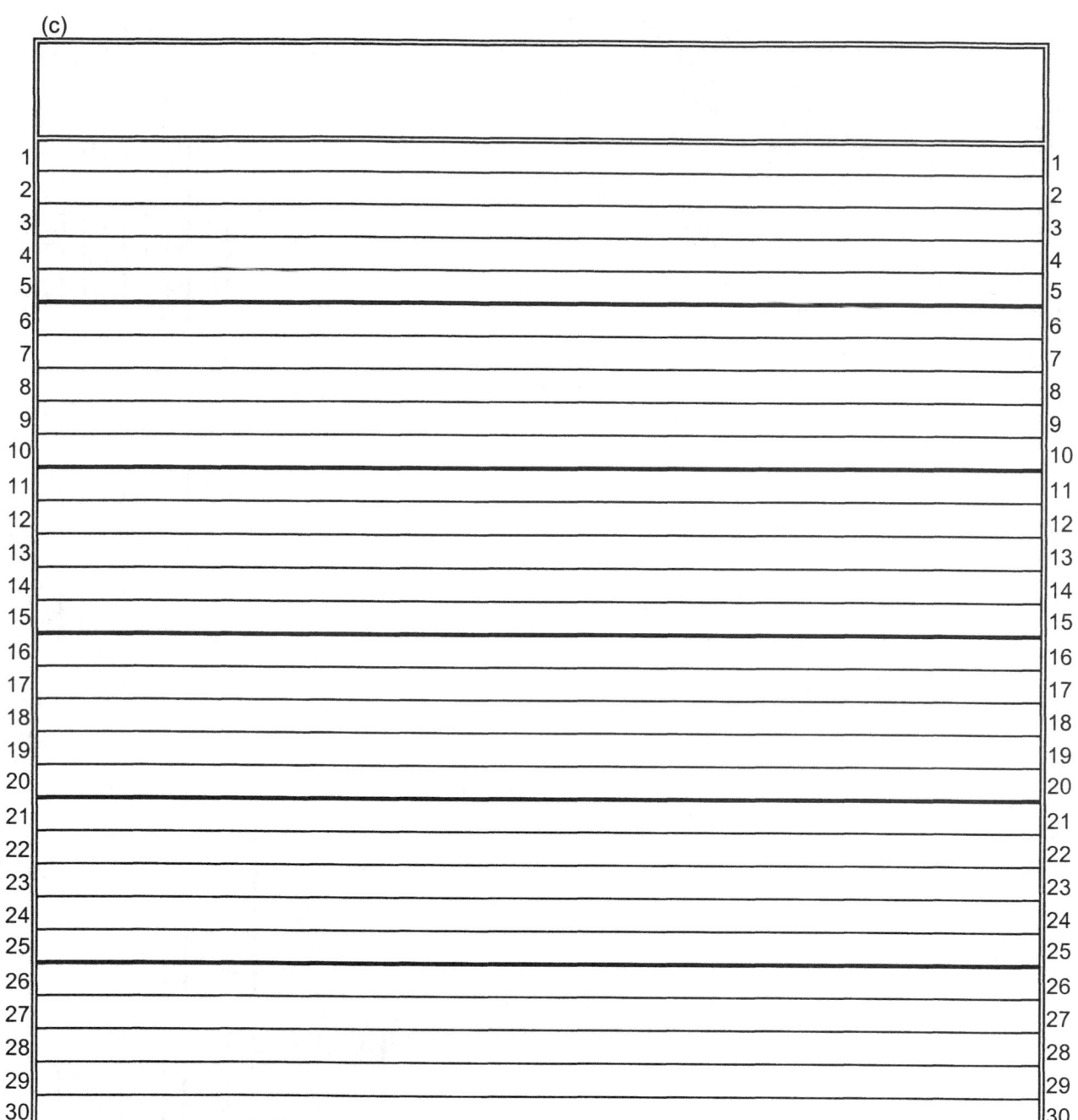

(a)

1		Retained earnings
2		Cost of goods sold
3		Selling and administrative expenses
4		Cash
5		Notes payable
6		Interest expense
7		Long-term debt
8		Inventories
9		Net sales
10		Accounts payable
11		Common stock
12		Income tax expense
13		Other revenue
14		
15		

(b)

KELLOGG COMPANY

Income Statement

For the Year Ended December 31, 2006

(in millions)

(a)

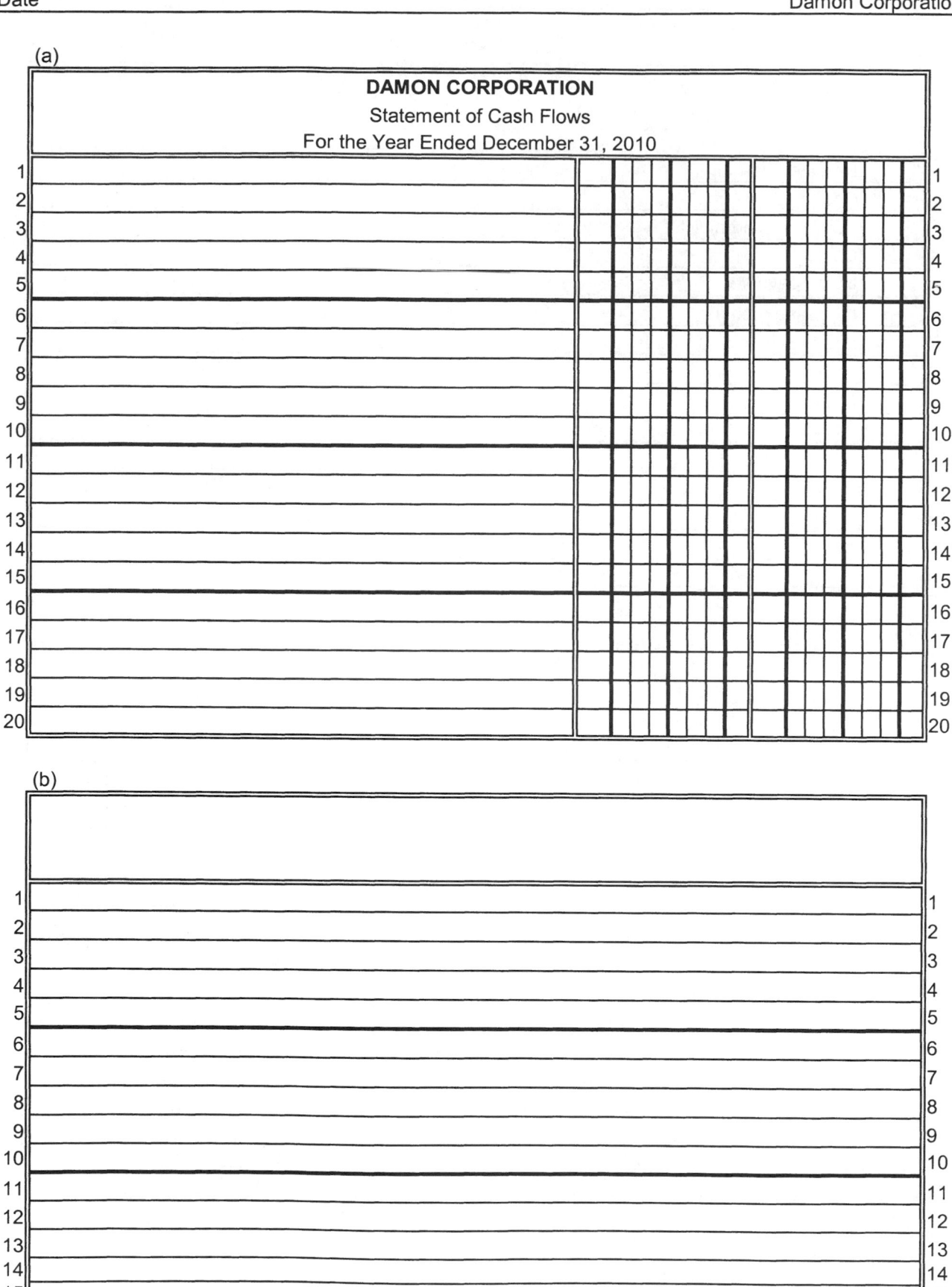

DAMON CORPORATION

Statement of Cash Flows

For the Year Ended December 31, 2010

(b)

(a)

SOUTHWEST AIRLINES
Statement of Cash Flows
For the Year Ended December 31, 2004
(in millions)

(b)

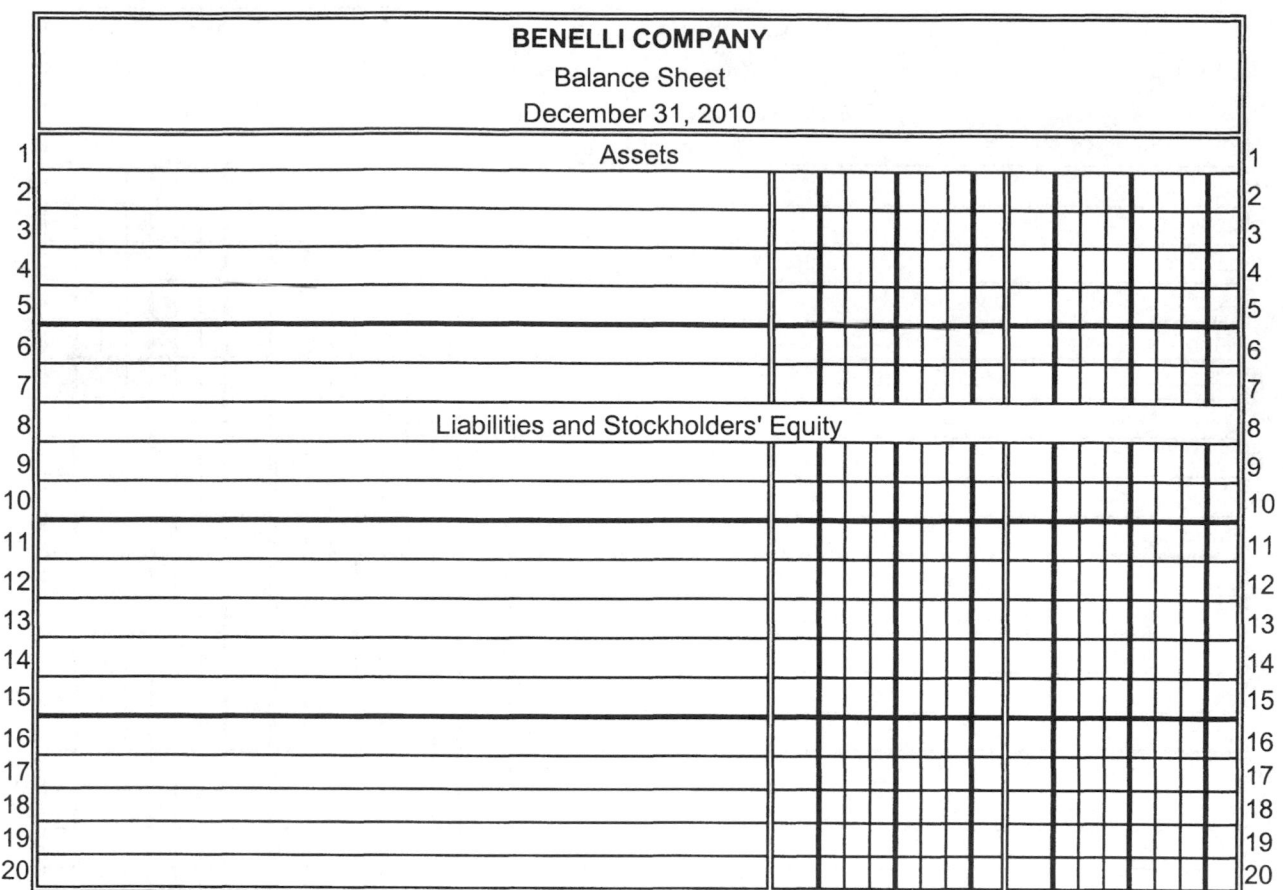

BENELLI COMPANY

Balance Sheet

December 31, 2010

Assets

Liabilities and Stockholders' Equity

(All dollars are in millions)

	(a)		Assets	=	Liabilities		Stockholders' Equity	
1	Assets:							1
2								2
3								3
4								4
5								5
6								6
7								7
8								8
9	Liabilities:							9
10								10
11								11
12								12
13								13
14								14
15								15
16	Stockholders' Equity:							16
17								17
18								18
19								19
20								20
21								21
22								22
23								23
24	(b)							24
25								25
26								26
27								27
28								28
29	(c)							29
30								30
31								31
32								32
33								33
34								34
35								35

		Elder Corporation	Holden Enterprises	
1	Beginning of year			1
2	Total assets	$ 1 1 0 0 0 0	$ 1 3 0 0 0 0	2
3	Total liabilities (d)	7 0 0 0 0		3
4	Total stockholders' equity (a)		7 0 0 0 0	4
5	End of year			5
6	Total assets (b)		1 8 0 0 0 0	6
7	Total liabilities	1 2 0 0 0 0	5 5 0 0 0	7
8	Total stockholders' equity (e)	5 0 0 0 0		8
9	Changes during year in retained earnings			9
10	Dividends (c)		5 0 0 0	10
11	Total revenues (f)	2 1 5 0 0 0		11
12	Total expenses	1 6 5 0 0 0	8 0 0 0 0	12
13				13

(a)

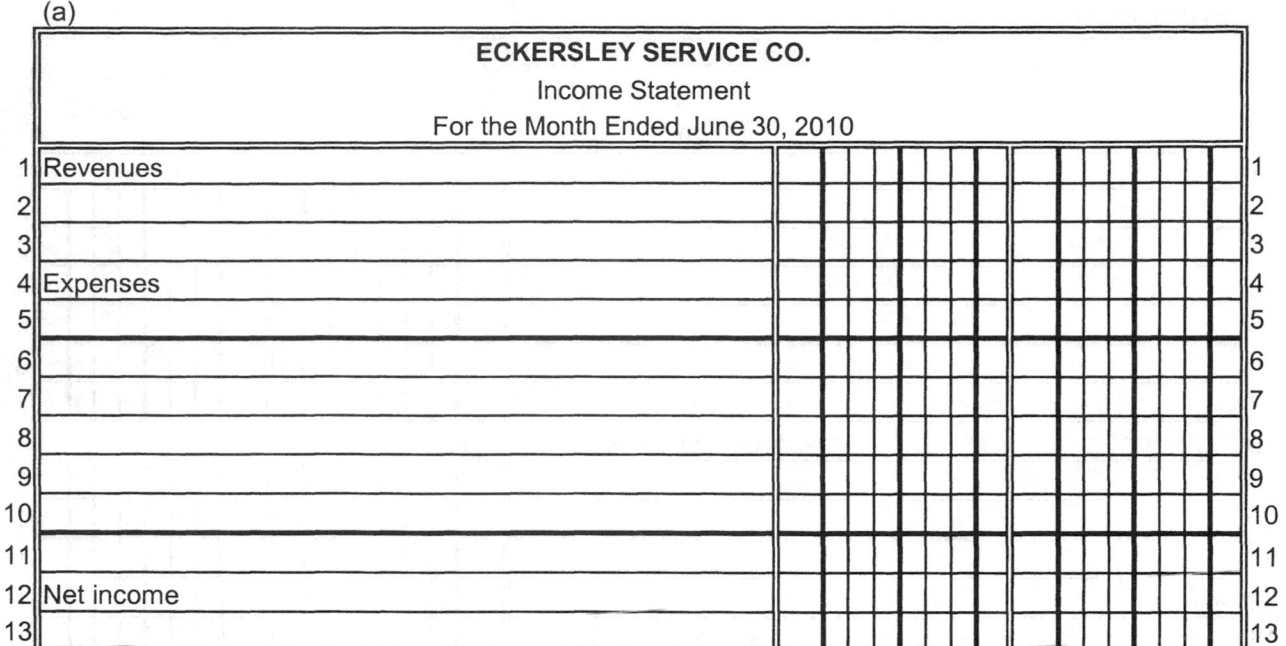

ECKERSLEY SERVICE CO.
Income Statement
For the Month Ended June 30, 2010

1 Revenues			1
2			2
3			3
4 Expenses			4
5			5
6			6
7			7
8			8
9			9
10			10
11			11
12 Net income			12
13			13

ECKERSLEY SERVICE CO.
Retained Earnings Statement
For the Month Ended June 30, 2010

1		1
2		2
3		3
4		4
5		5
6		6

(a) (Continued)

ECKERSLEY SERVICE CO.
Balance Sheet
June 30, 2010

Assets

Liabilities and Stockholders' Equity

(b) & (c)

(b)

(c)

(a)

	Items to be included:	
1		1
2		2
3		3
4		4
5		5
6		6
7		7

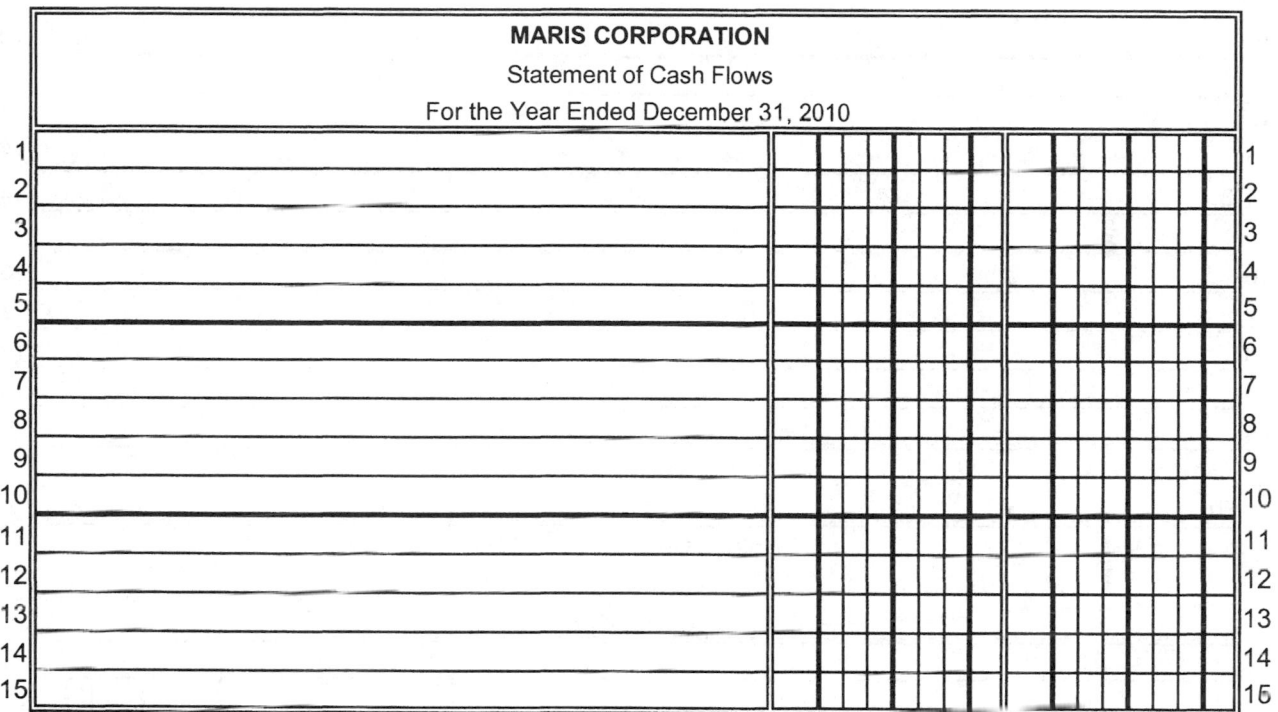

MARIS CORPORATION

Statement of Cash Flows

For the Year Ended December 31, 2010

(b)

(a)

	1.
1	
2	
3	
4	
5	
6	
7	
8	2.
9	
10	
11	
12	
13	
14	3.
15	
16	
17	
18	
19	
20	

(b)

PENINGTON CORPORATION

Balance Sheet

December 31, 2010

Assets

Liabilities and Stockholders' Equity

(a)

LABETTE DELIVERY			
Income Statement			
For the Month Ended May 31, 2010			
Revenues			
Expenses			
Net income			

LABETTE DELIVERY	
Retained Earnings Statement	
For the Month Ended May 31, 2010	

(a) (Continued)

LABETTE DELIVERY

Balance Sheet

May 31, 2010

Assets							
Liabilities and Stockholders' Equity							

(b) & (c)

(b)

(c)

(a)

Items to be included:

EATON CORPORATION

Statement of Cash Flows

For the Year Ended December 31, 2010

(b)

(a)

1	1.	1
2		2
3		3
4		4
5		5
6		6
7		7
8	2.	8
9		9
10		10
11		11
12		12
13		13
14		14
15	3.	15
16		16
17		17
18		18
19		19
20		20

(b)

HOUSTON CORPRATION

Income Statement

For the Year Ended December 31, 2010

1		1
2		2
3		3
4		4
5		5

Name

Section

Date

Chapter 1 Comparative Analysis Problem

Tootsie Roll Industries, Inc. vs. Hershey Foods Corporation

(a) (amounts in thousands)	Tootsie Roll Industries, Inc.	Hershey Foods Corporation
1. Total assets		
2. Net property, plant and equipment		
3. Sales revenue		
4. Net income		

(b)

1	1
2	2
3	3
4	4
5	5
6	6
7	7
8	8
9	9
10	10
11	11
12	12
13	13
14	14
15	15
16	16
17	17
18	18
19	19
20	20
21	21
22	22
23	23
24	24
25	25
26	26
27	27
28	28
29	29
30	30
31	31
32	32
33	33
34	34
35	35
36	36
37	37
38	38
39	39
40	40

BATES COMPANY, INC.
Balance Sheet
December 31, 2010

Assets		
Liabilities and Stockholders' Equity		
Computation of retained earnings:		

BE2-1

1		Accounts payable		Income tax payable	1
2		Accounts receivable		Investment in long-term bonds	2
3		Accumulated depreciation		Land	3
4		Building		Merchandise inventory	4
5		Cash		Patent	5
6		Goodwill		Supplies	6
7					7

BE2-2

RONDELLI COMPANY
Partial Balance Sheet

Current assets:

BE2-3

Earnings per share:

BE2-4

27		Issued new shares of common stock	27
28		Paid a cash dividend	28
29		Reported net income of $75,000	29
30		Reported a net loss of $20,000	30
31			31

BE2-5

Working capital:

Current ratio:

	BE2-6	
1	(a) Current ratio	1
2		2
3		3
4	(b) Debt to total assets	4
5		5
6		6
7	(c) Free cash flow	7
8		8
9		9
10		10
11		11
12	**BE2-7**	12
13	(a)	13
14		14
15	(b)	15
16		16
17	**BE2-8**	17
18	(a)	18
19	(b)	19
20	(c)	20
21	(d)	21
22	(e)	22
23		23
24	**BE2-9**	24
25	(a)	25
26	(b)	26
27	(c)	27
28		28
29	**BE2-10**	29
30	(a)	30
31	(b)	31
32	(c)	32
33	(d)	33
34		34
35	**BE2-11**	35
36		36
37	**BE2-12**	37
38	(a)	38
39	(b)	39
40	(c)	40

DO IT! 2-1

	THEREMIN CORPORATION	
	Balance Sheet (Partial)	
	December 31, 2010	

DO IT! 2-2

Trademarks

Current maturities of long-term debt

Interest revenue

Taxes payable

Long-term marketable debt securities

Unearned consulting fees

Inventories

Accumulated depreciation

Land improvements

Common stock

Advertising expense

Mortgage note payable due in 3 years.

DO IT! 2-3

(a)   Earnings per share:

2010	2009

DO IT! 2-3 (Concluded)

	(b)	2010	2009	
1	Current ratio:			1
2				2
3				3
4				4
5	Debt to total			5
6	assets ratio:			6
7				7
8				8
9				9
10				10
11				11
12				12
13	(c) Free cash flow:			13
14		2010	2009	14
15				15
16				16
17				17
18				18
19				19
20				20
21				21
22				22
23	**DO IT! 2-4**			23
24	1.			24
25	2.			25
26	3.			26
27	4.			27
28	5.			28
29	6.			29
30	7.			30
31	8.			31
32	9.			32
33	10.			33
34	11.			34
35	12.			35
36				36
37				37
38				38
39				39
40				40

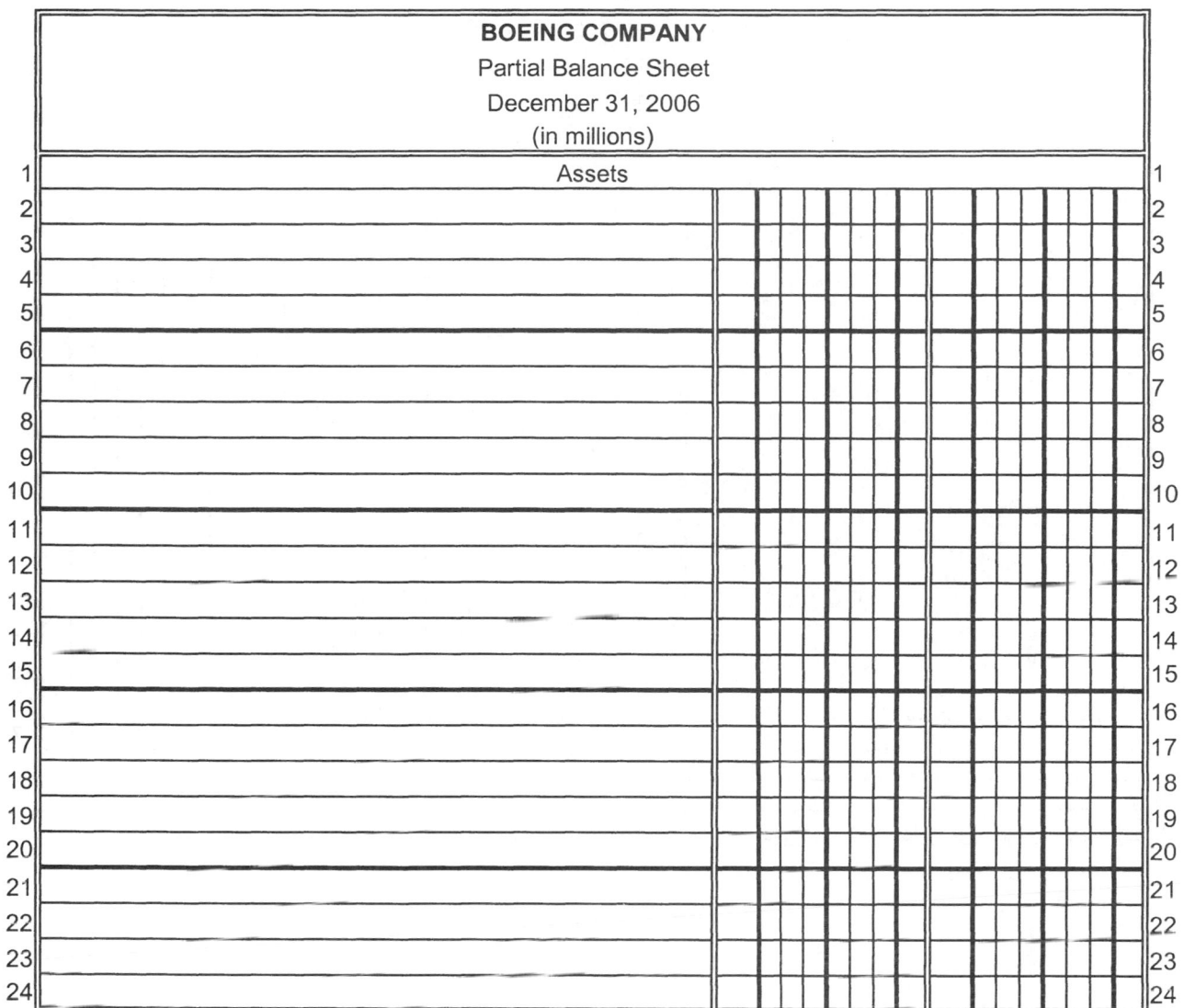

BOEING COMPANY						
Partial Balance Sheet						
December 31, 2006						
(in millions)						
Assets						

H.J. HEINZ COMPANY
Partial Balance Sheet
May 2, 2007
(in thousands)

	Assets				
1					
2					
3					
4					
5					
6					
7					
8					
9					
10					
11					
12					
13					
14					
15					
16					
17					
18					
19					
20					

CLELAND COMPANY				
Balance Sheet				
December 31, 2010				
Assets				

| TEXAS INSTRUMENTS, INC. |
| Balance Sheet |
| December 31, 2006 |
| (in millions) |

Assets

Liabilities and Stockholders' Equity

(a)

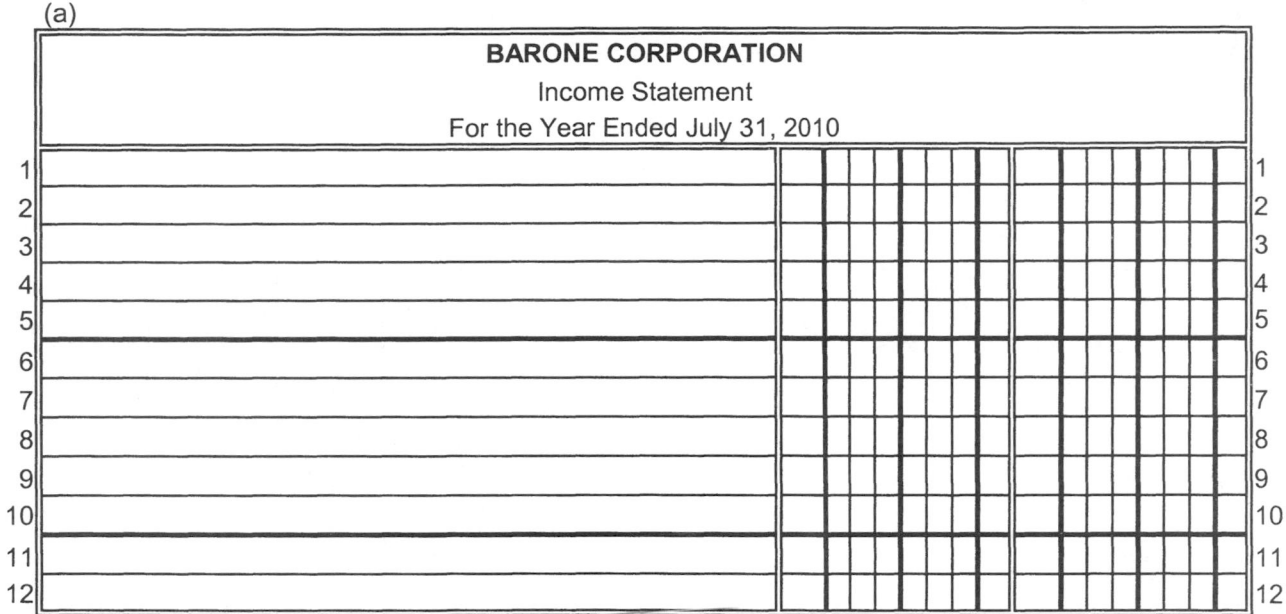

BARONE CORPORATION
Income Statement
For the Year Ended July 31, 2010

BARONE CORPORATION
Retained Earnings Statement
For the Year Ended July 31, 2010

(b)

BARONE CORPORATION		
Balance Sheet		
July 31, 2010		

	Assets			
1				
2				
3				
4				
5				
6				
7				
8				
9				
10				
11				
12				
13				
14	Liabilities and Stockholders' Equity			
15				
16				
17				
18				
19				
20				
21				
22				
23				
24				
25				
26				
27				
28				

(c)

1	Current ratio
2	
3	
4	Debt to total assets ratio
5	
6	
7	

(d)

	Beginning of Year	End of Year	
1 (a) Working capital			1
2			2
3			3
4			4
5			5
6 Current ratio			6
7			7
8			8
9			9
10			10
11 (b)			11
12			12
13			13
14			14
15 (c)			15
16			16
17			17
18			18
19			19
20			20

	(a) Preliminary Balance Sheet	(b) Proposed Actions	
1 Current ratio			1
2			2
3			3
4			4
5 Working capital			5
6			6
7			7
8			8
9			9
10			10
11 (c)			11
12			12
13			13
14			14
15			15
16			16
17			17
18			18
19			19
20			20
21			21
22			22
23			23
24			24
25			25
26			26
27			27
28 (d)			28
29			29
30			30
31			31
32			32
33			33
34			34
35			35
36			36
37			37
38			38
39			39
40			40

	2007	2006	
1 (a) Debt to total assets			1
2 ratio			2
3			3
4			4
5 (b) Free cash flow			5
6			6
7			7
8			8
9			9
10			10
11 (c)			11
12			12
13			13
14			14
15			15
16			16
17			17
18 (d)			18
19			19
20			20
21			21
22			22
23			23
24			24
25			25
26			26
27			27
28			28
29			29
30			30
31			31
32			32
33			33
34			34
35			35
36			36
37			37
38			38
39			39
40			40

YAHOO! INC.						
Balance Sheet						
December 31, 2006						

	Assets			
1				
2				
3				
4				
5				
6				
7				
8				
9				
10				
11				
12				
13				
14				
15	Liabilities and Stockholders' Equity			
16				
17				
18				
19				
20				
21				
22				
23				
24				
25				
26				
27				
28				
29				
30				
31				
32				
33				
34				
35				
36				
37				
38				
39				
40				

FINN CORPORATION				
Income Statement				
For the Year Ended December 31, 2010				
1	Revenues				1
2					2
3					3
4	Expenses				4
5					5
6					6
7					7
8					8
9					9
10					10
11	Net income				11
12					12
13					13

FINN CORPORATION		
Retained Earnings Statement		
For the Year Ended December 31, 2010		
1			1
2			2
3			3
4			4
5			5

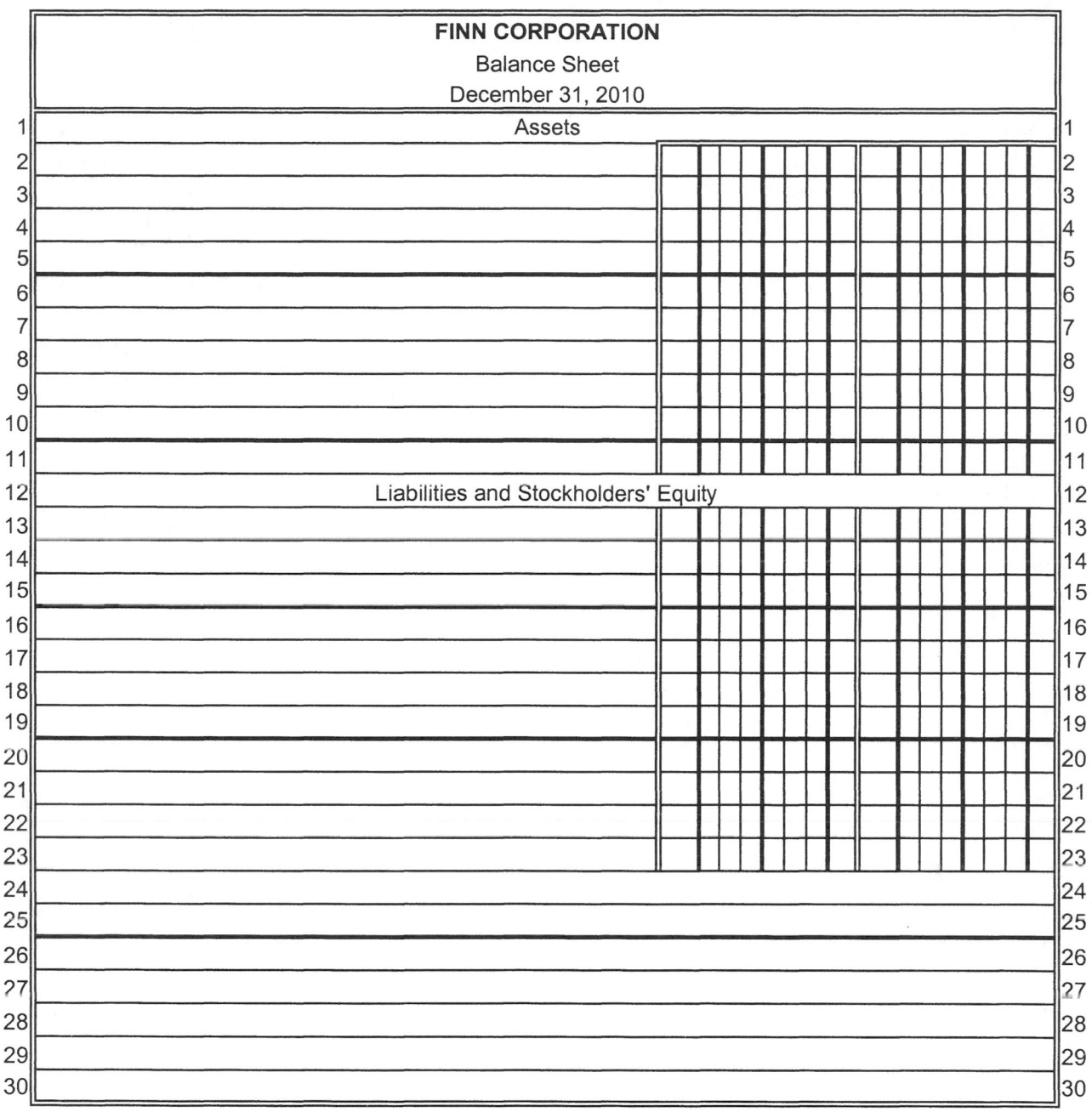

FINN CORPORATION

Balance Sheet

December 31, 2010

Assets

Liabilities and Stockholders' Equity

(a)

	KILEY ENTERPRISES				
	Income Statement				
	For the Year Ended April 30, 2010				
1	Revenues				1
2					2
3					3
4	Expenses				4
5					5
6					6
7					7
8					8
9					9
10					10
11					11
12	Net income				12
13					13
14					14

	KILEY ENTERPRISES		
	Retained Earnings Statement		
	For the Year Ended April 30, 2010		
1			1
2			2
3			3
4			4
5			5
6			6

(b)

	KILEY ENTERPRISES
	Balance Sheet
	April 30, 2010

Assets

1				
2				
3				
4				
5				
6				
7				
8				
9				
10				
11				
12				
13				
14				
15				
16				

Liabilities and Stockholders' Equity

17				
18				
19				
20				
21				
22				
23				
24				
25				
26				
27				
28				
29				
30				
31				
32				
33				
34				
35				
36				
37				
38				
39				
40				

(a)	Bedene Corporation		Groneman Corporation	
1				
2				
3				
4				
5				
6 Net income				
7				
8 Earnings per share				
9				
10				
11 Analysis:				
12				
13				
14				
15				
16 (b)				
17				
18				
19 Working capital				
20				
21 Current ratio				
22				
23				
24				
25 Analysis:				
26				
27				
28				
29				
30 (c)				
31 Debt to total assets ratio				
32				
33				
34				
35				
36				
37 Free Cash Flow				
38 Analysis:				
39				
40				

1	(a) (i) Working capital
2	
3	
4	
5	
6	(ii) Current ratio
7	
8	
9	
10	(iii) Free cash flow
11	
12	
13	
14	
15	
16	(iv) Debt to total assets ratio
17	
18	
19	
20	
21	(v) Earnings per share
22	
23	(b)
24	
25	
26	
27	
28	
29	
30	
31	
32	
33	
34	
35	
36	
37	

(a)	2009	2010
Earnings per share		
(b)		
Working capital		
(c)		
Current ratio		
(d)		
Debt to total assets ratio		
(e)		
Free cash flow		
(f)		

	Ratio	(All Dollars Are in Millions)	
		Target	Wal-Mart
1	(a) Working capital		
2			
3			
4			
5			
6	(b) Current ratio		
7			
8			
9			
10	(c) Debt to total assets		
11	ratio		
12			
13			
14	(d) Free cash flow		
15			
16			
17			
18			
19			
20	(e) Earnings per share		
21			
22			
23			
24			
25			
26			
27	(f)		
28			
29			
30			
31			
32			
33			
34			
35			
36			
37			
38			
39			
40			

KELLOGG COMPANY
Balance Sheet
December 31, 2006
(in millions)

	Assets											
1												
2												
3												
4												
5												
6												
7												
8												
9												
10												
11												
12	Liabilities and Stockholders' Equity											
13												
14												
15												
16												
17												
18												
19												
20												
21												
22												
23												
24												
25												
26												
27												
28												
29												
30												
31												
32												
33												
34												
35												
36												
37												
38												
39												

PINSON, INC.		
Income Statement		
For the Year Ended December 31, 2010		
Revenues		
Expenses		
Net income		

PINSON, INC.	
Retained Earnings Statement	
For the Year Ended December 31, 2010	

PINSON, INC. Balance Sheet December 31, 2010								
Assets								
Liabilities and Stockholders' Equity								

(a)

MILNER CORPORATION				
Income Statement				
For the Year Ended April 30, 2010				
1	Revenues				1
2					2
3					3
4	Expenses				4
5					5
6					6
7					7
8					8
9					9
10					10
11	Net income				11
12					12

MILNER CORPORATION		
Retained Earnings Statement		
For the Year Ended April 30, 2010		
1		1
2		2
3		3
4		4
5		5
6		6

(b)

MILNER CORPORATION
Balance Sheet
April 30, 2010

Assets

Liabilities and Stockholders' Equity

(c)

(a)	Smyth Company	James Company
1		
2		
3		
4		
5		
6 Net income		
7		
8 Earnings per share		
9		
10		
11 Analysis:		
12		
13		
14		
15		

(b)	Smyth Company	James Company
17		
18		
19 Working capital		
20		
21 Current ratio		
22		
23		
24 Analysis:		
25		
26		
27		

(c)	Smyth Company	James Company
29 Debt to total assets ratio		
30		
31 Free cash flow		
32		
33		
34		
35		
36		
37 Analysis:		
38		
39		
40		

(a)

1 (i) Current ratio
2
3
4
5 (ii) Working capital
6
7
8
9
10 (iii) Debt to total assets ratio
11
12
13
14 (iv) Free cash flow
15
16
17
18
19
20 (v) Earnings per share
21
22
23
24 (b)
25
26
27
28
29
30
31
32
33
34
35
36
37
38
39
40

	2009	2010
(a)		
1 Earnings per share		
2		
3		
4		
5 (b)		
6 Working capital		
7		
8		
9		
10		
11		
12		
13 (c)		
14 Current ratio		
15		
16		
17		
18 (d)		
19 Debt to total assets ratio		
20		
21		
22		
23 (e)		
24 Free cash flow		
25		
26		
27		
28		
29		
30		
31 (f)		
32		
33		
34		
35		
36		
37		
38		
39		
40		

	Ratio	Blockbuster Inc. (All Dollars Are in Millions)	Movie Gallery, Inc.	
1	(a) Working capital			1
2				2
3				3
4				4
5				5
6	(b) Current ratio			6
7				7
8				8
9				9
10	(c) Debt to total assets			10
11	ratio			11
12				12
13				13
14	(d) Free cash flow			14
15				15
16				16
17				17
18				18
19				19
20	(e) Earnings (Loss) per share			20
21				21
22				22
23				23
24				24
25				25
26				26
27	(f)			27
28				28
29				29
30				30
31				31
32				32
33				33
34				34
35				35
36				36
37				37
38				38
39				39
40				40

(a) ($ in thousands)	Hershey Foods Corporation	Tootsie Roll Industries, Inc.
(1) Working capital		
(2) Current ratio		
(3) Debt to total assets		
ratio		
(4) Free cash flow		
(5) Earnings per share		
(b)		

BE3-1	Assets	Liabilities	Stockholders' Equity
(a) Purchased supplies on account			
(b) Received cash for providing a service			
(c) Expenses paid in cash			
See next page for BE 3-2 and 3-3			

BE3-4	Debit Effect	Credit Effect	Normal Balance
(a) Accounts payable			
(b) Advertising expense			
(c) Service revenue			
(d) Accounts receivable			
(e) Retained earnings			
(f) Dividends			

BE3-5		Acct. Debited	Acct. Credited
June 1	Issues stock for $5,000 cash		
2	Buys equipment on account for $1,100		
3	Pays $500 to landlord for June rent		
12	Bills Jeff Gore $700 for welding work done		

BE3-6			
Date	Account Titles	Debit	Credit
June 1			
2			
3			
12			

BRIEF EXERCISES 3-2 AND 3-3

Bleeker Corp. and Estes Company

See Appendix

BE3-9

	Date	Account Titles	Debit	Credit	
1	Aug. 1				1
2					2
3					3
4					4
5	4				5
6					6
7					7
8					8
9	16				9
10					10
11					11
12					12
13	27				13
14					14
15					15
16					16

BE3-10

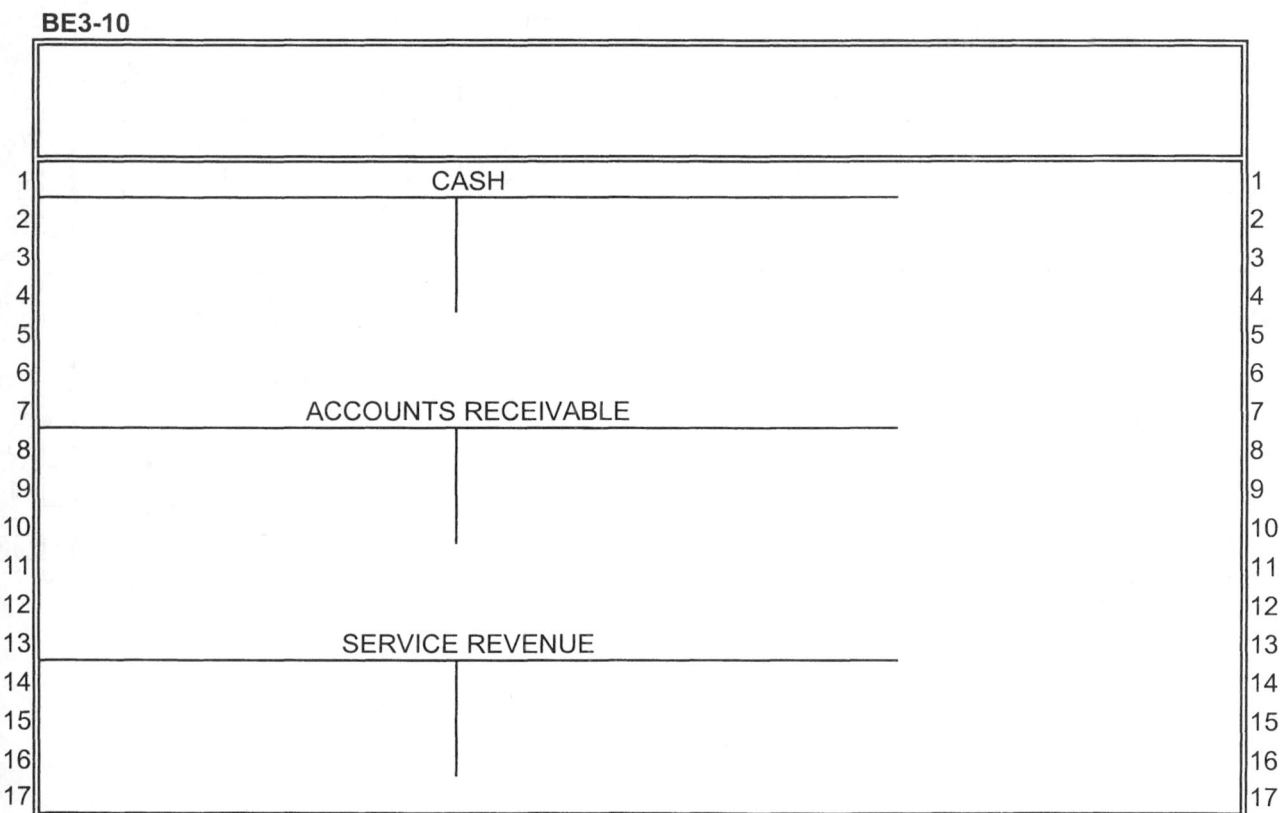

1	CASH		1
2			2
3			3
4			4
5			5
6			6
7	ACCOUNTS RECEIVABLE		7
8			8
9			9
10			10
11			11
12			12
13	SERVICE REVENUE		13
14			14
15			15
16			16
17			17

BE3-11

TROWMAN COMPANY Trial Balance June 30, 2010	Debit	Credit
1			1
2			2
3			3
4			4
5			5
6			6
7			7
8			8
9			9
10			10
11			11
12			12

BE3-12

PETTENGILL COMPANY Trial Balance December 31, 2010	Debit	Credit
1			1
2			2
3			3
4			4
5			5
6			6
7			7
8			8
9			9
10			10
11			11
12			12
13			13

ORLANDO CABRERA CO.

	Assets			=	Liabilities	+		+	Stockholders' Equity					
Trans-action	Cash	+	Accounts Receivable	=	Accounts Payable	+	Common Stock	+	Revenues	-	Retained Earnings Expenses	##	Dividends	
1.														1
														2
2.														3
														4
3.														5
														6
4.														7
														8

DO IT! 3-2

	Account Titles	Normal Balance	
1			1
2			2
3			3
4			4
5			5
6			6
7			7
8			8
9			9
10			10
11			11

DO IT! 3-3

	Trans.	Account Titles	Debit	Credit	
12					12
13					13
14					14
15					15
16					16
17					17
18					18
19					19
20					20
21					21
22					22
23					23
24					24
25					25
26					26

DO IT! 3-4

27		27
28		28
29	Cash	29
30		30
31		31
32		32
33		33
34		34
35		35
36		36
37		37
38		38
39		39
40		40

EXERCISES 3-1 & 3-2

Ruiz Advertising Company, Inc. and McBride Company

See Appendix

EXERCISE 3-3

Lopez Corp.

See Appendix

	(a)	
1	1.	1
2		2
3	2.	3
4		4
5	3.	5
6		6
7	4.	7
8		8
9	5.	9
10		10
11	**6.**	11
12		12
13	7.	13
14		14
15	8.	15
16		16
17	9.	17
18		18
19	10.	19
20		20
21	(b)	21
22		22
23		23
24		24
25		25
26		26
27		27
28		28
29		29
30		30
31	(c)	31
32		32
33		33
34		34
35		35
36		36
37		37
38		38
39		39
40		40

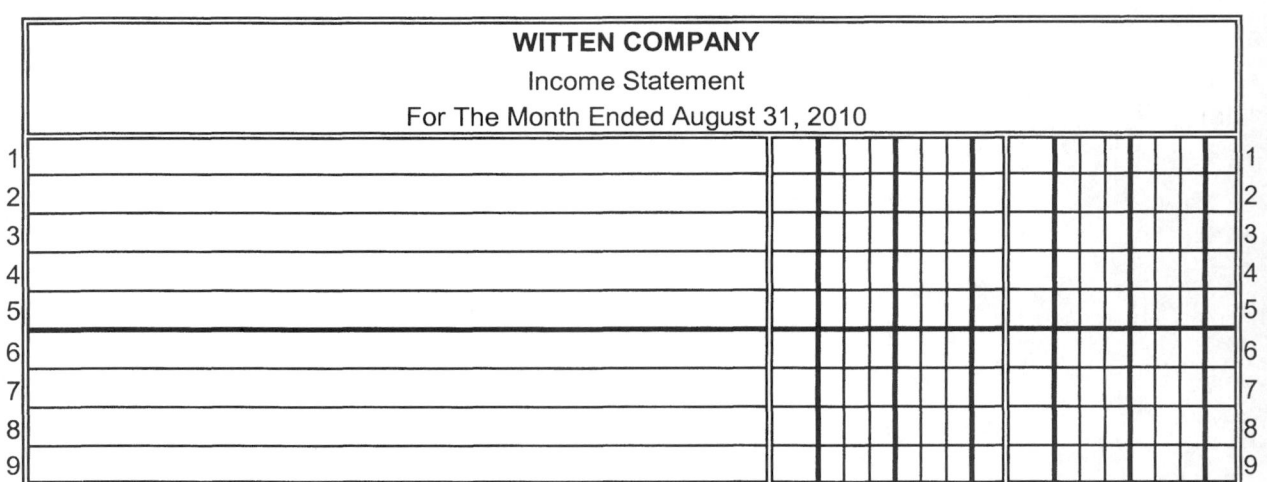

WITTEN COMPANY

Income Statement

For The Month Ended August 31, 2010

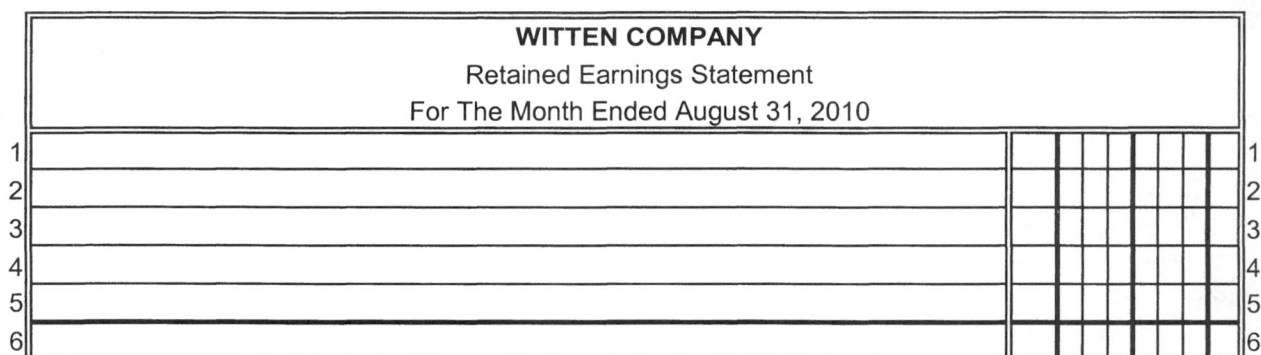

WITTEN COMPANY

Retained Earnings Statement

For The Month Ended August 31, 2010

WITTEN COMPANY

Balance Sheet

August 31, 2010

Assets

Liabilities and Stockholders' Equity

(a)

Trans-action No.	Account Debited				Account Credited			
	(a) Basic Type	(b) Specific Account	(c) Effect	(d) Normal Balance	(a) Basic Type	(b) Specific Account	(c) Effect	(d) Normal Balance
1								
1.	Asset	Cash	Increase	Debit	Stockholders' Equity	Common Stock	Increase	Credit
3								
4								
2.								
6								
7								
3.								
9								
10								
4.								
12								
13								
5.								
15								
16								
6.								
18								
19								
7.								
21								
22								
8.								
24								
25								

(b)

	Trans No.	Account Titles	Debit	Credit	
1	1.				1
2					2
3					3
4					4
5	2.				5
6					6
7					7
8					8
9	3.				9
10					10
11					11
12					12
13	4.				13
14					14
15					15
16					16
17	5.				17
18					18
19					19
20					20
21	6.				21
22					22
23					23
24					24
25	7.				25
26					26
27					27
28					28
29	8.				29
30					30
31					31
32					32
33					33
34					34
35					35
36					36
37					37
38					38
39					39
40					40

	Date	Account Titles	Debit	Credit	
1	Oct. 1				1
2					2
3					3
4					4
5	2				5
6					6
7					7
8	3				8
9					9
10					10
11					11
12	6				12
13					13
14					14
15					15
16	10				16
17					17
18					18
19					19
20	27				20
21					21
22					22
23					23
24	30				24
25					25
26					26
27					27
28					28
29					29
30					30

(a)

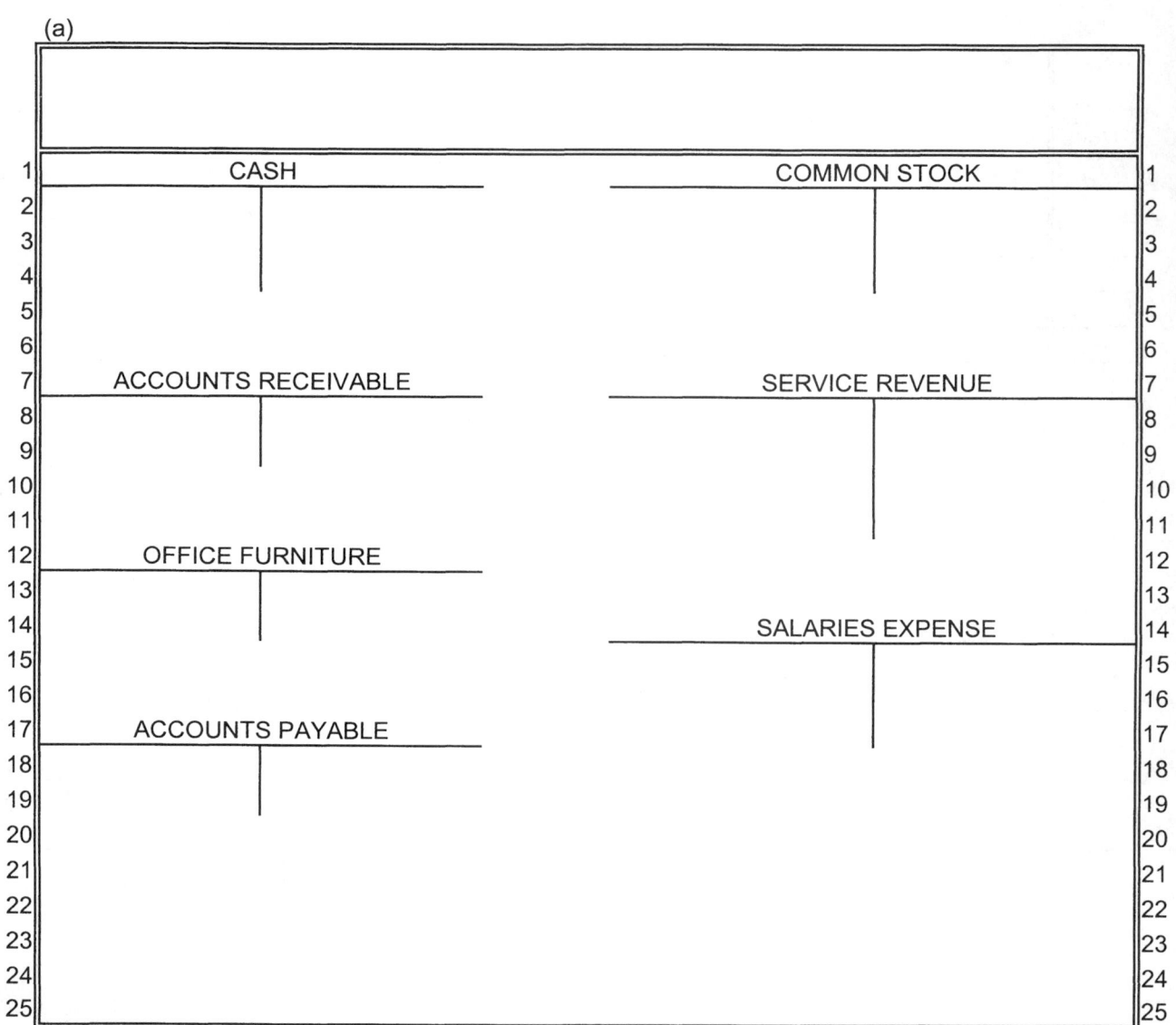

CASH	COMMON STOCK
ACCOUNTS RECEIVABLE	SERVICE REVENUE
OFFICE FURNITURE	SALARIES EXPENSE
ACCOUNTS PAYABLE	

(b)

RICKERT REAL ESTATE AGENCY

Trial Balance

October 31, 2010

	Debit	Credit

(a)

Date	Assets			=	Liabilities	+	Stockholders' Equity		Explanation
	Cash	+	Equipment	=	Accounts Payable	+	Stockholders' Equity		
Sept 1									1
									2
									3
5									4
									5
									6
									7
25									8
									9
									10
									11
30									12
									13
									14
									15

E3-10 (b)

	Date	Account Titles	Debit	Credit	
1	Sept 1				1
2					2
3					3
4					4
5	5				5
6					6
7					7
8					8
9					9
10	25				10
11					11
12					12
13					13
14	30				14
15					15
16					16
17					17
18					18
19					19
20					20

E3-11

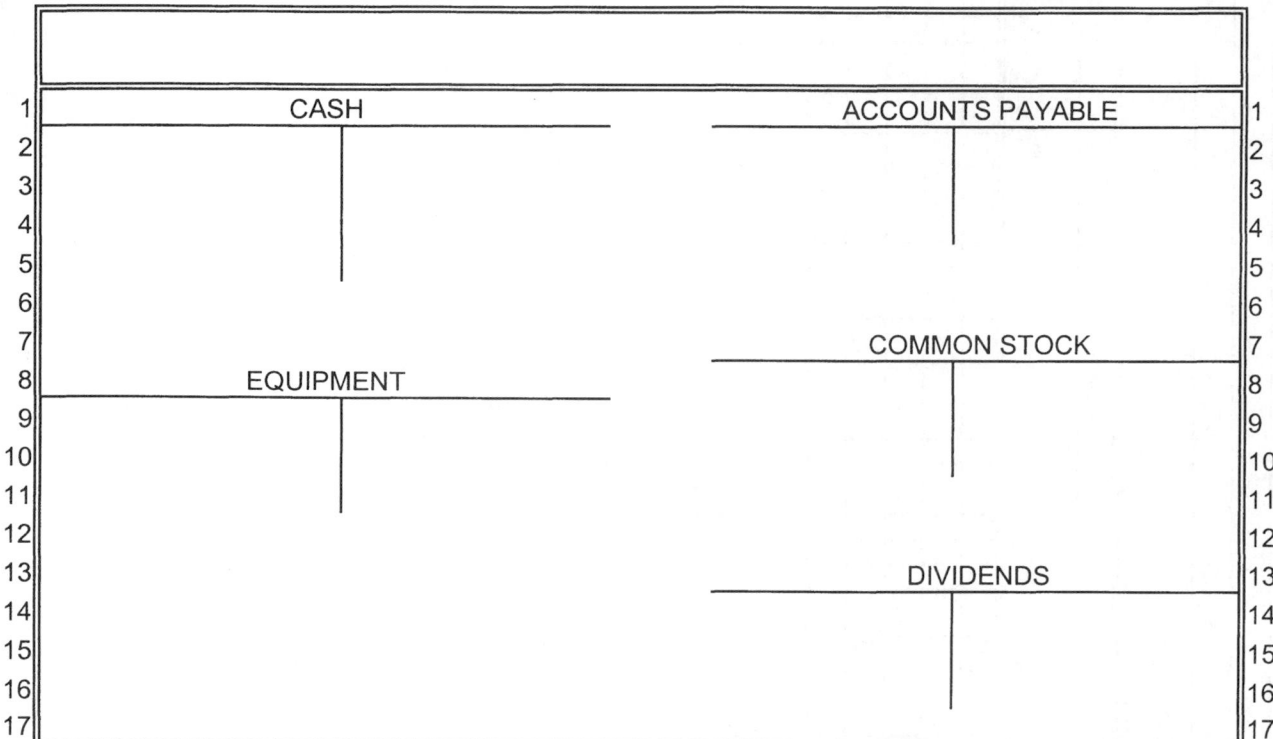

Name   Exercise 3-11

Section

Date   Sutton's Gardening Company Inc.

(a)

	Date	Account Titles	Debit	Credit
1	Apr 1			
2				
3				
4				
5				
6	4			
7				
8				
9				
10	7			
11				
12				
13				
14				
15	12			
16				
17				
18				
19				
20	15			
21				
22				
23				
24	25			
25				
26				
27				
28	29			
29				
30				
31				
32				
33	30			
34				
35				
36				
37				
38				
39				
40				

(b)

SUTTON'S GARDENING COMPANY INC. Trial Balance April 30, 2010	Debit	Credit
1		
2		
3		
4		
5		
6		
7		
8		
9		
10		
11		
12		
13		
14		
15		
16		
17		
18		
19		
20		
21		
22		
23		
24		
25		
26		
27		

(a)

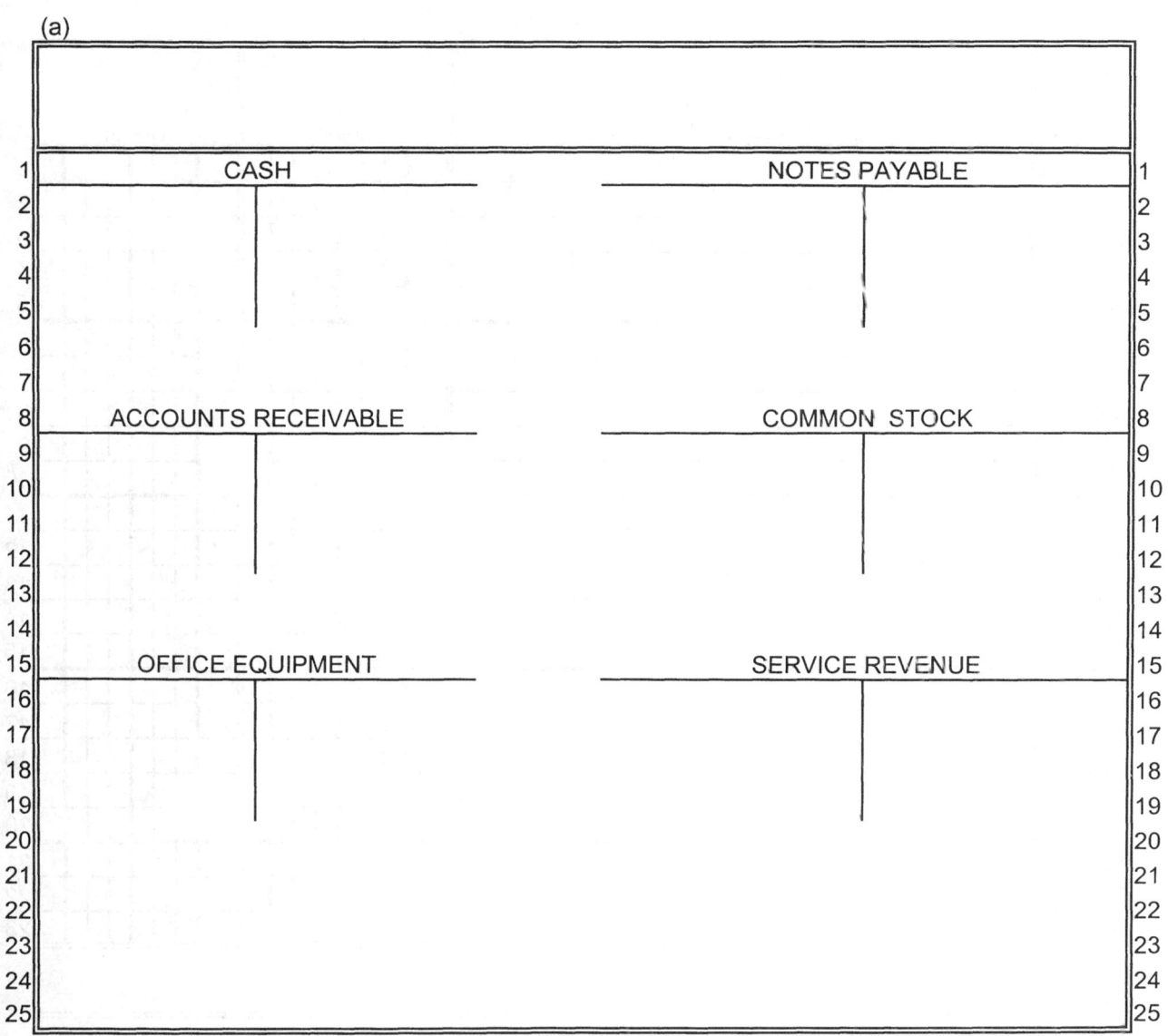

	CASH			NOTES PAYABLE	
1					1
2					2
3					3
4					4
5					5
6					6
7					7
8	ACCOUNTS RECEIVABLE			COMMON STOCK	8
9					9
10					10
11					11
12					12
13					13
14					14
15	OFFICE EQUIPMENT			SERVICE REVENUE	15
16					16
17					17
18					18
19					19
20					20
21					21
22					22
23					23
24					24
25					25

(b)

GIPSON INC.
Trial Balance
August 31, 2010

		Debit	Credit	
1				1
2				2
3				3
4				4
5				5
6				6
7				7
8				8
9				9

(a)

	Date	Account Titles	Debit	Credit	
1	Oct 1				1
2					2
3					3
4					4
5					5
6	10				6
7					7
8					8
9					9
10					10
11	10				11
12					12
13					13
14					14
15	20				15
16					16
17					17
18					18
19					19
20	20				20
21					21
22					22
23					23

(b)

BRUMBAUGH CO.
Trial Balance
October 31, 2010

		Debit	Credit	
1				1
2				2
3				3
4				4
5				5
6				6
7				7
8				8
9				9
10				10
11				11
12				12
13				13

(a)

THORNTON DELIVERY SERVICE
Trial Balance
July 31, 2010

	Debit	Credit
1		
2		
3		
4		
5		
6		
7		
8		
9		
10		
11		
12		
13		
14		
15		
16		
17		
18		
19		
20		

(b)

THORNTON DELIVERY SERVICE
Income Statement
For the Month Ended July 31, 2010

1		
2		
3		
4		
5		
6		
7		
8		
9		
10		
11		
12		
13		
14		
15		

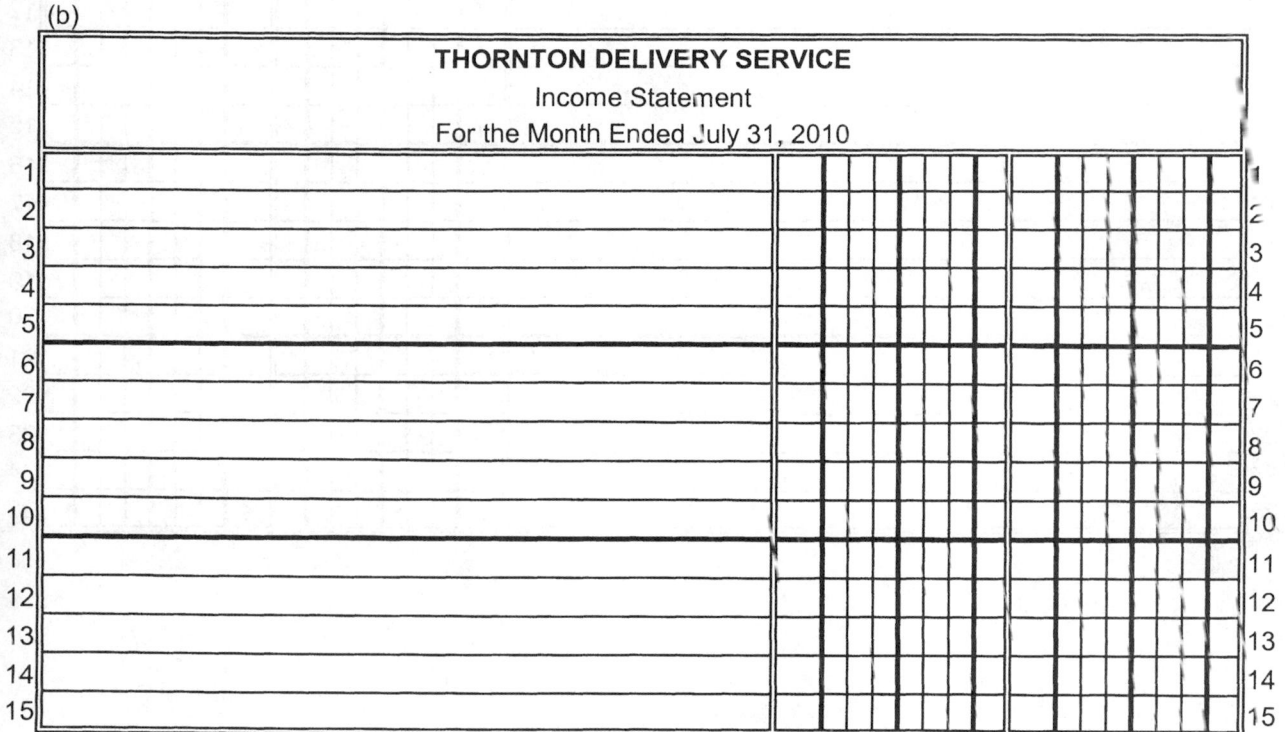

(b) (Continued)

THORNTON DELIVERY SERVICE

Retained Earnings Statement

For the Month Ended July 31, 2010

1		1
2		2
3		3
4		4
5		5
6		6

THORNTON DELIVERY SERVICE

Balance Sheet

July 31, 2010

	Assets	
1	Assets	1
2		2
3		3
4		4
5		5
6		6
7		7
8		8
9		9
10	Liabilities and Stockholders' Equity	10
11		11
12		12
13		13
14		14
15		15
16		16
17		17
18		18
19		19
20		20
21		21
22		22
23		23
24		24
25		25

PROBLEM 3 - 1A

Flint Hills Travel Agency Inc.

See Appendix

(b)

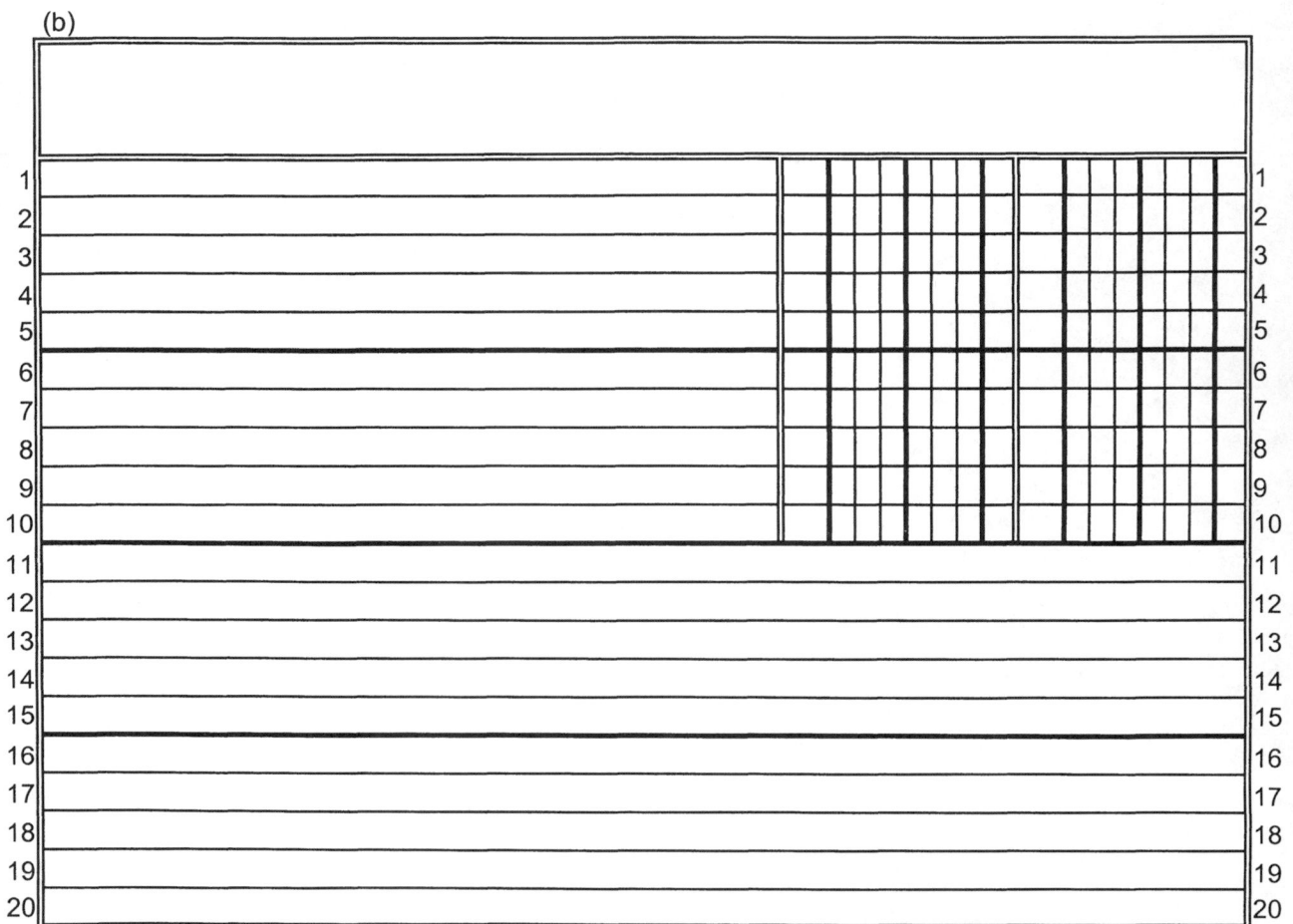

PROBLEM 3-2A

Kuhlmann Consulting Inc.

See Appendix

(b)

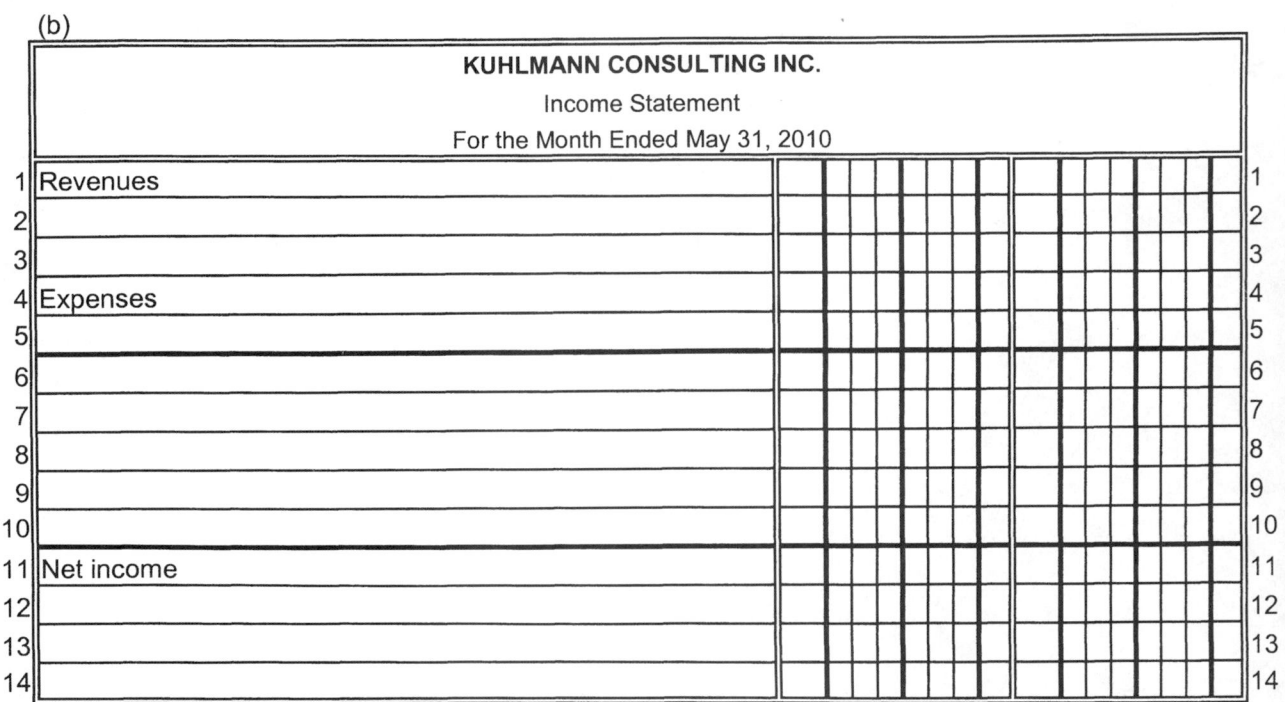

KUHLMANN CONSULTING INC.

Income Statement

For the Month Ended May 31, 2010

1	Revenues		
2			
3			
4	Expenses		
5			
6			
7			
8			
9			
10			
11	Net income		
12			
13			
14			

(c)

KUHLMANN CONSULTING INC.

Balance Sheet

May 31, 2010

1	Assets		
2			
3			
4			
5			
6			
7			
8			
9			
10	Liabilities and Stockholders' Equity		
11			
12			
13			
14			
15			
16			
17			
18			
19			
20			

PROBLEM 3-3A

Dick Reber Inc.

See Appendix

(b)

DICK REBER INC.			
Income Statement			
For the Month Ended August 31, 2010			
Revenues			
Expenses			
Net income			

DICK REBER INC.	
Retained Earnings Statement	
For the Month Ended August 31, 2010	

(b) (Continued)

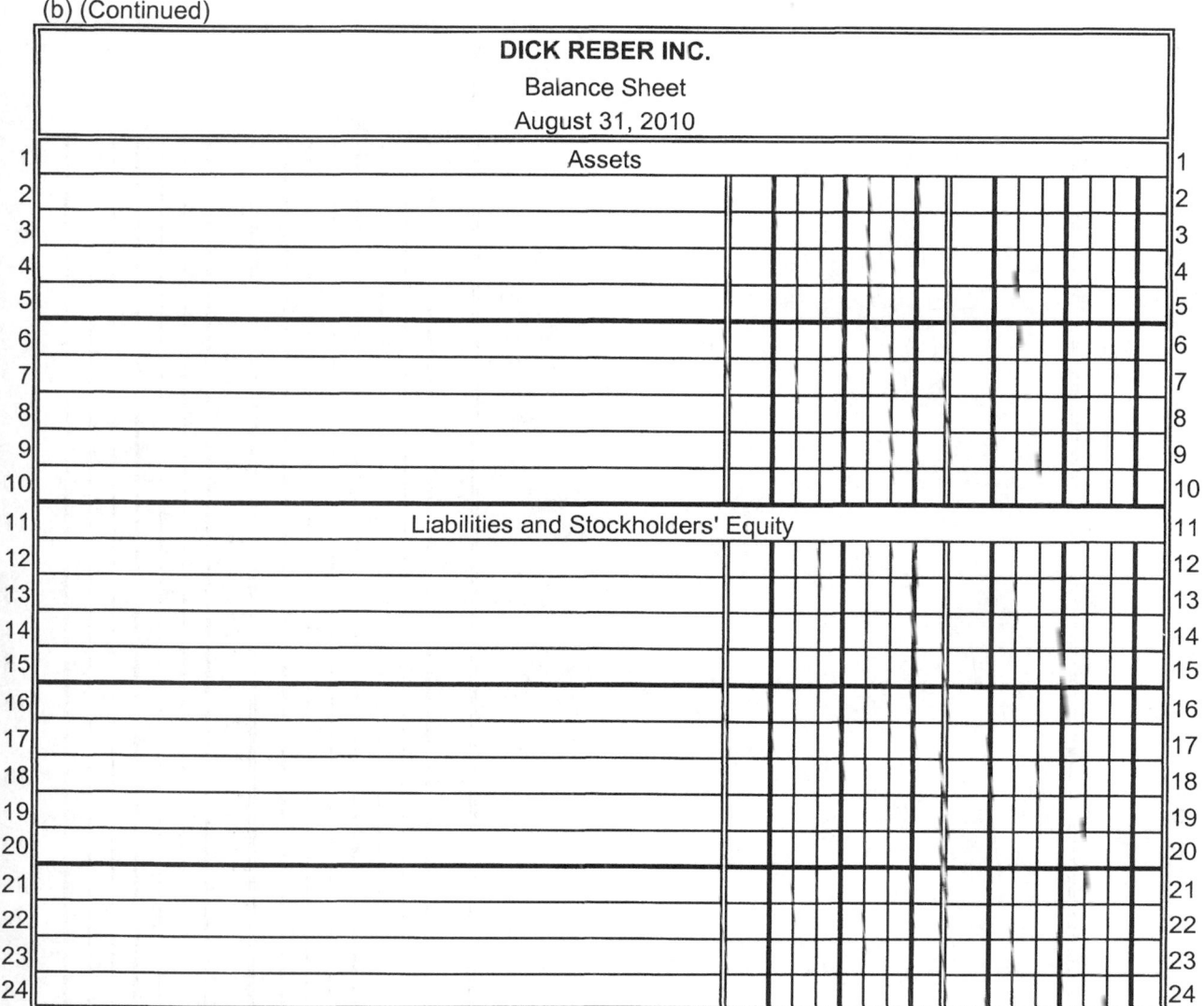

DICK REBER INC.

Balance Sheet

August 31, 2010

Assets

Liabilities and Stockholders' Equity

	Date	Account Titles	Debit	Credit	
1	Mar. 1				1
2					2
3					3
4					4
5	3				5
6					6
7					7
8					8
9					9
10					10
11	5				11
12					12
13					13
14					14
15	6				15
16					16
17					17
18					18
19	10				19
20					20
21					21
22					22
23	18				23
24					24
25					25
26					26
27	19				27
28					28
29					29
30					30
31					31
32	25				32
33					33
34					34
35					35
36	30				36
37					37
38					38
39					39
40					40

	Date	Account Titles	Debit	Credit	
1	Mar. 30				1
2					2
3					3
4					4
5	31				5
6					6
7					7
8					8
9					9
10					10
11					11
12					12
13					13
14					14
15					15
16					16
17					17
18					18
19					19
20					20
21					21
22					22
23					23
24					24
25					25
26					26
27					27
28					28
29					29
30					30
31					31
32					32
33					33
34					34
35					35
36					36
37					37
38					38
39					39
40					40

(a)

	Date	Account Titles	Debit	Credit	
1	Apr 1				1
2					2
3					3
4					4
5	1				5
6					6
7	2				7
8					8
9					9
10					10
11	3				11
12					12
13					13
14					14
15					15
16	10				16
17					17
18					18
19					19
20	11				20
21					21
22					22
23					23
24					24
25	20				25
26					26
27					27
28					28
29	30				29
30					30
31					31
32					32
33	30				33
34					34
35					35
36					36
37					37
38					38
39					39
40					40

(b)

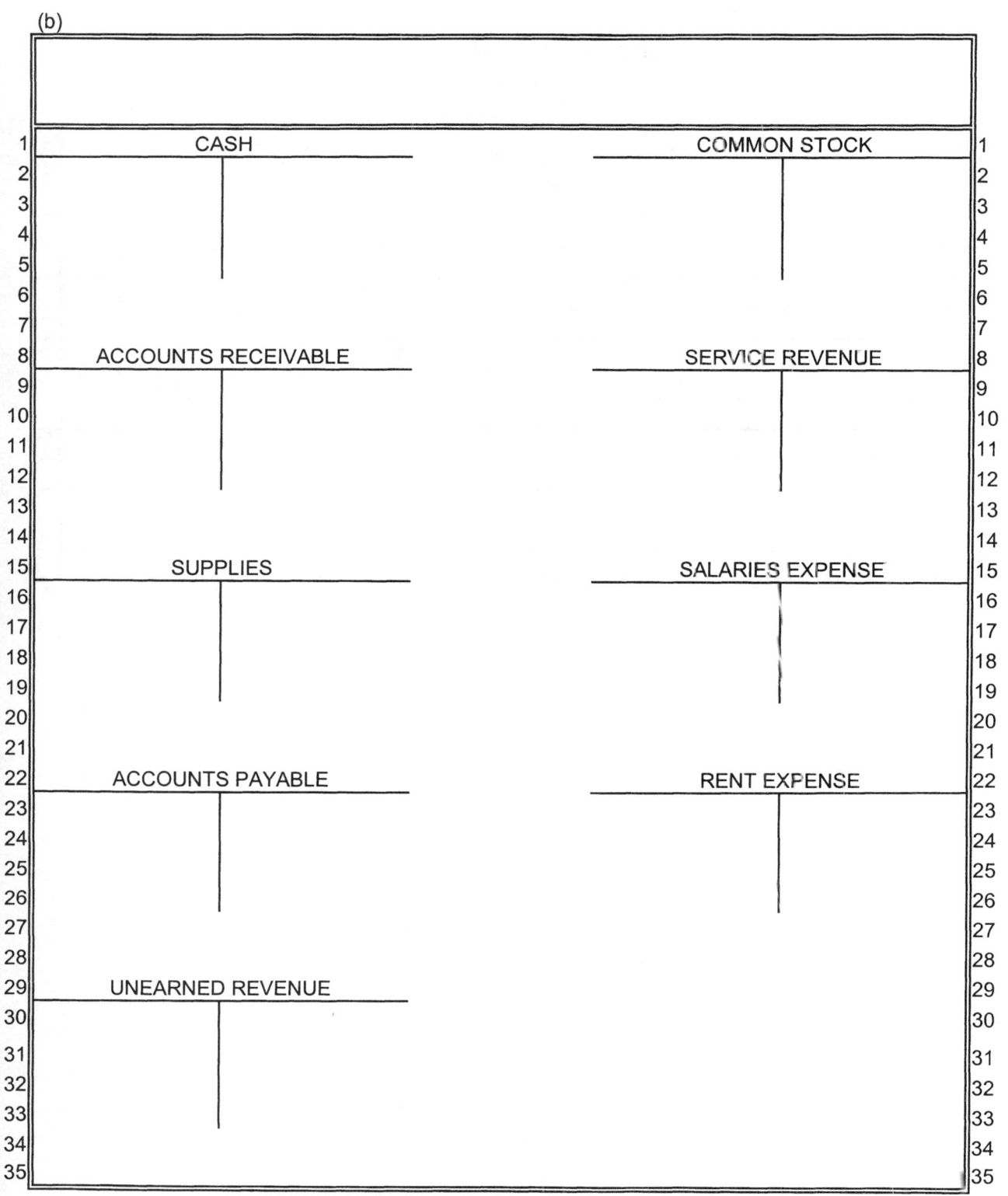

	CASH	COMMON STOCK	
1			1
2			2
3			3
4			4
5			5
6			6
7			7
8	ACCOUNTS RECEIVABLE	SERVICE REVENUE	8
9			9
10			10
11			11
12			12
13			13
14			14
15	SUPPLIES	SALARIES EXPENSE	15
16			16
17			17
18			18
19			19
20			20
21			21
22	ACCOUNTS PAYABLE	RENT EXPENSE	22
23			23
24			24
25			25
26			26
27			27
28			28
29	UNEARNED REVENUE		29
30			30
31			31
32			32
33			33
34			34
35			35

(c)

SUNFLOWER ARCHITETCTS INC. Trial Balance April 30, 2010		
	Debit	Credit
1		
2		
3		
4		
5		
6		
7		
8		
9		
10		
11		
12		
13		
14		
15		

(a) & (c)

	CASH			COMMON STOCK	
1					1
2	10/1 Bal. 8,300			10/1 Bal. 15,000	2
3					3
4					4
5					5
6					6
7					7
8					8
9	ACCOUNTS RECEIVABLE			DIVIDENDS	9
10	10/1 Bal. 2,600				10
11					11
12					12
13					13
14					14
15					15
16	SUPPLIES			SERVICE REVENUE	16
17	10/1 Bal. 2,100				17
18					18
19					19
20					20
21					21
22					22
23	EQUIPMENT			SALARIES EXPENSE	23
24	10/1 Bal. 8,000				24
25					25
26					26
27					27
28					28
29					29
30	ACCOUNTS PAYABLE			UTILITIES EXPENSE	30
31		10/1 Bal. 5,100			31
32					32
33					33
34					34
35					35
36					36
37	UNEARNED REVENUE				37
38		10/1 Bal. 900			38
39					39
40					40
41					41
42					42
43					43

(b)

	Date	Account Titles	Debit	Credit	
1	Oct 5				1
2					2
3					3
4					4
5					5
6	10				6
7					7
8					8
9					9
10					10
11	15				11
12					12
13					13
14					14
15	17				15
16					16
17					17
18					18
19					19
20	20				20
21					21
22					22
23					23
24	29				24
25					25
26					26
27					27
28	31				28
29					29
30					30
31					31
32					32
33					33
34					34
35					35
36					36
37					37
38					38
39					39
40					40

(d)

	Debit	Credit
SLOCOMBE COMPANY Trial Balance October 31, 2010		
1		
2		
3		
4		
5		
6		
7		
8		
9		
10		
11		
12		
13		
14		
15		
16		
17		
18		
19		
20		

	TITUS CO.		
	Trial Balance		
	June 30, 2010		
		Debit	Credit
1			
2			
3			
4			
5			
6			
7			
8			
9			
10			
11			
12			
13			
14			
15			
16			
17			
18			
19			
20			
21			
22			
23			
24			
25			
26			
27			
28			
29			
30			

(a) & (c)

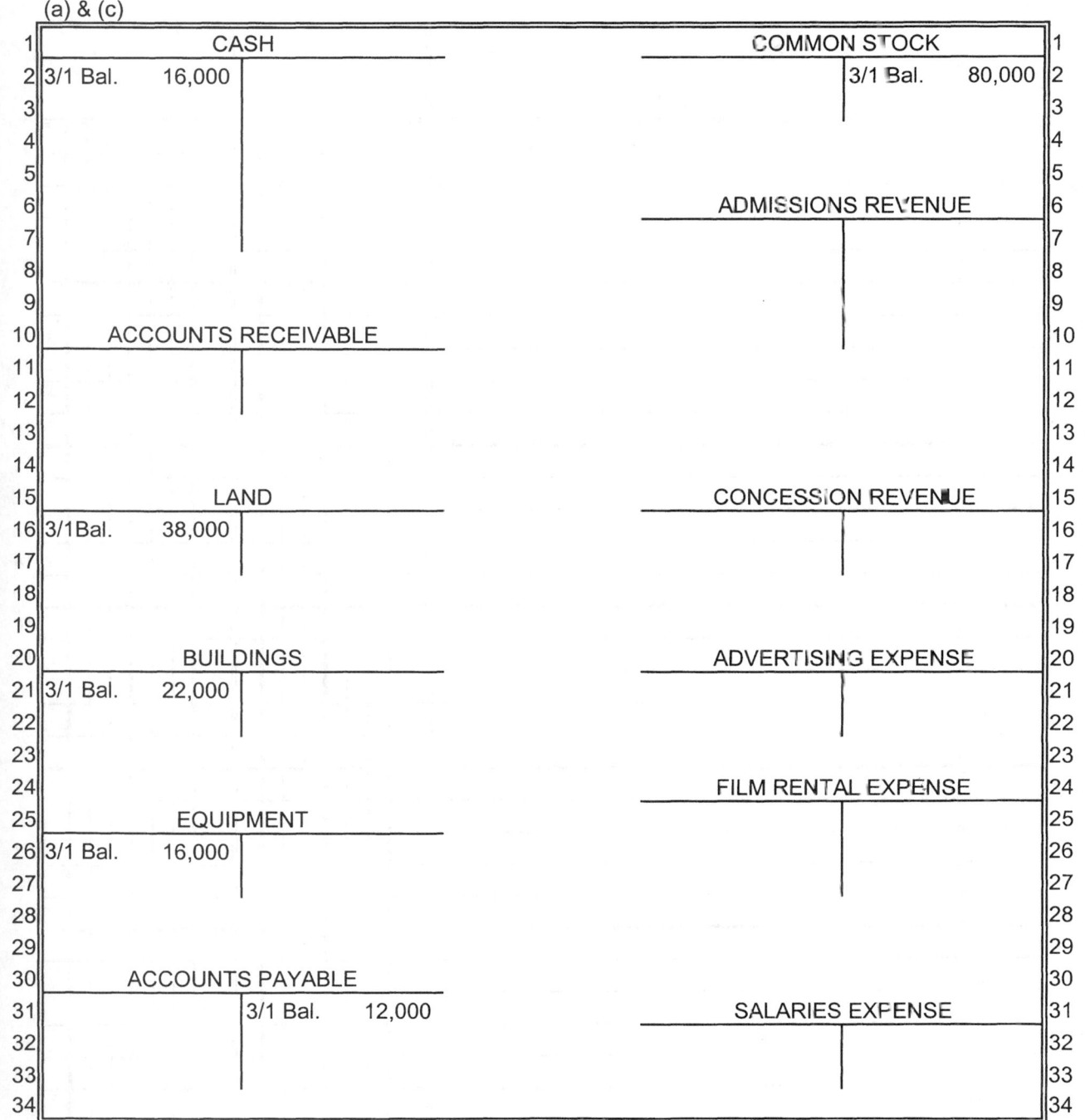

CASH		COMMON STOCK	
3/1 Bal. 16,000			3/1 Bal. 80,000

ACCOUNTS RECEIVABLE		ADMISSIONS REVENUE	

LAND		CONCESSION REVENUE	
3/1 Bal. 38,000			

BUILDINGS		ADVERTISING EXPENSE	
3/1 Bal. 22,000			

EQUIPMENT		FILM RENTAL EXPENSE	
3/1 Bal. 16,000			

ACCOUNTS PAYABLE		SALARIES EXPENSE	
	3/1 Bal. 12,000		

(b)

	Date	Account Titles	Debit	Credit	
1	Mar 2				1
2					2
3					3
4					4
5					5
6					6
7	3				7
8					8
9	9				9
10					10
11					11
12					12
13	10				13
14					14
15					15
16					16
17	11				17
18					18
19	12				19
20					20
21					21
22					22
23	20				23
24					24
25					25
26					26
27	20				27
28					28
29					29
30					30
31	31				31
32					32
33					33
34					34
35	31				35
36					36
37					37
38					38
39					39
40					40

(b) (Continued)

	Date	Account Titles	Debit	Credit	
1	Mar. 31				1
2					2
3					3
4					4
5					5
6					6
7					7
8					8
9					9
10					10

(d)

STAR-LITE THEATER INC.

Trial Balance

March 31, 2010

		Debit	Credit	
1				1
2				2
3				3
4				4
5				5
6				6
7				7
8				8
9				9
10				10
11				11
12				12
13				13
14				14
15				15
16				16
17				17
18				18
19				19
20				20

		Error	(a) In Balance	(b) Difference	(c) Larger Column		
1		1.	No	$600	Debit		1
2		2.					2
3		3.					3
4		4.					4
5		5.					5
6		6.					6
7		7.					7
8		8.					8
9							9
10							10
11							11
12							12
13							13
14							14
15							15
16							16
17							17
18							18
19							19
20							20

PROBLEM 3-1B

Hermesch Window Washing Inc.

See Appendix

(b)

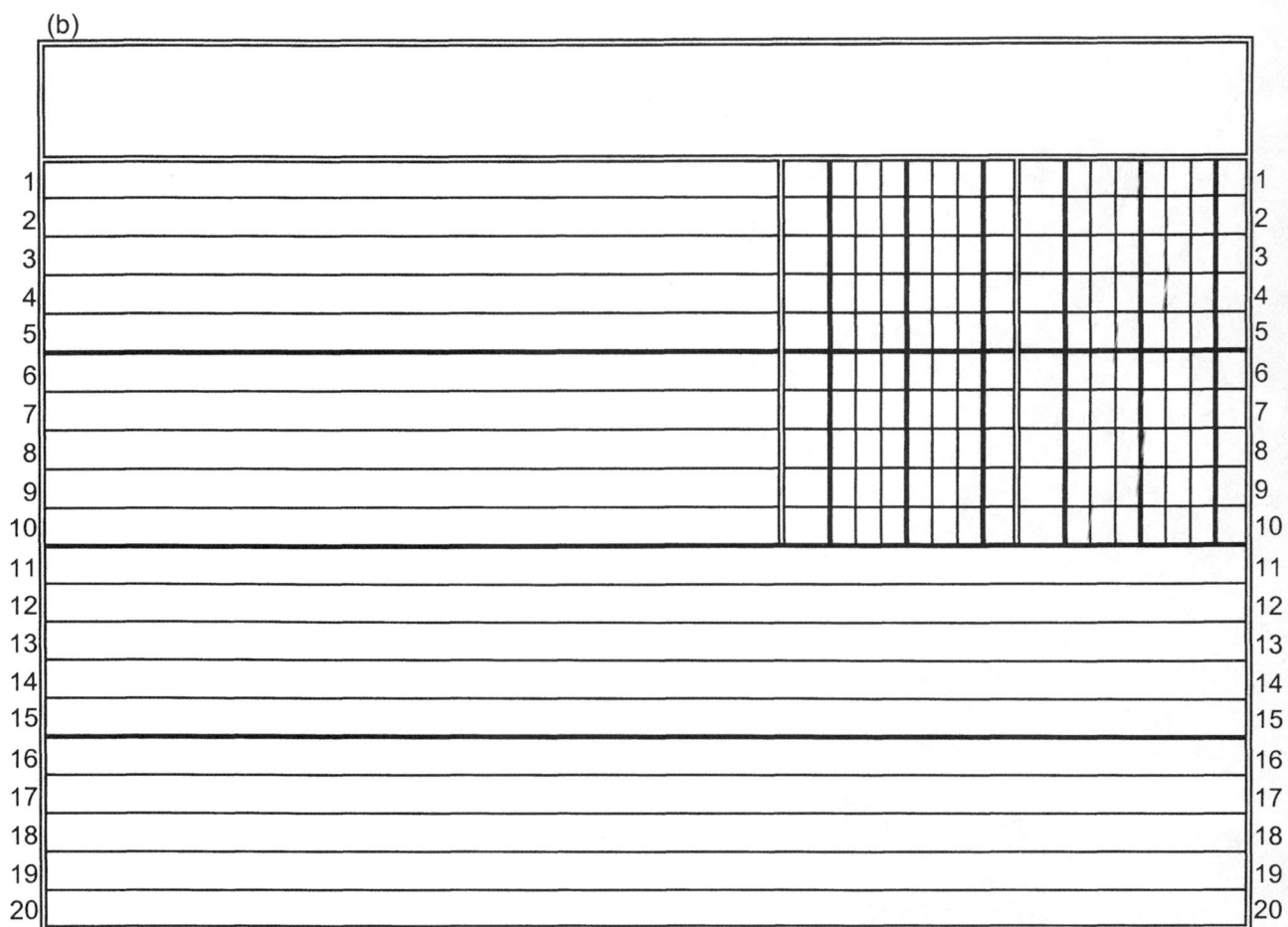

PROBLEM 3-2B

Speedy Service Inc.

See Appendix

(b)

	SPEEDY SERVICE INC.				
	Income Statement				
	For the Month Ended June 30, 2010				
1	Revenues				
2					
3					
4	Expenses				
5					
6					
7					
8					
9					
10					
11	Net income				
12					
13					
14					

(c)

	SPEEDY SERVICE INC.				
	Balance Sheet				
	June 30, 2010				
1	Assets				
2					
3					
4					
5					
6					
7					
8					
9					
10	Liabilities and Stockholders' Equity				
11					
12					
13					
14					
15					
16					
17					
18					
19					
20					

PROBLEM 3-3B

Grey Company

See Appendix

(b)

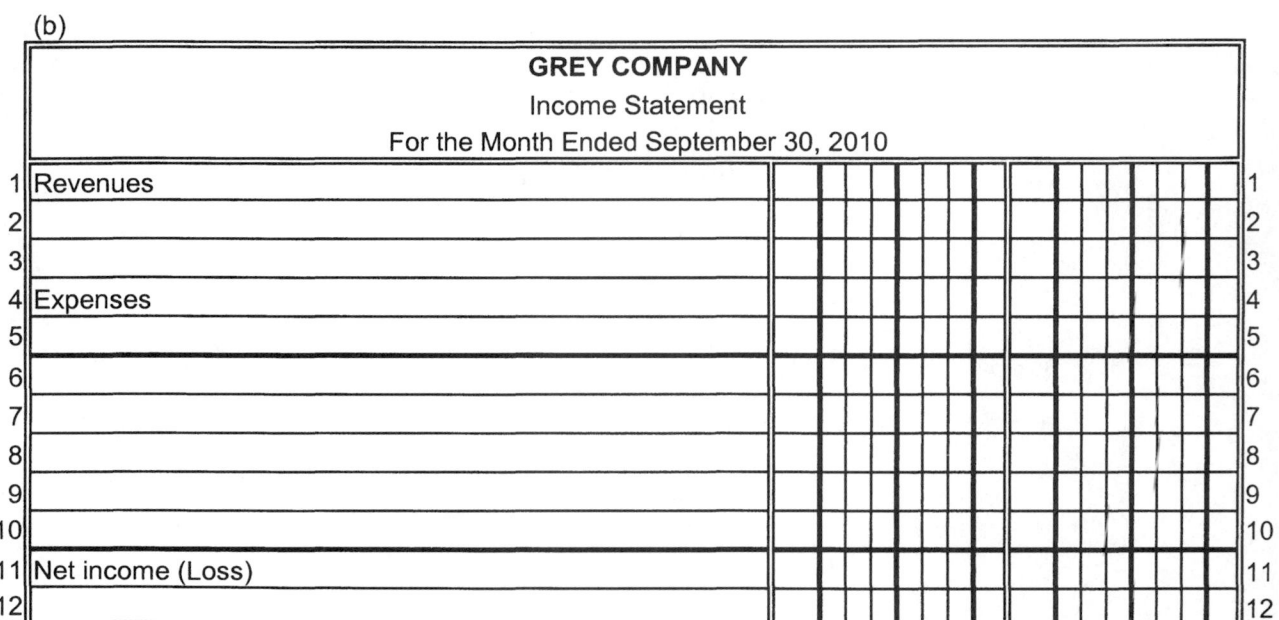

GREY COMPANY

Income Statement

For the Month Ended September 30, 2010

1	Revenues		
2			
3			
4	Expenses		
5			
6			
7			
8			
9			
10			
11	Net income (Loss)		
12			

GREY COMPANY

Retained Earnings Statement

For the Month Ended September 30, 2010

1		
2		
3		
4		
5		
6		

(b) (Continued)

GREY COMPANY
Balance Sheet
September 30, 2010

	Assets												
1													1
2													2
3													3
4													4
5													5
6													6
7													7
8													8
9													9
10													10
11	Liabilities and Stockholders' Equity												11
12													12
13													13
14													14
15													15
16													16
17													17
18													18
19													19
20													20
21													21
22													22
23													23
24													24

Section

Date

RV Haven

	Date	Account Titles	Debit	Credit	
1	Apr 1				1
2					2
3					3
4					4
5	4				5
6					6
7					7
8					8
9	8				9
10					10
11					11
12					12
13					13
14	11				14
15					15
16					16
17					17
18	12				18
19					19
20	13				20
21					21
22					22
23					23
24	17				24
25					25
26					26
27					27
28	20				28
29					29
30					30
31					31
32					32
33	25				33
34					34
35					35
36					36
37					37
38					38
39					39
40					40

	Date	Account Titles	Debit	Credit	
1	Apr 30				1
2					2
3					3
4					4
5					5
6	30				6
7					7
8					8
9					9
10					10
11					11
12					12
13					13
14					14
15					15
16					16
17					17
18					18
19					19
20					20
21					21
22					22
23					23
24					24
25					25
26					26
27					27
28					28
29					29
30					30
31					31
32					32
33					33
34					34
35					35
36					36
37					37
38					38
39					39
40					40

(a)

	Date	Account Titles	Debit	Credit	
1	May 1				1
2					2
3					3
4					4
5	2				5
6					6
7	3				7
8					8
9					9
10					10
11	7				11
12					12
13					13
14					14
15	11				15
16					16
17					17
18					18
19	12				19
20					20
21					21
22					22
23					23
24	17				24
25					25
26					26
27					27
28	31				28
29					29
30					30
31					31
32	31				32
33					33
34					34
35					35
36					36
37					37
38					38
39					39
40					40

(b)

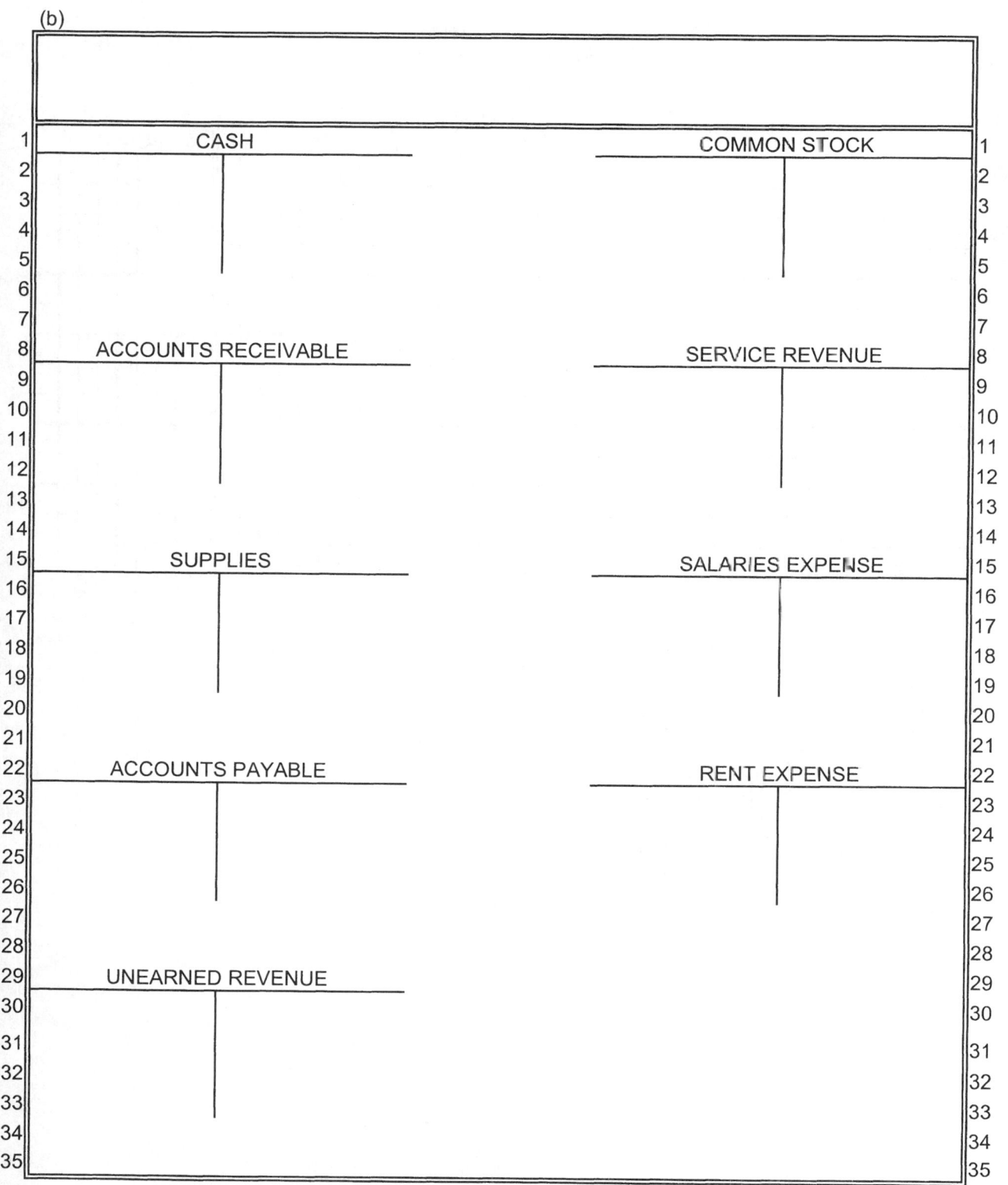

	CASH			COMMON STOCK	
1					1
2					2
3					3
4					4
5					5
6					6
7	ACCOUNTS RECEIVABLE			SERVICE REVENUE	7
8					8
9					9
10					10
11					11
12					12
13					13
14	SUPPLIES			SALARIES EXPENSE	14
15					15
16					16
17					17
18					18
19					19
20					20
21	ACCOUNTS PAYABLE			RENT EXPENSE	21
22					22
23					23
24					24
25					25
26					26
27					27
28	UNEARNED REVENUE				28
29					29
30					30
31					31
32					32
33					33
34					34
35					35

(c)

BADEN CONSULTING Trial Balance May 31, 2010	Debit	Credit
1		
2		
3		
4		
5		
6		
7		
8		
9		
10		
11		
12		
13		
14		
15		

(a) & (c)

#	CASH		COMMON STOCK	#
1	CASH		COMMON STOCK	1
2	7/1 Bal. 12,532		7/1 Bal. 35,000	2
3				3
4				4
5				5
6				6
7				7
8				8
9	ACCOUNTS RECEIVABLE		DIVIDENDS	9
10	7/1 Bal. 10,536			10
12				12
13				13
14				14
15				15
16	SUPPLIES		DRY CLEANING REVENUE	16
17	7/1 Bal. 3,512			17
18				18
19				19
20				20
21				21
22				22
23	EQUIPMENT		REPAIR EXPENSE	23
24	7/1 Bal. 25,950			24
26				26
27				27
28				28
29				29
30	ACCOUNTS PAYABLE		SALARIES EXPENSE	30
31	7/1 Bal. 15,800			31
32				32
33				33
34				34
35				35
36				36
37	UNEARNED REVENUE		UTILITIES EXPENSE	37
38	7/1 Bal. 1,730			38
40				40
41				41
42				42
43				43

(b)

	Date	Account Titles	Debit	Credit	
1	July 8				1
2					2
3					3
4					4
5	9				5
6					6
7					7
8					8
9	11				9
10					10
11					11
12					12
13					13
14	14				14
15					15
16					16
17					17
18	17				18
19					19
20					20
21					21
22	22				22
23					23
24					24
25					25
26	30				26
27					27
28					28
29					29
30					30
31					31
32	31				32
33					33
34					34
35					35
36					36
37					37
38					38
39					39
40					40

(d)

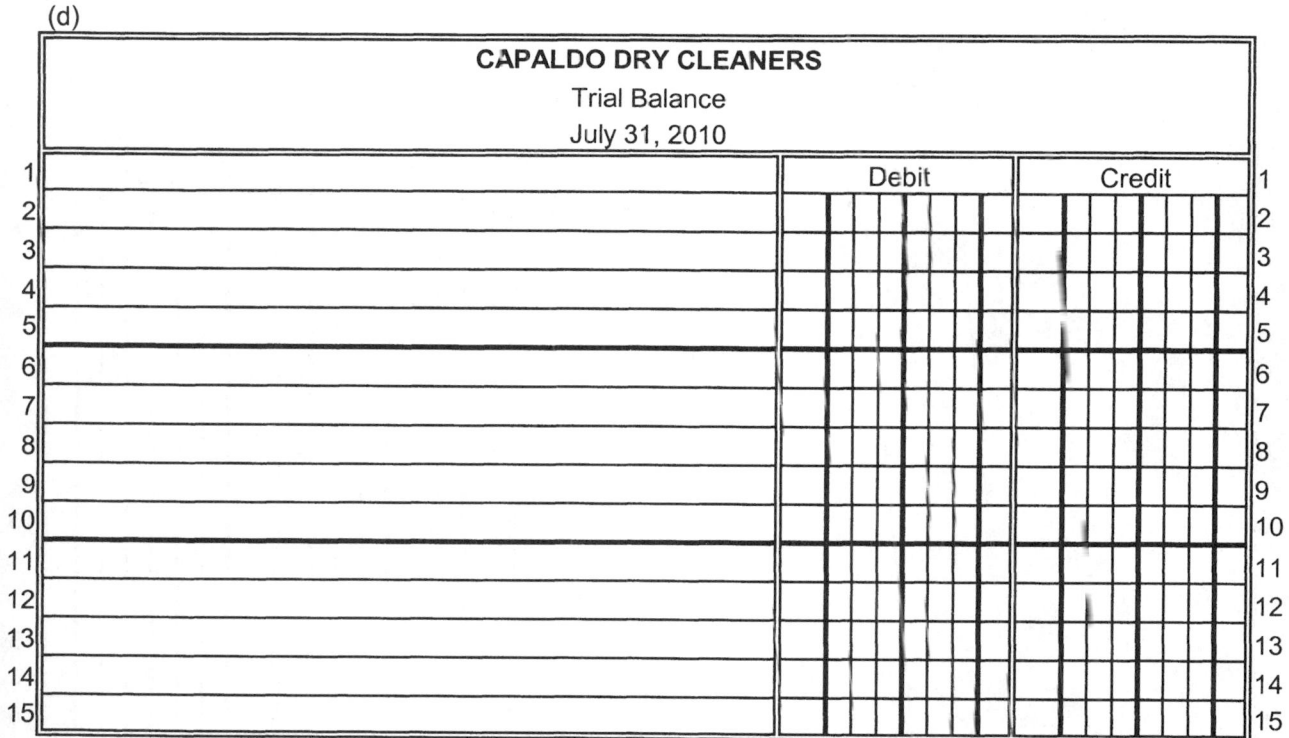

CAPALDO DRY CLEANERS
Trial Balance
July 31, 2010

	Debit	Credit

SCHUMAKER COMPANY Trial Balance May 31, 2010	Debit	Credit
1		
2		
3		
4		
5		
6		
7		
8		
9		
10		
11		
12		
13		
14		
15		
16		
17		
18		
19		
20		
21		
22		
23		
24		
25		
26		
27		
28		
29		
30		

(a) & (c)

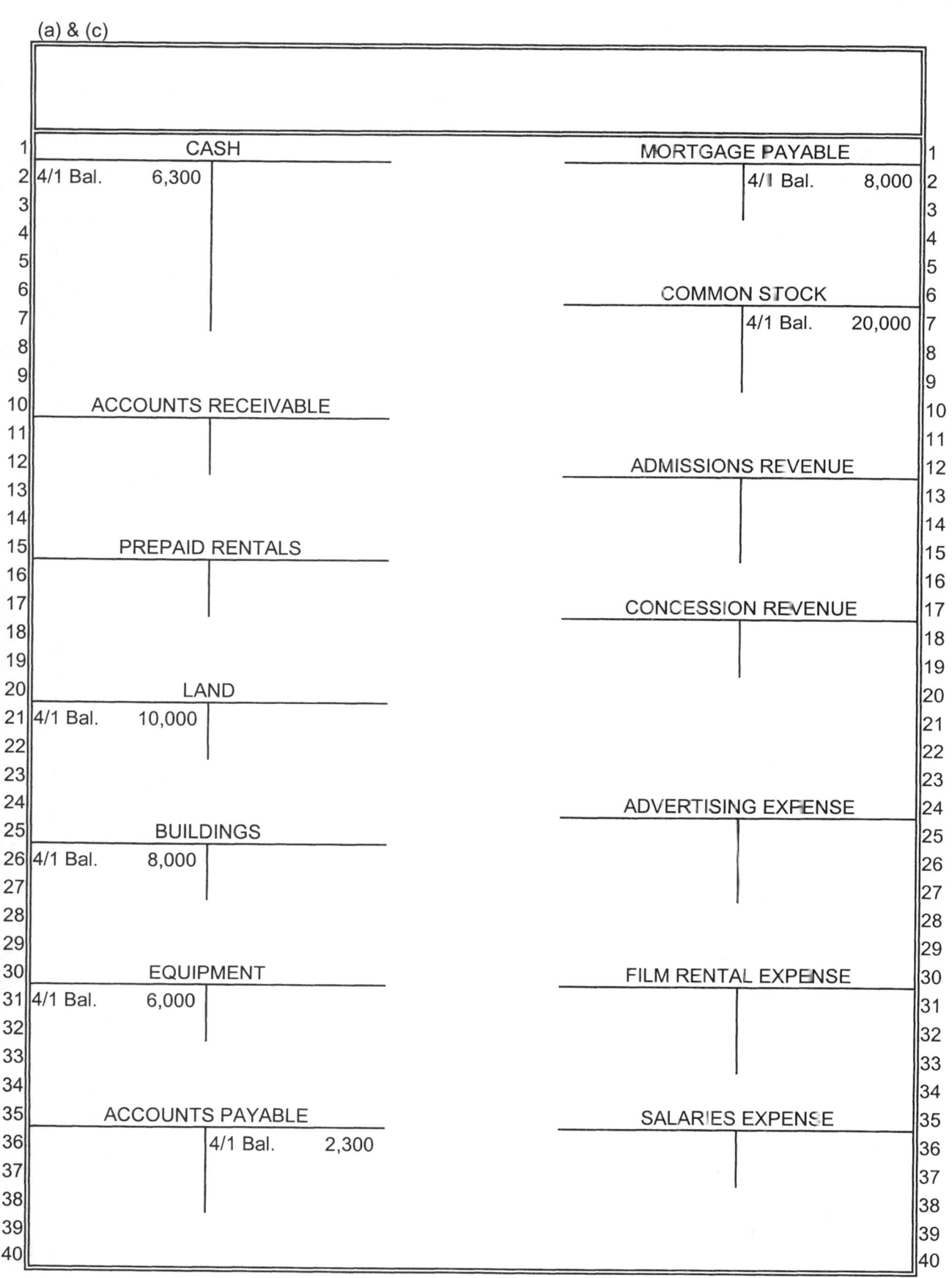

CASH		MORTGAGE PAYABLE	
4/1 Bal. 6,300			4/1 Bal. 8,000

		COMMON STOCK	
			4/1 Bal. 20,000

ACCOUNTS RECEIVABLE	

	ADMISSIONS REVENUE

PREPAID RENTALS	

	CONCESSION REVENUE

LAND	
4/1 Bal. 10,000	

	ADVERTISING EXPENSE

BUILDINGS	
4/1 Bal. 8,000	

	FILM RENTAL EXPENSE

EQUIPMENT	
4/1 Bal. 6,000	

ACCOUNTS PAYABLE		SALARIES EXPENSE	
	4/1 Bal. 2,300		

(b)

	Date	Account Titles	Debit	Credit	
1	Apr 2				1
2					2
3					3
4					4
5	3				5
6					6
7	9				7
8					8
9					9
10					10
11	10				11
12					12
13					13
14					14
15					15
16					16
17	11				17
18					18
19	12				19
20					20
21					21
22					22
23	20				23
24					24
25					25
26					26
27	25				27
28					28
29					29
30					30
31	29				31
32					32
33					33
34					34
35	30				35
36					36
37					37
38					38
39					39
40					40

(b) (Continued)

	Date	Account Titles	Debit	Credit	
1	Apr 30				1
2					2
3					3
4					4
5					5
6					6
7					7
8					8
9					9
10					10
11					11
12					12
13					13
14					14
15					15
16					16
17					17
18					18
19					19
20					20
21					21
22					22
23					23
24					24
25					25
26					26
27					27
28					28
29					29
30					30
31					31
32					32
33					33
34					34
35					35
36					36
37					37
38					38
39					39
40					40

(d)

GRANADA THEATER INC. Trial Balance April 30, 2010	Debit	Credit
1		
2		
3		
4		
5		
6		
7		
8		
9		
10		
11		
12		
13		
14		
15		
16		
17		
18		
19		
20		

(a)

1	1
2	2
3	3
4	4
5	5

(b)

	Error	(1) In Balance	(2) Difference	(3) Larger Column		
1	1.	No	$90	Credit		1
2	2.					2
3	3.					3
4	4.					4
5	5.					5
6	6.					6
7	7.					7
8	8.					8
9						9
10						10

(a)

	Date	Account Titles	Debit	Credit	
1	May 1				1
2					2
3					3
4	5				4
5					5
6	7				6
7					7
8					8
9	9				9
10					10
11					11
12	14				12
13					13
14					14
15	15				15
16					16
17					17
18	20				18
19					19
20					20
21	31				21
22					22
23					23
24					24

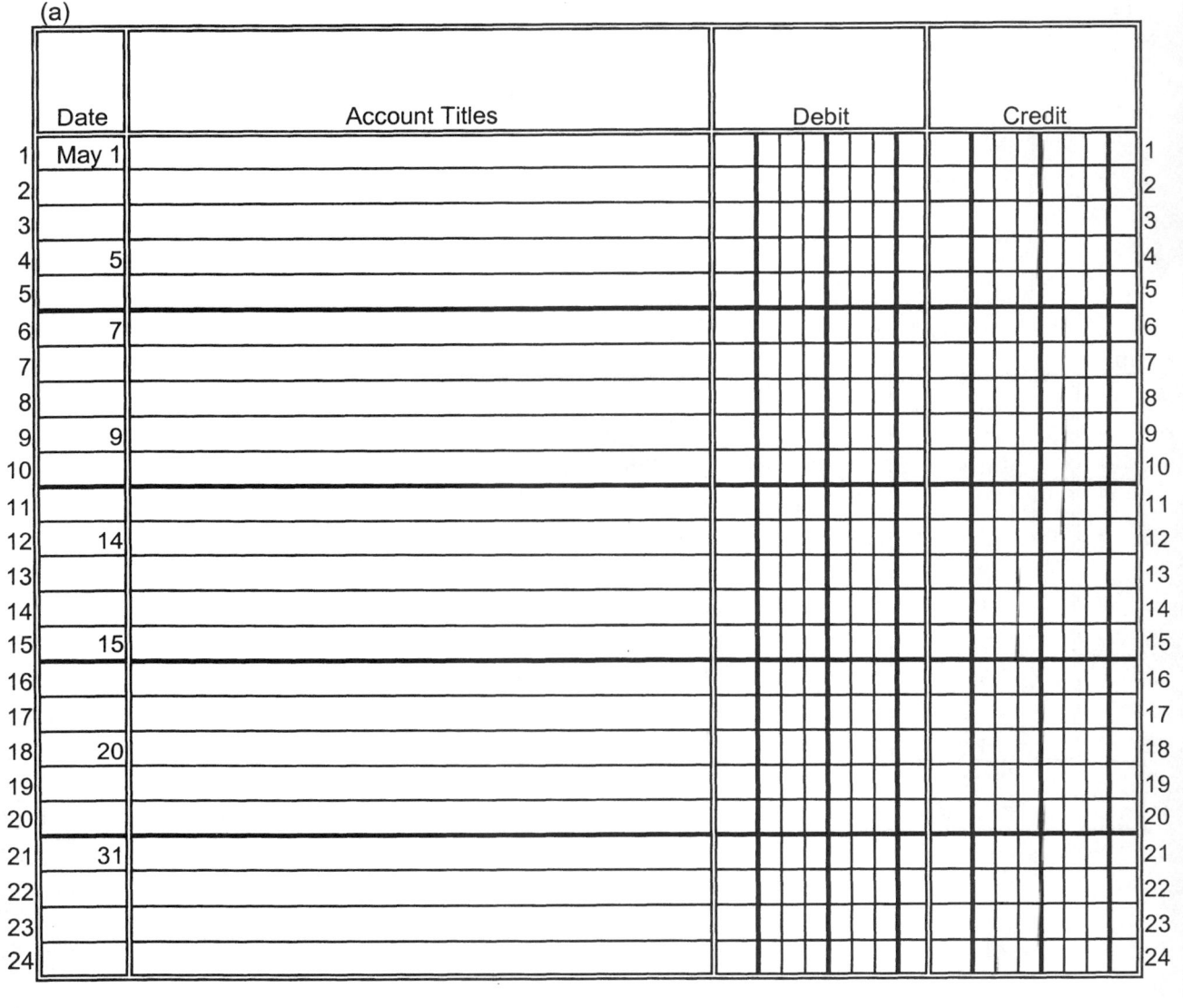

(b)

1		1
2		2
3		3
4		4
5		5
6		6
7		7
8		8
9		9
10		10
11		11

(c)

					1
1					1
2					2
3					3
4					4
5					5
6					6
7					7
8					8
9					9
10					10
11					11
12					12
13					13
14					14
15					15

(d)

1					1
2					2
3					3
4					4
5					5
6					6
7					7
8					8
9					9
10					10
11					11
12					12
13					13
14					14
15					15
16					16
17					17
18					18
19					19
20					20

BE4-1

	Cash	Net Income	
1 (a)			1
2 (b)			2
3 (c)			3
4 (d)			4
5 (e)			5
6 (f)			6
7			7
8			8

BE4-2

9 **BE4-2**		9
10 (a)		10
11		11
12		12
13 (b)		13
14		14
15		15
16 (c)		16
17		17
18		18
19 (d)		19
20		20
21		21
22		22
23		23

BE4-3

	(1) Type of Adjustment	(2) Accounts Before Adjustment	
24 **BE4-3**			24
25			25
26 (a)			26
27			27
28			28
29 (b)			29
30			30
31			31
32 (c)			32
33			33
34			34
35 (d)			35
36			36
37			37
38			38

BE4-4

	Date	Account Titles	Debit	Credit	
1		Account Titles	Debit	Credit	1
2	Dec 31				2
3					3
4					4

	ADVERTISING SUPPLIES		ADVERTISING SUPPLIES EXPENSE	
5				5
6				6
7				7
8				8
9				9
10				10

BE4-5

	Date	Account Titles	Debit	Credit	
12		Account Titles	Debit	Credit	12
13	Dec 31				13
14					14
15					15

	ACCUMULATED DEPRECIATION EQUIPMENT		DEPRECIATION EXPENSE EQUIPMENT	
16				16
17				17
18				18
19				19
20				20
21				21
22				22
23				23
24				24
25				25
26				26

BE4-6

	Date	Account Titles	Debit	Credit	
28		Account Titles	Debit	Credit	28
29	July 1				29
30					30
31					31
32	Dec 31				32
33					33
34					34

	PREPAID INSURANCE		INSURANCE EXPENSE	
35				35
36				36
37				37
38				38
39				39
40				40

BE4-7

	Date	Account Titles	Debit	Credit	
1					1
2	July 1				2
3					3
4					4
5	Dec 31				5
6					6
7					7
8					8
9					9

10	UNEARNED INSURANCE		10
11	REVENUE	INSURANCE REVENUE	11
12			12
13			13
14			14
15			15

BE4-8

	Date	Account Titles	Debit	Credit	
17					17
18	Dec 31				18
19	(a)				19
20					20
21					21
22	(b)				22
23					23
24					24
25	(c)				25
26					26

BE4-9

		Account	(1) Type of Adjustment	(2) Related Account	
28					28
29	(a)	Accounts receivable			29
30	(b)	Prepaid insurance			30
31	(c)	Equipment			31
32	(d)	Accumulated			32
33		depreciation-equipment			33
34	(e)	Notes payable			34
35	(f)	Interest payable			35
36	(g)	Unearned service			36
37		revenue			37
38					38
39					39
40					40

BE4-10

	ROSE CORPORATION								
	Income Statement								
	For the Year Ended December 31, 2010								
1									
2									
3									
4									
5									
6									
7									
8									
9									
10									
11									

BE4-11

	ROSE CORPORATION			
	Retained Earnings Statement			
	For the Year Ended December 31, 2010			
16				
17				
18				
19				
20				
21				
22				
23				
24				
25				
26				

BE4-12

	Account	Financial Statement Reported On
(a)	Accumulated depreciation	
(b)	Depreciation expense	
(c)	Retained earnings	
(d)	Dividends	
(e)	Service revenue	
(f)	Supplies	
(g)	Accounts payable	

BE4-13

1			
2			
3			
4			
5			

BE4-14

Date	Account Titles	Debit	Credit
(a)	Closing Entries		
July 31			

(b)   Retained Earnings

DO IT! 4-1

Date	Account Titles	Debit	Credit

DO IT! 4-2

Date	Account Titles	Debit	Credit

DO IT! 4-3

Income statement:

Balance sheet:

Name

Section

Date

Adams Company

	Date	Account Titles	Debit	Credit	
1					1
2					2
3					3
4					4
5					5
6					6
7					7
8					8
9					9
10					10
11					11
12					12
13					13
14					14
15					15
16					16
17					17
18					18
19					19
20					20
21					21
22					22
23					23
24					24
25					25
26					26
27					27
28					28
29					29
30					30
31					31
32					32
33					33
34					34
35					35
36					36
37					37
38					38
39					39
40					40

E4-4

	Amount	Explanation	
1	$ 3 3 6 4 0	Cash basis earnings	1
2			2
3			3
4			4
5			5
6			6
7			7
8			8
9			9
10			10
11			11
12			12
13			13
14			14
15			15
16			16
17			17
18			18
19			19
20			20
21			21
22			22
23			23
24			24
25			25

E4-5

(a)	Cash Basis	Accrual Basis	
1			1
2			2
3			3
4			4
5			5
6			6
7 (b)			7
8			8
9			9
10			10

(a)

BOULDER COMPANY
Income Statement
For the Six Months Ended April 30, 2010

1	Revenues		
2			
3	Expenses		
4			
5			
6			
7			
8			
9			
10			
11			
12			
13			
14			
15			

(b)

BOULDER COMPANY
Balance Sheet
April 30, 2010

1	Assets		
2			
3			
4			
5			
6			
7			
8			
9			
10			
11			
12	Liabilities and Stockholders' Equity		
13			
14			
15			
16			
17			
18			
19			
20			

E4-9

	Date	Account Titles	Debit	Credit	
1	Mar 31				1
2	1.				2
3					3
4					4
5	2.				5
6					6
7					7
8	3.				8
9					9
10					10
11	4.				11
12					12
13					13
14	5.				14
15					15
16					16

E4-10

	Date	Account Titles	Debit	Credit	
1	Jan 31				1
2	1.				2
3					3
4					4
5	2.				5
6					6
7					7
8	3.				8
9					9
10					10
11					11
12					12
13					13
14	4.				14
15					15
16					16
17	5.				17
18					18
19					19
20					20

E4-11

	Date	Account Titles	Debit	Credit	
1	Oct 31				1
2	1.				2
3					3
4					4
5	2.				5
6					6
7					7
8	3.				8
9					9
10					10
11	4.				11
12					12
13					13
14	5.				14
15					15
16					16
17	6.				17
18					18
19					19
20	7.				20
21					21
22					22
23					23
24					24
25					25

E4-12

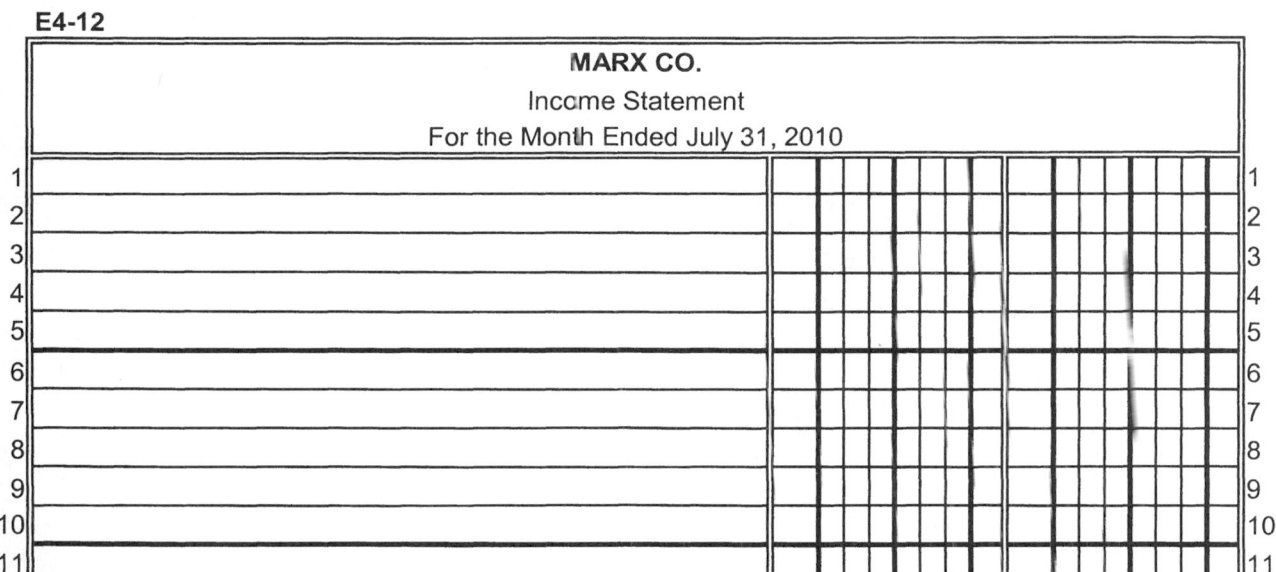

	MARX CO. Income Statement For the Month Ended July 31, 2010			
1				1
2				2
3				3
4				4
5				5
6				6
7				7
8				8
9				9
10				10
11				11

#11

		Answer	Computation		
1	(a)				1
2					2
3					3
4					4
5					5
6					6
7	(b)				7
8					8
9					9
10					10
11					11
12					12
13					13
14	(c)				14
15					15
16					16
17					17
18					18
19					19
20					20
21	(d)				21
22					22
23					23
24					24
25					25
26					26
27					27
28					28
29					29
30					30

E4-14

	Date	Account Titles	Debit	Credit	
1	Jan 31				1
2					2
3					3
4	31				4
5					5
6					6
7					7
8					8
9	31				9
10					10
11					11
12					12
13					13
14					14
15					15

E4-16

	Date	Account Titles	Debit	Credit	
1	Aug 31				1
2					2
3					3
4	31				4
5					5
6					6
7	31				7
8					8
9					9
10	31				10
11					11
12					12
13					13
14	31				14
15					15
16					16
17	31				17
18					18
19					19
20					20

	Date	Account Titles	Debit	Credit	
1	(a)				1
2	July 10				2
3					3
4					4
5	14				5
6					6
7					7
8	15				8
9					9
10					10
11	20				11
12					12
13					13
14					14
15					15
16	(b)				16
17	July 31				17
18					18
19					19
20	31				20
21					21
22					22
23	31				23
24					24
25					25
26	31				26
27					27
28					28
29					29
30					30

IVY COMPANY

Income Statement

For the Year Ended August 31, 2010

1	Revenue	
2		
3		
4		
5		
6	Expenses	
7		
8		
9		
10		
11		
12		
13		
14	Net income	
15		

IVY COMPANY

Retained Earnings Statement

For the Year Ended August 31, 2010

1	
2	
3	
4	
5	
6	
7	
8	
9	
10	

IVY COMPANY
Balance Sheet
August 31, 2010

Assets

Liabilities and Stockholders' Equity

	Date	Account Titles	Debit	Credit	
1	Aug 31				1
2					2
3					3
4					4
5	31				5
6					6
7					7
8					8
9					9
10					10
11					11
12					12
13					13
14					14
15					15
16					16
17	31				17
18					18
19					19
20					20
21	31				21
22					22
23					23
24					24
25					25
26					26
27					27
28					28
29					29
30					30

(a)

	Date	Account Titles	Debit	Credit	
1	1.				1
2					2
3					3
4					4
5	2.				5
6					6
7					7
8					8
9	3.				9
10					10
11					11
12					12
13					13
14					14
15					15
16					16
17	4.				17
18					18
19					19
20					20
21	5.				21
22					22
23					23
24					24
25					25

(b)

ACCOUNTS RECEIVABLE		**DUES REVENUE**
2009		
Bal. 11,000		2010
		Bal. 153,000
2010		
Bal. 18,000		**TICKET REVENUE**
UNEARNED TICKET REVENUE		
	2009	
	Bal. 26,000	2010
		Bal.
	2010	**CASH**
	Bal. 20,000	
		2010
		Bal.

(a)

	Date	Account Titles	Debit	Credit	
1	2010				1
2	Jun 30				2
3	1.				3
4					4
5					5
6	2.				6
7					7
8					8
9	3.				9
10					10
11					11
12	4.				12
13					13
14					14
15	5.				15
16					16
17					17
18	6.				18
19					19
20					20
21					21
22	7.				22
23					23
24					24
25					25
26					26

(b)

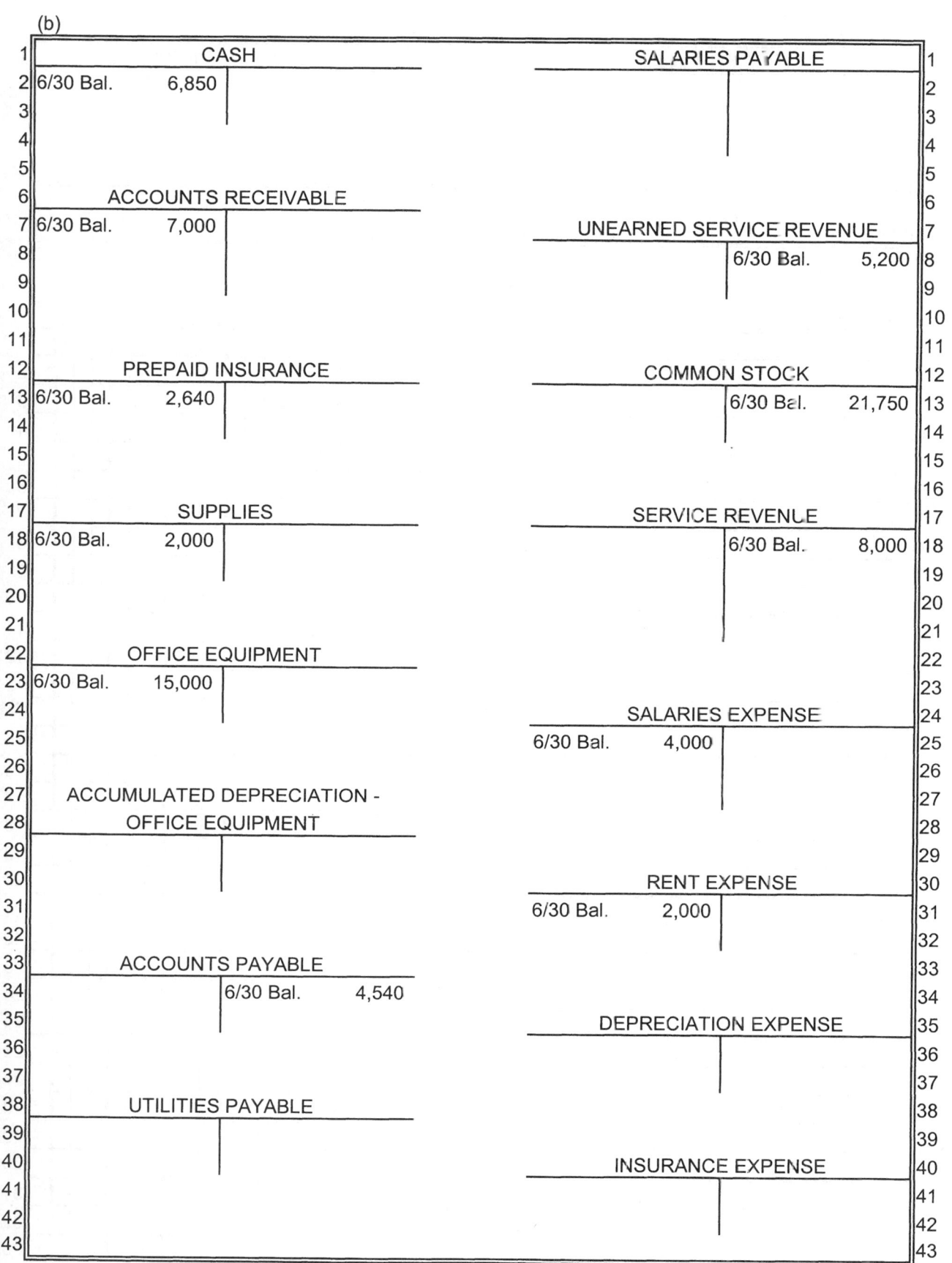

	CASH			SALARIES PAYABLE		
1						1
2	6/30 Bal.	6,850				2
3						3
4						4
5						5
6	ACCOUNTS RECEIVABLE					6
7	6/30 Bal.	7,000		UNEARNED SERVICE REVENUE		7
8				6/30 Bal.	5,200	8
9						9
10						10
11						11
12	PREPAID INSURANCE			COMMON STOCK		12
13	6/30 Bal.	2,640		6/30 Bal.	21,750	13
14						14
15						15
16						16
17	SUPPLIES			SERVICE REVENUE		17
18	6/30 Bal.	2,000		6/30 Bal.	8,000	18
19						19
20						20
21						21
22	OFFICE EQUIPMENT					22
23	6/30 Bal.	15,000				23
24				SALARIES EXPENSE		24
25				6/30 Bal. 4,000		25
26						26
27	ACCUMULATED DEPRECIATION -					27
28	OFFICE EQUIPMENT					28
29						29
30				RENT EXPENSE		30
31				6/30 Bal. 2,000		31
32						32
33	ACCOUNTS PAYABLE					33
34		6/30 Bal. 4,540				34
35				DEPRECIATION EXPENSE		35
36						36
37						37
38	UTILITIES PAYABLE					38
39				INSURANCE EXPENSE		39
40						40
41						41
42						42
43						43

(b) (Continued)

UTILITIES EXPENSE		SUPPLIES EXPENSE	

(c)

WAEGELEIN CONSULTING

Adjusted Trial Balance

June 30, 2010

(a)

	Date	Account Titles	Debit	Credit	
1	May 31				1
2	1.				2
3					3
4					4
5	2.				5
6					6
7					7
8	3.				8
9					9
10					10
11					11
12					12
13					13
14					14
15	4.				15
16					16
17					17
18	5.				18
19					19
20					20
21	6.				21
22					22
23					23
24					24
25					25

(b)

	CASH			ACCOUNTS PAYABLE	
5/31 Bal.	2,500			5/31 Bal.	4,700

	PREPAID INSURANCE			UNEARNED RENT REVENUE	
5/31 Bal.	1,800			5/31 Bal.	3,300

	SUPPLIES			SALARIES PAYABLE	
5/31 Bal.	2,600				

	LAND			INTEREST PAYABLE	
5/31 Bal.	15,000				

	LODGE			MORTGAGE PAYABLE	
5/31 Bal.	70,000			5/31 Bal.	36,000

ACCUMULATED DEPRECIATION - LODGE				COMMON STOCK	
				5/31 Bal.	60,000

				RENT REVENUE	
	FURNITURE			5/31 Bal.	9,000
5/31 Bal.	16,800				

ACCUMULATED DEPRECIATION - FURNITURE			SALARIES EXPENSE		
			5/31 Bal.	3,000	

(b) (Continued)

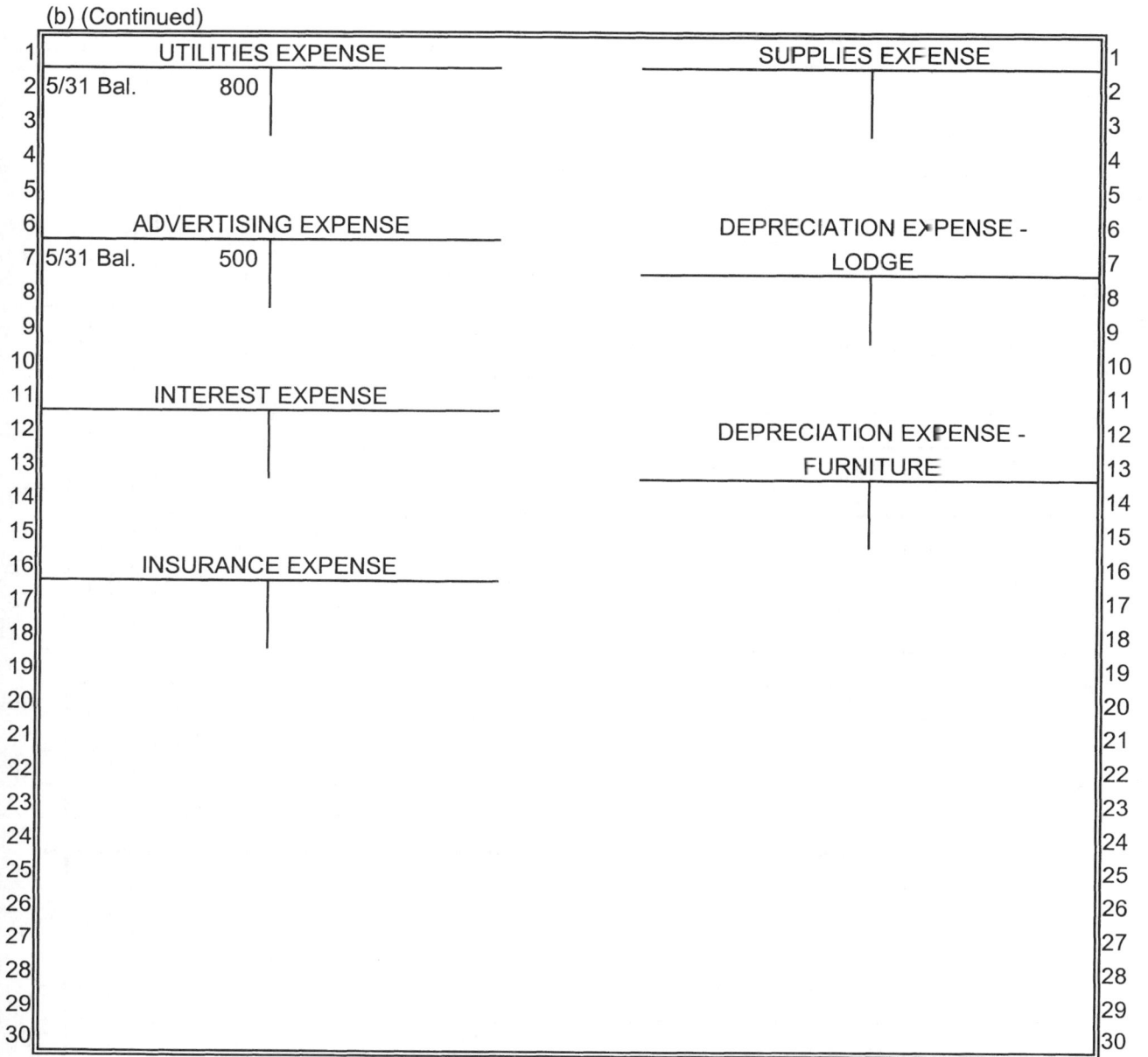

	UTILITIES EXPENSE			SUPPLIES EXPENSE	
1					1
2	5/31 Bal. 800				2
3					3
4					4
5					5
6	ADVERTISING EXPENSE			DEPRECIATION EXPENSE -	6
7	5/31 Bal. 500			LODGE	7
8					8
9					9
10					10
11	INTEREST EXPENSE				11
12				DEPRECIATION EXPENSE -	12
13				FURNITURE	13
14					14
15					15
16	INSURANCE EXPENSE				16

(c)

		OLATHE HOTEL			
		Adjusted Trial Balance			
		May 31, 2010			
			Debit	Credit	
1					1
2					2
3					3
4					4
5					5
6					6
7					7
8					8
9					9
10					10
11					11
12					12
13					13
14					14
15					15
16					16
17					17
18					18
19					19
20					20
21					21
22					22
23					23
24					24
25					25
26					26
27					27
28					28
29					29
30					30

(d)

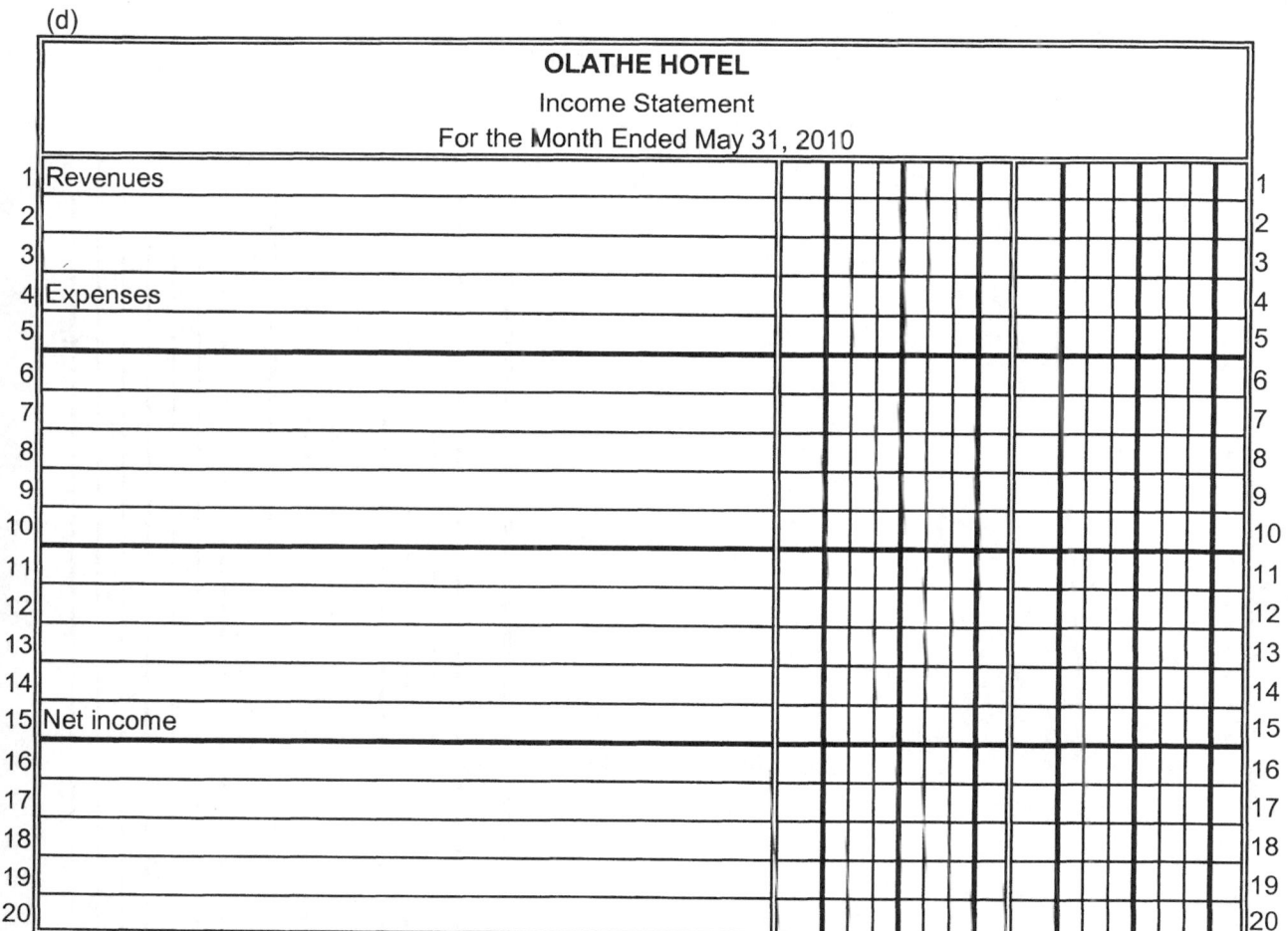

OLATHE HOTEL

Income Statement

For the Month Ended May 31, 2010

1	Revenues		
2			
3			
4	Expenses		
5			
6			
7			
8			
9			
10			
11			
12			
13			
14			
15	Net income		
16			
17			
18			
19			
20			

OLATHE HOTEL

Retained Earnings Statement

For the Month Ended May 31, 2010

1		
2		
3		
4		
5		

(d) (Continued) and (e)

OLATHE HOTEL

Balance Sheet

May 31, 2010

	Assets						
1							
2							
3							
4							
5							
6							
7							
8							
9							
10							
11							
12							
13							
14							
15							
16	Liabilities and Stockholders' Equity						
17							
18							
19							
20							
21							
22							
23							
24							
25							
26							
27							
28							
29							
30							
31							
32							
33							
34							
35	(e)						
36							
37							
38							
39							
40							

(a)

	Date	Accounts Titles	Debit	Credit	
1	Sept 30				1
2					2
3					3
4	30				4
5					5
6					6
7	30				7
8					8
9					9
10	30				10
11					11
12					12
13	30				13
14					14
15					15
16	30				16
17					17
18					18
19	30				19
20					20
21					21

(b)

FOUR OAKS GOLF INC.
Income Statement
For the Quarter Ended September 30, 2010

1	Revenues			1
2				2
3				3
4				4
5	Expenses			5
6				6
7				7
8				8
9				9
10				10
11				11
12				12
13	Net income			13
14				14

(b) (Continued)

FOUR OAKS GOLF INC.
Retained Earnings Statement
For the Quarter Ended September 30, 2010

1		
2		
3		
4		
5		
6		
7		

FOUR OAKS GOLF INC.
Balance Sheet
September 30, 2010

Assets		
1		
2		
3		
4		
5		
6		
7		
8		
9		
10		
11		
12		
Liabilities and Stockholders' Equity		
14		
15		
16		
17		
18		
19		
20		
21		
22		
23		
24		
25		
26		
27		
28		
29		

(c) and (d)

(c)

1		1
2		2
3		3
4		4
5		5

(d)

6		6
7		7
8		8
9		9
10		10
11		11
12		12
13		13
14		14
15		15
16		16
17		17
18		18
19		19
20		20
21		21
22		22
23		23
24		24
25		25
26		26
27		27
28		28
29		29
30		30
31		31
32		32
33		33
34		34
35		35
36		36
37		37
38		38

	Date	Account Titles	Debit	Credit	
1	Dec 31				1
2	1.				2
3					3
4					4
5					5
6					6
7					7
8					8
9					9
10					10
11	2.				11
12					12
13					13
14					14
15					15
16					16
17					17
18					18
19					19
20	3.				20
21					21
22					22
23					23
24					24
25					25
26					26
27					27
28	4.				28
29					29
30					30
31					31
32					32
33					33
34					34
35					35

(a)

	Date	Account Titles	Debit	Credit	
1	Jun 30				1
2	1.				2
3					3
4					4
5					5
6	2.				6
7					7
8					8
9					9
10	3.				10
11					11
12					12
13					13
14	4.				14
15					15
16					16
17					17
18					18
19					19
20	5.				20
21					21
22					22
23					23
24	6.				24
25					25
26					26
27					27
28	7.				28
29					29
30					30
31					31
32					32
33					33
34					34
35					35

(b)

HAPPY CAMPER TRAVEL COURT				
Income Statement				
For the Quarter Ended June 30, 2010				
1	Revenues:				
2					
3	Expenses:				
4					
5					
6					
7					
8					
9					
10					
11					
12					
13					
14					
15	Net income				
16					

(c)

(a), (c) & (e)

	CASH			UNEARNED SERVICE REVENUE		
1						1
2	11/1 Bal.	2,790			11/1 Bal. 400	2
3						3
4						4
5						5
6						6
7				SALARIES PAYABLE		7
8					11/1 Bal. 620	8
9	ACCOUNTS RECEIVABLE					9
10	11/1 Bal.	2,910				10
11						11
12						12
13				COMMON STOCK		13
14					11/1 Bal. 10,000	14
15	SUPPLIES					15
16	11/1 Bal.	1,120				16
17						17
18				RETAINED EARNINGS		18
19					11/1 Bal. 3,000	19
20						20
21						21
22	STORE EQUIPMENT					22
23	11/1 Bal.	10,000		SERVICE REVENUE		23
24						24
25						25
26						26
27						27
28	ACCUMULATED DEPRECIATION -					28
29	STORE EQUIPMENT					29
30		11/1 Bal. 500				30
31				DEPRECIATION EXPENSE		31
32						32
33						33
34						34
35	ACCOUNTS PAYABLE					35
36		11/1 Bal. 2,300		SUPPLIES EXPENSE		36
37						37
38						38
39						39
40						40

(a), (c) & (e) (Continued)

	SALARIES EXPENSE			RENT EXPENSE	
1					1
2					2
3					3
4					4
5					5
6					6

(b)

	Date	Account Titles	Debit	Credit	
1	Nov 8				1
2					2
3					3
4					4
5	10				5
6					6
7					7
8	12				8
9					9
10					10
11	15				11
12					12
13					13
14	17				14
15					15
16					16
17	20				17
18					18
19					19
20	22				20
21					21
22					22
23	25				23
24					24
25					25
26	27				26
27					27
28					28
29	29				29
30					30
31					31
32					32

(d) & (f)

MONTANA EQUIPMENT REPAIR
Trial Balances
November 30, 2010

	Before Adjustment		After Adjustment	
	Dr.	Cr.	Dr.	Cr.
1				
2				
3				
4				
5				
6				
7				
8				
9				
10				
11				
12				
13				
14				
15				
16				
17				
18				
19				
20				

(e)

Date	Account Titles	Debit	Credit
Nov 30			
1.			
2.			
3.			
4.			

(g)

MONTANA EQUIPMENT REPAIR			
Income Statement			
For the Month Ended November 30, 2010			
1			
2 Revenues			
3			
4			
5 Expenses			
6			
7			
8			
9			
10			
11			
12 Net income			
13			
14			
15			
16			
17			

MONTANA EQUIPMENT REPAIR	
Retained Earnings Statement	
For the Month Ended November 30, 2010	
1	
2	
3	
4	
5	

(g) (Continued)

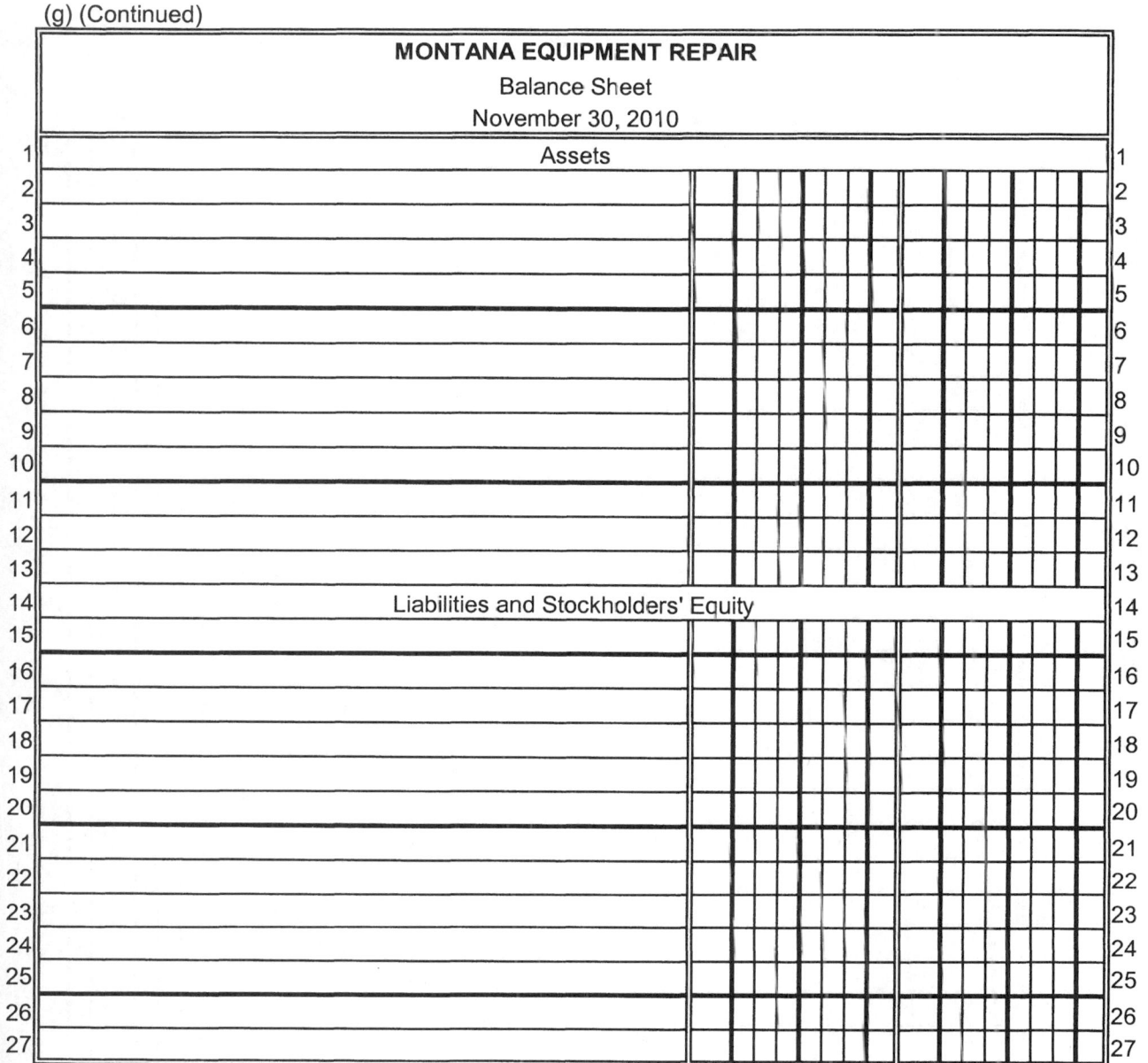

MONTANA EQUIPMENT REPAIR

Balance Sheet

November 30, 2010

Assets

Liabilities and Stockholders' Equity

(a)

	Date	Account Titles	Debit	Credit	
1	July 1				1
2					2
3					3
4	1				4
5					5
6					6
7					7
8	3				8
9					9
10					10
11	5				11
12					12
13					13
14	12				14
15					15
16					16
17	18				17
18					18
19					19
20	20				20
21					21
22					22
23	21				23
24					24
25					25
26	25				26
27					27
28					28
29	31				29
30					30
31					31
32	31				32
33					33
34					34
35					35

(b), (e) & (h)

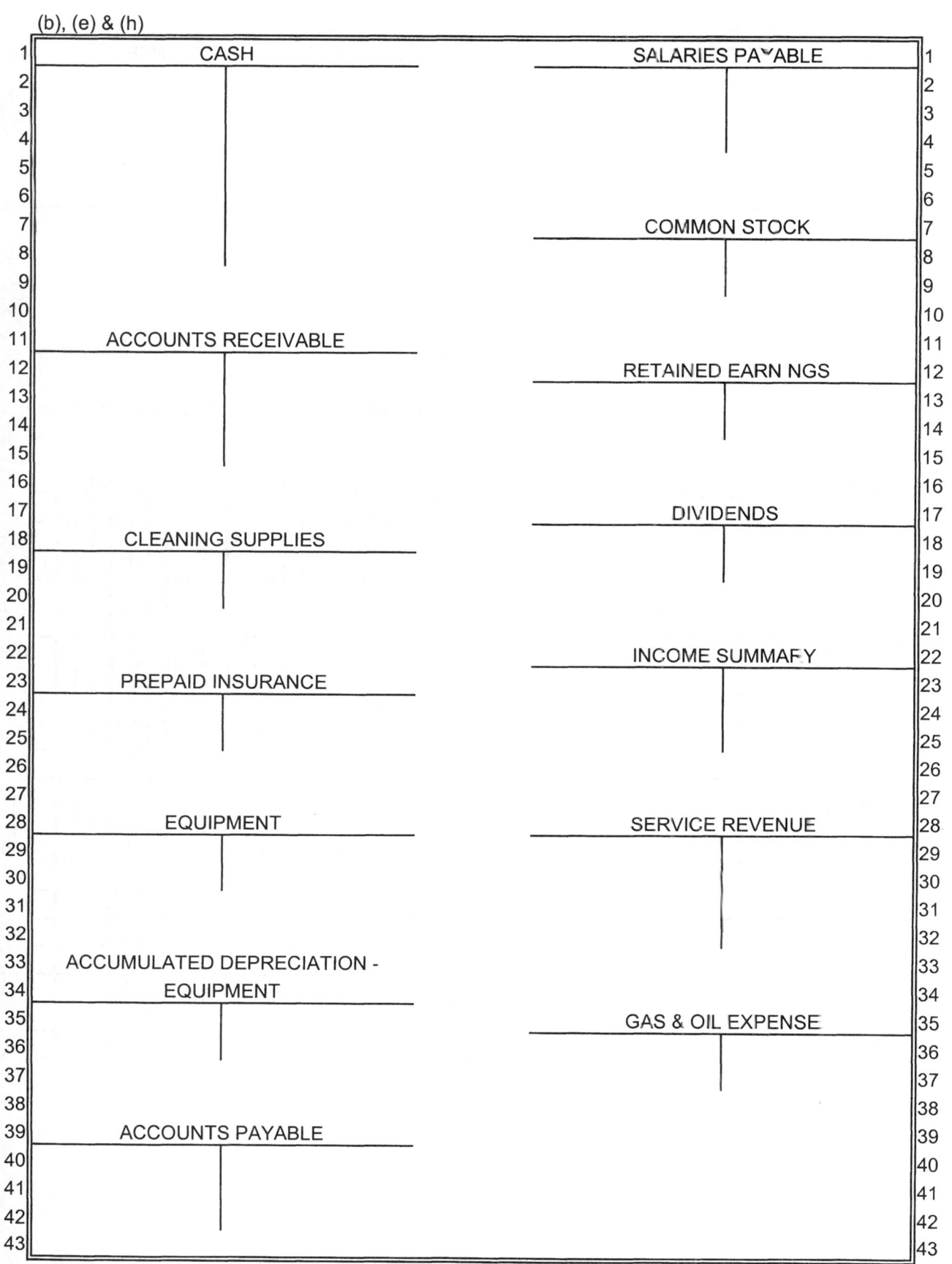

CASH	SALARIES PAYABLE
ACCOUNTS RECEIVABLE	COMMON STOCK
	RETAINED EARNINGS
CLEANING SUPPLIES	DIVIDENDS
PREPAID INSURANCE	INCOME SUMMARY
EQUIPMENT	SERVICE REVENUE
ACCUMULATED DEPRECIATION - EQUIPMENT	GAS & OIL EXPENSE
ACCOUNTS PAYABLE	

(b), (e) & (h) (Continued)

	CLEANING SUPPLIES EXPENSE	INSURANCE EXPENSE	
1			1
2			2
3			3
4			4
5			5
6	DEPRECIATION EXPENSE	SALARIES EXPENSE	6
7			7
8			8
9			9
10			10
11			11

(d)

	Date	Account Titles	Debit	Credit	
1	July 31				1
2	1.				2
3					3
4					4
5	2.				5
6					6
7					7
8	3.				8
9					9
10					10
11	4.				11
12					12
13					13
14	5.				14
15					15
16					16
17					17
18					18
19					19
20					20

( ) & (f)

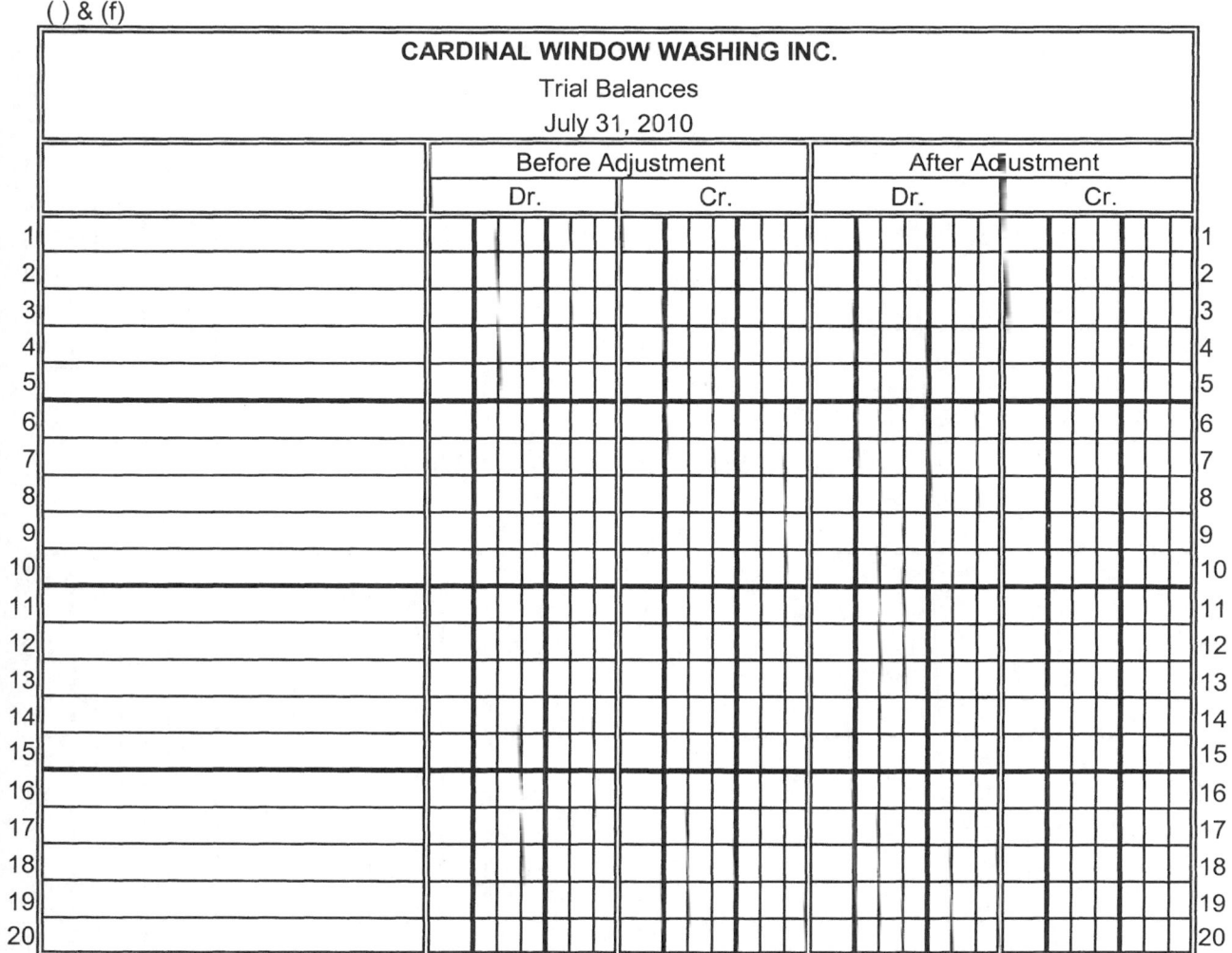

CARDINAL WINDOW WASHING INC.

Trial Balances

July 31, 2010

	Before Adjustment		After Adjustment	
	Dr.	Cr.	Dr.	Cr.
1				
2				
3				
4				
5				
6				
7				
8				
9				
10				
11				
12				
13				
14				
15				
16				
17				
18				
19				
20				

(g)

CARDINAL WINDOW WASHING INC.

Income Statement

For the Month Ended July 31, 2010

1 Revenues	
2	
3 Expenses	
4	
5	
6	
7	
8	
9	
10	
11 Net income	
12	
13	

(g) (Continued)

CARDINAL WINDOW WASHING INC.		
Retained Earnings Statement		
For the Month Ended July 31, 2010		
1		1
2		2
3		3
4		4
5		5
6		6

CARDINAL WINDOW WASHING INC.		
Balance Sheet		
July 31, 2010		
1	Assets	1
2		2
3		3
4		4
5		5
6		6
7		7
8		8
9		9
10		10
11		11
12		12
13	Liabilities and Stockholders' Equity	13
14		14
15		15
16		16
17		17
18		18
19		19
20		20
21		21
22		22
23		23
24		24
25		25
26		26
27		27

(h)

	Date	Account Titles	Debit	Credit	
1	July 31				1
2					2
3					3
4	31				4
5					5
6					6
7					7
8					8
9					9
10					10
11	31				11
12					12
13					13
14	31				14
15					15
16					16

(i)

CARDINAL WINDOW WASHING INC.

Post-Closing Trial Balance

July 31, 2010

		Debit	Credit	
1				1
2				2
3				3
4				4
5				5
6				6
7				7
8				8
9				9
10				10
11				11
12				12
13				13
14				14

(a)

	Date	Account Titles	Debit	Credit	
1	1.				1
2					2
3					3
4	2.				4
5					5
6					6
7	3.				7
8					8
9					9
10					10
11					11
12					12
13					13
14					14
15	4.				15
16					16
17					17
18	5.				18
19					19
20					20
21					21
22					22
23					23
24					24
25					25

(b)

		1
		2
		3
		4
		5

		6
		7
		8
		9
		10

ACCOUNTS RECEIVABLE		FEES REVENUE		1
2009				2
Bal.	6,000			3
				4
		2010		5
2010		Bal.	162,000	6
Bal.	20,000			7

UNEARNED FEES REVENUE		CASH		10
	2009			11
	Bal. 18,000			12
				13
		2010		14
		Bal.		15
	2010			16
	Bal. 17,000			17

(a)

	Date	Account Titles	Debit	Credit	
1	May 31				1
2	1.				2
3					3
4					4
5	2.				5
6					6
7					7
8	3.				8
9					9
10					10
11	4.				11
12					12
13					13
14	5.				14
15					15
16					16
17	6.				17
18					18
19					19
20	7.				20
21					21
22					22
23					23
24					24
25					25

(b)

CASH			SALARIES PAYABLE	
5/31 Bal. 7,500				

ACCOUNTS RECEIVABLE			UNEARNED SERVICE REVENUE	
5/31 Bal. 3,000			5/31 Bal. 4,000	

PREPAID INSURANCE			COMMON STOCK	
5/31 Bal. 3,600			5/31 Bal. 19,100	

SUPPLIES			SERVICE REVENUE	
5/31 Bal. 2,500			5/31 Bal. 7,500	

OFFICE FURNITURE			SALARIES EXPENSE	
5/31 Bal. 12,000			5/31 Bal. 4,000	

ACCUMULATED DEPRECIATION - OFFICE FURNITURE			RENT EXPENSE	
			5/31 Bal. 1,500	

ACCOUNTS PAYABLE			DEPRECIATION EXPENSE	
	5/31 Bal. 3,500			

TRAVEL PAYABLE			INSURANCE EXPENSE	

(b) (Continued)

TRAVEL EXPENSE		SUPPLIES EXPENSE	
1			1
2			2
3			3
4			4
5			5

(c)

GOREN CONSULTING
Adjusted Trial Balance
May 31, 2010

1		
2		
3		
4		
5		
6		
7		
8		
9		
10		
11		
12		
13		
14		
15		
16		
17		
18		
19		
20		
21		
22		
23		
24		
25		
26		
27		
28		
29		
30		
31		
32		
33		

(a)

	Date	Account Titles	Debit	Credit	
1	Aug 31				1
2	1.				2
3					3
4					4
5	2.				5
6					6
7					7
8	3.				8
9					9
10					10
11					11
12					12
13					13
14	4.				14
15					15
16					16
17	5.				17
18					18
19					19
20	6.				20
21					21
22					22
23	7.				23
24					24
25					25

(b)

CASH	**ACCUMULATED DEPRECIATION - FURNITURE**
8/31 Bal. 24,600	
ACCOUNTS RECEIVABLE	
	ACCOUNTS PAYABLE
	8/31 Bal. 6,500
PREPAID INSURANCE	**UNEARNED RENT REVENUE**
8/31 Bal. 5,400	8/ 31 Bal. 6,800
SUPPLIES	**SALARIES PAYABLE**
8/31 Bal. 4,300	
LAND	**INTEREST PAYABLE**
8/31 Bal. 40,000	
COTTAGES	**MORTGAGE PAYABLE**
8/31 Bal. 132,000	8/31 Bal. 120,000
ACCUMULATED DEPRECIATION - COTTAGES	**COMMON STOCK**
	8/31 Bal. 100,000
	DIVIDENDS
FURNITURE	8/31 Bal. 5,000
8/31 Bal. 36,000	

(b) (Continued)

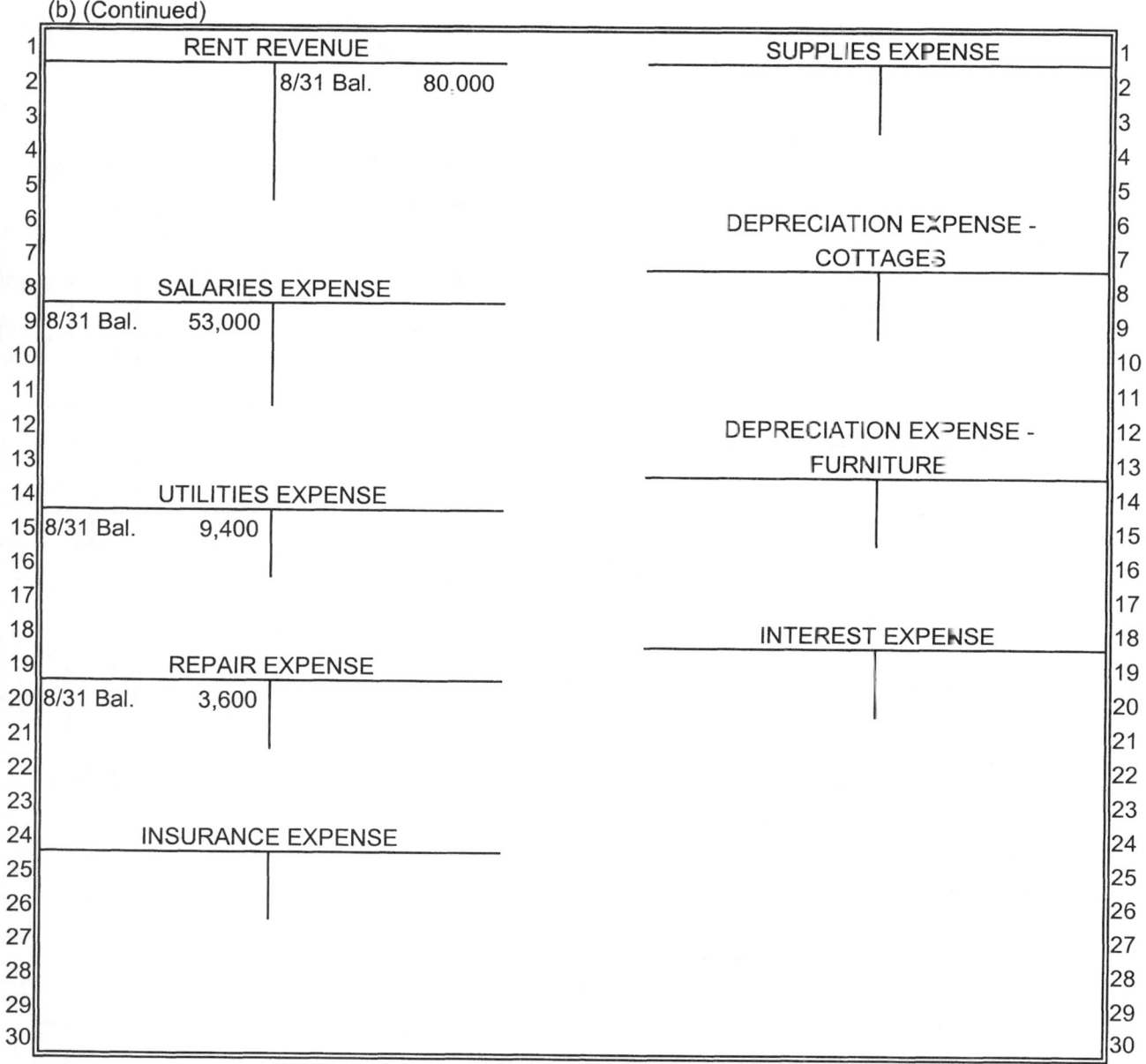

	RENT REVENUE	
		8/31 Bal. 80.000

	SALARIES EXPENSE	
8/31 Bal. 53,000		

	UTILITIES EXPENSE	
8/31 Bal. 9,400		

	REPAIR EXPENSE	
8/31 Bal. 3,600		

INSURANCE EXPENSE

SUPPLIES EXPENSE

DEPRECIATION EXPENSE - COTTAGES

DEPRECIATION EXPENSE - FURNITURE

INTEREST EXPENSE

(c)

FLINT HILLS RESORT
Adjusted Trial Balance
August 31, 2010

	Debit	Credit
1		
2		
3		
4		
5		
6		
7		
8		
9		
10		
11		
12		
13		
14		
15		
16		
17		
18		
19		
20		
21		
22		
23		
24		
25		
26		
27		
28		
29		
30		

(d)

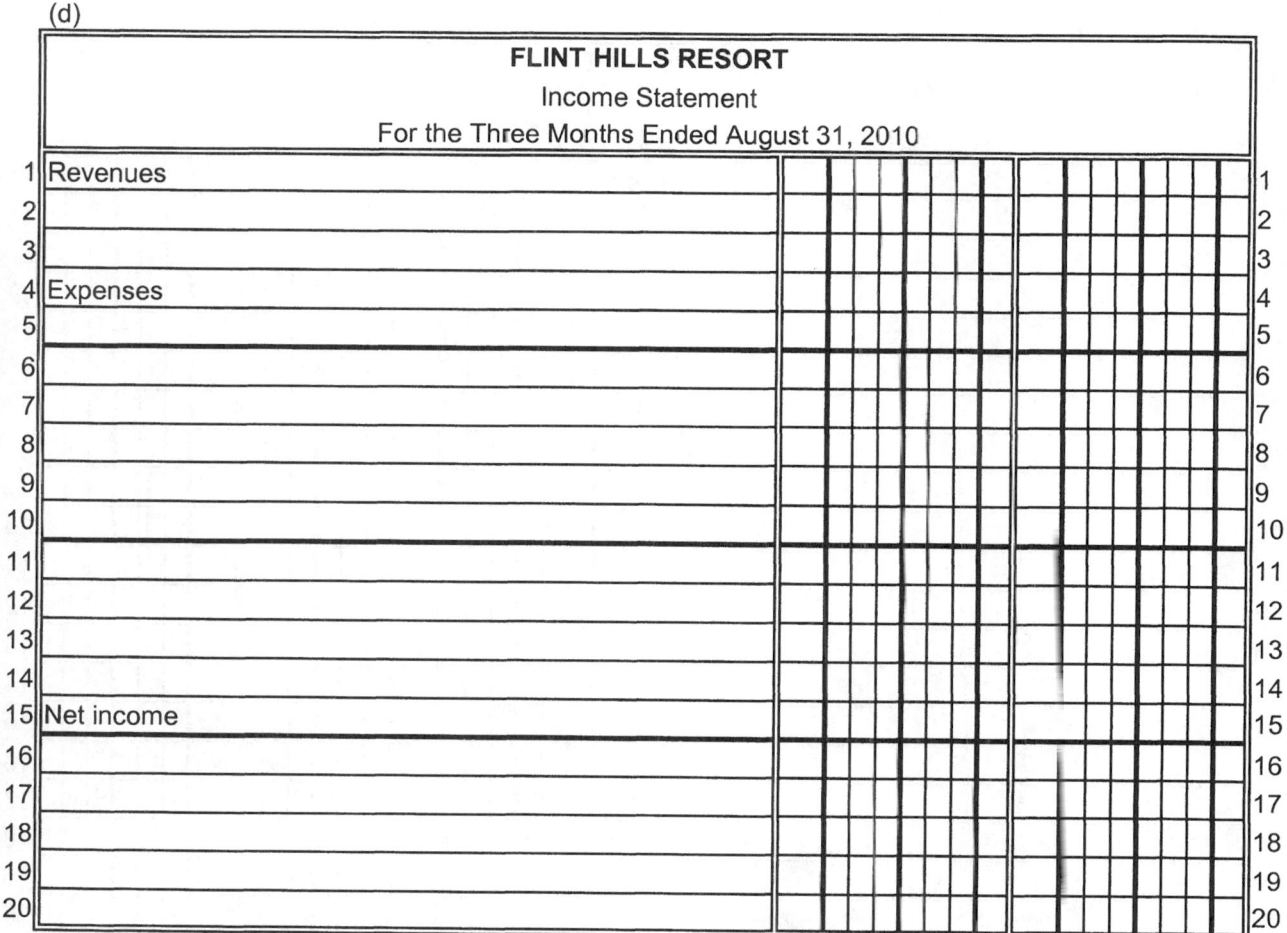

FLINT HILLS RESORT

Income Statement

For the Three Months Ended August 31, 2010

1 Revenues		
2		
3		
4 Expenses		
5		
6		
7		
8		
9		
10		
11		
12		
13		
14		
15 Net income		
16		
17		
18		
19		
20		

FLINTR HILLS RESORT

Retained Earnings Statement

For the Three Months Ended August 31, 2010

1	
2	
3	
4	
5	
6	
7	
8	
9	
10	

(d) (Continued) and (e)

FLINT HILLS RESORT

Balance Sheet

August 31, 2010

Assets

Liabilities and Stockholders' Equity

(e)

(a)

	Date	Accounts Titles	Debit	Credit	
1	Dec 31				1
2					2
3					3
4	31				4
5					5
6					6
7	31				7
8					8
9					9
10	31				10
11					11
12					12
13	31				13
14					14
15					15
16	31				16
17					17
18					18
19	31				19
20					20
21					21

(b)

LONGLY ADVERTISING AGENCY

Income Statement

For The Year Ended December 31, 2010

1	Revenues			1
2				2
3				3
4	Expenses			4
5				5
6				6
7				7
8				8
9				9
10				10
11				11
12				12
13	Net income			13
14				14

(b) (Continued)

LONGLY ADVERTISING AGENCY
Retained Earnings Statement
For the Year Ended December 31, 2010

1	
2	
3	
4	
5	
6	
7	

LONGLY ADVERTISING AGENCY
Balance Sheet
December 31, 2010

Assets		
1		
2		
3		
4		
5		
6		
7		
8		
9		
10		
11		
12		
13		
Liabilities and Stockholders' Equity		
15		
16		
17		
18		
19		
20		
21		
22		
23		
24		
25		
26		
27		
28		
29		

(c), (d) & (e)

1	(c)	1
2		2
3		3
4		4
5		5
6	(d)	6
7		7
8		8
9		9
10		10
11	(e)	11
12		12
13		13
14		14
15		15
16		16
17		17
18		18
19		19
20		20
21		21
22		22
23		23
24		24
25		25
26		26
27		27
28		28
29		29
30		30
31		31
32		32
33		33
34		34
35		35
36		36
37		37
38		38

	Date	Account Titles	Debit	Credit	
1	Dec 31				1
2	1.				2
3					3
4					4
5					5
6					6
7					7
8					8
9					9
10					10
11	2.				11
12					12
13					13
14					14
15					15
16					16
17					17
18					18
19					19
20					20
21	3.				21
22					22
23					23
24					24
25					25
26					26
27					27
28					28
29	4.				29
30					30
31					31
32					32
33					33
34					34
35					35

(a)

	Date	Account Titles	Debit	Credit	
1	Mar 31				1
2	1.				2
3					3
4					4
5					5
6	2.				6
7					7
8					8
9					9
10					10
11	3.				11
12					12
13					13
14					14
15					15
16	4.				16
17					17
18					18
19					19
20					20
21	5.				21
22					22
23					23
24					24
25					25
26	6.				26
27					27
28					28
29					29
30					30
31					31
32					32
33					33
34					34
35					35

(b)

WYANDOTTE TRAVEL AGENCY
Income Statement
For the Quarter Ended March 31, 2010

	Revenues:						
1	Revenues:						
2							
3	Expenses:						
4							
5							
6							
7							
8							
9							
10							
11							
12							
13							
14							
15	Net income						
16							

(c)

1			
2			
3			
4			
5			
6			
7			
8			
9			
10			
11			
12			
13			
14			
15			
16			
17			
18			
19			
20			

(a), (c) & (e)

	CASH				UNEARNED SERVICE REVENUE		
1							1
2	9/1 Bal.	4,880			9/1 Bal.	400	2
3							3
4							4
5							5
6							6
7					SALARIES PAYABLE		7
8					9/1 Bal.	700	8
9	ACCOUNTS RECEIVABLE						9
10	9/1 Bal.	3,820					10
11							11
12							12
13					COMMON STOCK		13
14					9/1 Bal.	10,000	14
15	SUPPLIES						15
16	9/1 Bal.	800					16
17							17
18					RETAINED EARNINGS		18
19					9/1 Bal.	8,700	19
20							20
21							21
22	STORE EQUIPMENT						22
23	9/1 Bal.	15,000			SERVICE REVENUE		23
24							24
25							25
26							26
27							27
28	ACCUMULATED DEPRECIATION						28
29		9/1 Bal.	1,600				29
30					DEPRECIATION EXPENSE		30
31							31
32							32
33							33
34	ACCOUNTS PAYABLE						34
35		9/1 Bal.	3,100		SUPPLIES EXPENSE		35
36							36
37							37
38							38
39							39
40							40
41							41
42							42
43							43

(a), (c) & (e) (Continued)

	SALARIES EXPENSE		RENT EXPENSE	
1				1
2				2
3				3
4				4
5				5
6				6

(b)

	Date	Account Titles	Debit	Credit	
1	Sept 8				1
2					2
3					3
4					4
5	10				5
6					6
7					7
8	12				8
9					9
10					10
11	15				11
12					12
13					13
14	17				14
15					15
16					16
17	20				17
18					18
19					19
20	22				20
21					21
22					22
23	25				23
24					24
25					25
26	27				26
27					27
28					28
29	29				29
30					30
31					31
32					32

(d) & (f)

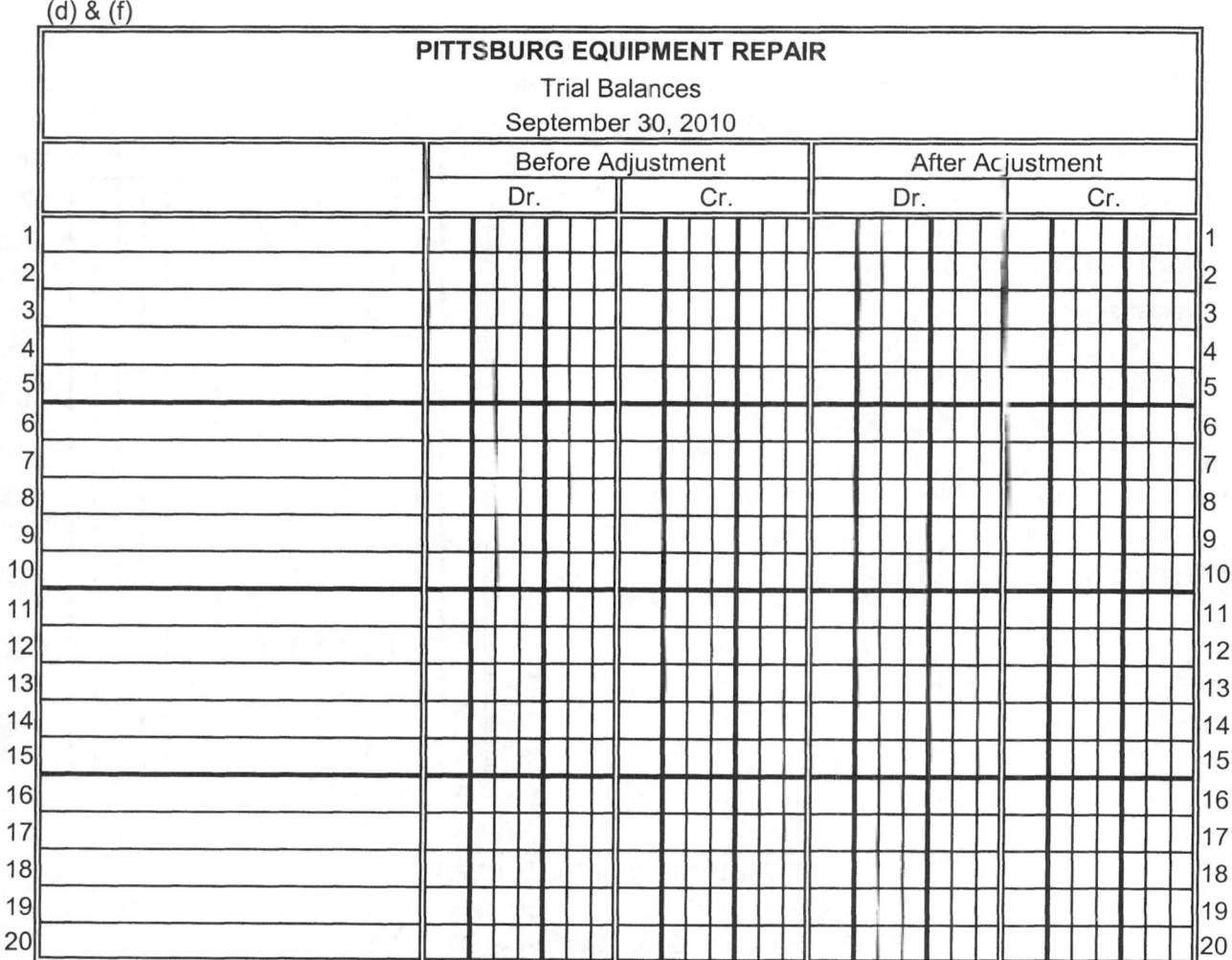

	Before Adjustment		After Adjustment	
	Dr.	Cr.	Dr.	Cr.
1				
2				
3				
4				
5				
6				
7				
8				
9				
10				
11				
12				
13				
14				
15				
16				
17				
18				
19				
20				

PITTSBURG EQUIPMENT REPAIR
Trial Balances
September 30, 2010

(e)

	Date	Account Titles	Debit	Credit
1	Sept 30			
2	1.			
3				
4				
5	2.			
6				
7				
8	3.			
9				
10				
11	4.			
12				
13				

(g)

PITTSBURG EQUIPMENT REPAIR

Income Statement

For the Month Ended September 30, 2010

Revenues			
Expenses			
Net income			

PITTSBURG EQUIPMENT REPAIR

Retained Earnings Statement

For the Month Ended September 30, 2010

(g) (Continued)

PITTSBURG EQUIPMENT REPAIR
Balance Sheet
September 30, 2010

Assets							
1							1
2							2
3							3
4							4
5							5
6							6
7							7
8							8
9							9
10							10
11							11
12							12
Liabilities and Stockholders' Equity							13
14							14
15							15
16							16
17							17
18							18
19							19
20							20
21							21
22							22
23							23
24							24
25							25

(a)

	Date	Account Titles	Debit	Credit	
1	Mar 1				1
2					2
3					3
4	1				4
5					5
6					6
7					7
8	3				8
9					9
10					10
11	5				11
12					12
13					13
14	14				14
15					15
16					16
17	18				17
18					18
19					19
20	20				20
21					21
22					22
23	21				23
24					24
25					25
26	28				26
27					27
28					28
29	31				29
30					30
31					31
32	31				32
33					33
34					34
35					35

(b), (e) & (h)

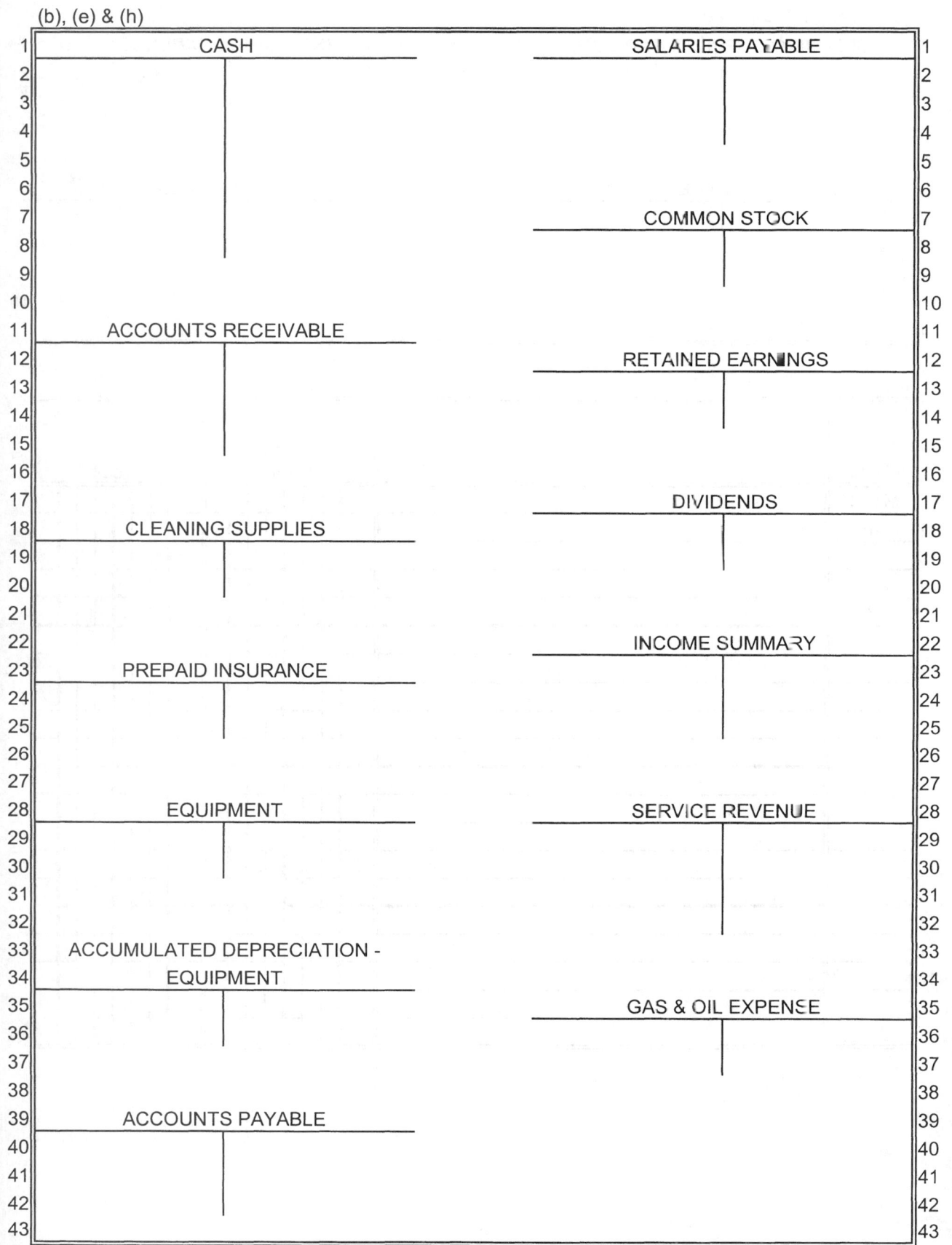

CASH	SALARIES PAYABLE
ACCOUNTS RECEIVABLE	COMMON STOCK
	RETAINED EARNINGS
CLEANING SUPPLIES	DIVIDENDS
PREPAID INSURANCE	INCOME SUMMARY
EQUIPMENT	SERVICE REVENUE
ACCUMULATED DEPRECIATION - EQUIPMENT	GAS & OIL EXPENSE
ACCOUNTS PAYABLE	

(b), (e) & (h) (Continued)

	CLEANING SUPPLIES EXPENSE		INSURANCE EXPENSE	
1				1
2				2
3				3
4				4
5				5
6	DEPRECIATION EXPENSE		SALARIES EXPENSE	6
7				7
8				8
9				9
10				10
11				11

(d)

	Date	Account Titles	Debit	Credit	
1	Mar 31				1
2	1.				2
3					3
4					4
5	2.				5
6					6
7					7
8	3.				8
9					9
10					10
11	4.				11
12					12
13					13
14	5.				14
15					15
16					16
17					17
18					18
19					19
20					20

(c) & (f)

KWIK CLEANERS
Trial Balances
March 31, 2010

	Before Adjustment		After Adjustment	
	Dr.	Cr.	Dr.	Cr.
1				
2				
3				
4				
5				
6				
7				
8				
9				
10				
11				
12				
13				
14				
15				
16				
17				
18				
19				
20				

(g)

KWIK CLEANERS
Income Statement
For the Month Ended March 31, 2010

1	Revenues	
2		
3	Expenses	
4		
5		
6		
7		
8		
9		
10		
11	Net income	
12		
13		

(g) (Continued)

KWIK CLEANERS
Retained Earnings Statement
For the Month Ended March 31, 2010

1									1
2									2
3									3
4									4
5									5
6									6

KWIK CLEANERS
Balance Sheet
March 31, 2010

	Assets								
1									1
2									2
3									3
4									4
5									5
6									6
7									7
8									8
9									9
10									10
11									11
12									12
13									13
14									14
15	Liabilities and Stockholders' Equity								15
16									16
17									17
18									18
19									19
20									20
21									21
22									22
23									23
24									24
25									25
26									26
27									27
28									28
29									29
30									30

(h)

	Date	Account Titles	Debit	Credit	
1	Mar 31				1
2					2
3					3
4	31				4
5					5
6					6
7					7
8					8
9					9
10					10
11	31				11
12					12
13					13
14	31				14
15					15
16					16

(i)

KWIK CLEANERS
Post-Closing Trial Balance
March 31, 2010

		Debit	Credit	
1				1
2				2
3				3
4				4
5				5
6				6
7				7
8				8
9				9
10				10
11				11
12				12
13				13
14				14

(a)

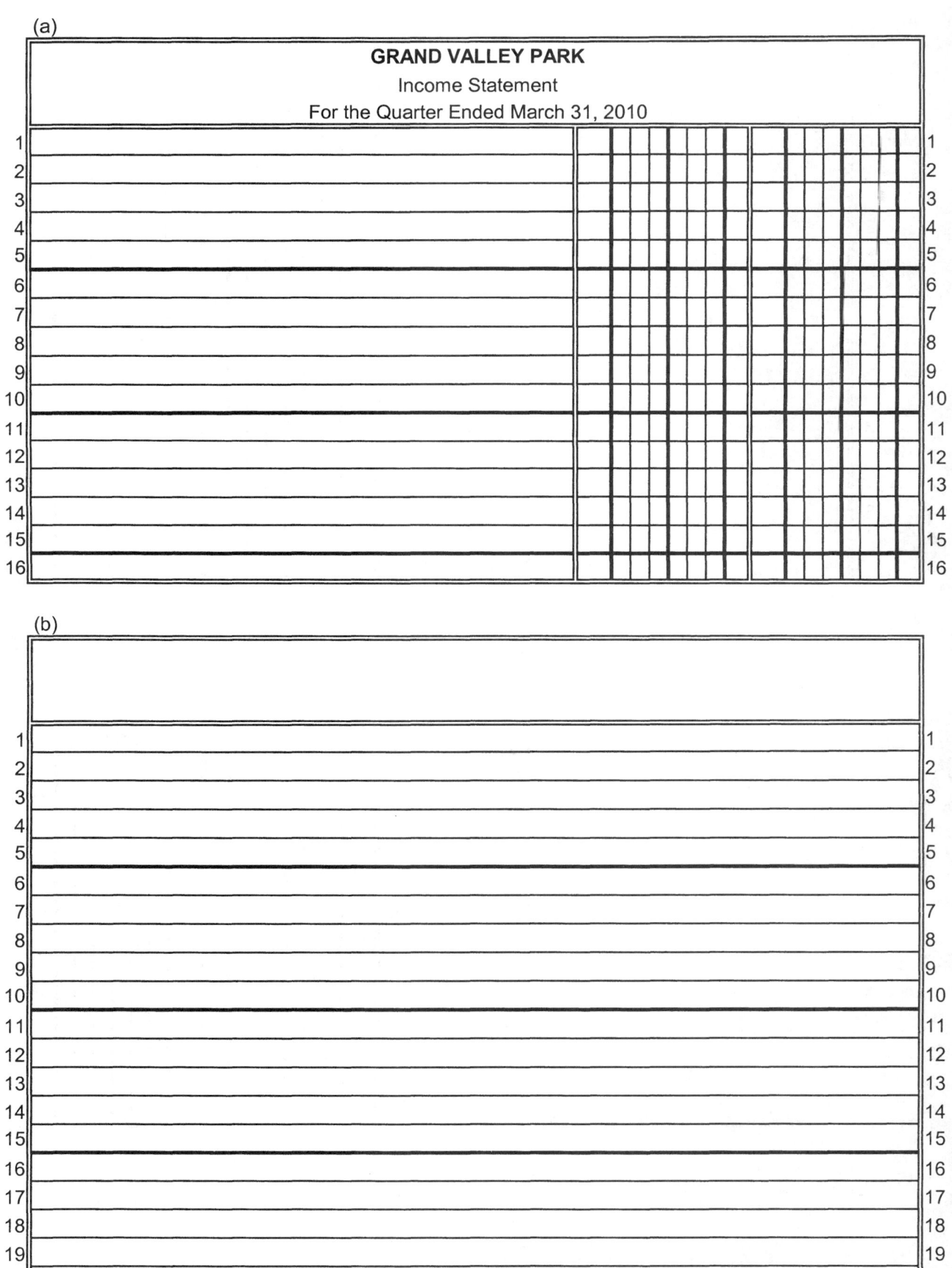

GRAND VALLEY PARK

Income Statement

For the Quarter Ended March 31, 2010

(b)

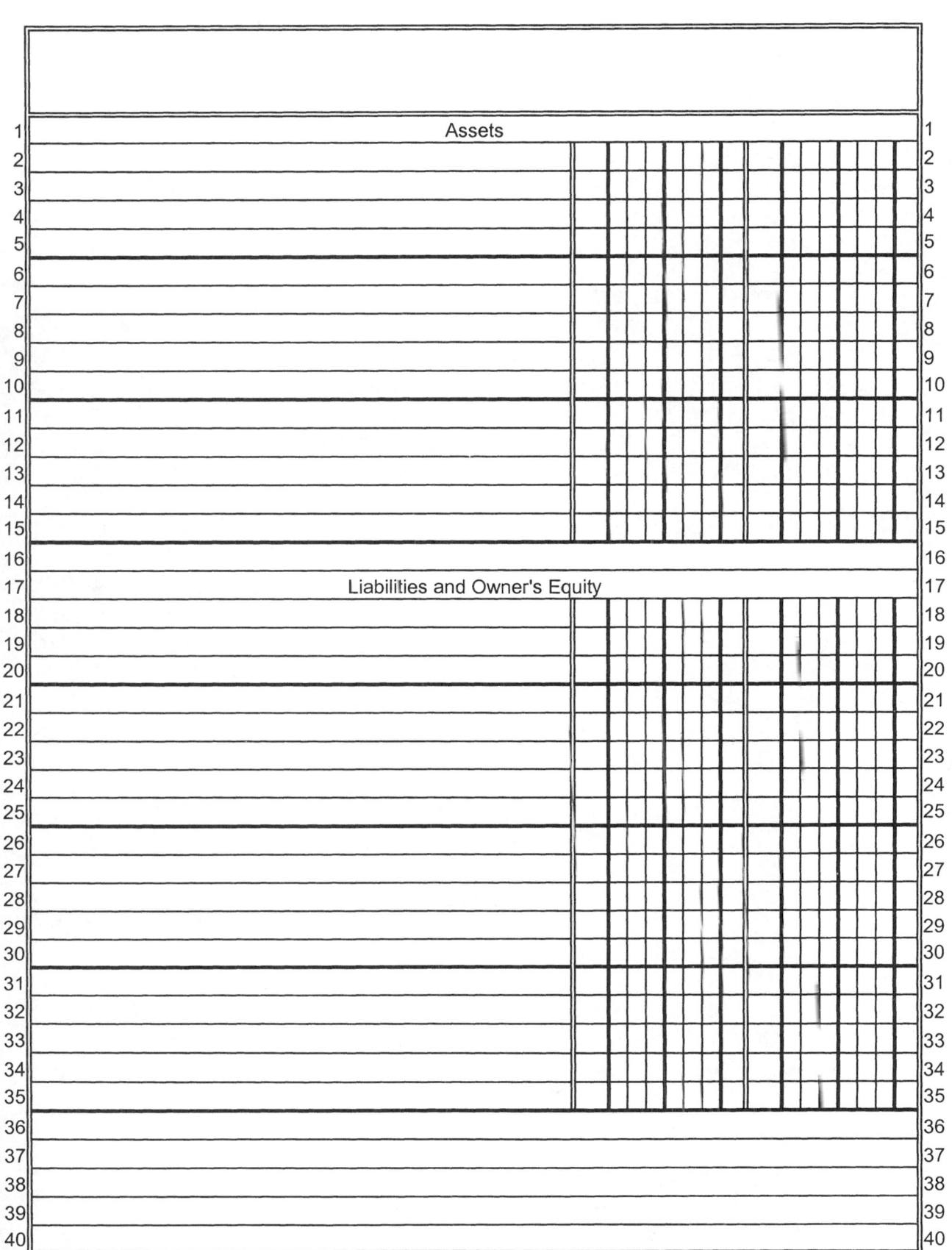

Assets

Liabilities and Owner's Equity

BE5-1

	Sales	Cost of Goods Sold	Gross Profit	Operating Expenses	Net Income	
1						1
2	$ 71,200	(b)	$ 39,000	(d)	$ 10,800	2
3						3
4	$ 108,000	$ 65,000	(c)	(e)	$ 29,500	4
5						5
6	(a)	$ 71,900	$ 109,600	$ 46,200	(f)	6
7						7
8						8
9						9
10						10

	BE5-2			
11				11
12	Account Titles	Debit	Credit	12
13	Prior Company:			13
14				14
15				15
16				16
17	Wood Company:			17
18				18
19				19
20				20
21				21
22				22

	BE5-3			
23				23
24	Account Titles	Debit	Credit	24
25	(a)			25
26				26
27				27
28				28
29				29
30				30
31	(b)			31
32				32
33				33
34				34
35				35
36				36
37	(c)			37
38				38
39				39
40				40

BE5-4

		Account Titles	Debit	Credit	
1	(a)				1
2					2
3					3
4					4
5	(b)				5
6					6
7					7
8	(c)				8
9					9
10					10
11					11
12					12
13					13
14					14

BE5-5

CARPENTER COMPANY

Income Statement (Partial)

For the Month Ended October 31, 2010

19		
20		
21		
22		
23		
24		
25		
26		

BE5-6

Item	Income Statement Section	
Gain on sale of equipment		29
		30
Cost of goods sold		31
		32
Depreciation expense		33
		34
Sales returns and allowances		35
		36
		37
		38
		39
		40

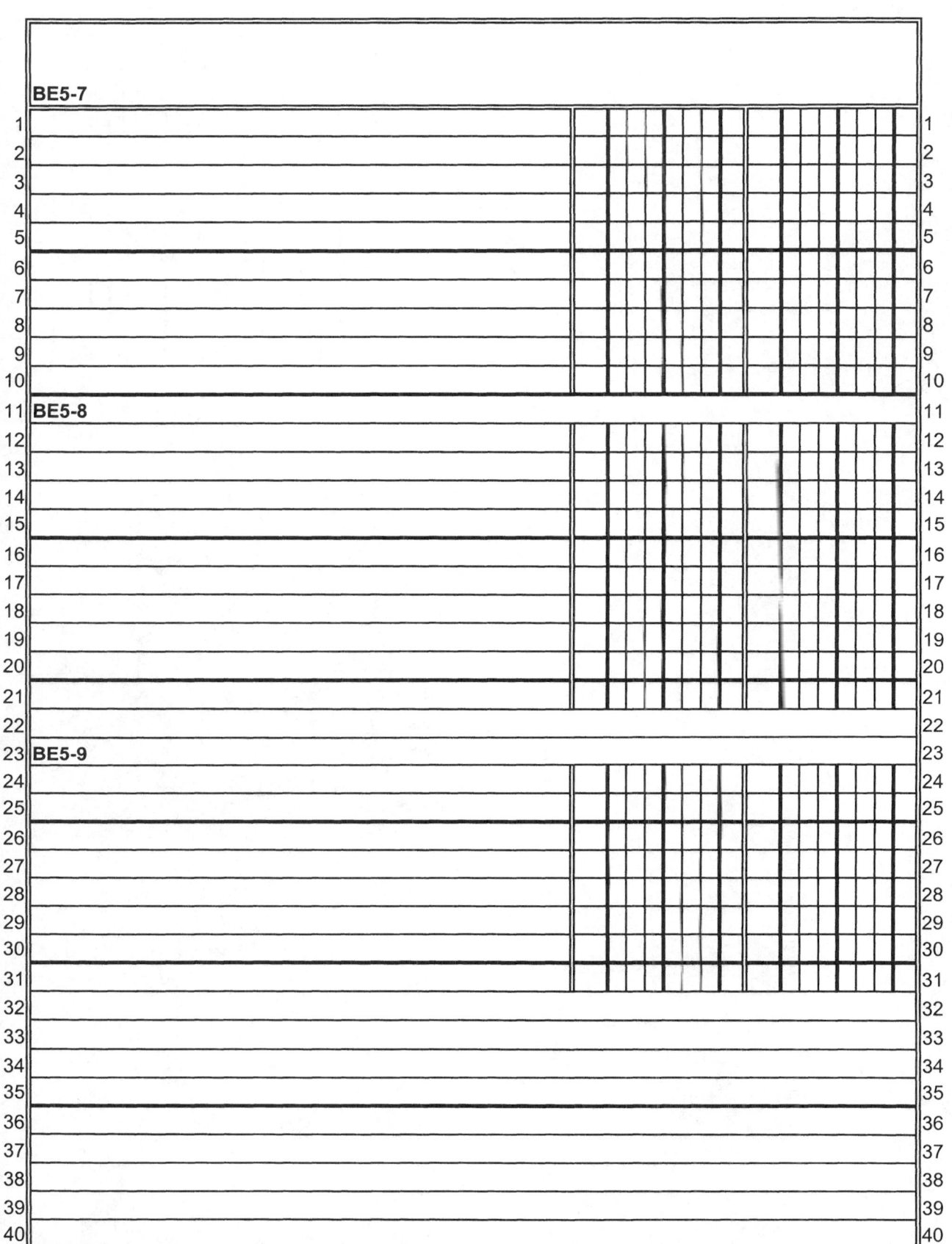

BE5-7

BE5-8

BE5-9

*BE5-13

	Account Titles	Debit	Credit	
1	(a)			1
2				2
3				3
4	(b)			4
5				5
6				6
7	(c)			7
8				8
9				9
10				10
11				11
12				12
13				13
14				14
15				15
16				16
17				17
18				18
19				19
20				20
21				21
22				22
23				23
24				24
25				25
26				26
27				27
28				28
29				29
30				30
31				31
32				32
33				33
34				34
35				35
36				36
37				37
38				38
39				39
40				40

DO IT! 5-1

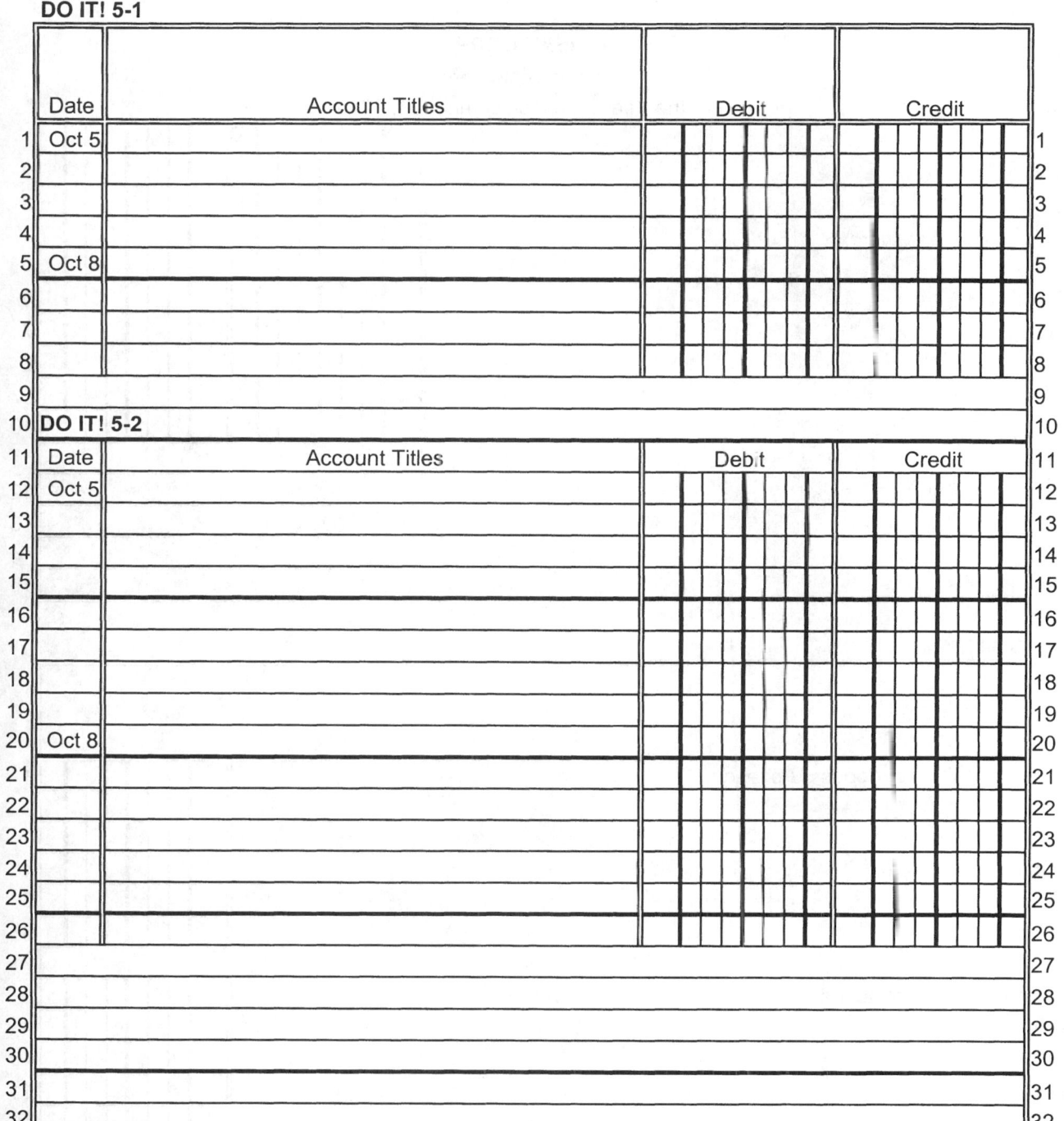

	Date	Account Titles	Debit	Credit	
1	Oct 5				1
2					2
3					3
4					4
5	Oct 8				5
6					6
7					7
8					8
9					9

DO IT! 5-2

	Date	Account Titles	Debit	Credit	
11	Date	Account Titles	Debit	Credit	11
12	Oct 5				12
13					13
14					14
15					15
16					16
17					17
18					18
19					19
20	Oct 8				20
21					21
22					22
23					23
24					24
25					25
26					26
27					27
28					28
29					29
30					30
31					31
32					32

DO IT! 5-3

	JUNEAU CORP.				
	Income Statement				
	For the Year Ended December 31, 2010				
1					1
2					2
3					3
4					4
5					5
6					6
7					7
8					8
9					9
10					10
11					11
12					12
13					13
14					14
15					15

DO IT! 5-4

1	(a) Cost of goods purchased:		1
2			2
3			3
4			4
5			5
6			6
7			7
8	(b) Cost of goods sold:		8
9			9
10			10
11			11
12			12
13			13
14			14
15			15
16			16
17			17
18			18
19			19
20			20

E5-1

	Date	Account Titles	Debit	Credit	
1	(a)				1
2	Dec 3				2
3					3
4					4
5					5
6					6
7					7
8	8				8
9					9
10					10
11	13				11
12					12
13					13
14					14
15	(b)				15
16	Jan 2				16
17					17

E5-2

	Date	Account Titles	Debit	Credit	
1	Sept 6				1
2					2
3					3
4	9				4
5					5
6					6
7	10				7
8					8
9					9
10	12				10
11					11
12					12
13					13
14					14
15					15
16	14				16
17					17
18					18

E5-2 (Continued)

	Date	Account Titles	Debit	Credit	
1	Sept. 14				1
2					2
3					3
4	20				4
5					5
6					6
7					7
8					8
9					9

E5-3

	Date	Account Titles	Debit	Credit	
1	(a)				1
2	Apr 5				2
3					3
4					4
5	6				5
6					6
7					7
8	7				8
9					9
10					10
11	8				11
12					12
13					13
14	15				14
15					15
16					16
17					17
18	(b)				18
19	May 4				19
20					20
21					21

	Date	Account Titles	Debit	Credit	
1	(a)	Hopson Company			1
2	June 10				2
3					3
4					4
5	11				5
6					6
7					7
8	12				8
9					9
10					10
11	19				11
12					12
13					13
14					14
15	(b)	Gore Company			15
16	June 10				16
17					17
18					18
19					19
20					20
21					21
22	11				22
23					23
24	12				24
25					25
26					26
27					27
28					28
29					29
30	19				30
31					31
32					32
33					33
34					34
35					35
36					36
37					37
38					38
39					39
40					40

E5-5

	DAVISEN COMPANY											
	Income Statement (Partial)											
	For the Year Ended October 31, 2010											
1												1
2												2
3												3
4												4
5												5
6												6

E5-6 (a)

	YATES COMPANY																	
	Income Statement																	
	For the Month Ended January 31, 2010																	
1	Sales revenues:																	1
2																		2
3																		3
4																		4
5																		5
6																		6
7																		7
8																		8
9	Operating expenses:																	9
10																		10
11																		11
12																		12
13																		13
14																		14
15																		15
16	Net income																	16
17																		17

(b)

1	Profit margin ratio =	1
2		2
3		3
4	Gross profit rate =	4
5		5
6		6
7		7

(a)

	Iwig Company	Pratt Company	
Sales	$ 90000	$	
Sales Returns		5000	
Net Sales	84000	100000	
Cost of Goods Sold	56700		
Gross Profit		40000	
Operating Expenses	14580		
Net Income	$	$ 18000	

(b)

	Iwig Company	Pratt Company
Profit margin ratio		
Gross profit rate		

(c)

(a)

MARIS COMPANY
Income Statement
For the Year Ended December 31, 2010

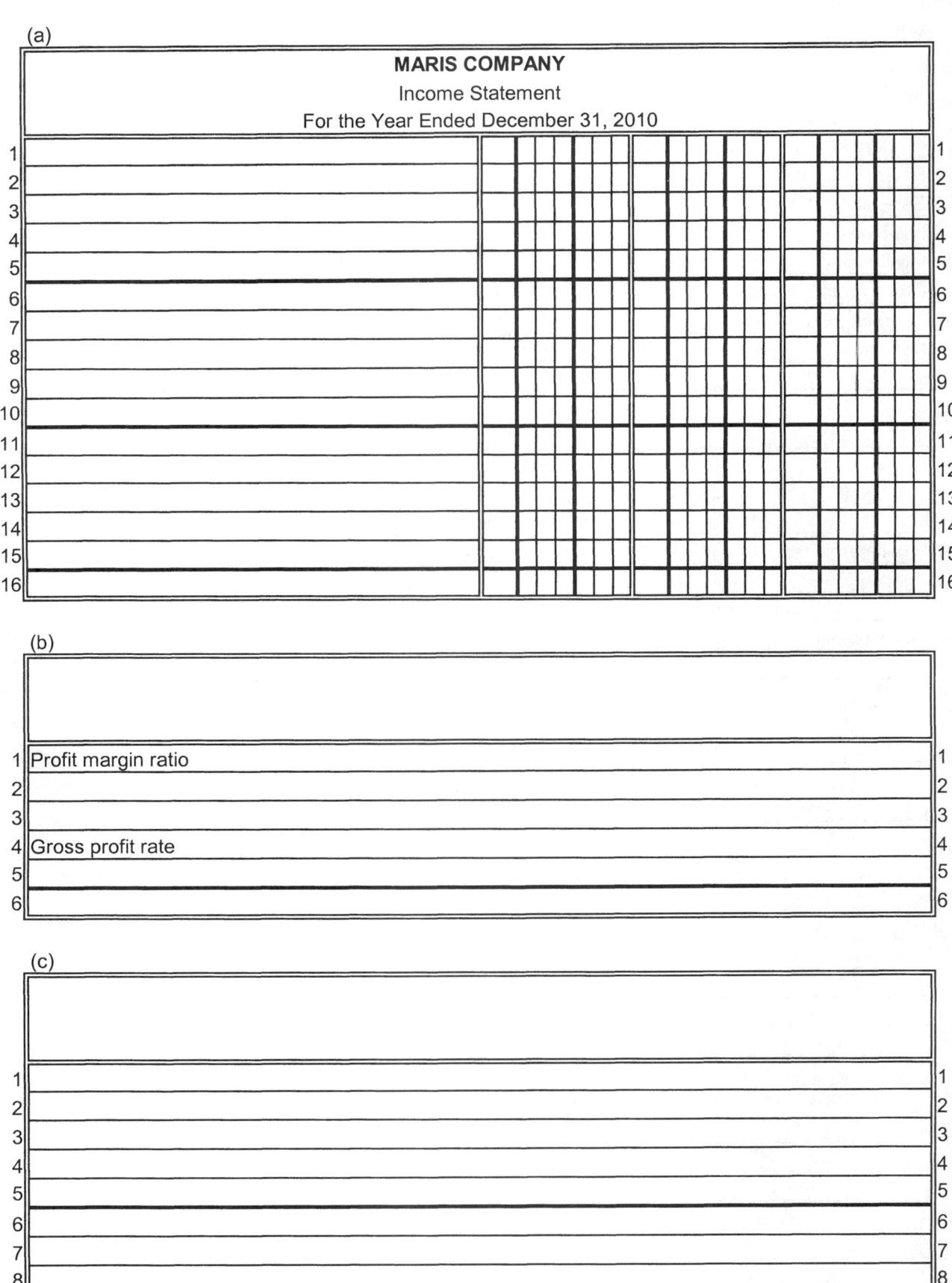

(b)

Profit margin ratio

Gross profit rate

(c)

(a)

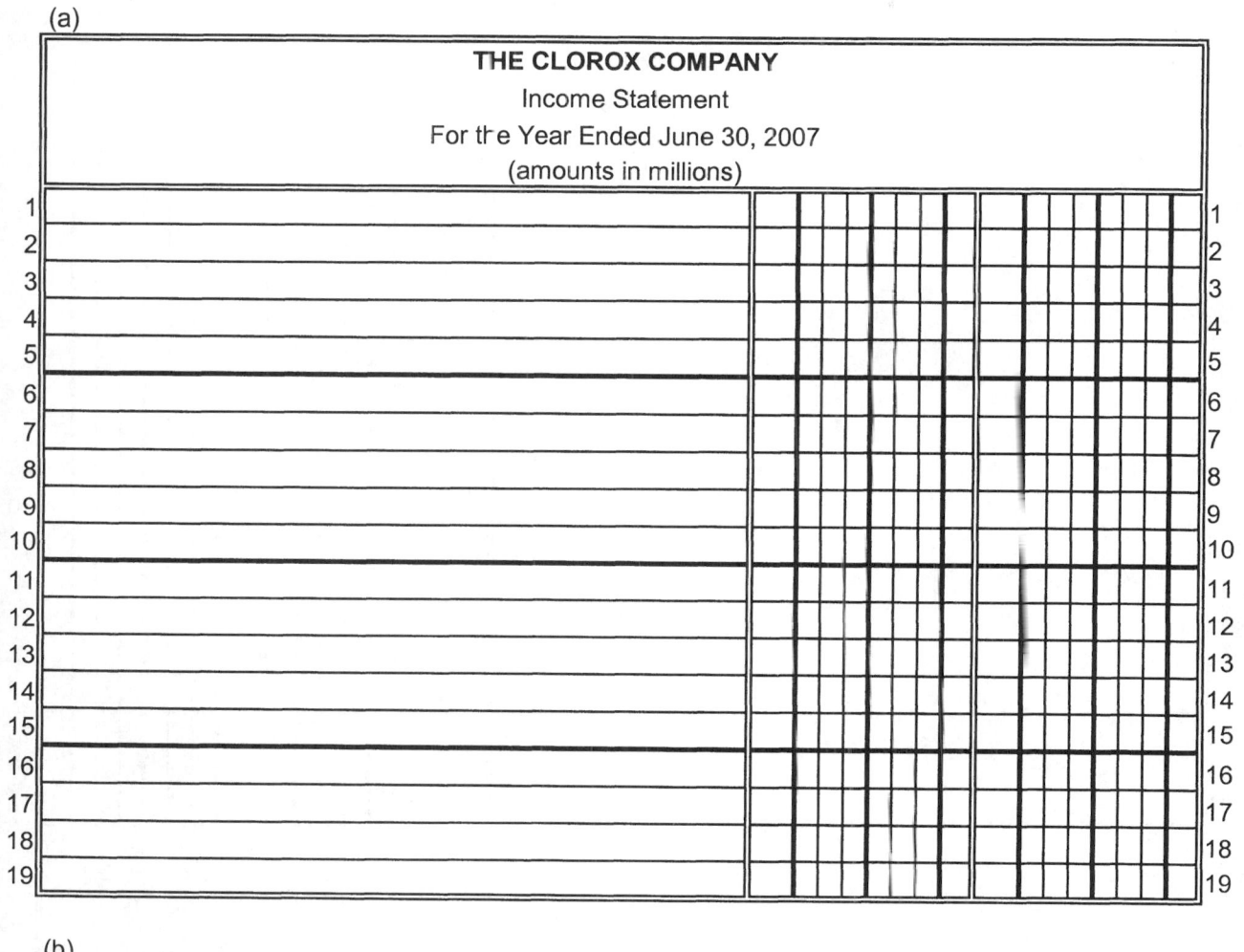

THE CLOROX COMPANY
Income Statement
For the Year Ended June 30, 2007
(amounts in millions)

(b)

1 Gross profit rate	
2	
3	
4 Gross profit rate indicates:	
5	
6 Profit margin ratio	
7	
8 Profit margin ratio indicates:	
9	
10	
11	
12	
13	
14	
15	

(c)

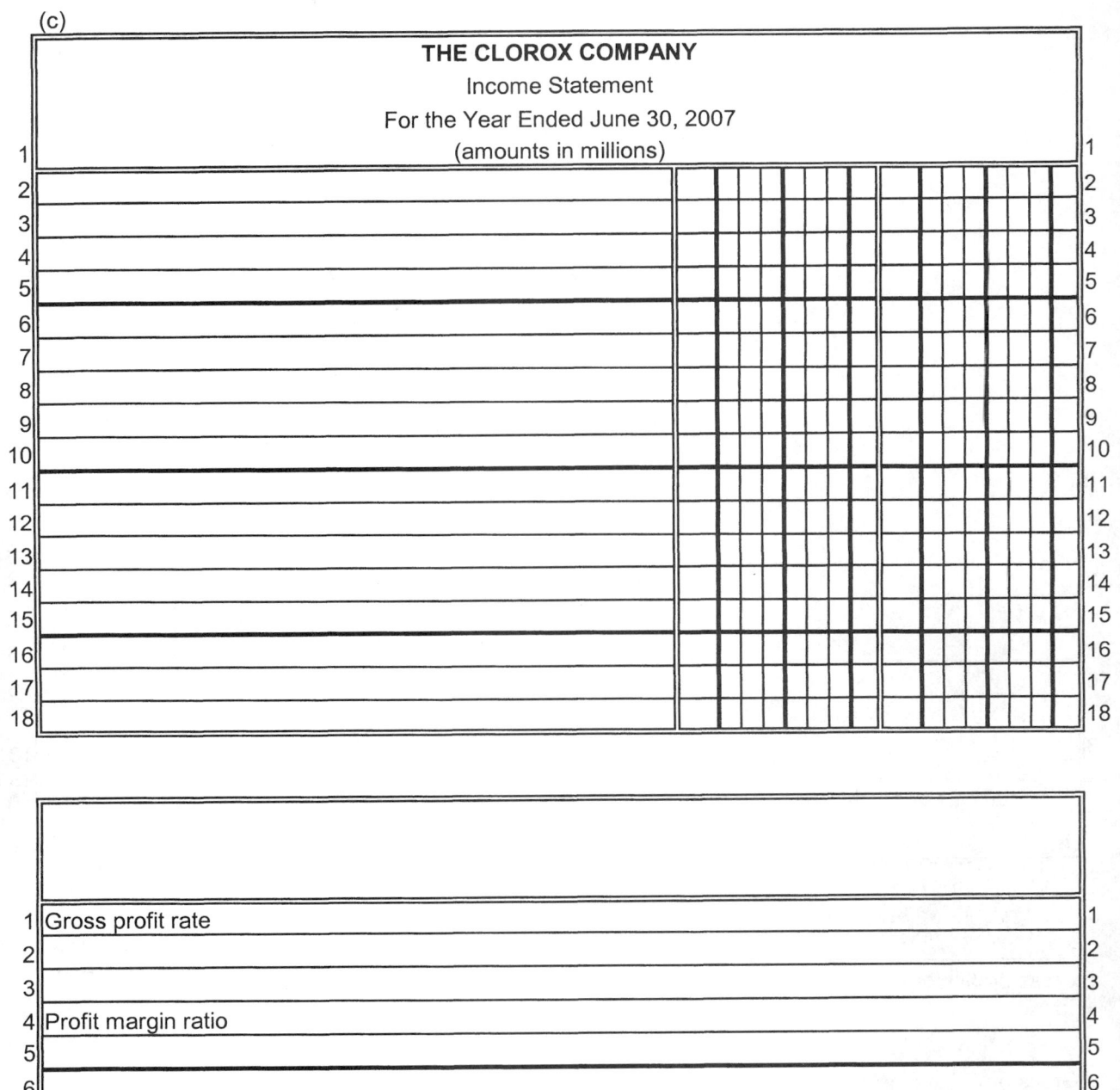

THE CLOROX COMPANY
Income Statement
For the Year Ended June 30, 2007
(amounts in millions)

Gross profit rate

Profit margin ratio

E5-10

	PERINE COMPANY		
	Cost of Goods Sold		
	For the Year Ended August 31, 2010		
1				1
2				2
3				3
4				4
5				5
6				6
7				7
8				8
9				9
10				10

E5-11

		Company X	Company F	Company L	Company S	
1	Beginning inventory	$250	$120	$1,000	(j)	1
2						2
3	Purchases	1,500	1,080	(g)	43,590	3
4						4
5	Purchase returns and					5
6	allowances	60	(d)	290	(k)	6
7						7
8	Net purchases	(a)	1,040	7,410	42,290	8
9						9
10	Freight-in	130	(e)	(h)	2,240	10
11						11
12	Cost of goods purchased	(b)	1,230	8,050	(l)	12
13						13
14	Cost of goods available					14
15	for sale	1,820	1,350	(i)	49,530	15
16						16
17	Ending inventory	310	(f)	1,450	6,230	17
18						18
19	Cost of goods sold	(c)	1,230	7,600	43,300	19
20						20

	Date	Account Titles	Debit	Credit	
1	(a)				1
2	Apr 5				2
3					3
4					4
5	6				5
6					6
7					7
8	7				8
9					9
10					10
11	8				11
12					12
13					13
14	15				14
15					15
16					16
17					17
18					18
19					19
20	(b)				20
21	May 4				21
22					22
23					23
24					24
25					25

(a)

	Date		Account Titles	Debit	Credit	
1	May	1				1
2						2
3						3
4		2				4
5						5
6						6
7						7
8						8
9						9
10		5				10
11						11
12						12
13		9				13
14						14
15						15
16						16
17		10				17
18						18
19						19
20						20
21		11				21
22						22
23						23
24		12				24
25						25
26						26
27		15				27
28						28
29						29
30		17				30
31						31
32						32
33		19				33
34						34
35						35
36		24				36
37						37
38						38
39						39
40						40

(a) (Continued)

	Date	Account Titles	Debit	Credit	
1	25				1
2					2
3					3
4	27				4
5					5
6					6
7					7
8	29				8
9					9
10					10
11					11
12					12
13					13
14	31				14
15					15
16					16
17					17
18					18
19					19
20					20
21					21
22					22
23					23
24					24
25					25
26					26
27					27
28					28
29					29
30					30
31					31
32					32
33					33
34					34
35					35
36					36
37					37
38					38
39					39
40					40

(b)

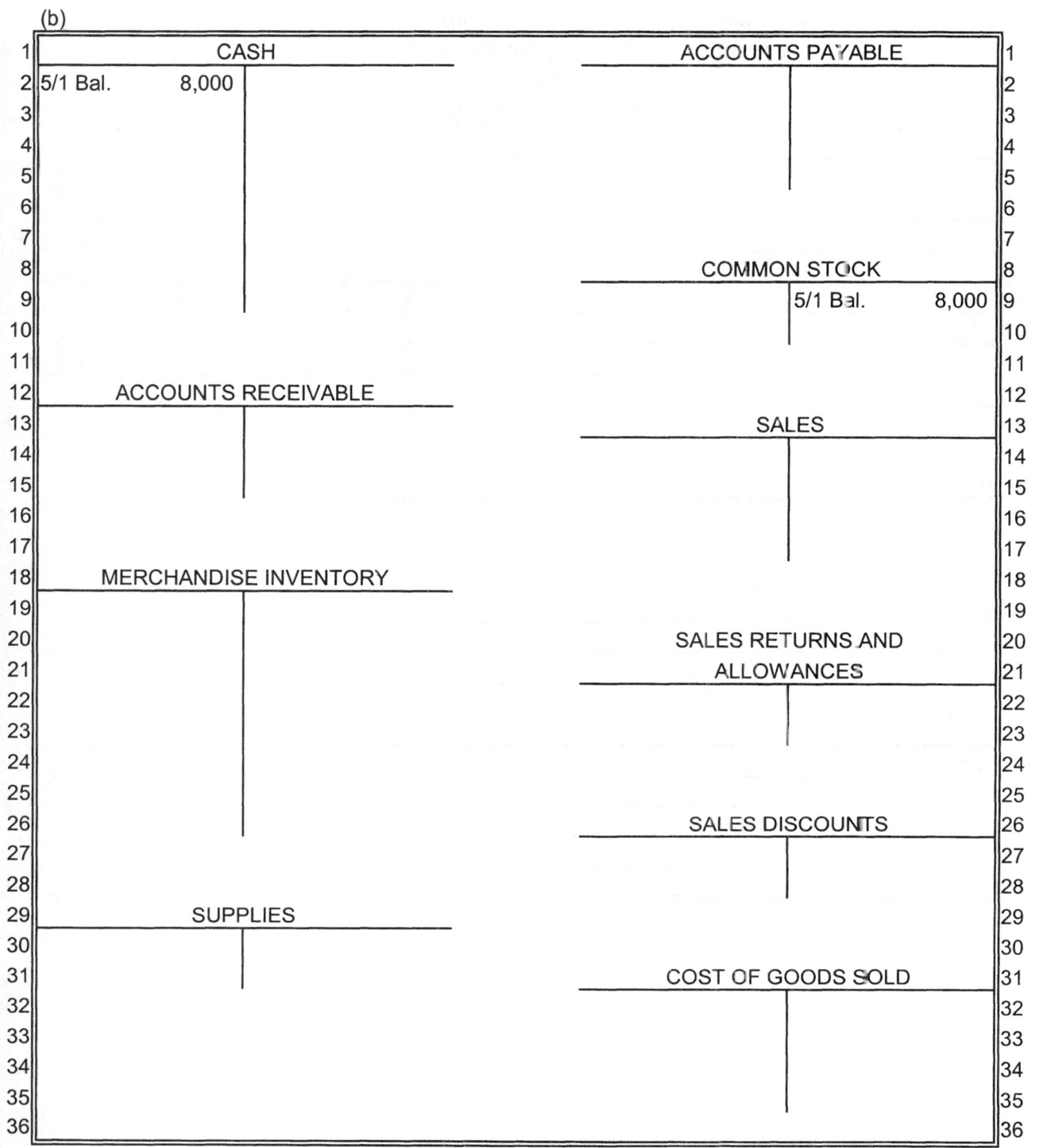

CASH		ACCOUNTS PAYABLE
5/1 Bal. 8,000		

		COMMON STOCK
		5/1 Bal. 8,000

ACCOUNTS RECEIVABLE

SALES

MERCHANDISE INVENTORY

SALES RETURNS AND ALLOWANCES

SALES DISCOUNTS

SUPPLIES

COST OF GOODS SOLD

(c)

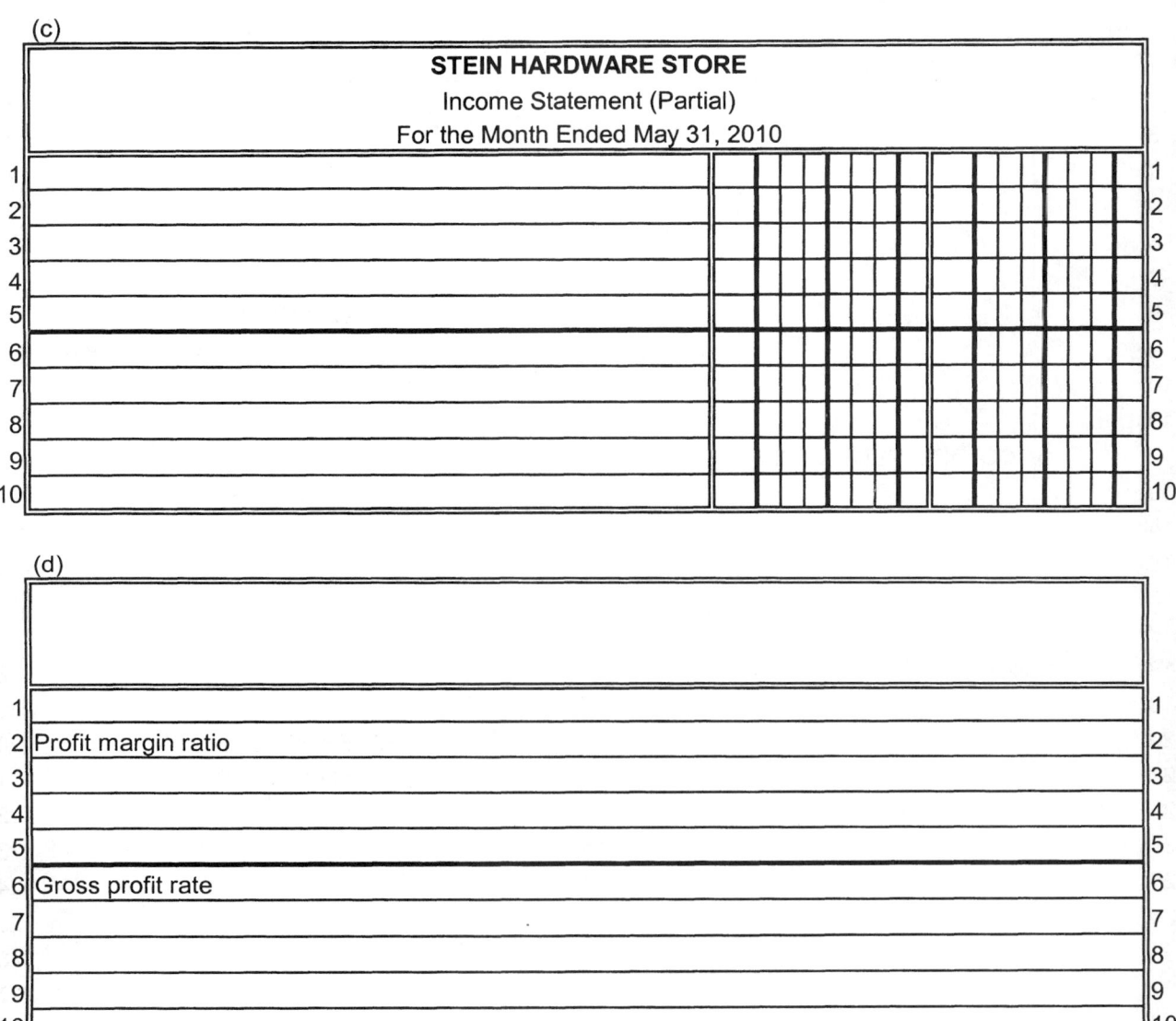

STEIN HARDWARE STORE

Income Statement (Partial)

For the Month Ended May 31, 2010

(d)

Profit margin ratio		
Gross profit rate		

	Date	Account Titles	Debit	Credit	
1	June 1				1
2					2
3					3
4					4
5					5
6					6
7	3				7
8					8
9					9
10					10
11					11
12					12
13	6				13
14					14
15					15
16	9				16
17					17
18					18
19					19
20	15				20
21					21
22					22
23	17				23
24					24
25					25
26					26
27					27
28					28
29	20				29
30					30
31					31
32	24				32
33					33
34					34
35					35
36	26				36
37					37
38					38
39					39
40					40

	Date	Account Titles	Debit	Credit	
1	28				1
2					2
3					3
4					4
5					5
6					6
7	30				7
8					8
9					9
10					10
11					11
12					12
13					13
14					14
15					15
16					16
17					17
18					18
19					19
20					20
21					21
22					22
23					23
24					24
25					25
26					26
27					27
28					28
29					29
30					30
31					31
32					32
33					33
34					34
35					35
36					36
37					37
38					38
39					39
40					40

(a)

Date	Account Titles	Debit	Credit
Apr 5			
7			
9			
10			
12			
14			
17			
20			
21			
27			

(a) (Continued)

	Date		Debit	Credit	
1	Apr. 30				1
2					2
3					3
4					4
5					5
6					6
7					7
8					8

(b)

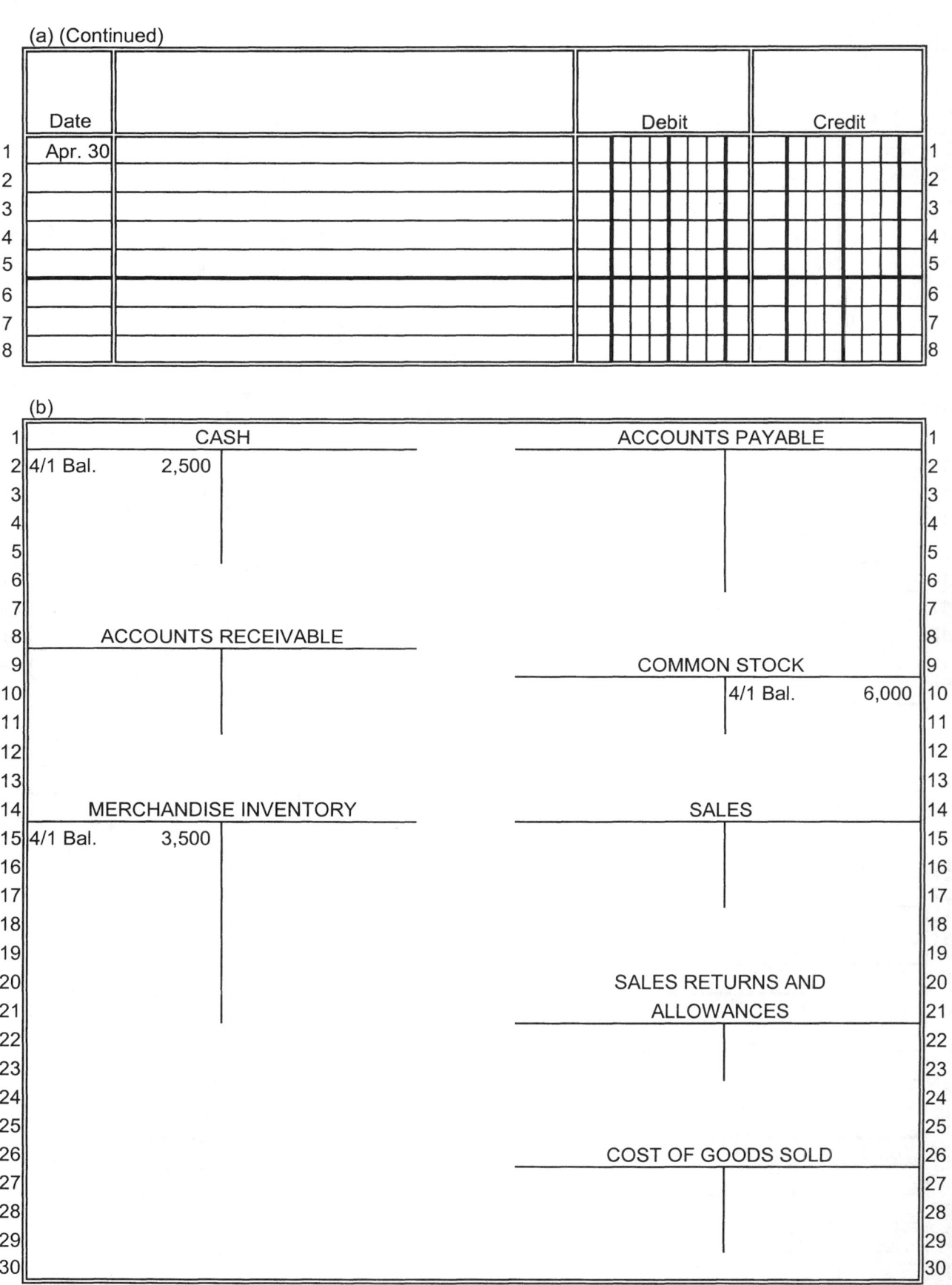

	CASH		ACCOUNTS PAYABLE	
1				1
2	4/1 Bal. 2,500			2
3				3
4				4
5				5
6				6
7				7
8	ACCOUNTS RECEIVABLE			8
9			COMMON STOCK	9
10			4/1 Bal. 6,000	10
11				11
12				12
13				13
14	MERCHANDISE INVENTORY		SALES	14
15	4/1 Bal. 3,500			15
16				16
17				17
18				18
19				19
20			SALES RETURNS AND	20
21			ALLOWANCES	21
22				22
23				23
24				24
25				25
26			COST OF GOODS SOLD	26
27				27
28				28
29				29
30				30

(c)

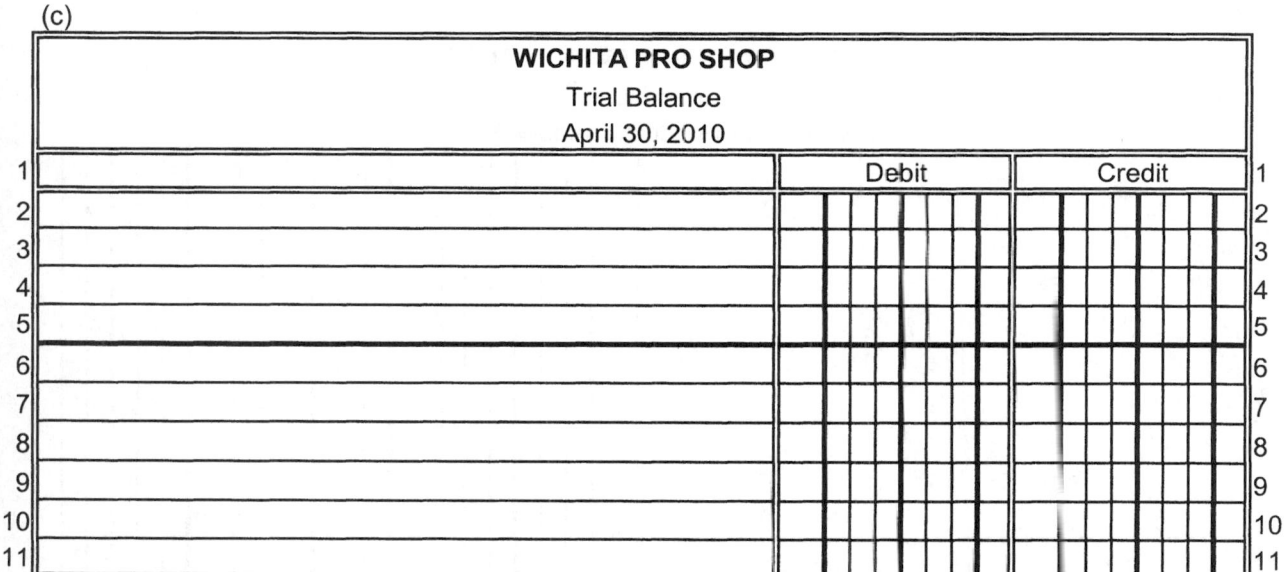

WICHITA PRO SHOP
Trial Balance
April 30, 2010

	Debit	Credit
1		
2		
3		
4		
5		
6		
7		
8		
9		
10		
11		

(d)

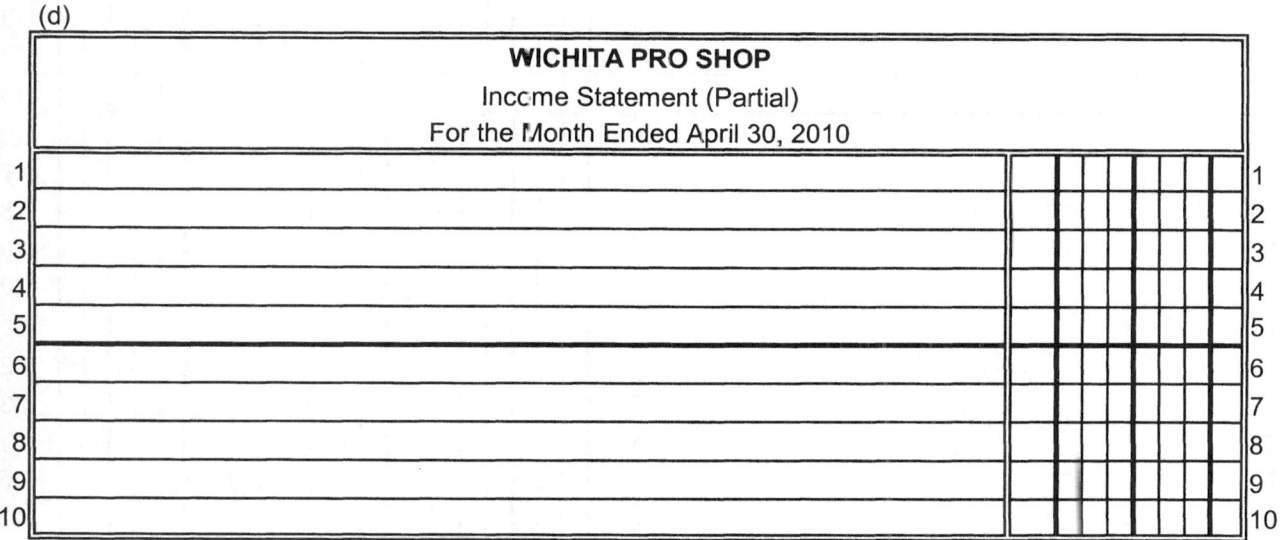

WICHITA PRO SHOP
Income Statement (Partial)
For the Month Ended April 30, 2010

1	
2	
3	
4	
5	
6	
7	
8	
9	
10	

(a)

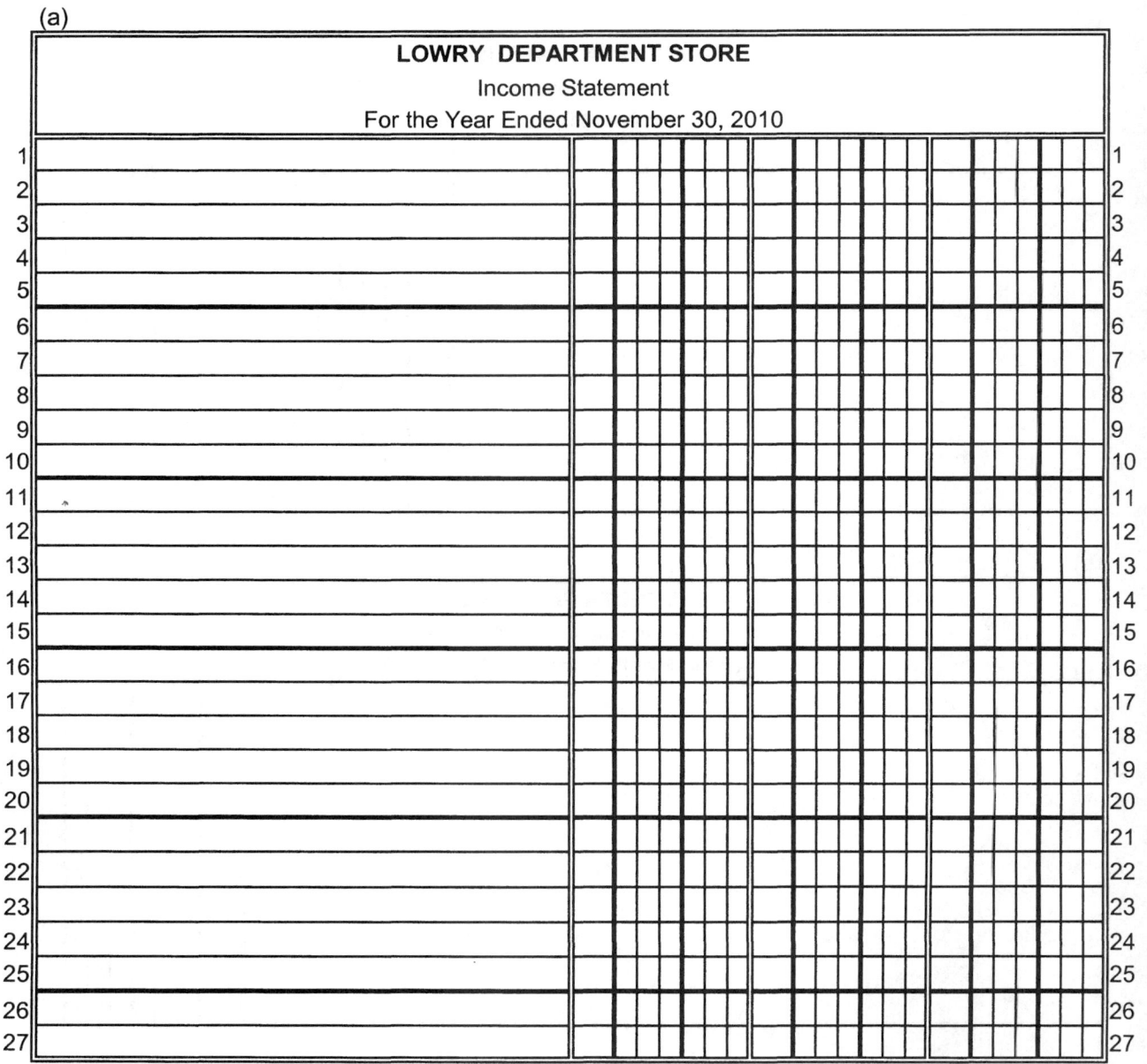

LOWRY DEPARTMENT STORE

Income Statement

For the Year Ended November 30, 2010

LOWRY DEPARTMENT STORE

Retained Earnings Statement

For the Year Ended November 30, 2010

(a) (Continued)

LOWRY DEPARTMENT STORE
Balance Sheet
November 30, 2010

Assets

Liabilities and Stockholders' Equity

(b)

1	Profit margin ratio	1
2		2
3	Gross profit rate	3
4		4

(c)

1	Revised net income:	1
2		2
3		3
4		4
5		5
6		6
7	Revised net sales:	7
8		8
9		9
10		10
11		11
12		12
13	Revised gross profit:	13
14		14
15		15
16		16
17		17
18		18
19	Revised profit margin ratio:	19
20		20
21		21
22		22
23	Revised gross profit rate:	23
24		24
25		25
26		26
27		27
28		28
29		29
30		30
31		31
32		32
33		33
34		34
35		35
36		36
37		37
38		38
39		39
40		40

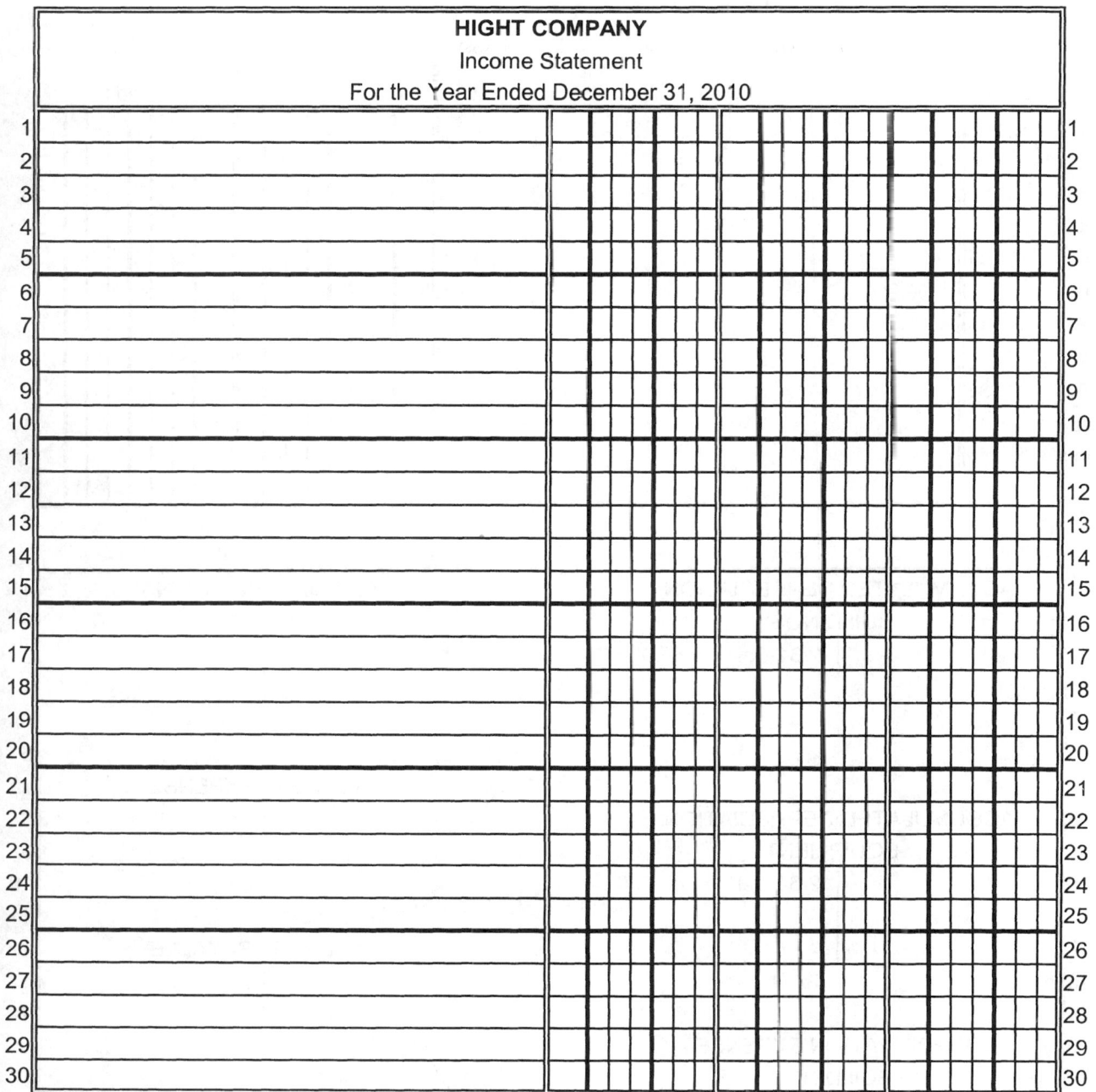

HIGHT COMPANY
Income Statement
For the Year Ended December 31, 2010

(a)

	Date	Account Titles	Debit	Credit	
1	Dec 31				1
2					2
3					3
4					4
5	31				5
6					6
7					7
8					8
9	31				9
10					10
11					11
12					12

(b)

1	ACCUMULATED DEPRECIATION -	DEPRECIATION EXPENSE -
2	BUILDINGS	EQUIPMENT
3		12/31 Bal 60,000	
4		
5		
6		
7		INTEREST EXPENSE
8	ACCUMULATED DEPRECIATION -	
9	EQUIPMENT	
10		12/31 Bal 40,500	
11		
12		INTEREST PAYABLE
13		
14		
15	DEPRECIATION EXPENSE -	
16	BUILDINGS	
17		
18		
19		
20		
21		
22		
23		
24		

(c)

SAVE-Mart WHOLESALE COMPANY Adjusted Trial Balance December 31, 2007	Debit	Credit
1		
2		
3		
4		
5		
6		
7		
8		
9		
10		
11		
12		
13		
14		
15		
16		
17		
18		
19		
20		
21		
22		
23		
24		
25		
26		
27		
28		
29		
30		
31		
32		
33		
34		
35		

(d)

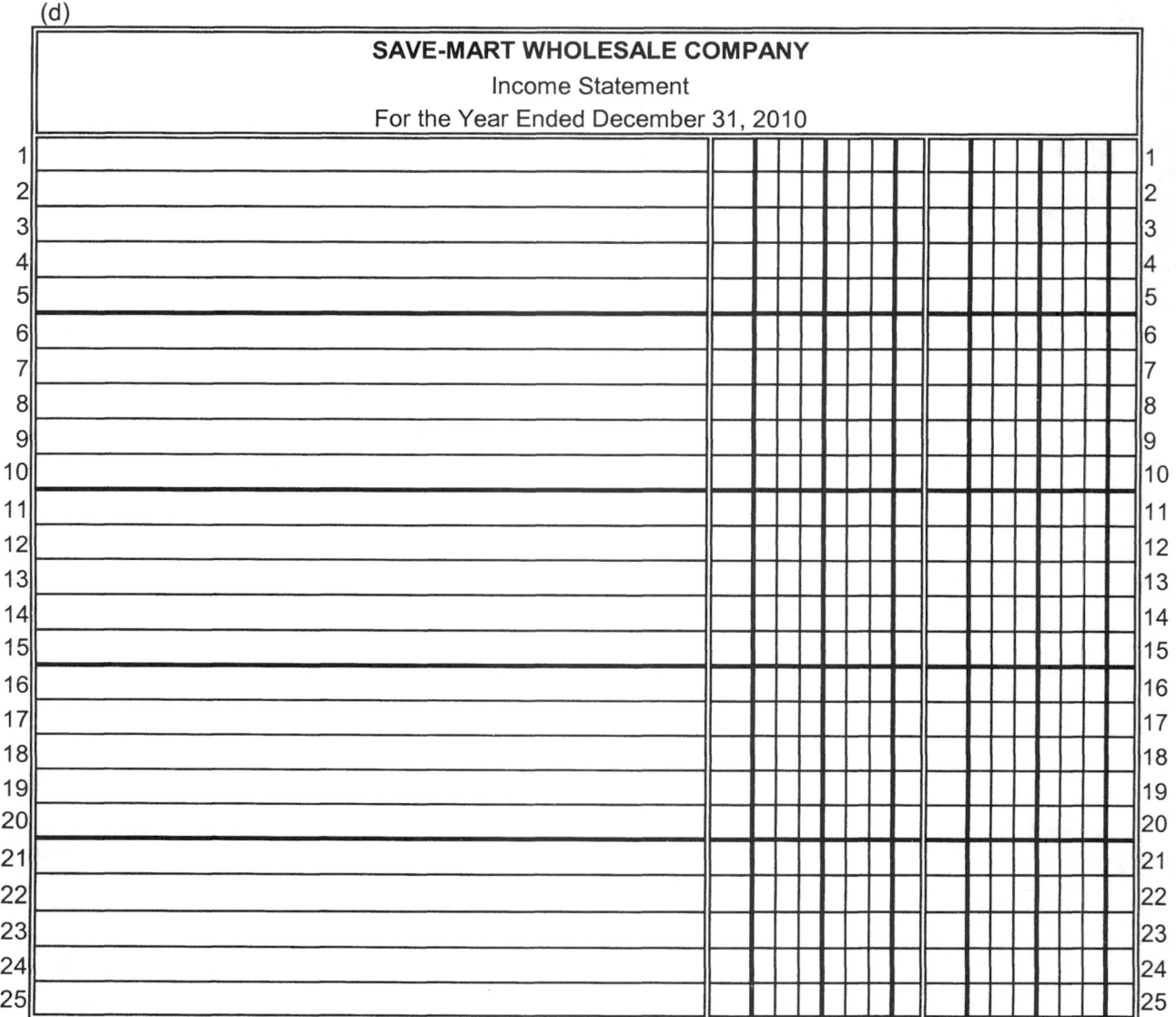

SAVE-MART WHOLESALE COMPANY
Income Statement
For the Year Ended December 31, 2010

SAVE-MART WHOLESALE COMPANY
Retained Earnings Statement
For the Year Ended December 31, 2010

(d) (Continued)

SAVE-Mart WHOLESALE COPANY

Balance Sheet

December 31, 2010

	Assets						
1							
2							
3							
4							
5							
6							
7							
8							
9							
10							
11							
12							
13							
14							
15							
16	Liabilities and Stockholders' Equity						
17							
18							
19							
20							
21							
22							
23							
24							
25							
26							
27							
28							
29							
30							
31							
32							
33							
34							
35							

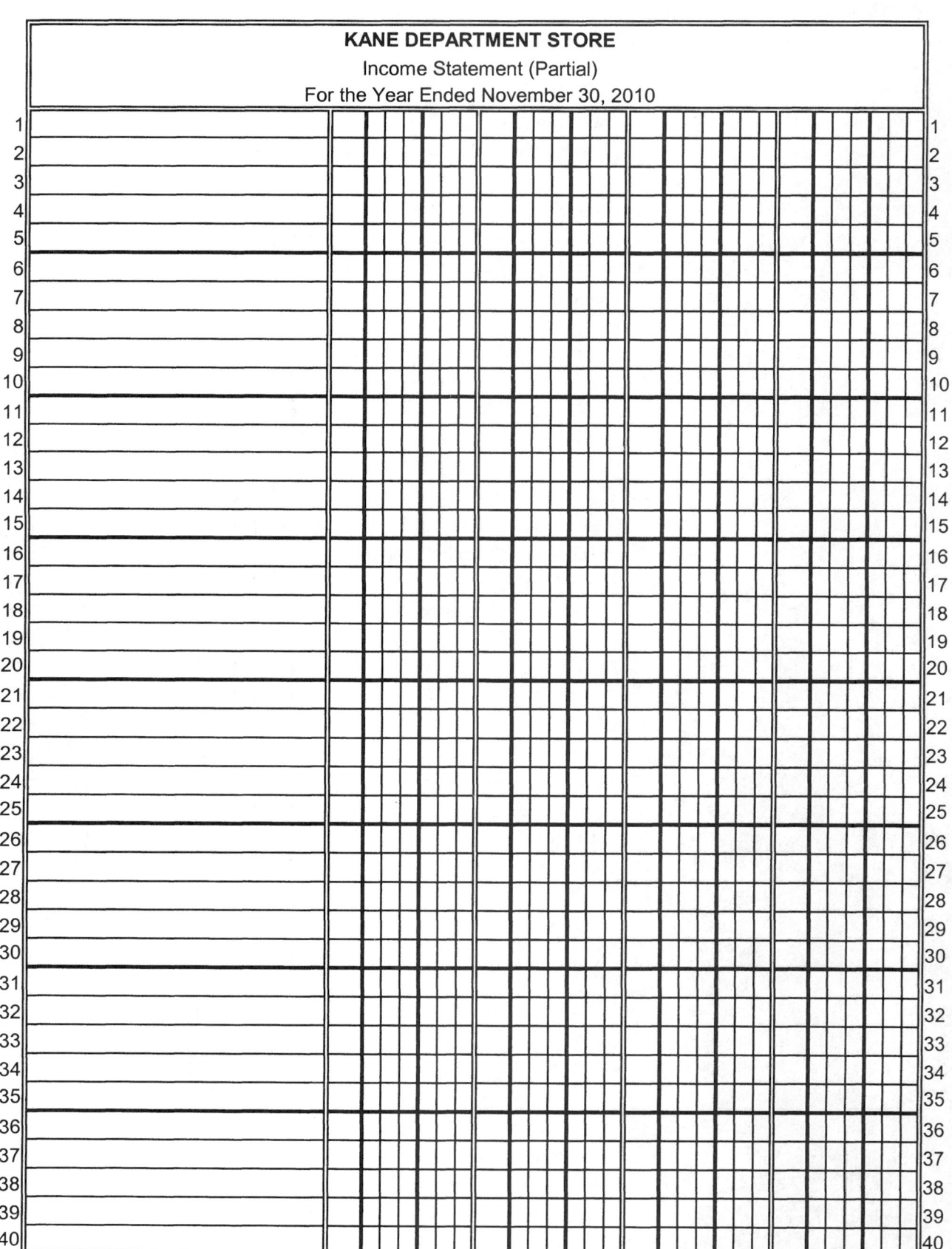

KANE DEPARTMENT STORE
Income Statement (Partial)
For the Year Ended November 30, 2010

(a)	2008	2009	2010	2011	
1 Income statement data:					1
2 Sales	$	$ 96850	$	$ 82220	2
3 Cost of goods sold			25140	26490	3
4 Gross profit		67260	59540		4
5 Operating expenses		63640		52870	5
6 Net income	$	$	$ 4570	$	6
7					7
8 Balance sheet data:					8
9 Merchandise inventory	$ 13000	$	$ 14700	$	9
10 Accounts payable	5800	6500	4600		10
11					11
12 Additional information:					12
13 Purchases of merchandise					13
14 inventory on account		$ 25890	$	$ 24050	14
15 Cash payments to suppliers				24650	15
16					16
17					17
18					18
19 (b)					19
20					20
21					21
22					22
23					23
24					24
25					25
26					26
27					27
28		2009	2010	2011	28
29					29
30 Gross profit rate					30
31					31
32 Profit margin ratio					32
33					33
34					34
35					35

(a)

	Date	Account Titles	Debit	Credit	
1	Apr. 5				1
2					2
3					3
4	7				4
5					5
6					6
7	9				7
8					8
9					9
10	10				10
11					11
12					12
13	12				13
14					14
15					15
16	14				16
17					17
18					18
19					19
20	17				20
21					21
22					22
23	20				23
24					24
25					25
26	21				26
27					27
28					28
29					29
30	27				30
31					31
32					32
33	30				33
34					34
35					35
36					36
37					37
38					38
39					39
40					40

(b)

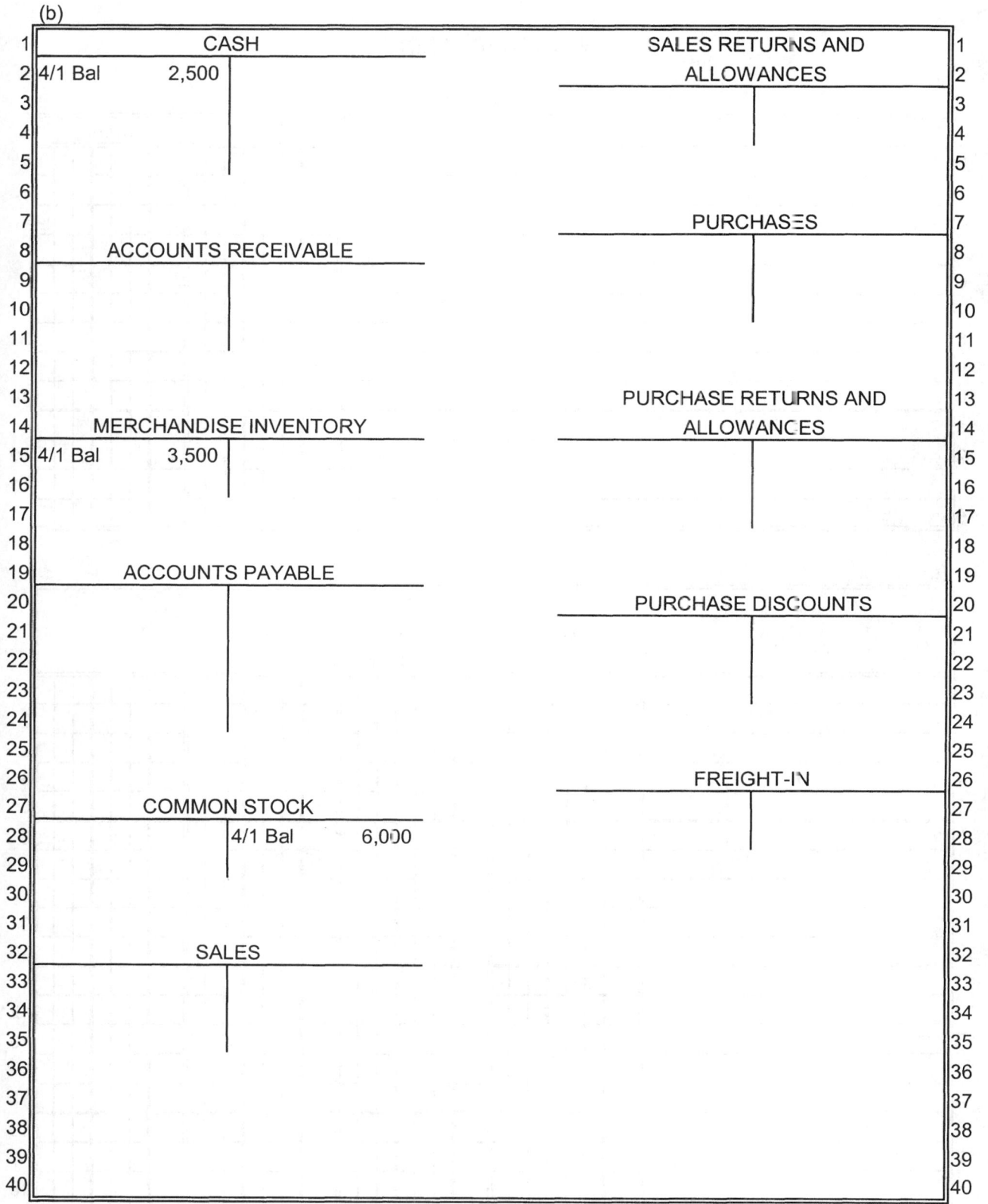

CASH		SALES RETURNS AND ALLOWANCES
4/1 Bal 2,500		
ACCOUNTS RECEIVABLE		PURCHASES
MERCHANDISE INVENTORY		PURCHASE RETURNS AND ALLOWANCES
4/1 Bal 3,500		
ACCOUNTS PAYABLE		PURCHASE DISCOUNTS
COMMON STOCK		FREIGHT-IN
4/1 Bal 6,000		
SALES		

(c)

WICHITA PRO SHOP Trial Balance April 30, 2010	Debit	Credit

(d)

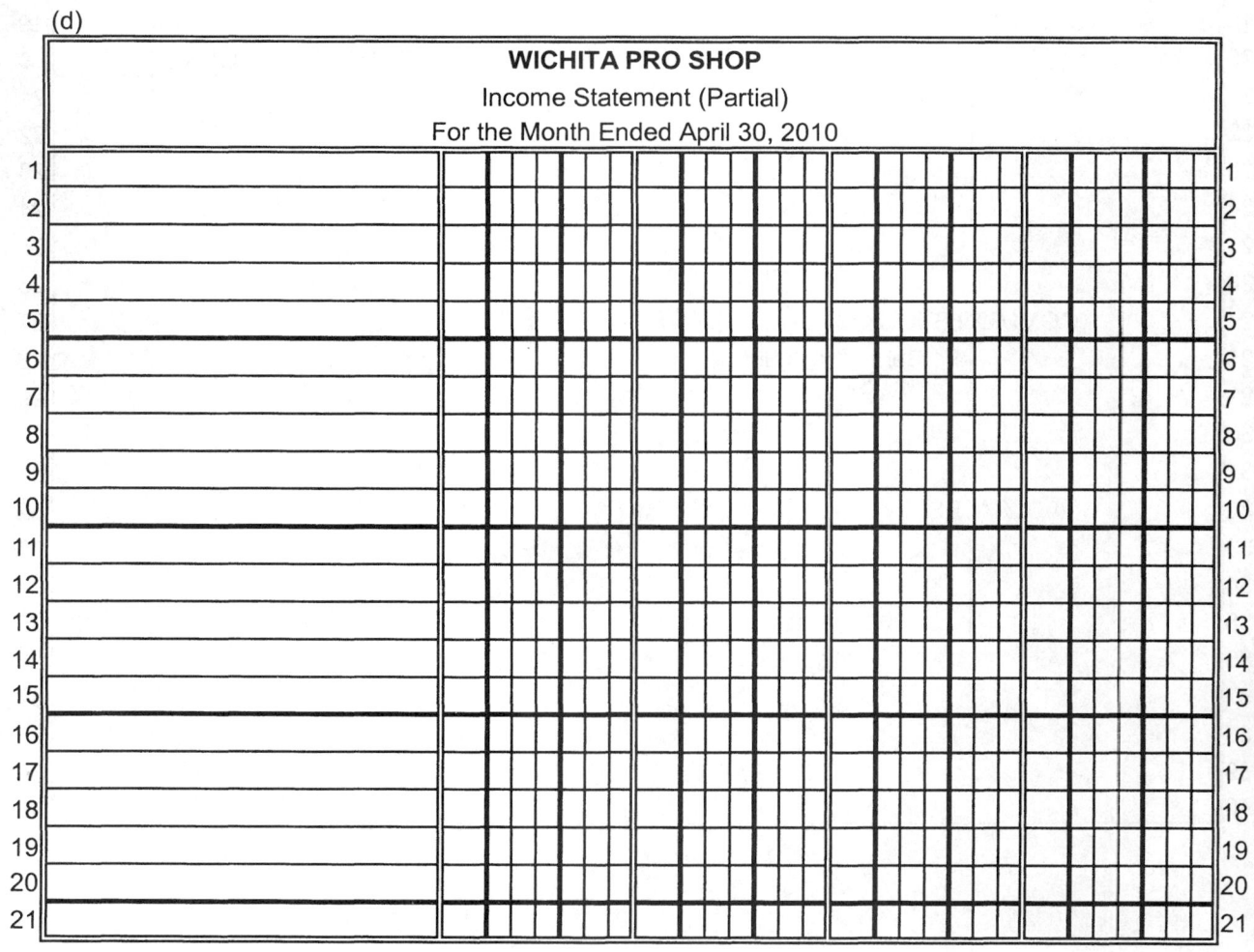

WICHITA PRO SHOP Income Statement (Partial) For the Month Ended April 30, 2010				

(a)

	Date	Account Titles	Debit	Credit	
1	Apr 2				1
2					2
3					3
4	4				4
5					5
6					6
7					7
8					8
9					9
10	5				10
11					11
12					12
13	6				13
14					14
15					15
16	11				16
17					17
18					18
19					19
20	13				20
21					21
22					22
23					23
24	14				24
25					25
26					26
27	16				27
28					28
29					29
30	18				30
31					31
32					32
33	20				33
34					34
35					35
36	23				36
37					37
38					38
39					39
40					40

(a) (Continued)

	Date	Account Titles	Debit	Credit	
1	26				1
2					2
3					3
4	27				4
5					5
6					6
7					7
8	29				8
9					9
10					10
11					11
12					12
13					13
14	30				14
15					15
16					16
17					17
18					18
19					19
20					20
21					21
22					22
23					23
24					24
25					25
26					26
27					27
28					28
29					29
30					30
31					31
32					32
33					33
34					34
35					35
36					36
37					37
38					38
39					39
40					40

(b)

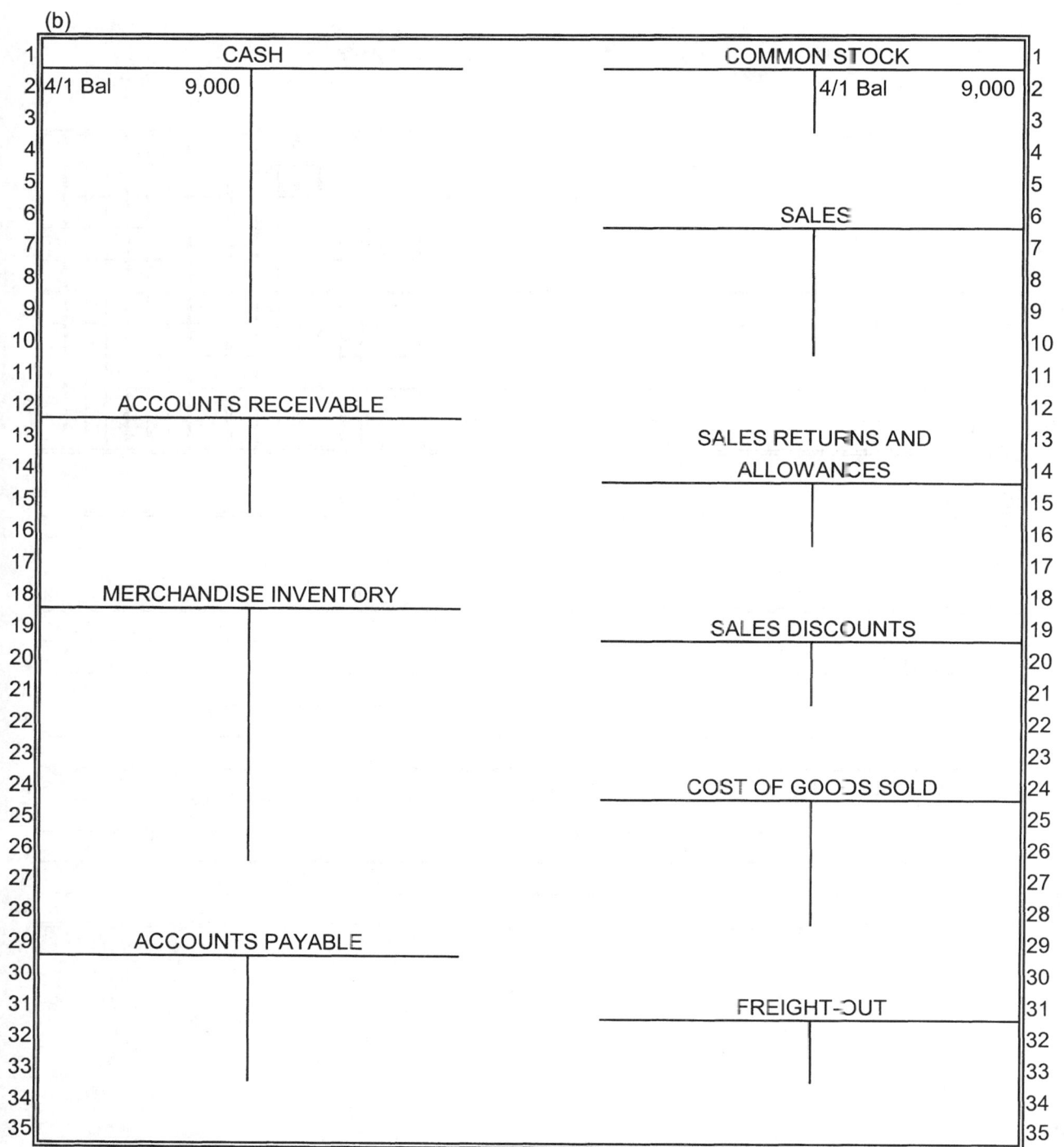

CASH		COMMON STOCK	
4/1 Bal 9,000		4/1 Bal 9,000	
		SALES	
ACCOUNTS RECEIVABLE		SALES RETURNS AND ALLOWANCES	
		SALES DISCOUNTS	
MERCHANDISE INVENTORY		COST OF GOODS SOLD	
ACCOUNTS PAYABLE		FREIGHT-OUT	

(c)

CORDELL DISTRIBUTING COMPANY
Income Statement (Partial)
For the Month Ended April 30, 2010

(d)

Profit margin ratio

Gross profit rate

	Date	Account Titles	Debit	Credit	
1	July 1				1
2					2
3					3
4	3				4
5					5
6					6
7					7
8					8
9					9
10	9				10
11					11
12					12
13					13
14	12				14
15					15
16					16
17					17
18	17				18
19					19
20					20
21					21
22					22
23					23
24	18				24
25					25
26					26
27					27
28					28
29					29
30	20				30
31					31
32					32
33	21				33
34					34
35					35
36					36
37					37
38					38
39					39
40					40

	Date	Account Titles	Debit	Credit	
1	July 22				1
2					2
3					3
4					4
5					5
6					6
7	30				7
8					8
9					9
10	31				10
11					11
12					12
13					13
14					14
15					15
16					16
17					17
18					18
19					19
20					20
21					21
22					22
23					23
24					24
25					25
26					26
27					27
28					28
29					29
30					30
31					31
32					32
33					33
34					34
35					35
36					36
37					37
38					38
39					39
40					40

(a)

	Date	Account Titles	Debit	Credit	
1	Apr 4				1
2					2
3					3
4	6				4
5					5
6					6
7	8				7
8					8
9					9
10					10
11					11
12					12
13	10				13
14					14
15					15
16	11				16
17					17
18					18
19	13				19
20					20
21					21
22					22
23	14				23
24					24
25					25
26	15				26
27					27
28					28
29	17				29
30					30
31					31
32	18				32
33					33
34					34
35					35
36					36
37					37
38	20				38
39					39
40					40

(a) (Continued)

	Date	Account Titles	Debit	Credit	
1	Apr 21				1
2					2
3					3
4					4
5	27				5
6					6
7					7
8	30				8
9					9
10					10

(b)

1	CASH	ACCOUNTS PAYABLE	1
2	4/1 Bal 2,500		2
3			3
4			4
5			5
6			6
7			7
8		COMMON STOCK	8
9		4/1 Bal. 4,200	9
10	ACCOUNTS RECEIVABLE		10
11			11
12			12
13		SALES	13
14			14
15			15
16			16
17	MERCHANDISE INVENTORY		17
18	4/1 Bal 1,700		18
19		SALES RETURNS AND	19
20		ALLOWANCES	20
21			21
22			22
23			23
24			24
25		COST OF GOODS SOLD	25
26			26
27			27
28			28

(c)

COLORADO TENNIS SHOP Trial Balance April 30, 2010	Debit	Credit

(d)

COLORADO TENNIS SHOP Income Statement (Partial) For the Month Ended April 30, 2010	

(a)

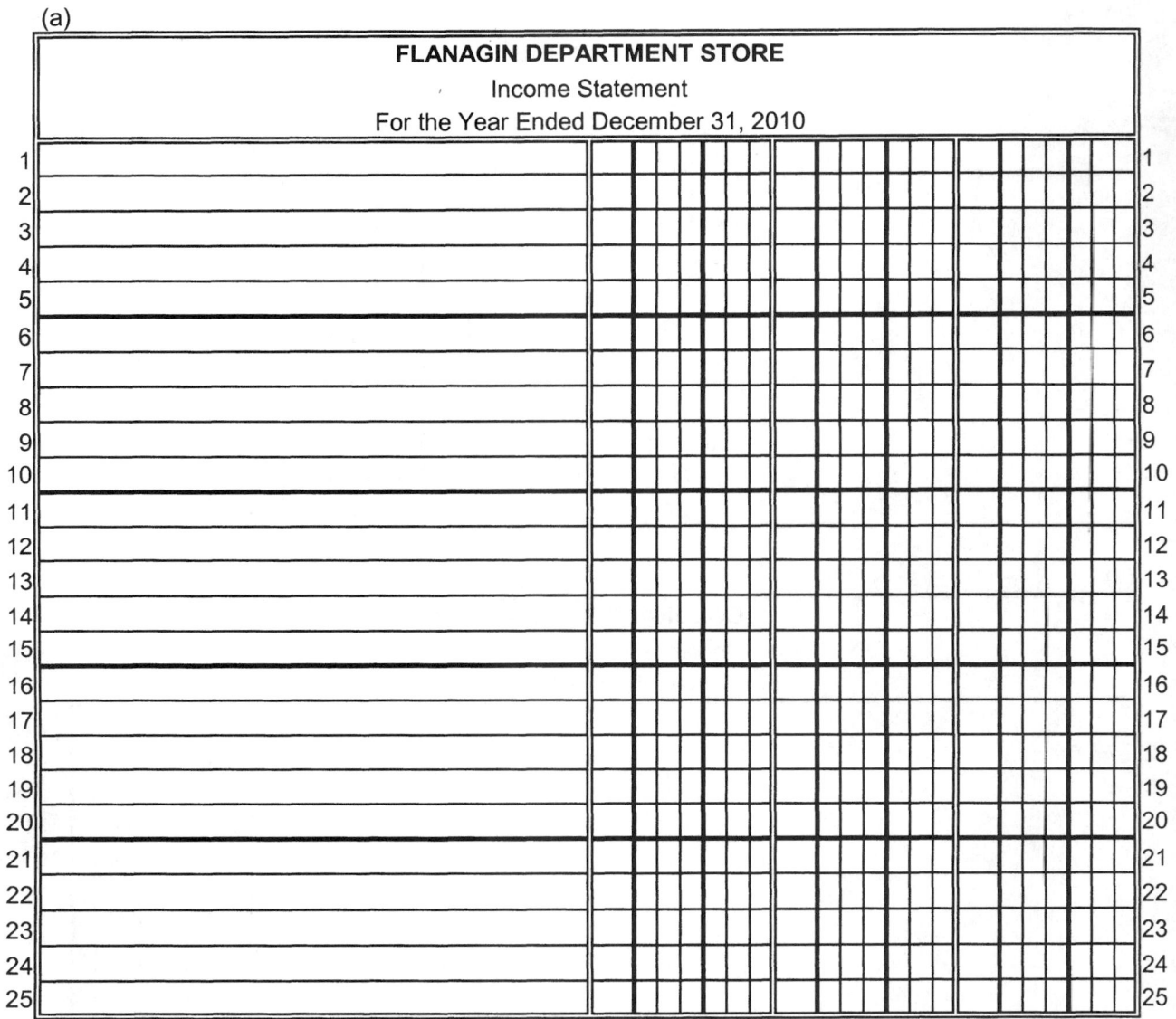

FLANAGIN DEPARTMENT STORE
Income Statement
For the Year Ended December 31, 2010

FLANAGIN DEPARTMENT STORE
Retained Earnings Statement
For the Year Ended December 31, 2010

(a) (Continued)

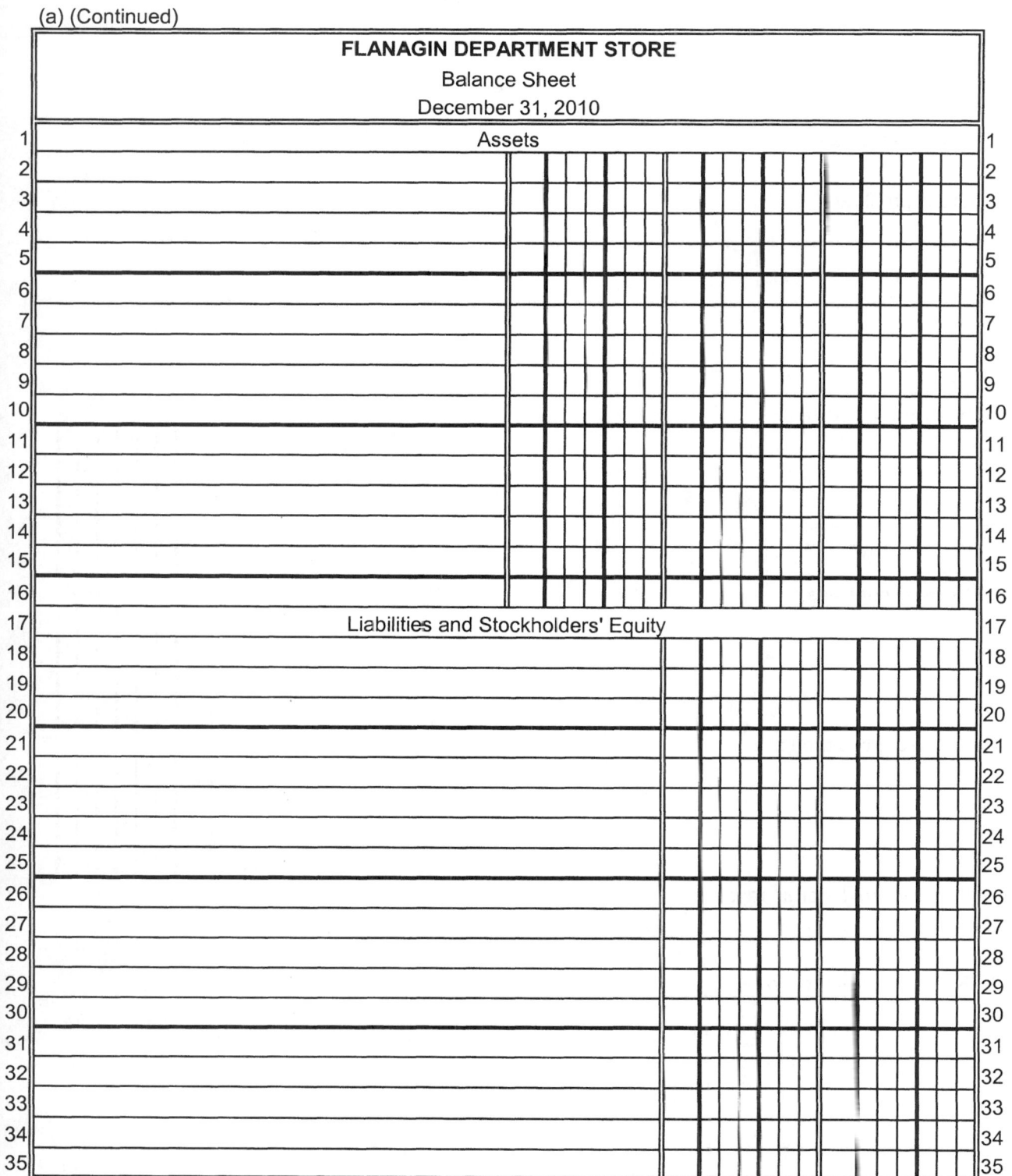

FLANAGIN DEPARTMENT STORE

Balance Sheet

December 31, 2010

Assets

Liabilities and Stockholders' Equity

(b)

Profit margin ratio	
Gross profit rate	

(c)

1	Revised net income:
2	
3	
4	
5	
6	
7	Revised net sales:
8	
9	
10	
11	
12	Revised gross profit:
13	
14	
15	
16	
17	Revised profit margin ratio:
18	
19	
20	Revised gross profit rate:
21	
22	
23	
24	
25	
26	
27	
28	
29	
30	
31	

(c) (Continued)

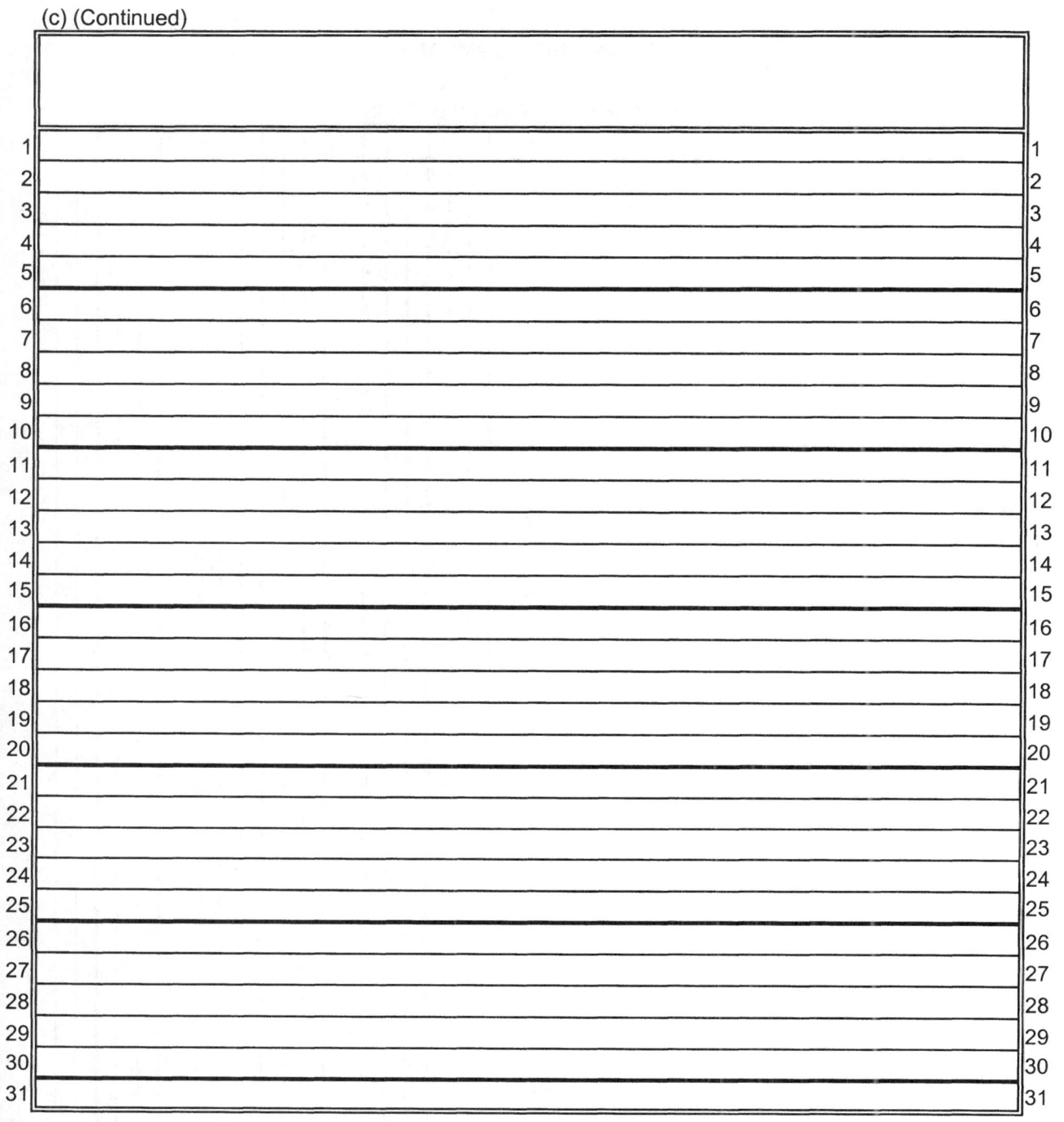

	CHOWDHURY COMPANY						
	Income Statement						
	For the Year Ended December 31, 2010						
1							1
2							2
3							3
4							4
5							5
6							6
7							7
8							8
9							9
10							10
11							11
12							12
13							13
14							14
15							15
16							16
17							17
18							18
19							19
20							20
21							21
22							22
23							23
24							24
25							25
26							26
27							27
28							28
29							29
30							30
31							31
32							32
33							33
34							34
35							35

(a)

	Date	Account Titles	Debit	Credit	
1	Nov 30				1
2					2
3					3
4	30				4
5					5
6					6
7					7
8	30				8
9					9
10					10
11					11
12	30				12
13					13
14					14

(b)

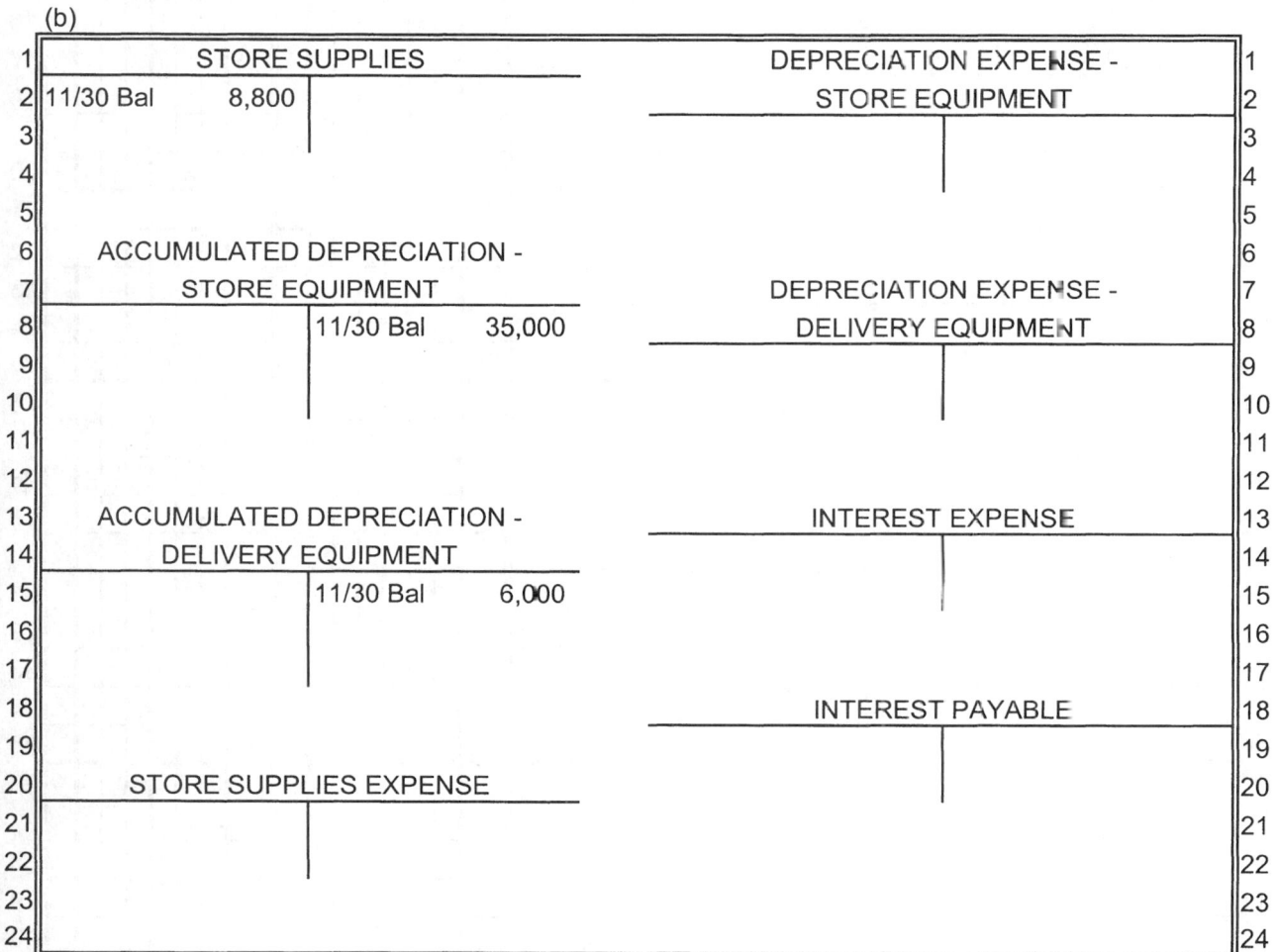

	STORE SUPPLIES		DEPRECIATION EXPENSE -	
2	11/30 Bal	8,800	STORE EQUIPMENT	2
6	ACCUMULATED DEPRECIATION -			6
7	STORE EQUIPMENT		DEPRECIATION EXPENSE -	7
8		11/30 Bal 35,000	DELIVERY EQUIPMENT	8
13	ACCUMULATED DEPRECIATION -		INTEREST EXPENSE	13
14	DELIVERY EQUIPMENT			14
15		11/30 Bal 6,000		15
18			INTEREST PAYABLE	18
20	STORE SUPPLIES EXPENSE			20

(c)

CALHOUN FASHION CENTER
Adjusted Trial Balance
November 30, 2010

	Debit	Credit

(d)

CALHOUN FASHION CENTER

Income Statement

For the Year Ended November 30, 2010

1			
2			
3			
4			
5			
6			
7			
8			
9			
10			
11			
12			
13			
14			
15			
16			
17			
18			
19			
20			
21			
22			
23			
24			
25			

CALHOUN FASHION CENTER

Retained Earnings Statement

For the Year Ended November 30, 2010

1	
2	
3	
4	
5	
6	
7	
8	

(d) (Continued)

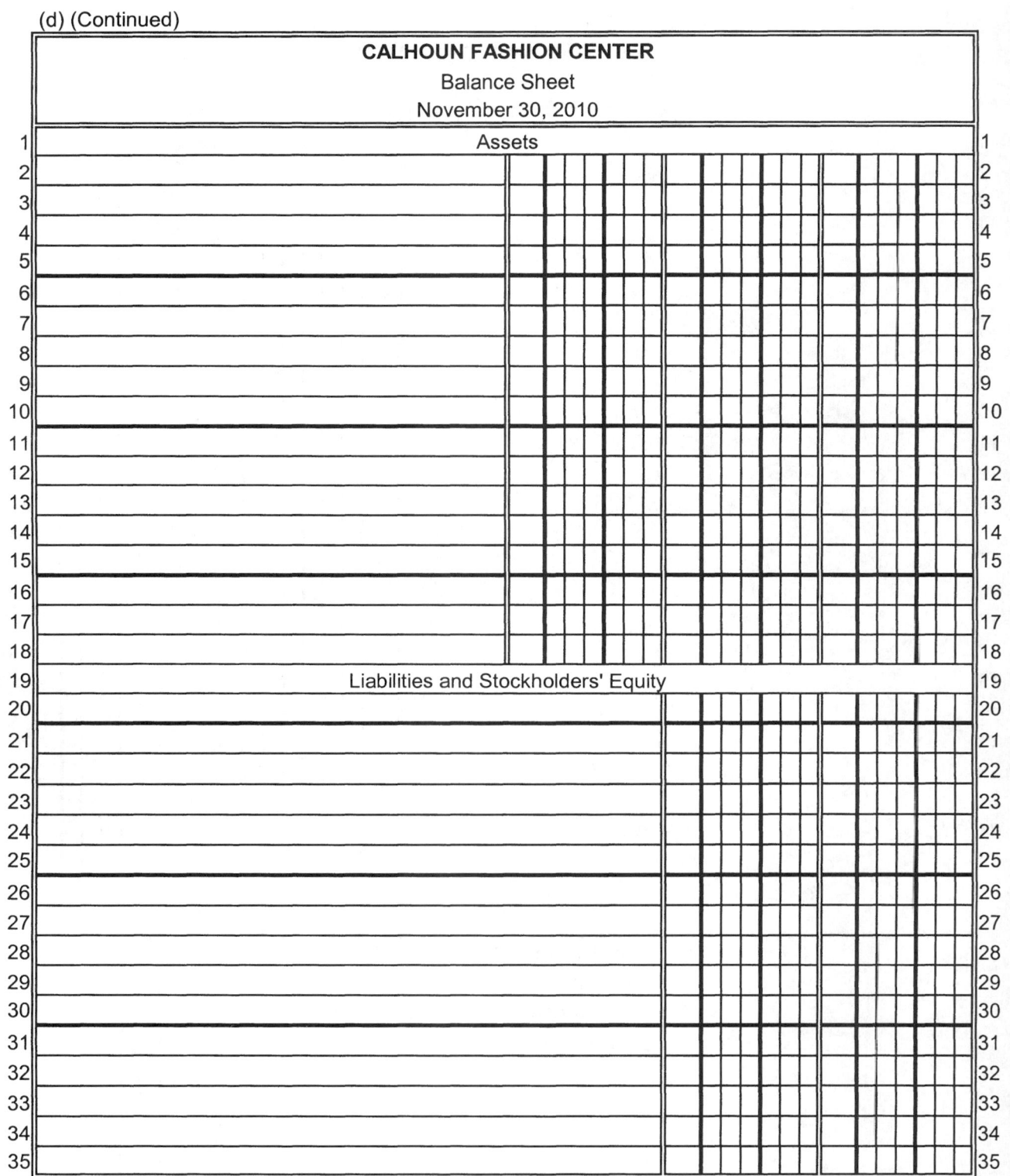

CALHOUN FASHION CENTER
Balance Sheet
November 30, 2010

Assets

Liabilities and Stockholders' Equity

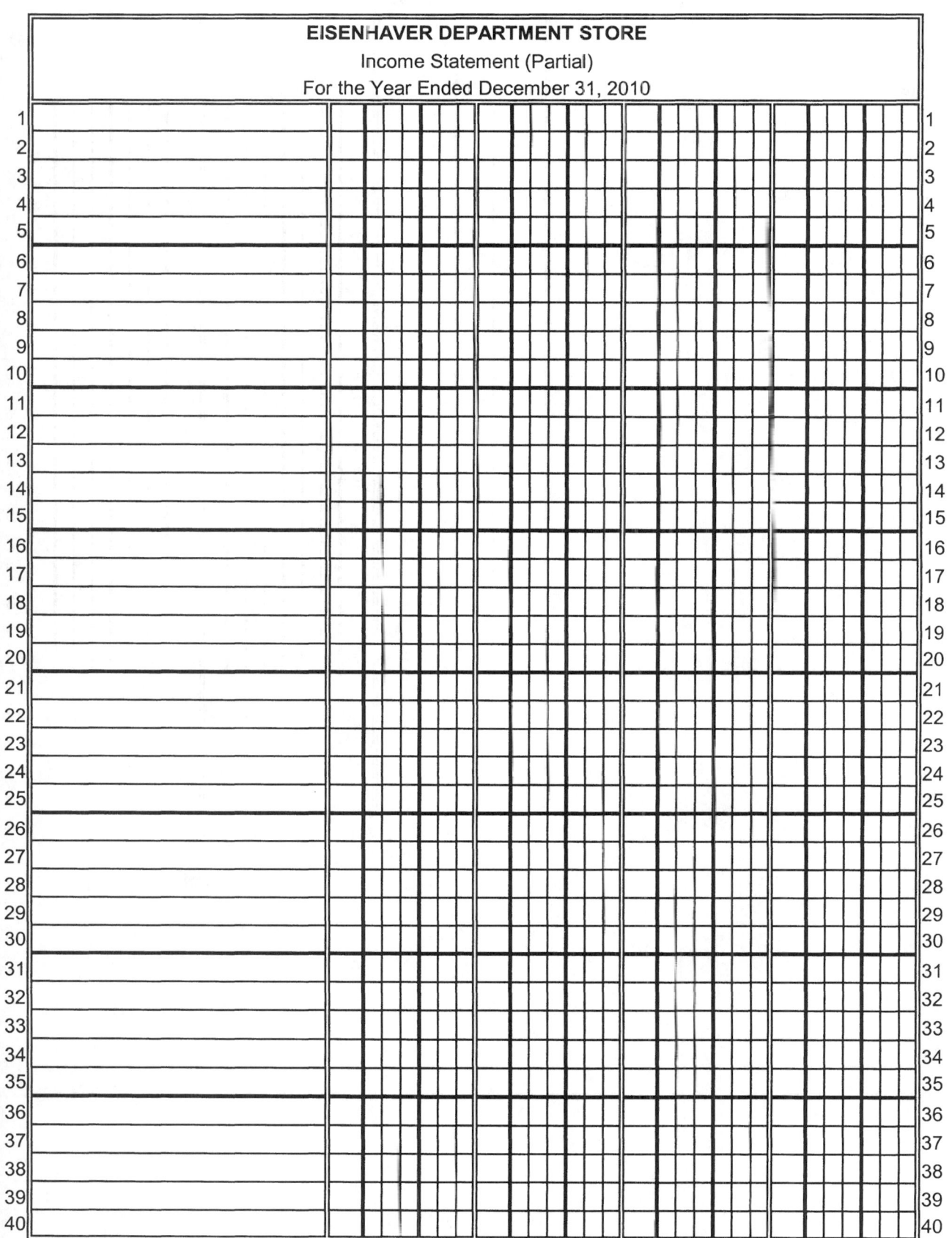

EISENHAVER DEPARTMENT STORE
Income Statement (Partial)
For the Year Ended December 31, 2010

(a)	2009	2010	2011
1			
2			
3			
4			
5			
6			
7			
8			
9			
10 (b)			
11			
12			
13			
14			
15 (c)			
16			
17			
18			
19			
20			
21 (d)			
22			
23			
24			
25			
26			
27			
28			
29			
30			
31			
32			
33			
34			
35			

(a)

	Date	Account Titles	Debit	Credit	
1	Apr 4				1
2					2
3					3
4	6				4
5					5
6					6
7	8				7
8					8
9					9
10	10				10
11					11
12					12
13	11				13
14					14
15					15
16	13				16
17					17
18					18
19					19
20	14				20
21					21
22					22
23	15				23
24					24
25					25
26	17				26
27					27
28					28
29	18				29
30					30
31					31
32	20				32
33					33
34					34
35	21				35
36					36
37					37
38					38
39					39
40					40

(a) (Continued)   General Journal

	Date	Account Titles	Debit	Credit	
1	Apr 27				1
2					2
3					3
4	30				4
5					5
6					6
7					7
8					8
9					9
10					10
11					11
12					12
13					13
14					14
15					15
16					16
17					17
18					18
19					19
20					20
21					21
22					22
23					23
24					24
25					25
26					26
27					27
28					28
29					29
30					30
31					31
32					32
33					33
34					34
35					35
36					36
37					37
38					38
39					39
40					40

(b)

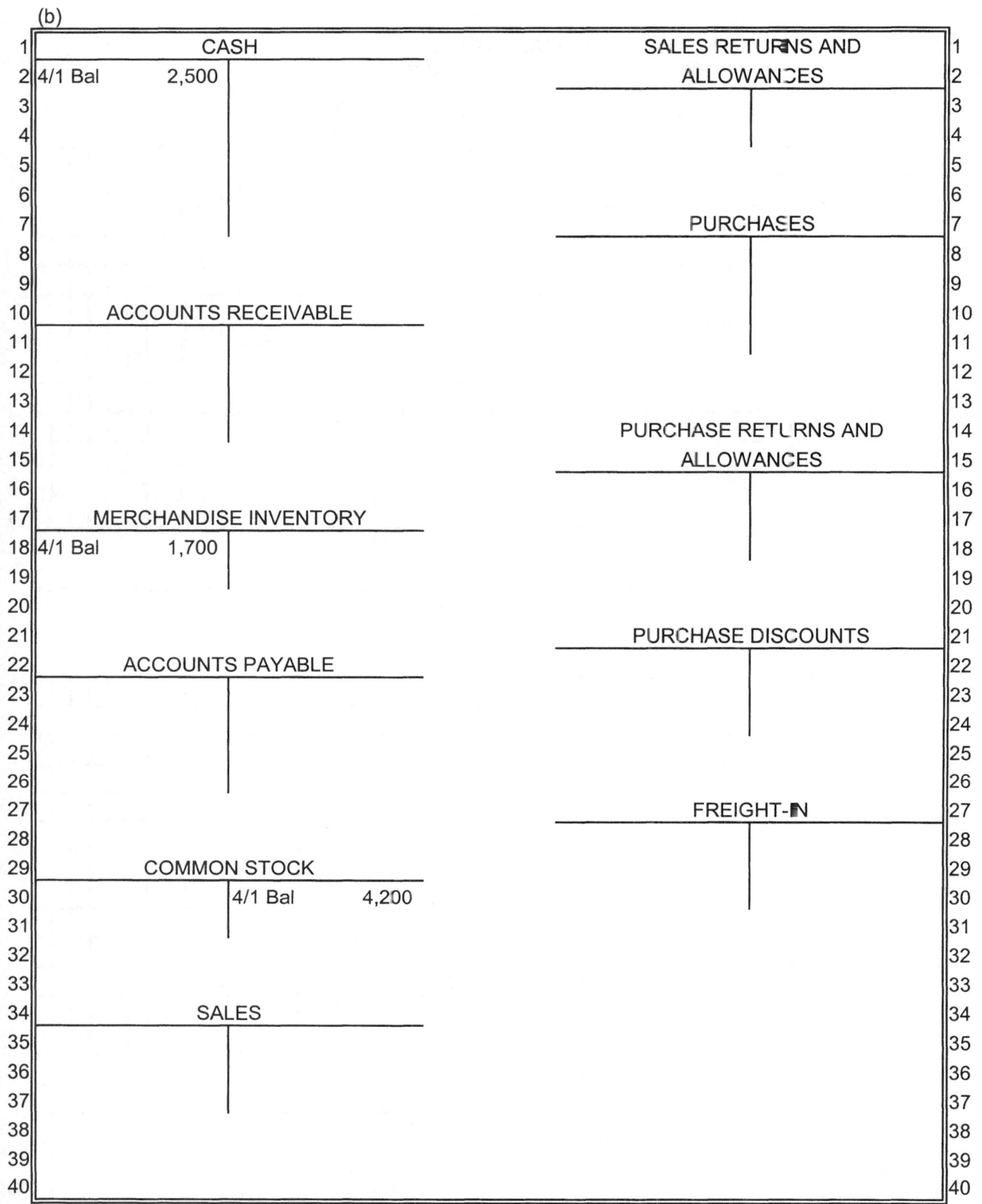

CASH		SALES RETURNS AND ALLOWANCES
4/1 Bal 2,500		

ACCOUNTS RECEIVABLE		PURCHASES

MERCHANDISE INVENTORY		PURCHASE RETURNS AND ALLOWANCES
4/1 Bal 1,700		

ACCOUNTS PAYABLE		PURCHASE DISCOUNTS

COMMON STOCK		FREIGHT-IN
4/1 Bal 4,200		

SALES	

(c)

COLORADO TENNIS SHOP Trial Balance April 30, 2010			Debit	Credit
1				
2				
3				
4				
5				
6				
7				
8				
9				
10				
11				
12				
13				
14				

(d)

COLORADO TENNIS SHOP Income Statement (Partial) For the Month Ended April 30, 2010				
1				
2				
3				
4				
5				
6				
7				
8				
9				
10				
11				
12				
13				
14				
15				
16				
17				
18				
19				
20				
21				

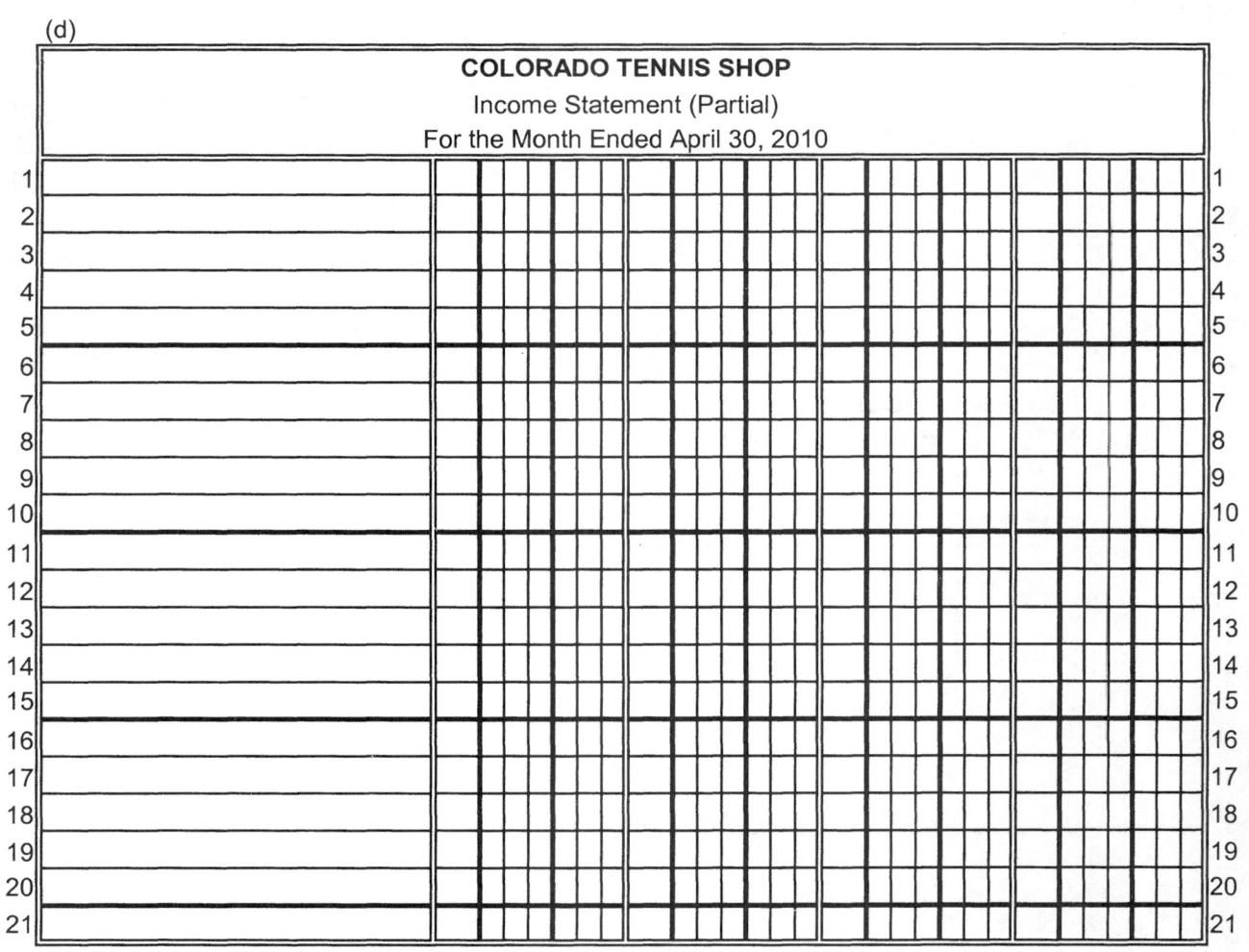

(a)

	Date	Account Titles	Debit	Credit	
1	Dec. 6				1
2					2
3					3
4					4
5	8				5
6					6
7					7
8	10				8
9					9
10					10
11					11
12					12
13					13
14	13				14
15					15
16					16
17	15				17
18					18
19					19
20	18				20
21					21
22					22
23					23
24					24
25					25
26	20				26
27					27
28					28
29	23				29
30					30
31					31
32					32
33	27				33
34					34
35					35
36					36
37					37
38					38
39					39
40					40

(b) & (c)

	CASH			ACCOUNTS PAYABLE		
1						1
2	12/1 Bal	7,300			12/1 Bal	4,600	2
3						3
4						4
5						5
6						6
7				SALARIES PAYABLE		7
8					12/1 Bal	1,000	8
9	ACCOUNTS RECEIVABLE					9
10	12/1 Bal	5,600				10
11						11
12						12
13				COMMON STOCK		13
14					12/1 Bal	15,000	14
15	MERCHANDISE INVENTORY					15
16	12/1 Bal	12,000				16
17				RETAINED EARNINGS		17
18					12/1 Bal	25,300	18
19						19
20						20
21				SALES		21
22	SUPPLIES					22
23	12/1 Bal	1,200				23
24						24
25						25
26						26
27				SALES DISCOUNTS		27
28	EQUIPMENT					28
29	12/1 Bal	22,000				29
30						30
31						31
32	ACCUMULATED DEPRECIATION			COST OF GOODS SOLD		32
33		12/1 Bal	2,200			33
34						34
35						35
36						36
37						37
38						38
39						39
40						40

(b) & (c) (Continued)

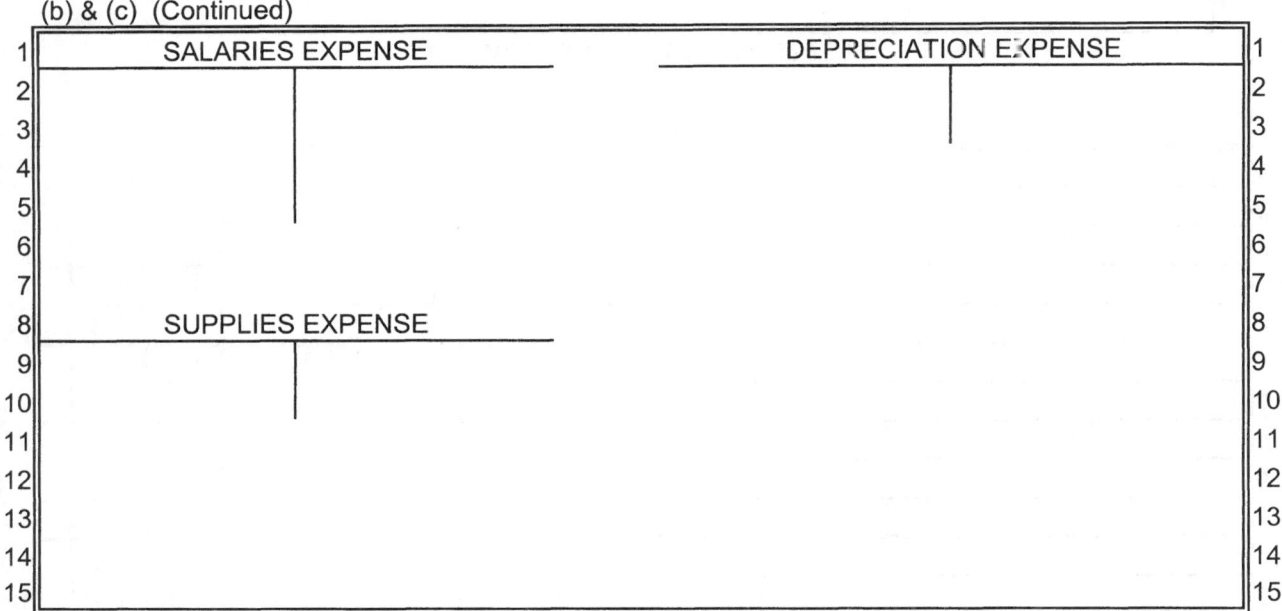

	SALARIES EXPENSE		DEPRECIATION EXPENSE	
1				1
2				2
3				3
4				4
5				5
6				6
7				7
8	SUPPLIES EXPENSE			8
9				9
10				10
11				11
12				12
13				13
14				14
15				15

(c)

	Date	Account Titles	Debit	Credit	
1	Dec. 31				1
2					2
3					3
4	31				4
5					5
6					6
7	31				7
8					8
9					9
10					10
11					11
12					12
13					13
14					14
15					15
16					16
17					17
18					18
19					19
20					20

(d)

SLEEZER DISTRIBUTING COMPANY Adjusted Trial Balance December 31, 2010	Debit	Credit
1		
2		
3		
4		
5		
6		
7		
8		
9		
10		
11		
12		
13		
14		
15		
16		
17		
18		
19		
20		

(e)

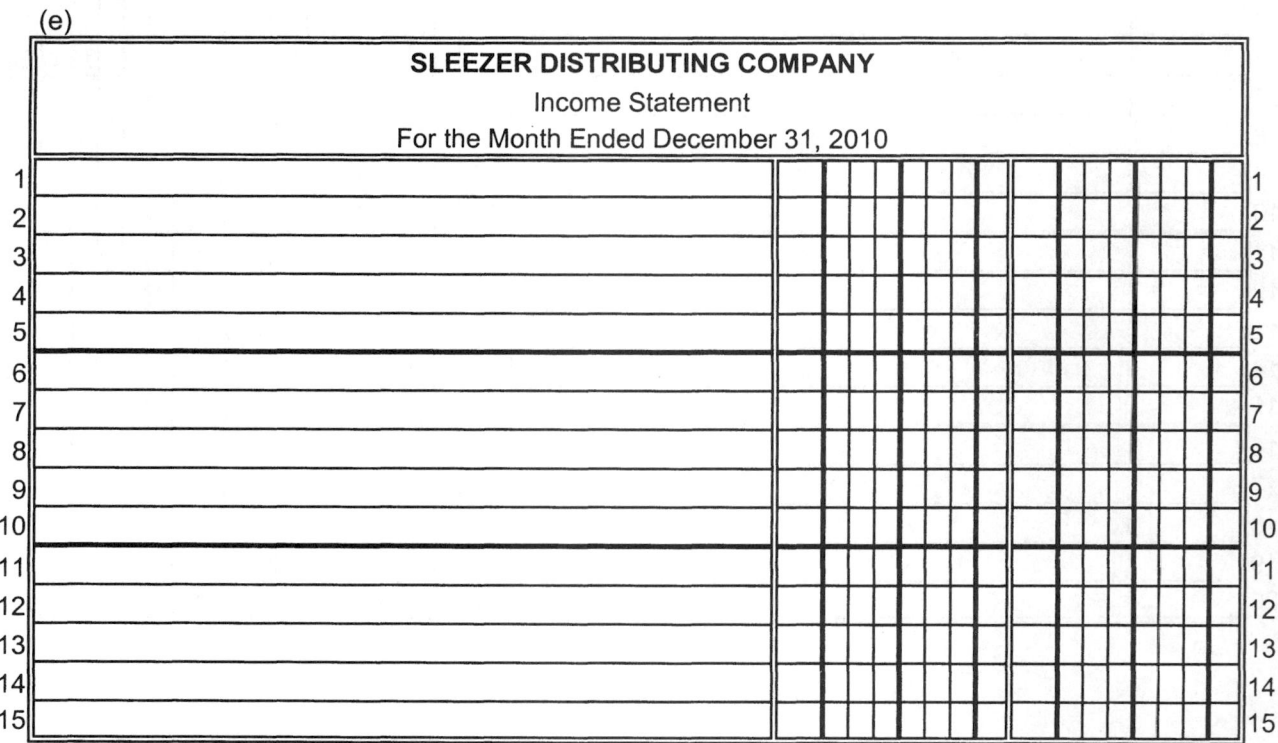

SLEEZER DISTRIBUTING COMPANY Income Statement For the Month Ended December 31, 2010		
1		
2		
3		
4		
5		
6		
7		
8		
9		
10		
11		
12		
13		
14		
15		

(e) (Continued)

SLEEZER DISTRIBUTING COMPANY

Retained Earnings Statement

For the Month Ended December 31, 2010

1				1
2				2
3				3
4				4
5				5
6				6

SLEEZER DISTRIBUTING COMPANY

Balance Sheet

December 31, 2010

	Assets			
1	Assets			1
2				2
3				3
4				4
5				5
6				6
7				7
8				8
9				9
10				10
11				11
12				12
13				13
14				14
15	Liabilities and Stockholders' Equity			15
16				16
17				17
18				18
19				19
20				20
21				21
22				22
23				23
24				24
25				25
26				26
27				27
28				28
29				29

(a) (1)

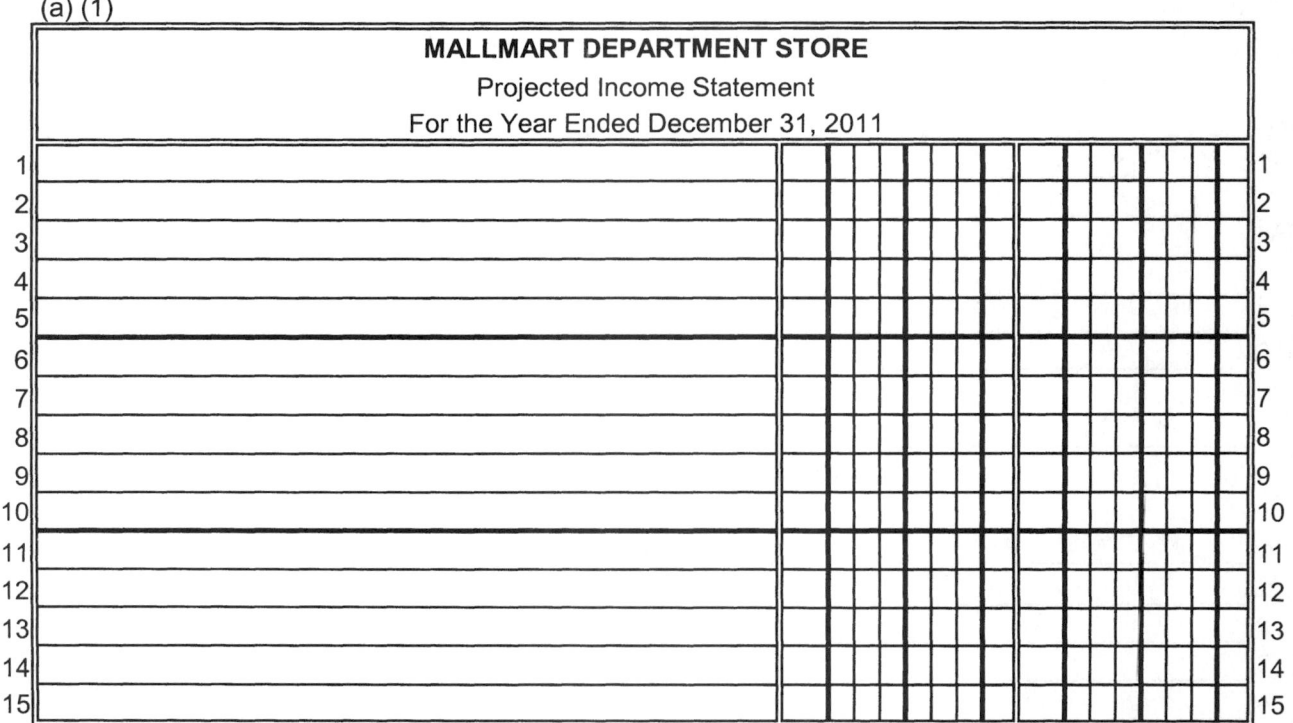

MALLMART DEPARTMENT STORE
Projected Income Statement
For the Year Ended December 31, 2011

(2)

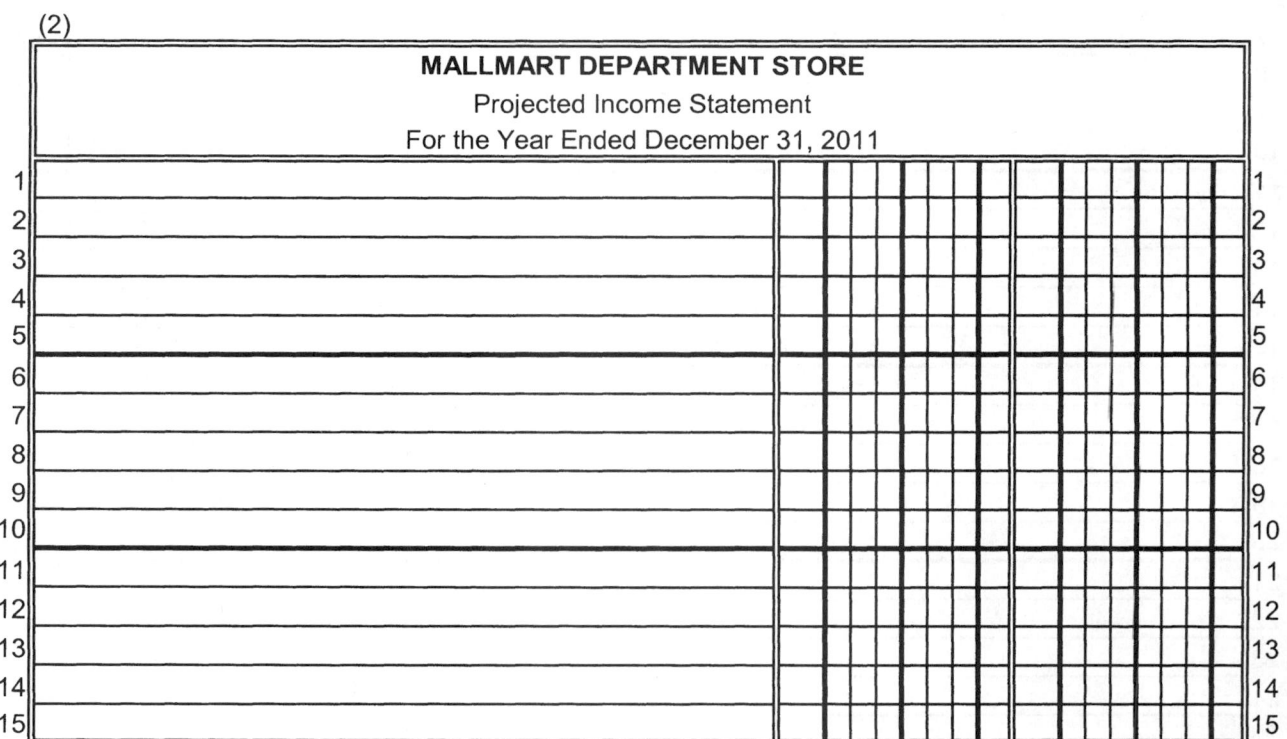

MALLMART DEPARTMENT STORE
Projected Income Statement
For the Year Ended December 31, 2011

(b)

	1
1	
2	
3	
4	
5	
6	
7	
8	
9	
10	

(c)

MALLMART DEPARTMENT STORE

Projected Income Statement

For the Year Ended December 31, 2011

1		
2		
3		
4		
5		
6		
7		
8		
9		
10		
11		
12		
13		
14		
15		
16		
17		
18		
19		
20		

(d)

1	1
2	2
3	3
4	4
5	5
6	6
7	7
8	8
9	9
10	10
11	11
12	12
13	13
14	14
15	15
16	16
17	17
18	18
19	19
20	20
21	21
22	22
23	23
24	24
25	25
26	26
27	27
28	28
29	29
30	30
31	31
32	32
33	33
34	34
35	35
36	36
37	37
38	38

BE6-1

1	(a)
2	
3	
4	(b)
5	
6	
7	(c)
8	
9	
10	(d)
11	
12	
13	
14	

BE6-2

16	(a)
17	
18	
19	(b)
20	

BE6-3

	Units	Unit Cost	Total Cost
21			
22			
23			
24			
25			
26			
27			
28			
29			

BE6-4

31	(a)
32	
33	(b)
34	
35	(c)
36	
37	
38	(d)
39	
40	

BE6-5

	LIFO	FIFO
1		
2		
3		
4		
5		
6		
7		
8		
9		
10		
11		
12		
13		
14		

BE6-7

	Cost	Market	LCM
Inventory categories:			
Cameras			
Camcorders			
DVDs			
Total valuation			

BE6-8

Inventory turnover ratio =

Days in inventory

BE6-9

*BE6-10

Product E2-D2

(1) FIFO Method

Date	Purchases	Cost of Goods Sold	Balance
May 7	50 units @ $10		
June 1			
July 28			
Aug. 27			

(2) LIFO Method

Date	Purchases	Cost of Goods Sold	Balance
May 7	50 units @ $10		
June 1			
July 28			
Aug. 27			

(3) Average Cost

Date	Purchases	Cost of Goods Sold	Balance
May 7	50 units @ $10		
June 1			
July 28			
Aug. 27			

DO IT! 6-1

1	
2	
3	
4	
5	
6	

DO IT! 6-2

8	Cost of goods available for sale:
13	Ending inventory:
19	(a) FIFO:
24	(b) LIFO:
29	(c) Average-cost:

DO IT! 6-3

	Cost	Market	LCM
1 Small	$ 64 000	$ 73 000	
2 Medium	29 000	26 000	
3 Large	152 000	171 000	

E6-1

1	Ending Inventory - physical count					1
2						2
3						3
4						4
5						5
6						6
7						7
8						8
9						9
10						10
11						11
12						12
13	Correct inventory					13
14	**E6-2**					14
15	Ending inventory - as reported					15
16						16
17						17
18						18
19						19
20						20
21						21
22						22
23						23
24						24
25						25
26						26
27						27
28						28
29						29
30						30
31						31
32						32
33						33
34						34
35						35
36						36
37						37
38						38
39						39
40	Correct inventory					40

(a)

	FIFO			
1				
2				
3				
4				
5				
6				
7				
8				

Proof:

Date	Units	Unit Cost	Total Cost

	LIFO			

Proof:

Date	Units	Unit Cost	Total Cost

(b)   Cost of Goods Available for Sale:

FIFO:

LIFO:

	(a)									

FIFO

1	
2	
3	
4	
5	
6	
7	
8	

Proof:

	Date	Units	Unit Cost	Total Cost

(b) AVERAGE COST

Proof

	Date	Units	Unit Cost	Total Cost

(c) LIFO

Proof

	Date	Units	Unit Cost	Total Cost

(a) (1)	FIFO	
(2)	LIFO	
(3)	AVERAGE COST	
Weighted average unit cost =		
Ending inventory =		
Cost of goods sold =		
(b)		
(c)		
(d)		

	LIFO	FIFO
(a)		

	LIFO	FIFO
(b)		

	LIFO	FIFO
(c)		

	Units	Cost/Unit	Market Value/Unit	(a) Total Cost	(b) Total Market Value	(c) Lower of Cost or Market
1 Cameras:						
2 Minolta	5	$175	$160			
3						
4 Canon	7	$145	$152			
5						
6 Light Meters:						
7 Vivitar	12	$125	$119			
8						
9 Kodak	10	$120	$135			
10						
11 Total						
12						
13						
14						
15						
16						
17						
18						
19						
20						

(a)

FIFO

Date	Purchases	Cost of Goods Sold	Balance
June 1			(125 units @ $5)
12			
15			
23			
27			

Ending inventory =

Cost of goods sold =

(a) (Continued)

LIFO

	Date	Purchases		Cost of Goods Sold		Balance	
1	June 1					(125 units @ $5)	6 2 5
2	12						
3							
4	15						
5							
6	23						
7							
8	27						
9							
10							
11							
12	Ending inventory =			Cost of Goods Sold =			

Moving Average

	Date	Purchases		Cost of Goods Sold		Balance	
1	June 1					(125 units @ $5)	6 2 5
2	12						
3	15						
4	23						
5	27						
6							
7							
8	Ending inventory =			Cost of Goods Sold =			

	Periodic	Perpetual	
1 (b)			1
2 Ending inventory, FIFO			2
3 Ending inventory, LIFO			3
4			4
5			5
6			6
7			7
8			8
9 (c)			9
10			10
11			11
12			12
13			13
14			14
15			15
16			16
17			17
18			18
19			19
20			20
21			21
22			22
23			23
24			24
25			25
26			26
27			27
28			28
29			29
30			30
31			31
32			32
33			33
34			34
35			35
36			36
37			37
38			38
39			39
40			40

(a)

FIFO

Date	Purchases			Sales			Balance		
9/1							(14 units @ $100)		1 4 0 0
9/5									
9/12									
9/16									
9/19									
9/26									
9/29									

(a) (Continued)

LIFO

Date	Purchases			Cost of Goods Sold			Balance		
1	9/1						(14 units @ $100)	1 4 0 0
2	9/5							
3	9/12							
4								
5	9/16							
6								
7	9/19							
8								
9	9/26							
10								
11								
12	9/29							
13								

Average Cost

Date	Purchases			Cost of Goods Sold			Balance		
1	9/1						(14 units @ $100)	1 4 0 0
2	9/5							
3	9/12							
4	9/16							
5	9/19							
6	9/26							
7	9/29							
8								

	Periodic	Perpetual
(b)		
1 Ending inventory FIFO		
2		
3 Ending inventory LIFO		
4		

(c)

		2007	2008	
1				1
2				2
3				3
4				4
5				5
6				6
7				7
8				8
9				9
10				10
11				11
12				12
13				13
14				14
15				15
16				16
17				17
18				18
19				19
20				20

Notson Company

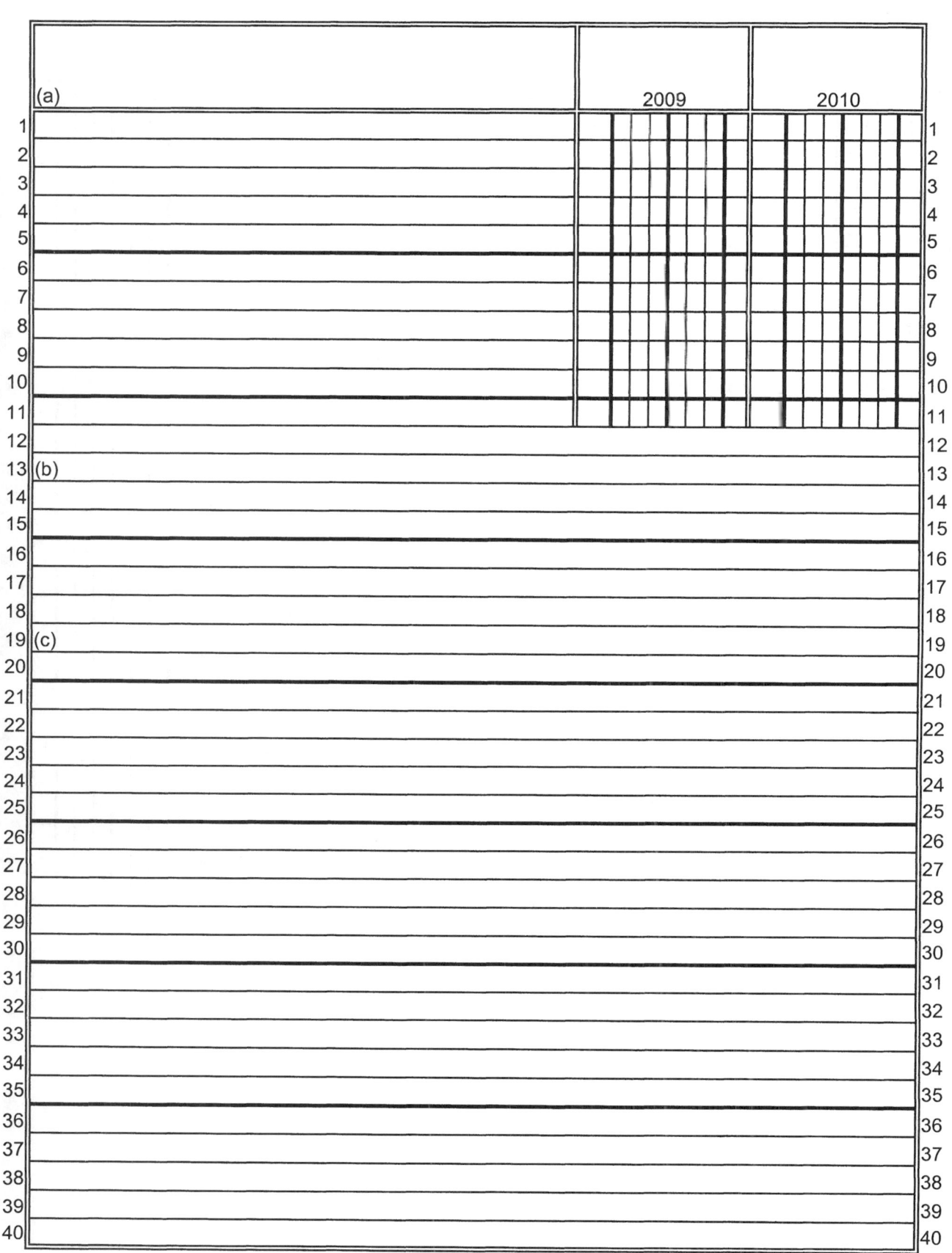

	2009	2010
(a)		

(b)

(c)

(a)

COST OF GOODS AVAILABLE FOR SALE

	Date	Explanation	Units	Unit Cost	Total Cost
1	March 1				
2	5				
3	13				
4	21				
5	26				
6					
7					

(b) **FIFO**

(1) Ending Inventory

	Date		Units	Unit Cost	Total Cost
10	Date		Units	Unit Cost	Total Cost
11					
12					
13					
14					
15					

(2) Cost of Goods Sold

Proof of Cost of Goods Sold

	Date		Units	Unit Cost	Total Cost
23	Date		Units	Unit Cost	Total Cost
24					
25					
26					
27					
28					

(b) (Continued)

LIFO

(1) Date	Ending Inventory	Units	Unit Cost	Total Cost

(2)	Cost of Goods Sold			

	Proof of Cost of Goods Sold			
Date		Units	Unit Cost	Total Cost

Average Cost

(1)	Ending Inventory			
Average Cost Per Unit		Units	Unit Cost	Total Cost

(2)	Cost of Goods Sold			

(c)

(1)

(2)

(a)

COST OF GOODS AVAILABLE FOR SALE

	Date	Explanation	Units	Unit Cost	Total Cost	
1	1/1					1
2	2/20					2
3	5/5					3
4	8/12					4
5	12/8					5
6						6
7						7

(b)   **FIFO**

(1) Ending Inventory

	Date		Units	Unit Cost	Total Cost	
10						10
11						11
12						12
13						13
14						14
15						15

(2) Cost of Goods Sold

16		16
17		17
18		18
19		19
20		20
21		21

Proof of Cost of Goods Sold

	Date		Units	Unit Cost	Total Cost	
23						23
24						24
25						25
26						26
27						27
28						28

(b) (Continued)

LIFO

(1) Ending Inventory

Date		Units	Unit Cost	Total Cost

(2) Cost of Goods Sold

Proof of Cost of Goods Sold

Date		Units	Unit Cost	Total Cost

Average Cost

(1) Ending Inventory

Average Cost Per Unit	Units	Unit Cost	Total Cost

(2) Cost of Goods Sold

Proof of Cost of Goods Sold

(c)

(1)

(2)

(a)

	KIRCHNER INC. Condensed Income Statements For the Year Ended December 31, 2010	FIFO	LIFO
1			
2			
3			
4			
5			
6			
7			
8			
9			
10			
11			
12			
13			
14			
15			
16			

(b)

(a)

Cost of Goods Available For Sale

	Date	Explanation	Units	Unit Cost	Total Cost	
1	Oct. 1					1
2	9					2
3	17					3
4	25					4
5						5

Ending Inventory in Units

6			6
7			7
8			8
9			9
10			10
11			11

Sales Revenue

	Date		Units	Unit Price	Total Sales	
12						12
13	Date		Units	Unit Price	Total Sales	13
14	Oct. 11					14
15	22					15
16	29					16
17						17
18						18

	(1)	LIFO				
19	(1)	LIFO				19
20	(i) Ending Inventory					20
21	Date		Units	Unit Cost	Total Cost	21
22						22
23						23
24						24
25						25

	(ii) Cost of Goods Sold		
26	(ii) Cost of Goods Sold		26
27			27
28			28
29			29
30			30
31			31

	(iii) Gross Profit		
32	(iii) Gross Profit		32
33			33
34			34
35			35
36			36

	(iv) Gross Profit Rate		
37	(iv) Gross Profit Rate		37
38			38
39			39
40			40

(a) (Continued)

(2) (i)	FIFO Ending Inventory			
Date		Units	Unit Cost	Total Cost
(ii)	Cost of Goods Sold			
(iii)	Gross Profit			
(iv)	Gross Profit Rate			
(3)	Average Cost Weighted Average Cost Per Unit			
(i)	Ending Inventory			
(ii)	Cost of Goods Sold			
(iii)	Gross Profit			

(a) (Continued)

	Average Cost	
1		1
2	(iv) Gross Profit Rate	2
3		3
4		4
5		5
6		6
7	(b)	7
8		8
9		9
10		10
11		11
12		12
13		13
14		14
15		15
16		16
17		17
18		18
19		19
20		20
21		21
22		22
23		23
24		24
25		25
26		26
27		27
28		28
29		29
30		30
31		31
32		32
33		33
34		34
35		35
36		36
37		37
38		38
39		39
40		40

(a)

Specific Identification

(1) To maximize gross profit

Sales Revenue

Date		Units	Unit Price	Sales Revenue
Mar. 5				
25				

Cost of Goods Sold

Date		Units	Unit Cost	Total Cost
Mar. 5				
25				

Sales Revenue	
Cost of Goods Sold	
Gross profit	

(2) To minimize gross profit

Sales Revenue

Date		Units	Unit Price	Sales Revenue
Mar. 5				
25				

Cost of Goods Sold

Date		Units	Unit Cost	Total Cost
Mar. 5				
25				

Sales Revenue	
Cost of Goods Sold	
Gross profit	

(b)

	FIFO			
	Cost of Goods Available for Sale			
Date		Units	Unit Cost	Total Cost
Mar. 1				
3				
10				

	Units	Unit Cost	Total Cost
Goods available for sale			
Units sold			
Ending inventory			

	Total Cost
Goods available for sale	
Ending inventory	
Cost of goods sold	

	Total Cost
Sales revenue	
Cost of goods sold	
Gross profit	

(c)

	LIFO	
Cost of Goods Available for Sale		
Ending inventory		
Cost of goods sold		

Sales revenue	
Cost of goods sold	
Gross profit	

(d)

	2006
(a) Inventory turnover ratio:	
Days in inventory:	
(b) Current ratio:	

(c)		2006
Current ratio:		
(d)		

(a)

Cost of Goods Available for Sale			
	Units	Unit Cost	Total Cost
1 Inventory			
2 Purchases:			
3 January 2			
4 January 9			
5 January 10 return			
6 Januarty 23			
7			
8			
9 Sales:			
10			
11 January 6			
12 January 9			
13 January 10			
14 January 30			
15			

(a) (Continued)

LIFO

(1) Date	Purchases	Cost of Goods Sold	Balance
Jan. 1			(160 units @ $18) 2880
2			
6			
9			
10			
10			
23			
30			

(i) Cost of goods sold =

(ii) Ending inventory =

(iii) Gross profit =

(a) (Continued)

FIFO

(2) Date	Purchases	Cost of Goods Sold	Balance
Jan. 1			(160 units @ $18) 2 8 8 0
2			
6			
9			
10			
10			
23			
30			

(i) Cost of goods sold =

(ii) Ending inventory =

(iii) Gross profit =

(a) (Continued)

Moving Average

(3)

Date	Purchases	Cost of Goods Sold	Balance
Jan. 1			(160 units @ $18) 2 8 8 0
2			
6			
9			
9			
10			
10			
23			
30			

(i) Cost of goods sold =

(ii) Ending inventory =

(iii) Gross profit =

(b)

	LIFO	FIFO	Moving Average
1			
2			
3			
4			
5			
6			
7			
8			
9			
10			
11			
12			
13			
14			
15			
16			
17			
18			
19			
20			
21			
22			
23			
24			
25			
26			
27			
28			
29			
30			
31			
32			
33			
34			
35			
36			
37			
38			
39			
40			

(a)

FIFO

(1)

Date	Purchases	Cost of Goods Sold	Balance
July 1			
6			
11			
14			
21			
27			

Average Cost

(2)

Date	Purchases	Cost of Goods Sold	Balance
July 1			
6			
11			
14			
21			
27			

(a) (Continued)

LIFO

(3) Date	Purchases	Cost of Goods Sold	Balance
July 1			
6			
11			
14			
21			
27			

(b)

(a)

COST OF GOODS AVAILABLE FOR SALE

	Date	Explanation	Units	Unit Cost	Total Cost	
1	Oct. 1					1
2	3					2
3	9					3
4	19					4
5	25					5
6						6
7						7

(b)   **FIFO**

(1)   Ending Inventory

	Date		Units	Unit Cost	Total Cost	
10	Date		Units	Unit Cost	Total Cost	10
11						11
12						12
13						13
14						14
15						15

(2)   Cost of Goods Sold

16			16
17			17
18			18
19			19
20			20
21			21

Proof of Cost of Goods Sold

	Date		Units	Unit Cost	Total Cost	
23	Date		Units	Unit Cost	Total Cost	23
24						24
25						25
26						26
27						27
28						28

29	29
30	30
31	31
32	32
33	33
34	34
35	35
36	36
37	37
38	38
39	39
40	40

(b) (Continued)

LIFO			
(1)	Ending Inventory		
Date		Units	Unit Cost	Total Cost

(2)	Cost of Goods Sold		

Proof of Cost of Goods Sold			
Date		Units	Unit Cost	Total Cost

Average Cost			
(1)	Ending Inventory		
Average Cost Per Unit		Units	Unit Cost	Total Cost

(2)	Cost of Goods Sold		

(c)

(1)

(2)

(a)

COST OF GOODS AVAILABLE FOR SALE

	Date	Explanation	Units	Unit Cost	Total Cost	
1	1/1					1
2	3/15					2
3	7/20					3
4	9/4					4
5	12/2					5
6						6
7						7

(b)   **FIFO**

(1)   Ending Inventory

	Date		Units	Unit Cost	Total Cost	
10						10
11						11
12						12
13						13
14						14
15						15

(2)   Cost of Goods Sold

16			16
17			17
18			18
19			19
20			20
21			21

Proof of Cost of Goods Sold

	Date		Units	Unit Cost	Total Cost	
23						23
24						24
25						25
26						26
27						27
28						28

29	29
30	30
31	31
32	32
33	33
34	34
35	35
36	36
37	37
38	38
39	39
40	40

(b) (Continued)

LIFO

(1) Ending Inventory

Date		Units	Unit Cost	Total Cost

(2) Cost of Goods Sold

				Total Cost

Proof of Cost of Goods Sold

Date		Units	Unit Cost	Total Cost

Average Cost

(1) Ending Inventory

Average Cost Per Unit		Units	Unit Cost	Total Cost

(2) Cost of Goods Sold

				Total Cost

Proof of Cost of Goods Sold

(c)

(a)

HADAWAY INC. Condensed Income Statements For the Year Ended December 31, 2010	FIFO	LIFO
1		
2		
3		
4		
5		
6		
7		
8		
9		
10		
11		
12		
13		
14		
15		

(b)

(a)

Cost of Goods Available For Sale

	Date	Explanation	Units	Unit Cost	Total Cost	
1	June 1					1
2	4					2
3	18					3
4	18					4
5	28					5
6						6
7						7

Ending Inventory in Units

8				8
9				9
10				10
11				11

Sales Revenue

	Date		Units	Unit Price	Total Sales	
13	Date		Units	Unit Price	Total Sales	13
14	June 10					14
15	11					15
16	25					16
17						17
18						18

	(1)	**LIFO**		19
20	(i)	Ending Inventory		20

	Date		Units	Unit Cost	Total Cost	
21	Date		Units	Unit Cost	Total Cost	21
22						22
23						23
24						24
25						25

	(ii)	Cost of Goods Sold		
26	(ii)	Cost of Goods Sold		26
27				27
28				28
29				29
30				30
31				31

	(iii)	Gross Profit		
32	(iii)	Gross Profit		32
33				33
34				34
35				35
36				36

	(iv)	Gross Profit Rate		
37	(iv)	Gross Profit Rate		37
38				38
39				39
40				40

(a) (Continued)

(2)   **FIFO**

(i)   Ending Inventory

Date		Units	Unit Cost	Total Cost

(ii)   Cost of Goods Sold

(iii)   Gross Profit

(iv)   Gross Profit Rate

(3)   **Average Cost**

Weighted Average Cost Per Unit

(i)   Ending Inventory

(ii)   Cost of Goods Sold

(iii)   Gross Profit

(a) (Continued)

Average Cost

(iv)   Gross Profit Rate

(b)

(a)

GAS SAVER PLUS
Income Statement (Partial)
For the Month Ended March 30, XXXX

	Specific Identification	FIFO	LIFO

Specific identification ending inventory consists of:

	Units	Unit Cost	Total Cost

FIFO ending inventory consists of:

LIFO ending inventory consists of:

(b)

	2006	
(a)	Inventory turnover ratio:	
1		1
2		2
3		3
4		4
5		5
6	Days in inventory:	6
7		7
8		8
9		9
10	(b) Current ratio:	10
11		11
12		12
13		13
14		14

	(c)	2006	
15			15
16			16
17			17
18			18
19			19
20			20
21	Current ratio:		21
22			22
23			23
24			24
25	(d)		25
26			26
27			27
28			28
29			29
30			30
31			31
32			32
33			33
34			34
35			35
36			36
37			37
38			38
39			39

(a)

	Units	Unit Cost	Total Cost	
1	Sales:				1
2	January 8				2
3	January 10 return				3
4	January 20				4
5					5
6					6
7					7
8					8
9					9
10					10
11					11
12					12
13					13
14					14
15					15
16					16
17					17
18					18
19					19
20					20
21					21
22					22
23					23
24					24
25					25
26					26
27					27
28					28
29					29
30					30
31					31
32					32

(a) (Continued)

LIFO

(1) Date	Purchases	Cost of Goods Sold	Balance
Jan. 1			(40 units @ $12) 4 8 0
5			
8			
10			
15			
16			
20			
25			

(i) Cost of goods sold =

(ii) Ending inventory =

(iii) Gross profit =

(a) (Continued)

FIFO

(2) Date	Purchases	Cost of Goods Sold	Balance
Jan. 1			480 (40 units @ $12)
5			
8			
10			
15			
16			
20			
25			

(i) Cost of goods sold =

(ii) Ending inventory =

(iii) Gross profit =

(a) (Continued)

(3)

Moving Average

Date	Purchases	Cost of Goods Sold	Balance
Jan. 1			(40 units @ $12) 4 8 0
5			
8			
10			
15			
16			
20			
25			

(i) Cost of goods sold =

(ii) Ending inventory =

(iii) Gross profit =

(b)

	LIFO	FIFO	Weighted Average
1			
2			
3			
4			
5			
6			
7			
8			
9			
10			
11			
12			
13			
14			
15			
16			
17			
18			
19			
20			
21			
22			
23			
24			
25			
26			
27			
28			
29			
30			
31			
32			
33			
34			
35			
36			
37			
38			
39			
40			

*Problem 6-9B

U-Save-More Center

(a)

FIFO

(1)

Date	Purchases	Sales	Balance
July 1			
6			
11			
14			
21			
27			

Average Cost

(2)

Date	Purchases	Sales	Balance
July 1			
6			
11			
14			
21			
27			

(a) (Continued)

LIFO

(3) Date	Purchases			Sales			Balance		
July 1									
6									
11									
14									
21									
27									

(b)

Name _____

Section _____

Date _____ Gonzalez Company

(a)

	Date	Account Titles	Debit	Credit	
1	Dec 3				1
2					2
3					3
4	5				4
5					5
6					6
7					7
8					8
9					9
10	7				10
11					11
12					12
13					13
14					14
15					15
16	17				16
17					17
18					18
19	22				19
20					20
21					21
22					22
23					23
24					24
25	31				25
26					26
27					27
28					28
29					29
30					30
31					31
32					32
33					33
34					34
35					35
36					36
37					37
38					38
39					39
40					40

(b)

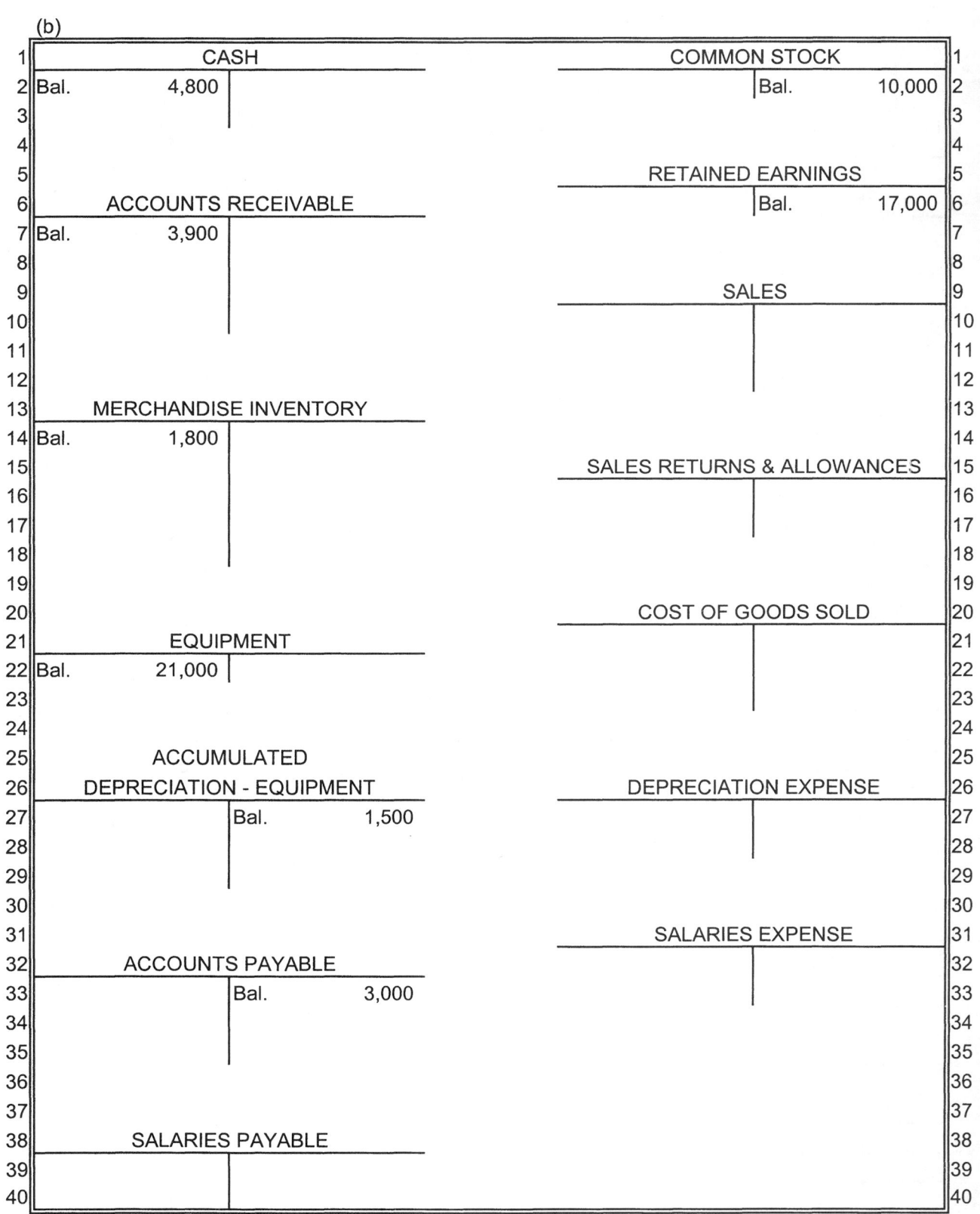

CASH			COMMON STOCK	
Bal.	4,800		Bal.	10,000
			RETAINED EARNINGS	
ACCOUNTS RECEIVABLE			Bal.	17,000
Bal.	3,900			
			SALES	
MERCHANDISE INVENTORY				
Bal.	1,800		SALES RETURNS & ALLOWANCES	
			COST OF GOODS SOLD	
EQUIPMENT				
Bal.	21,000			
ACCUMULATED				
DEPRECIATION - EQUIPMENT			DEPRECIATION EXPENSE	
	Bal.	1,500		
			SALARIES EXPENSE	
ACCOUNTS PAYABLE				
	Bal.	3,000		
SALARIES PAYABLE				

(c)

GONZALEZ COMPANY		
Adjusted Trial Balance		
December 31, 2010		
	Debit	Credit
1		
2		
3		
4		
5		
6		
7		
8		
9		
10		
11		
12		
13		
14		
15		
16		
17		
18		
19		
20		

(d)

GONZALEZ COMPANY		
Income Statement		
For the Month Ended December 31, 2010		
1		
2		
3		
4		
5		
6		
7		
8		
9		
10		
11		
12		
13		
14		
15		

(d) (Continued)

GONZALEZ COMPANY
Balance Sheet
December 31, 2010

	Assets					
1						
2						
3						
4						
5						
6						
7						
8						
9						
10						
11						
12						
13						
14						
15						
16						
17	Liabilities and Stockholders' Equity					
18						
19						
20						
21						
22						
23						
24						
25						
26						
27						
28						
29						
30						
31						
32						
33						
34						
35						

(e)   FIFO Method

	Units	Unit Cost	Cost of Goods Available for Sale
1			
2			
3			
4			

5

6   Ending Inventory

Date		Units	Unit Cost	Total Cost
7				
8				
9				
10				

11

12   Cost of Goods Sold

13

14

15

16

17

18

19

20

(f)   LIFO Method

Ending Inventory	Units	Unit Cost	Total Cost
1			
2			
3			
4			

5

6 Cost of Goods Sold

7

8

9

10

(a)

(b)

(c)	2007	2006
Inventory turnover:		
Days in inventory:		

(d)

(e)

1	Current ratio:	1
2		2
3		3
4		4
5		5
6		6
7		7
8		8
9	Current ratio:	9
10		10
11		11
12		12
13		13
14		14
15		15
16		16
17		17
18		18
19		19
20		20
21		21
22		22
23		23
24		24
25		25
26		26
27		27
28		28
29		29
30		30
31		31
32		32
33		33
34		34
35		35
36		36
37		37
38		38
39		39
40		40

BE7-5

		Account Titles	Debit	Credit	
1					1
2					2
3					3
4					4

BE7-10

5				5
6				6
7				7
8				8
9				9
10				10
11				11
12				12

BE7-11

13				13
14				14
15				15
16				16
17				17
18				18
19				19
20				20
21				21

BE7-13

22			22
23	**EUSEY COMPANY**		23
24	Cash Budget		24
25	For January		25
26			26
27			27
28			28
29			29
30			30
31			31
32			32
33			33

*BE7-14

	Date	Account Titles	Debit	Credit	
35	Date	Account Titles	Debit	Credit	35
36	Mar 20				36
37					37
38					38
39					39
40					40

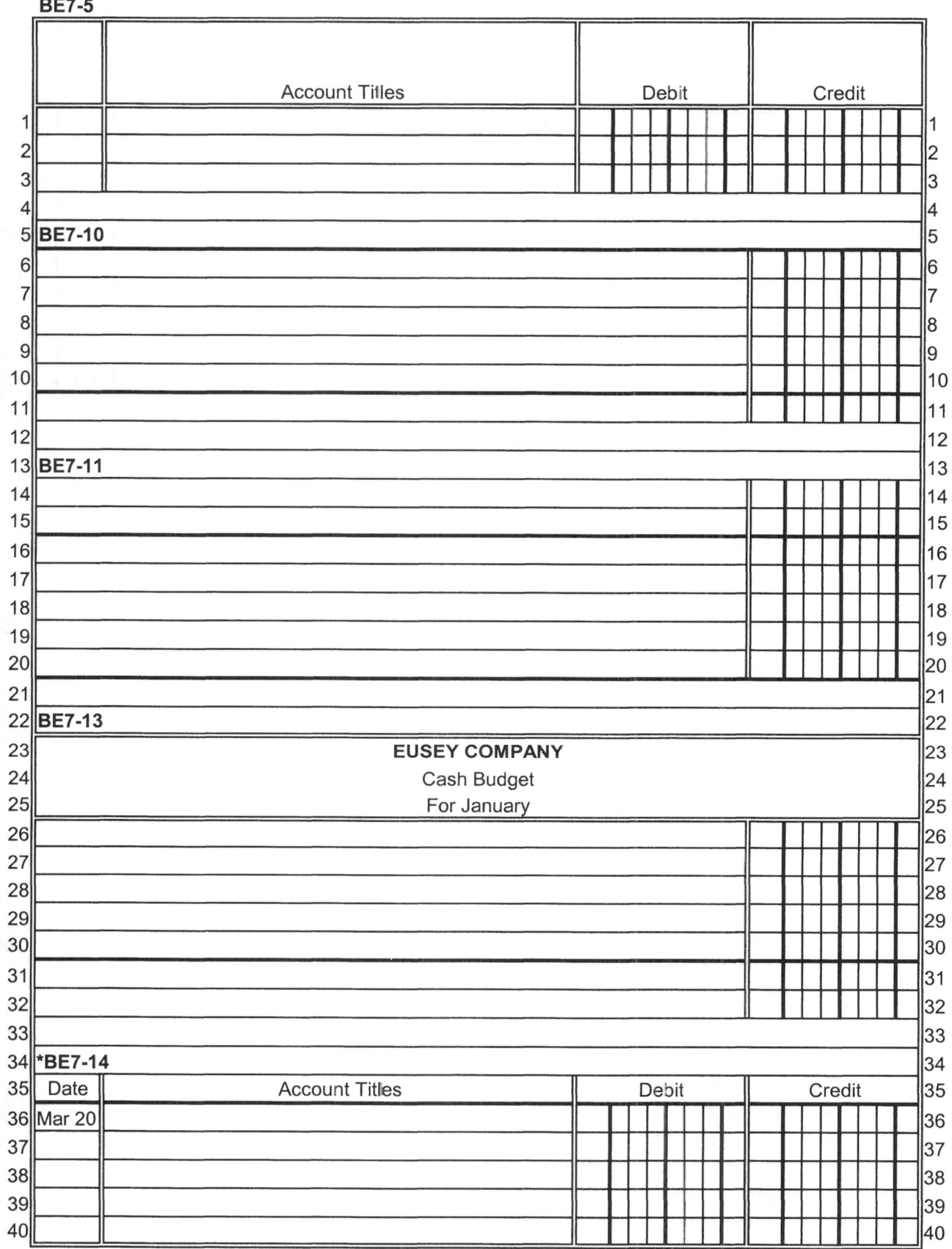

			1
1			1
2			2
3			3
4			4
5			5
6			6
7			7
8			8
9			9
10			10
11			11
12			12
13			13
14			14
15			15
16			16
17			17
18			18
19			19
20			20
21			21
22			22
23			23
24			24
25			25
26			26
27			27
28			28
29			29
30			30
31			31
32			32
33			33
34			34
35			35
36			36
37			37
38			38
39			39
40			40

E7-6

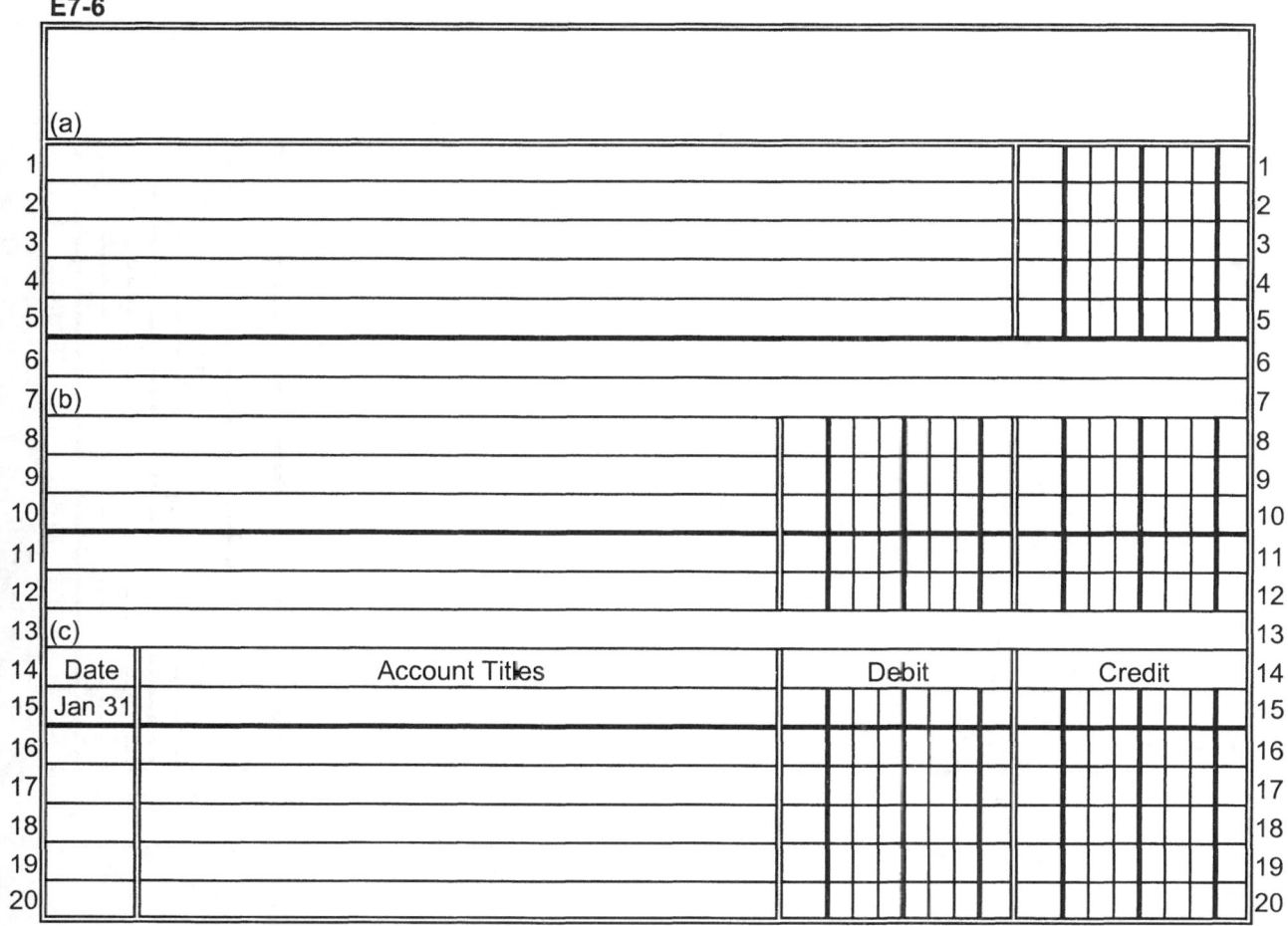

(a)

(b)

(c)

Date	Account Titles	Debit	Credit
Jan 31			

E7-7

	Check Number	Amount

(a)

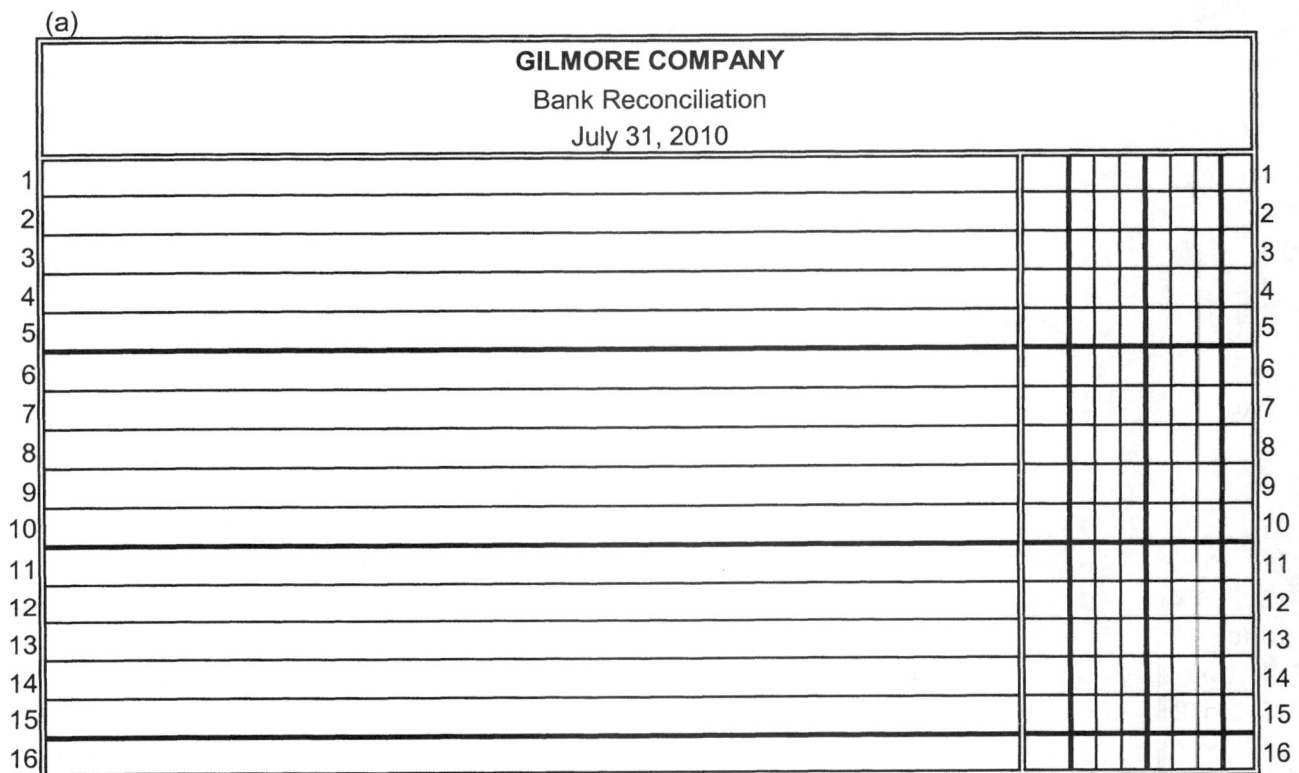

GILMORE COMPANY
Bank Reconciliation
July 31, 2010

(b)

	Date	Account Titles	Debit	Credit	
1	July 31				1
2					2
3					3
4					4
5					5
6	31				6
7					7
8					8
9					9
10					10

(a)

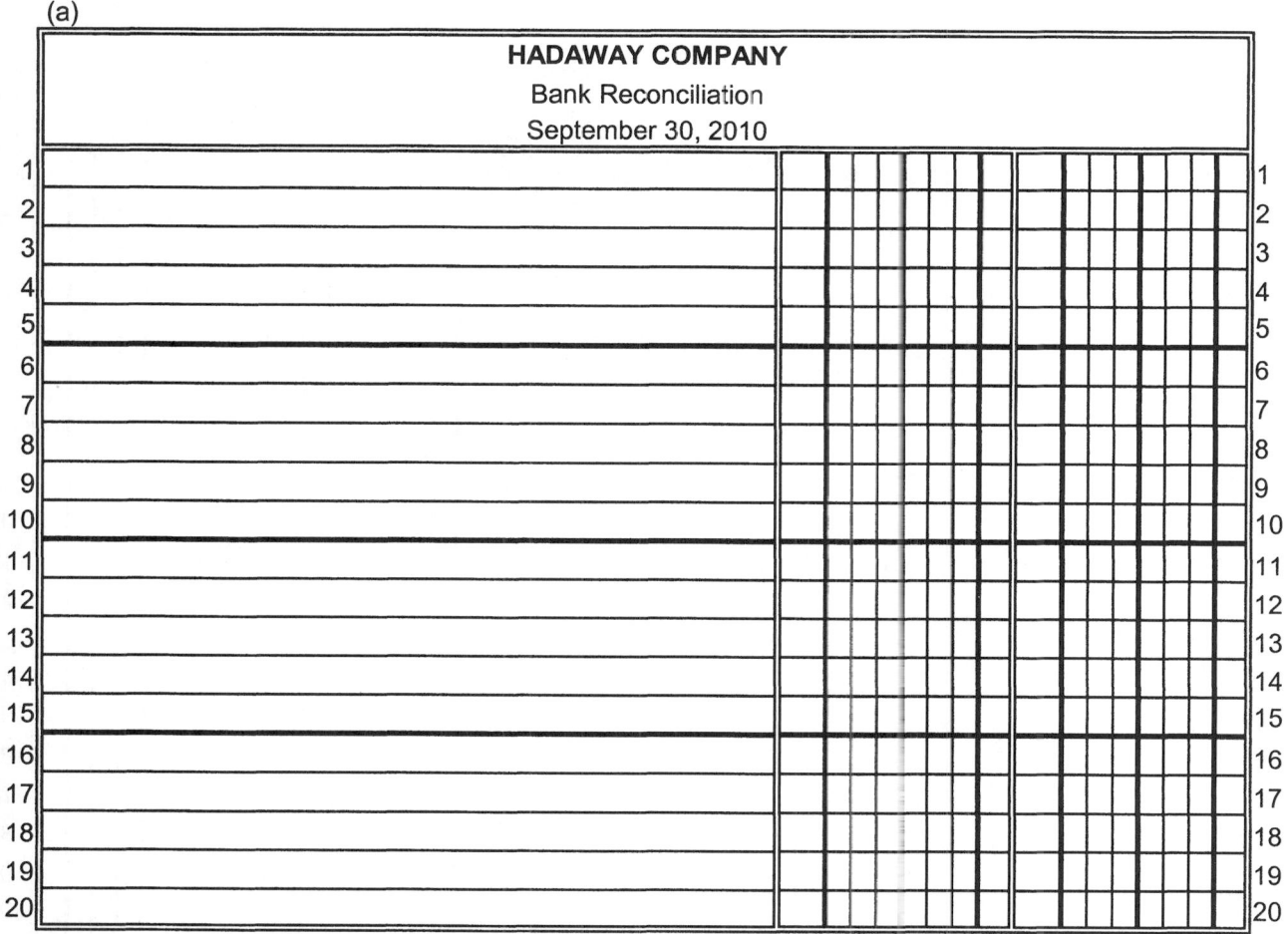

HADAWAY COMPANY
Bank Reconciliation
September 30, 2010

(b)

	Date	Account Titles	Debit	Credit
1	Sept 30			
2				
3				
4				
5	30			
6				
7				
8	30			
9				
10				
11	30			
12				
13				
14				
15				

1	(a) Deposits in transit at July 31:										1
2											2
3											3
4											4
5											5
6											6
7											7
8											8
9											9
10											10
11	(b) Outstanding checks at July 31:										11
12											12
13											13
14											14
15											15
16											16
17											17
18											18
19											19
20											20
21	(c) Deposits in transit at August 31:										21
22											22
23											23
24											24
25											25
26											26
27											27
28											28
29											29
30											30
31	(d) Outstanding checks at August 31:										31
32											32
33											33
34											34
35											35
36											36
37											37
38											38
39											39
40											40

(a) & (b)

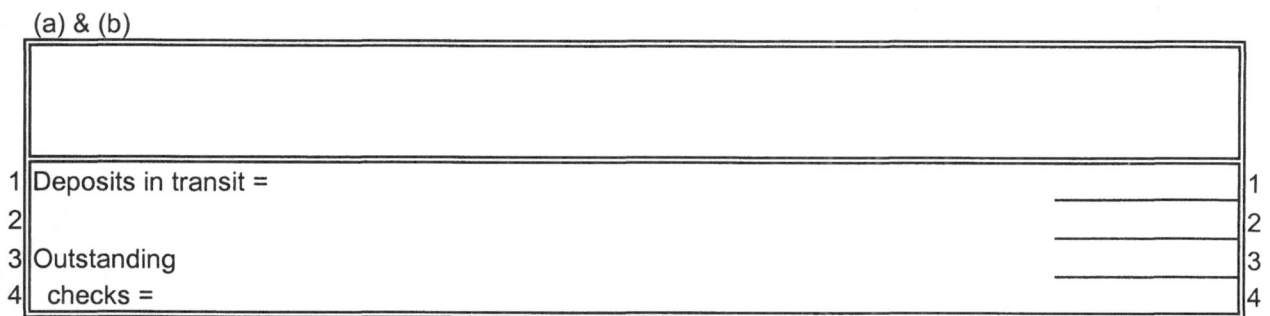

1	Deposits in transit =	1
2		2
3	Outstanding	3
4	checks =	4

(c)

KANE INC.

Bank Reconciliation

August 31, 2010

1	1
2	2
3	3
4	4
5	5
6	6
7	7
8	8
9	9
10	10
11	11
12	12
13	13
14	14
15	15
16	16
17	17
18	18
19	19
20	20
21	21

(d)

	Date	Account Titles	Debit	Credit	
1	Aug 31				1
2					2
3					3
4					4
5					5

E7-12

1	(a)　　　Cash and Cash Equivalents:
2	
3	
4	
5	
6	
7	
8	
9	
10	(b)
11	
12	
13	
14	
15	
16	
17	
18	
19	
20	

E7-13

1	
2	
3	
4	
5	
6	
7	
8	
9	
10	
11	
12	
13	
14	
15	

E7-14

MAYFIELD COMPANY
Cash Budget
For the Two Months Ending February 28, 2010

	January	February
Beginning cash balance	$ 4 6 0 0 0	

***E7-15**

	Date	Account Titles	Debit	Credit
1	Oct. 1			
2				
3				
4	31			
5				
6				
7				
8				
9				
10				
11	31			
12				
13				

(a)

	Date		Debit	Credit	
1	Aug. 1				1
2					2
3					3
4	15				4
5					5
6					6
7					7
8					8
9					9
10					10
11	16				11
12					12
13					13
14	31				14
15					15
16					16
17					17
18					18
19					19
20					20

(b)   Petty Cash

(c)

(a)

FENTON COMPANY				
Bank Reconciliation				
July 31, 2010				
1				1
2				2
3				3
4				4
5				5
6				6
7				7
8				8
9				9
10				10
11				11
12				12
13				13
14				14
15				15
16				16
17				17

(b)

	Date	Account Titles	Debit	Credit	
1	July 31				1
2					2
3					3
4					4
5					5
6	31				6
7					7
8					8
9	31				9
10					10
11					11
12	31				12
13					13
14					14
15					15
16					16
17					17
18					18
19					19

(a)

HUNSAKER COMPANY
Bank Reconciliation
November 30, 2010

1			
2			
3			
4			
5			
6			
7			
8			
9			
10			
11			
12			
13			
14			
15			
16			
17			
18			
19			
20			
21			
22			

(b)

	Date	Account Titles	Debit	Credit
1	Nov. 30			
2				
3				
4				
5				
6	30			
7				
8				
9	30			
10				
11				
12	30			
13				
14				

(a)

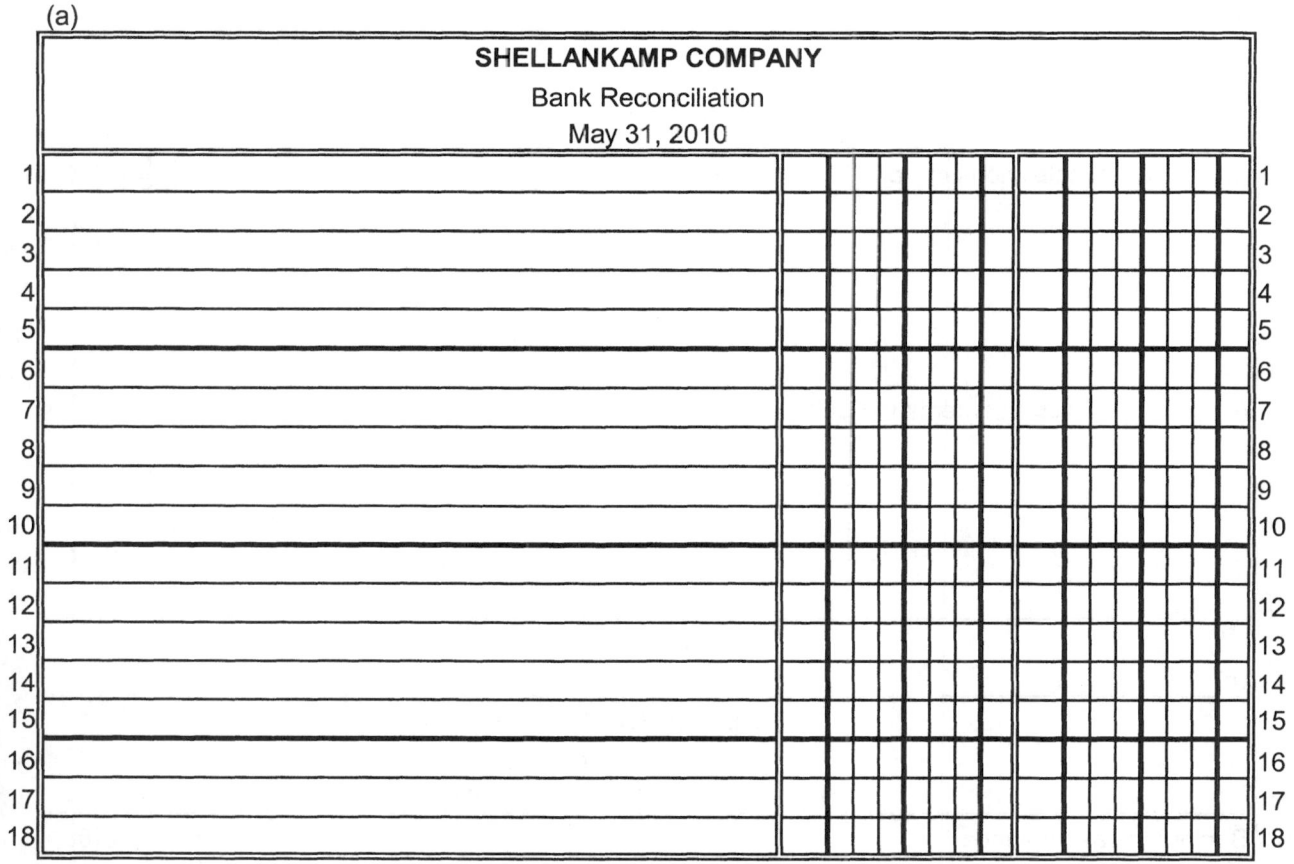

	SHELLANKAMP COMPANY		
	Bank Reconciliation		
	May 31, 2010		
1			
2			
3			
4			
5			
6			
7			
8			
9			
10			
11			
12			
13			
14			
15			
16			
17			
18			

(b)

	Date	Account Titles	Debit	Credit
1	May 31			
2				
3				
4				
5				
6	31			
7				
8				
9	31			
10				
11				
12	31			
13				
14				
15	31			
16				
17				

(a) and (b)

1	(a) Cash collections in April:	
2		
3		
4		
5		
6		
7	(b) Cash disbursements in April:	
8		
9		
10		
11		
12		

(c)

WEINBERGER INC.

Cash Budget

For the Month Ending April 30, 2007

1	Beginning cash balance	$ 8 0 0 0
2		
3		
4		
5		
6		
7		
8		
9		
10		
11		
12		
13		
14		
15		
16		
17		
18		
19		
20		
21		
22		
23		

FOGELBERG CORPORATION					
Cash Budget					
For the Two Months Ending February 28, 2010					
	January		February	
Beginning cash balance	$	5 2 0 0 0			

(a)

FREDERICKSON COMPANY
Bank Reconciliation
October 31, 2010

	No.	Amount	No.	Amount	

(b) and (c)

(b)

(c)

(a)

	LOMBARD COMPANY		
	Bank Reconciliation		
	May 31, 2010		
1			
2			
3			
4			
5			
6			
7			
8			
9			
10			
11			
12			
13			
14			
15			
16			
17			

(b)

	Date	Account Titles	Debit	Credit
1	May 31			
2				
3				
4				
5				
6	31			
7				
8				
9	31			
10				
11				
12	31			
13				
14				
15	31			
16				
17				
18				
19				

(a)

	CHRISTIANSEN COMPANY		
	Bank Reconciliation		
	December 31, 2010		
1			
2			
3			
4			
5			
6			
7			
8			
9			
10			
11			
12			
13			
14			
15			
16			
17			
18			
19			
20			
21			
22			

(b)

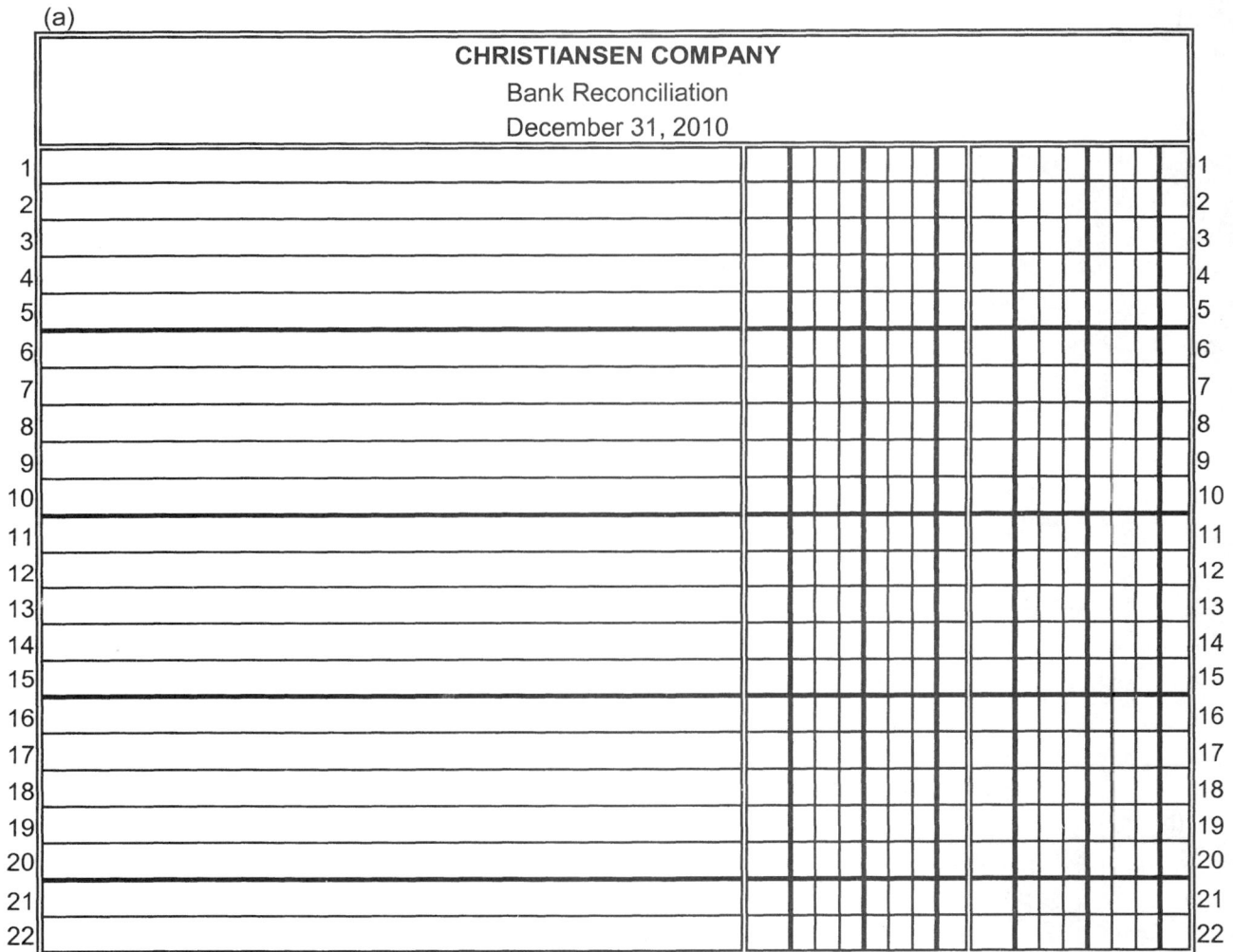

	Date	Account Titles	Debit	Credit
1	Dec 31			
2				
3				
4				
5				
6	31			
7				
8				
9	31			
10				
11				
12	31			
13				
14				

(a)

		Debit	Credit
GREENWOOD COMPANY			
Bank Reconciliation			
July 31, 2010			
1			
2			
3			
4			
5			
6			
7			
8			
9			
10			
11			
12			
13			
14			
15			
16			
17			
18			

(b)

	Date	Account Titles	Debit	Credit
1	July 31			
2				
3				
4				
5				
6	31			
7				
8				
9	31			
10				
11				
12	31			
13				
14				
15				
16				
17				

(a)

	POLK CO. Cash Budget For the Two Months Ending February 28, 2010						
		January				February	
2	Beginning cash balance	$	2 6 0 0 0				
3							
4							
5							
6							
7							
8							
9							
10							
11							
12							
13							
14							
15							
16							
17							
18							
19							
20							

(b)

YBARRA INC.

Cash Budget

For the Two Months Ending February 28, 2010

	January	February
Beginning cash balance	$ 6 0 0 0 0	

(a)

MCNALLY COMPANY				
Bank Reconciliation				
October 31, 2010				

	No.	Amount	No.	Amount

(b) and (c)

(b)

(c)

(a)

	Date	Account Titles	Debit	Credit	
1	Dec. 7				1
2					2
3					3
4	12				4
5					5
6					6
7	17				7
8					8
9					9
10					10
11					11
12					12
13	19				13
14					14
15					15
16	22				16
17					17
18					18
19					19
20	26				20
21					21
22					22
23					23
24					24
25					25
26					26
27					27
28					28
29					29
30					30
31					31
32					32
33					33
34					34
35					35
36					36
37					37
38					38
39					39
40					40

(b) & (e)

	CASH			ACCOUNTS PAYABLE		
1						1
2	Bal.	18,200			Bal. 6,100	2
3						3
4						4
5						5
6						6
7						7
8				INCOME TAX PAYABLE		8
9						9
10	NOTES RECEIVABLE					10
11	Bal.	2,500				11
12				COMMON STOCK		12
13					Bal. 20,000	13
14						14
15	ACCOUNTS RECEIVABLE					15
16	Bal.	7,500		RETAINED EARNINGS		16
17					Bal. 44,700	17
18						18
19						19
20						20
21				SALES		21
22	MERCHANDISE INVENTORY					22
23	Bal.	16,000				23
24						24
25						25
26				SALES DISCOUNTS		26
27						27
28	PREPAID INSURANCE					28
29	Bal.	1,600				29
30						30
31				COST OF GOODS SOLD		31
32						32
33	EQUIPMENT					33
34	Bal.	28,000				34
35						35
36				DEPRECIATION EXPENSE		36
37	ACCUMULATED DEPRECIATION					37
38		Bal. 3,000				38
39						39
40				SALARIES EXPENSE		40
41						41
42						42
43						43

(b) & (e) (Continued)

	INSURANCE EXPENSE		INCOME TAX EXPENSE	
1				1
2				2
3				3
4				4
5				5
6				6
7				7
8				8
9				9
10				10
11				11
12				12
13				13
14				14
15				15
16				16
17				17
18				18
19				19
20				20
21				21
22				22
23				23
24				24
25				25
26				26
27				27
28				28
29				29
30				30
31				31
32				32
33				33
34				34
35				35
36				36
37				37
38				38
39				39
40				40

(c)

MORELAND COMPANY		
Bank Reconciliation		
December 31, 2010		

1			
2			
3			
4			
5			
6			
7			
8			
9			
10			
11			
12			
13			
14			
15			
16			
17			
18			
19			
20			

(d)

	Date	Account Titles	Debit	Credit
1	Dec. 31			
2				
3				
4				
5				
6	31			
7				
8				
9	31			
10				
11				
12	31			
13				
14				
15				

(d)

	Date	Account Titles	Debit	Credit	
1	Dec. 31				1
2					2
3					3
4	31				4
5					5
6					6
7					7
8					8
9					9
10					10

(f)

MORELAND COMPANY
Adjusted Trial Balance
December 31, 2010

		Debit	Credit	
1				1
2				2
3				3
4				4
5				5
6				6
7				7
8				8
9				9
10				10
11				11
12				12
13				13
14				14
15				15
16				16
17				17
18				18
19				19
20				20
21				21
22				22
23				23
24				24
25				25

(g)

MORELAND COMPANY

Income Statement

For the Month Ending December 31, 2010

1					
2					
3					
4					
5					
6					
7					
8					
9					
10					
11					
12					
13					
14					
15					
16					
17					
18					
19					
20					

(g) (Continued)

MORELAND COMPANY

Balance Sheet

December 31, 2010

	Assets			
1				
2				
3				
4				
5				
6				
7				
8				
9				
10				
11				
12				
13				
14				
15	Liabilities and Stockholders' Equity			
16				
17				
18				
19				
20				
21				
22				
23				
24				
25				
26				
27				
28				
29				
30				
31				
32				
33				
34				
35				
36				
37				
38				
39				
40				

BE8-1

1 (a)
2
3 (b)
4
5 (c)

BE8-2	Account Titles	Debit	Credit
(a)			
(b)			
(c)			

BE8-3

	Account Titles	Debit	Credit
(a)			

(b)		Before Write-Off	After Write-Off

BE8-4

	Account Titles	Debit	Credit

BE8-5

		Account Titles	Debit	Credit	
1	(a)				1
2					2
3					3
4	(b)				4
5					5
6					6
7					7

BE8-6

			Annual Interest Rate	Total Interest	
9					9
10					10
11	(a)				11
12					12
13	(b)				13
14					14
15	(c)				15

BE8-7

	Date	Account Titles	Debit	Credit	
18	Jan 10				18
19					19
20					20
21	Feb 9				21
22					22

BE8-8

		Account Titles	Debit	Credit	
25	(a)				25
26					26
27					27
28	(b)	Current assets:			28
29					29
30					30
31					31
32					32
33					33
34					34
35					35
36	(c)	Receivables turnover ratio:			36
37					37
38					38
39		Average collection period:			39
40					40

BE8-8 (Continued)

1		1
2		2
3		3
4		4
5		5
6		6
7		7
8	**BE8-9**	8
9	Accounts receivable turnover ratio:	9
10		10
11		11
12		12
13	Average collection period:	13
14		14
15		15
16		16
17		17
18		18

	BE8-10	Account Titles	Debit	Credit	
19					19
20	(a)				20
21					21
22					22
23					23
24	(b)				24
25					25
26					26
27					27
28					28
29					29
30					30

31		31
32	**BE8-11**	32
33	Accounts Receivable	33
34		34
35		35
36		36
37		37
38		38
39		39
40		40

DO IT! 8-1

		Account Titles	Debit	Credit	
1					1
2					2
3					3
4					4

DO IT! 8-2

5	5
6	6
7	Interest payable at maturity:	7
8	8
9	9

		Account Titles	Debit	Credit	
10					10
11					11
12					12
13					13
14					14
15					15

DO IT! 8-3

16	16
17	(a) Accounts receivable	17
18	turnover:	18
19	19
20	20
21	21
22	(b) Average collection	22
23	period in days:	23
24	24
25	25

DO IT! 8-4

		Account Titles	Debit	Credit	
26					26
27					27
28					28
29					29
30					30
31					31
32					32
33					33
34					34
35					35
36					36
37					37
38					38
39					39
40					40

E8-1

	Date	Account Titles	Debit	Credit	
1					1
2	Jan. 6				2
3					3
4					4
5	16				5
6					6
7					7
8					8
9					9
10					10
11	**E8-2**				11
12	Jan 10				12
13					13
14					14
15	Feb 12				15
16					16
17					17
18	Mar. 10				18
19					19
20					20
21					21
22					22
23	**E8-3**	See next page			23
24					24
25	**E8-4**				25
26	Dec 31				26
27	(a)				27
28					28
29					29
30	(b)				30
31					31
32					32
33	(c)				33
34					34
35					35
36					36
37					37
38					38
39					39
40					40

(a) - (d)

	Account Titles	Debit	Credit	
1	(a)			1
2				2
3				3
4				4
5				5
6				6
7	(b)			7
8				8
9				9
10	(c)			10
11				11
12				12
13				13
14				14
15				15
16	(d)			16
17				17
18				18
19				19
20				20

(e) & (f)

(e)

ACCOUNTS RECEIVABLE

ALLOWANCE FOR DOUBTFUL ACCOUNTS

(f)

E8-5

Aging Schedule

(a) Accounts Receivable	Amount	%	Estimated Uncollectibles

(b)

Date	Account Titles	Debit	Credit
Mar 31			

(c)

E8-6

Date	Account Titles	Debit	Credit
2009			
Dec 31			
2010			
May 11			
June 12			

E8-7

	Date	Account Titles	Debit	Credit	
1	Nov 1				1
2					2
3					3
4	Dec 11				4
5					5
6					6
7	16				7
8					8
9					9
10	31				10
11					11
12					12
13	Calculation of interest revenue:				13
14	Younger's note:				14
15	Meier's note:				15
16	Chen's note:				16
17	Total accrued interest				17
18					18
19	**E8-8**	May 1, 2009			19
20					20
21					21
22					22
23		December 31, 2009			23
24					24
25					25
26					26
27		May 1, 2010			27
28					28
29					29
30					30
31					31
32					32
33					33
34					34
35					35

E8-9

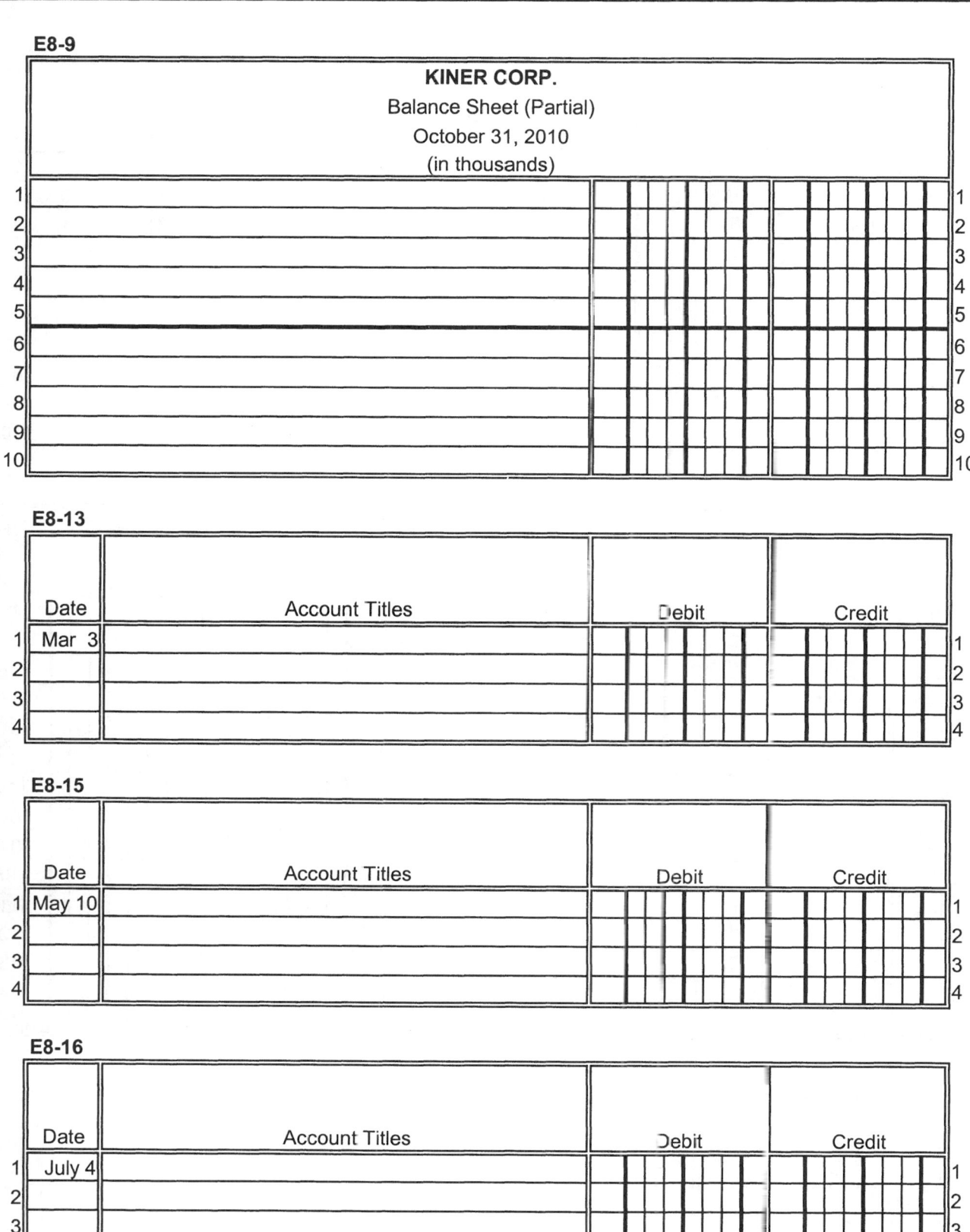

	KINER CORP.		
	Balance Sheet (Partial)		
	October 31, 2010		
	(in thousands)		

E8-13

Date	Account Titles	Debit	Credit
Mar 3			

E8-15

Date	Account Titles	Debit	Credit
May 10			

E8-16

Date	Account Titles	Debit	Credit
July 4			

(a)

	Total Estimated Bad Debts					
		Number of Days Outstanding				
	Total	0 -30	31 - 60	61 - 90	91 - 120	Over 120
1 Accounts						
2 Receivable	$375,000	$222, 000	$90,000	$38,000	$10,000	$15,000
3 % uncollectible		1%	4%	5%	6%	10%
4 Estimated						
5 Bad debts						
6						
7						
8						
9						
10						

	Account Titles	Debit	Credit
1 (b)			
2			
3			
4			
5 (c)			
6			
7			
8			
9 (d)			
10			
11			
12			
13			
14			
15			

(e)

1	
2	
3	
4	
5	

(a)

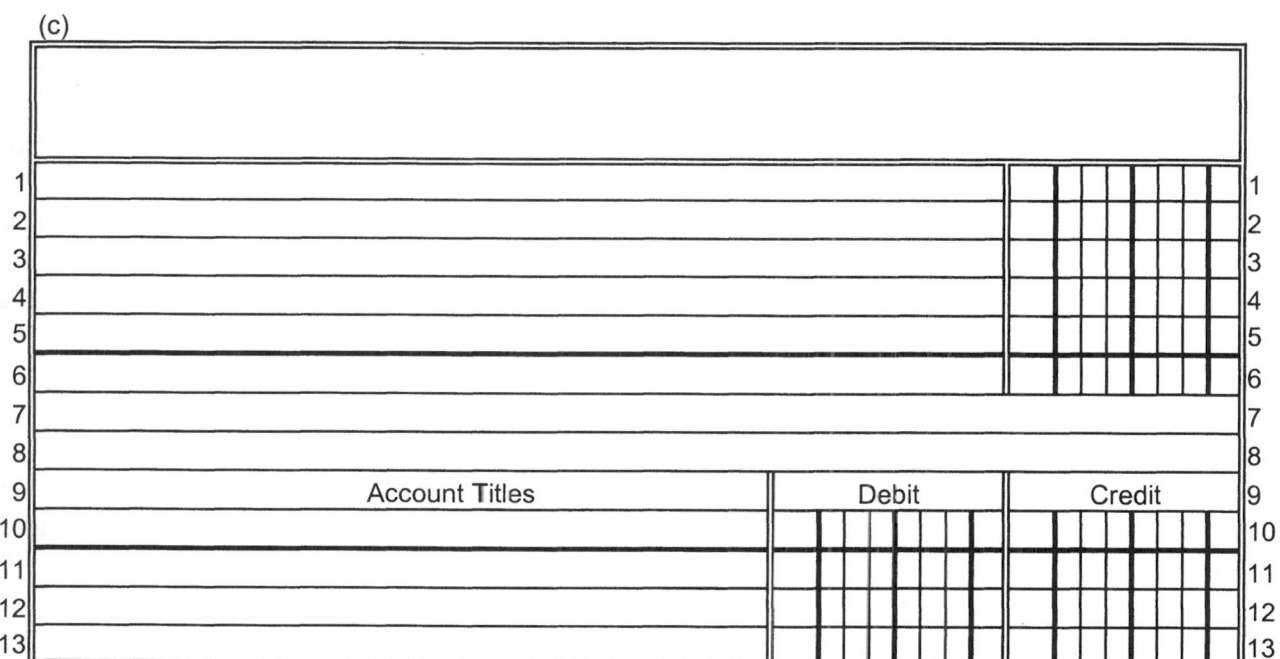

		Account Titles	Debit	Credit
1	1.			
2				
3				
4	2.			
5				
6				
7	3.			
8				
9				
10	4.			
11				
12				
13	5.			
14				
15				
16				
17				
18				
19				
20				

See (b) and (d) on next page

(c)

		Account Titles	Debit	Credit
1				
2				
3				
4				
5				
6				
7				
8				
9				
10				
11				
12				
13				

(b)

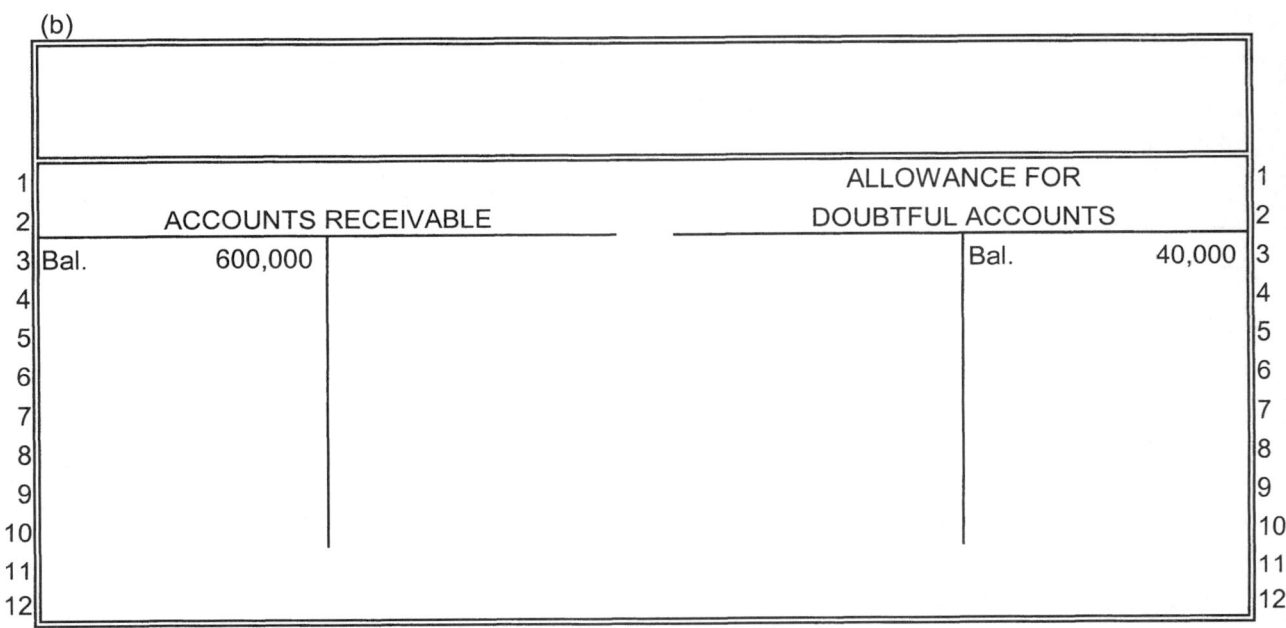

	ACCOUNTS RECEIVABLE		ALLOWANCE FOR DOUBTFUL ACCOUNTS	
1				1
2				2
3	Bal. 600,000		Bal. 40,000	3
4				4
5				5
6				6
7				7
8				8
9				9
10				10
11				11
12				12

(d)

1	Receivables turnover ratio:	1
2		2
3		3
4		4
5		5
6		6
7		7
8		8
9		9
10	Average collection period:	10
11		11
12		12
13		13
14		14

(a), (b), and (c)

	Date	Account Titles	Debit	Credit	
1	(a)	2009			1
2	Dec 31				2
3					3
4					4
5					5
6	(b)	2010			6
7	Mar 1				7
8					8
9					9
10					10
11	May 1				11
12					12
13					13
14					14
15	1				15
16					16
17					17
18					18
19	(c)	2010			19
20	Dec 31				20
21					21
22					22

(a) & (b)

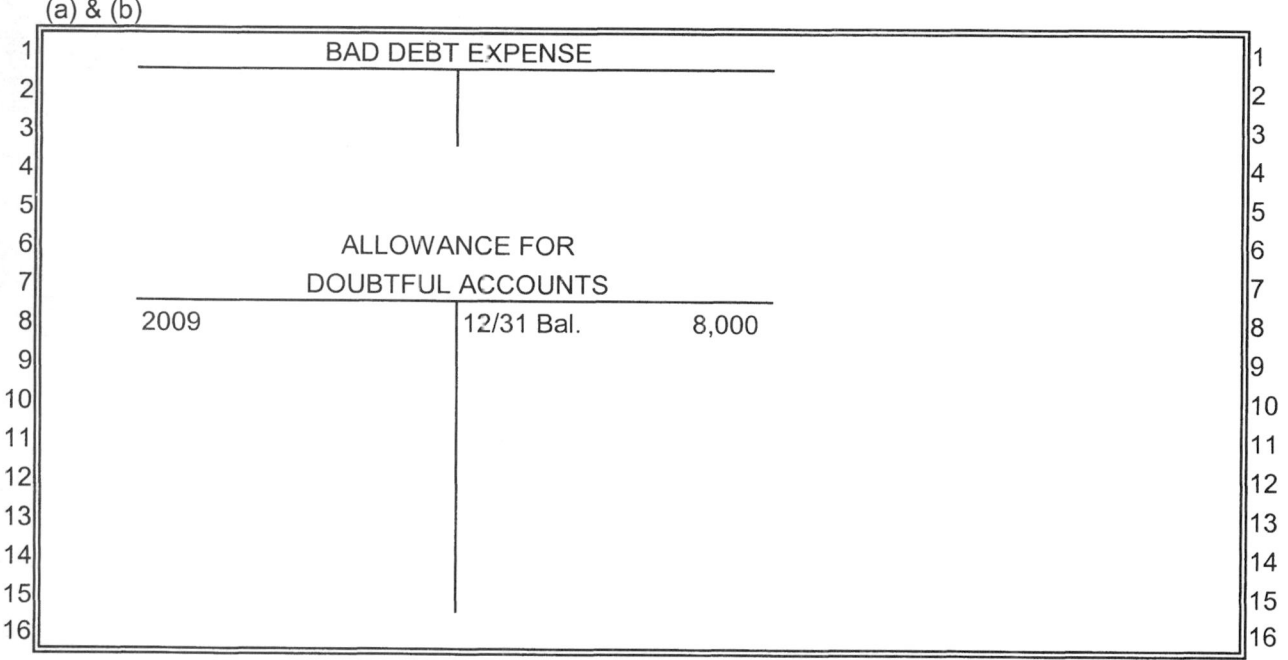

BAD DEBT EXPENSE

ALLOWANCE FOR
DOUBTFUL ACCOUNTS

| 2009 | 12/31 Bal. | 8,000 |

	Date	Account Titles	Debit	Credit	
1	(a)				1
2	Dec 31				2
3					3
4					4
5	(b)				5
6	Dec 31				6
7					7
8					8
9					9
10	(c)				10
11					11
12					12
13					13
14					14
15	(d)				15
16					16
17					17
18					18
19					19
20					20
21					21
22					22
23					23
24					24
25					25

(e)

	Date	Account Titles	Debit	Credit	
1	Jan 5				1
2					2
3					3
4					4
5					5
6					6
7	Feb 2				7
8					8
9					9
10	12				10
11					11
12					12
13					13
14					14
15					15
16	26				16
17					17
18					18
19					19
20					20
21					21
22	Apr 5				22
23					23
24					24
25	12				25
26					26
27					27
28					28
29	June 2				29
30					30
31					31
32					32
33	15				33
34					34
35					35
36					36
37					37
38					38
39					39
40					40

		Transaction	Current Ratio (2 : 1)	Receivables Turnover (10X)	Average Collection Period (36.5 Days)	
1						1
2	1.	Recorded cash sale.				2
3						3
4	2.	Recorded bad debts expense.				4
5						5
6	3.	Wrote off an account from a customer				6
7		as uncollectible.				7
8						8
9	4.	Recorded sales on account.				9
10						10
11						11
12						12
13						13

(a)

	Date	Account Titles	Debit	Credit	
1	July 5				1
2					2
3					3
4	14				4
5					5
6					6
7					7
8	20				8
9					9
10					10
11					11
12	24				12
13					13
14					14
15					15
16	31				16
17					17
18					18
19					19
20					20

(b)

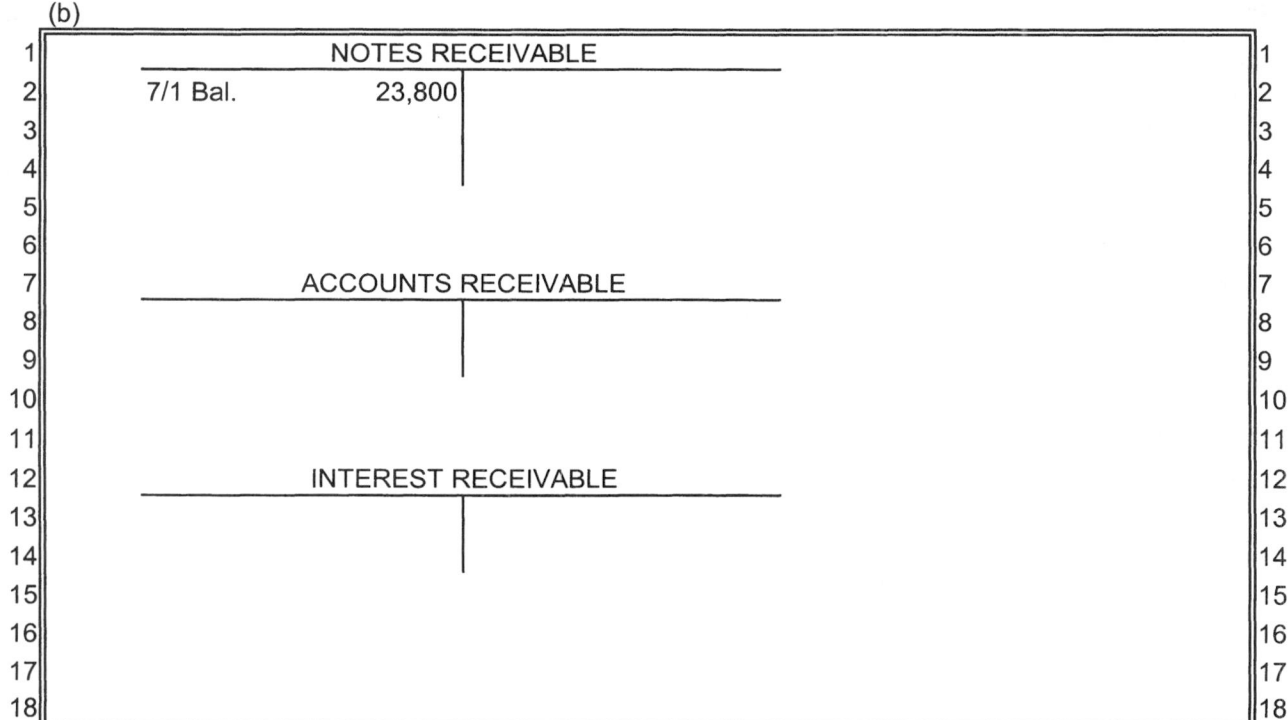

	NOTES RECEIVABLE		
1			1
2	7/1 Bal.	23,800	2
3			3
4			4
5			5
6	ACCOUNTS RECEIVABLE		6
7			7
8			8
9			9
10			10
11			11
12	INTEREST RECEIVABLE		12
13			13
14			14
15			15
16			16
17			17
18			18

(c)

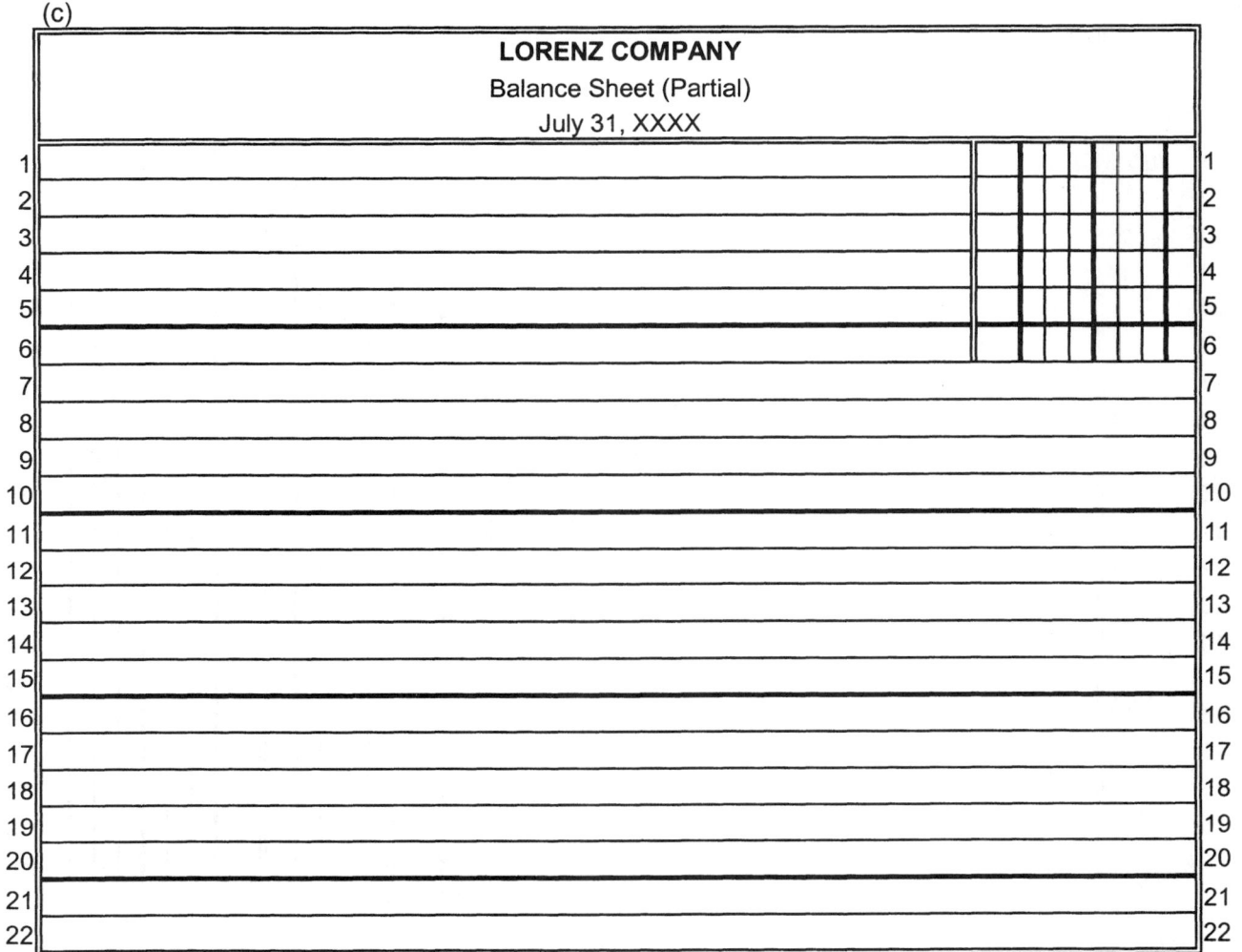

LORENZ COMPANY
Balance Sheet (Partial)
July 31, XXXX

(a)

		Total Estimated Bad Debts				
			Number of Days Outstanding			
	Total	0 - 30	31 - 60	61 - 90	91 - 120	Over 120
1 Accounts						
2 Receivable	$285,000	$107,000	$60,000	$50,000	$38 000	$30,000
3 % uncollectible		1%	5%	7.5%	10%	12%
4 Estimated						
5 Bad debts						

	Account Titles	Debit	Credit
1 (b)			
2			
3			
4			
5 (c)			
6			
7			
8			
9 (d)			
10			
11			
12			
13			
14			
15			

(e)

		Account Titles	Debit	Credit	
1	1.				1
2					2
3					3
4	2.				4
5					5
6					6
7	3.				7
8					8
9					9
10	4.				10
11					11
12					12
13	5.				13
14					14
15					15
16					16
17					17
18					18
19					19
20					20

See (b) and (d) on next page.

(c)

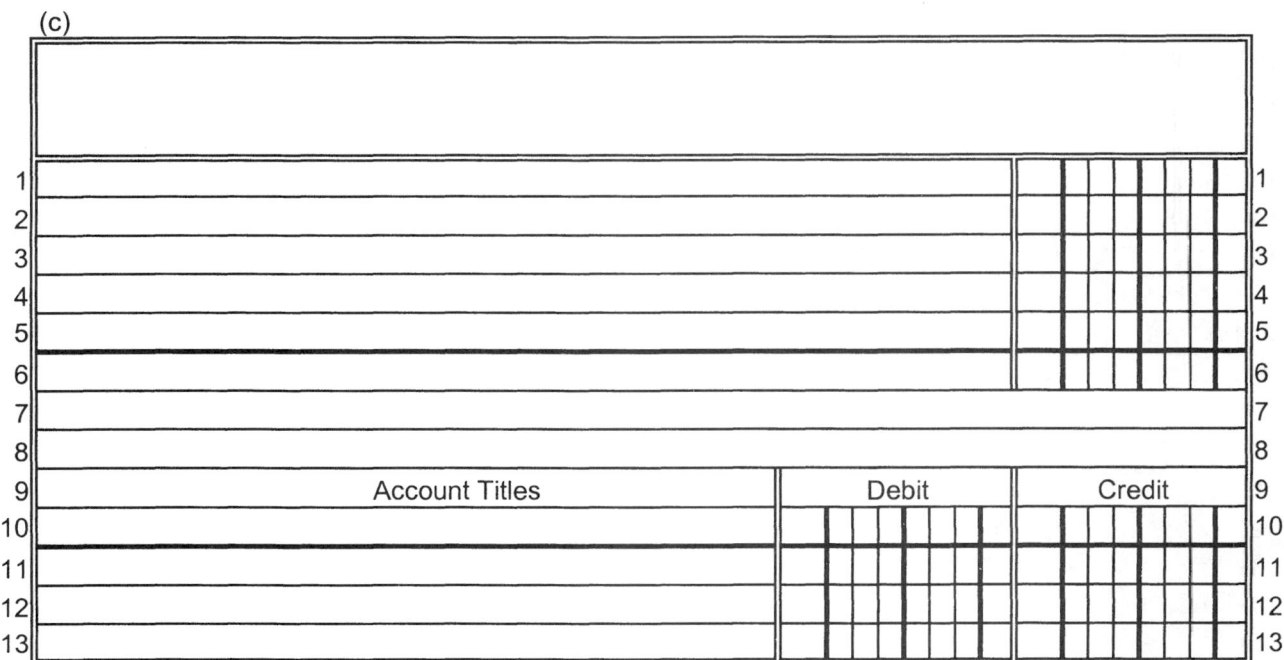

(b)

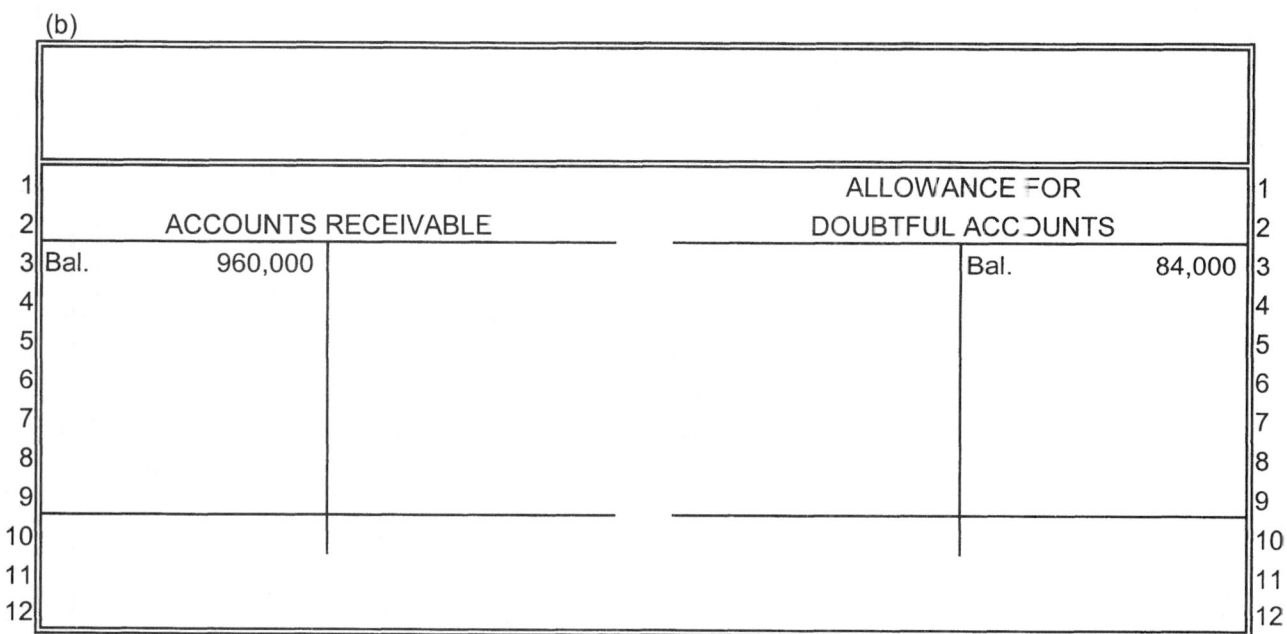

	ACCOUNTS RECEIVABLE				ALLOWANCE FOR DOUBTFUL ACCOUNTS		
3	Bal.	960,000				Bal.	84,000

(d)

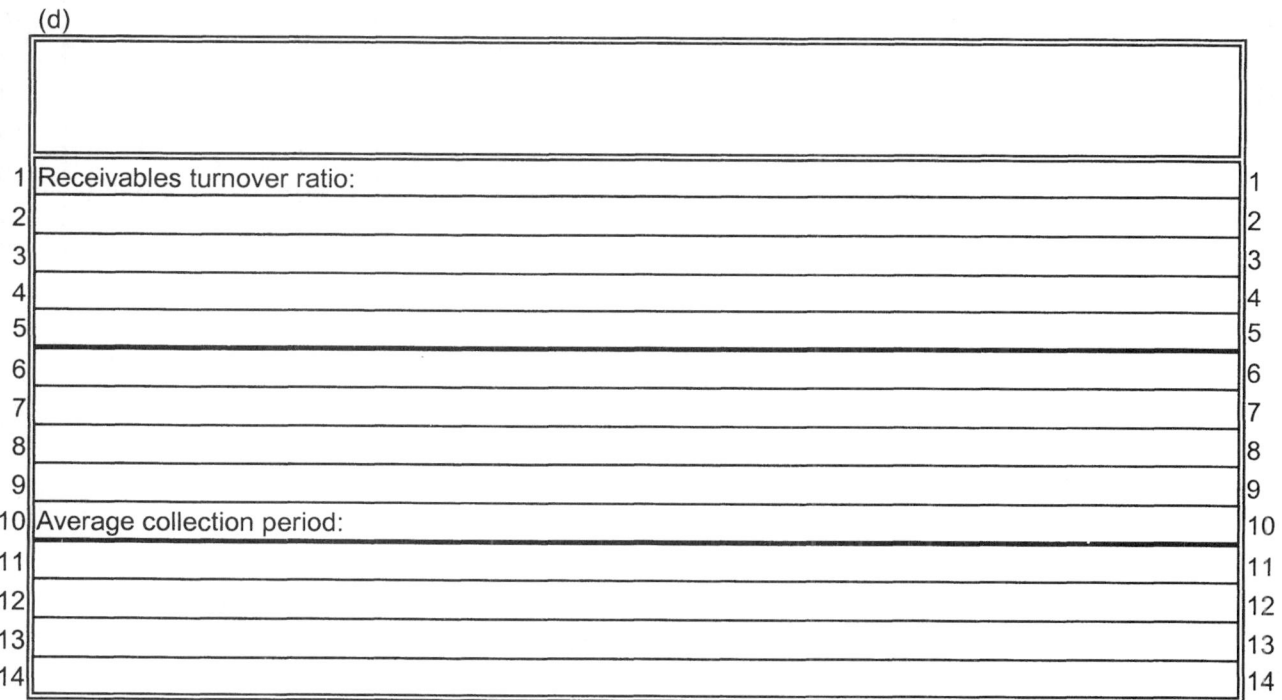

Receivables turnover ratio:

Average collection period:

(a), (b), and (c)

	Date	Account Titles	Debit	Credit	
1	(a)	2009			1
2	Dec 31				2
3					3
4					4
5					5
6	(b)	2010			6
7	Mar 1				7
8					8
9					9
10					10
11	May 31				11
12					12
13					13
14					14
15	31				15
16					16
17					17
18					18
19	(c)	2010			19
20	Dec 31				20
21					21
22					22

(a) & (b)

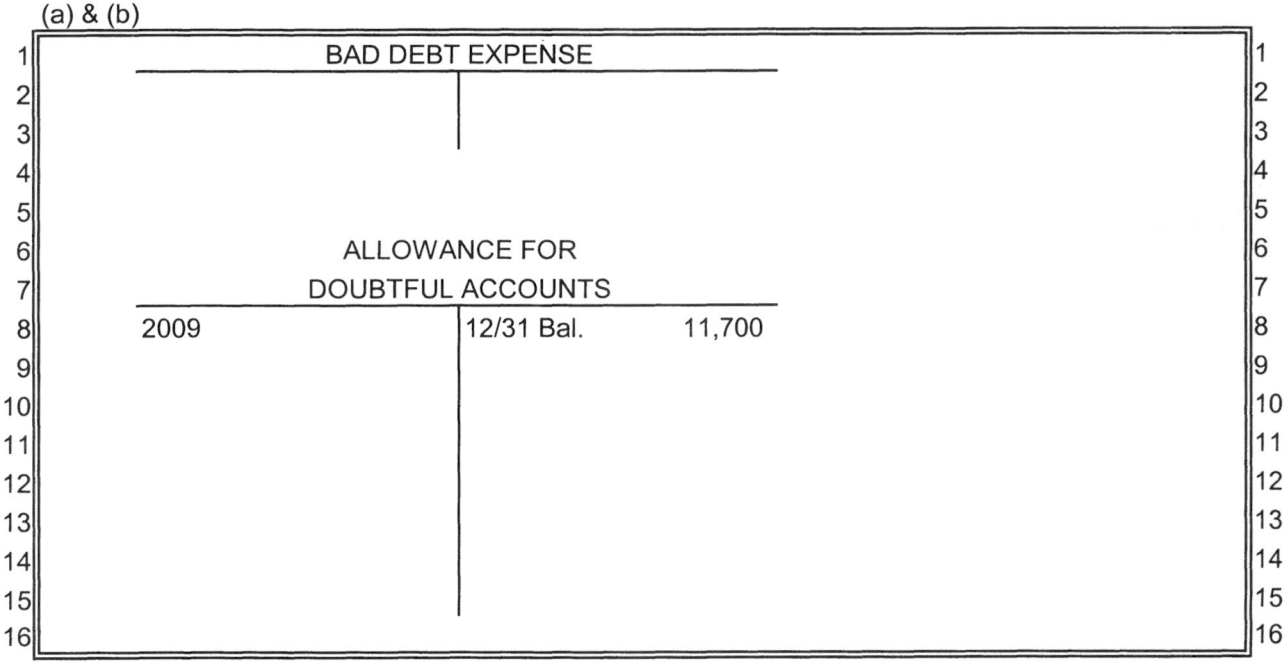

	BAD DEBT EXPENSE		

	ALLOWANCE FOR DOUBTFUL ACCOUNTS		
2009		12/31 Bal.	11,700

			(a)									
1												1
2												2
3												3
4												4
5	(b)											5
6	Date	Account Titles				Debit			Credit			6
7	Dec 31											7
8												8
9												9
10												10
11												11
12												12
13												13
14												14
15	(c)											15
16	Dec 31											16
17												17
18												18
19												19
20												20
21												21
22												22
23												23
24	·											24
25												25
26	(d)											26
27												27
28												28
29												29
30												30
31	(e)											31
32												32
33												33
34												34
35												35
36	(f)											36
37												37
38												38
39												39
40												40

	Date	Account Titles	Debit	Credit	
1	Jan 5				1
2					2
3					3
4	20				4
5					5
6					6
7	Feb 18				7
8					8
9					9
10	Apr 20				10
11					11
12					12
13					13
14	30				14
15					15
16					16
17					17
18	May 25				18
19					19
20					20
21	Aug 18				21
22					22
23					23
24					24
25	Sept 1				25
26					26
27					27
28					28
29					29
30					30
31					31
32					32
33					33
34					34
35					35
36					36
37					37
38					38
39					39
40					40

(a)

	Transaction	Receivables Turnover (6X)	Average Collection Period (61 days)	
1	1. Made sales on account			1
2				2
3	2. Collected amounts owing from customers.			3
4				4
5	3. Wrote off an account receivable as uncollectible.			5
6				6
7				7
8	4. Recorded sales returns and credited the			8
9	customers' accounts.			9
10				10
11	5. Recorded bad debts expense for the year using the			11
12	allowance method.			12
13				13

(b)

1		1
2		2
3		3
4		4
5		5
6		6
7		7
8		8
9		9
10		10
11		11
12		12
13		13
14		14
15		15
16		16
17		17
18		18
19		19
20		20
21		21
22		22

(a)

	Date	Account Titles	Debit	Credit	
1	Oct. 7				1
2					2
3					3
4	12				4
5					5
6					6
7					7
8	15				8
9					9
10					10
11					11
12	25				12
13					13
14					14
15					15
16	31				16
17					17
18					18
19					19
20					20

(b)

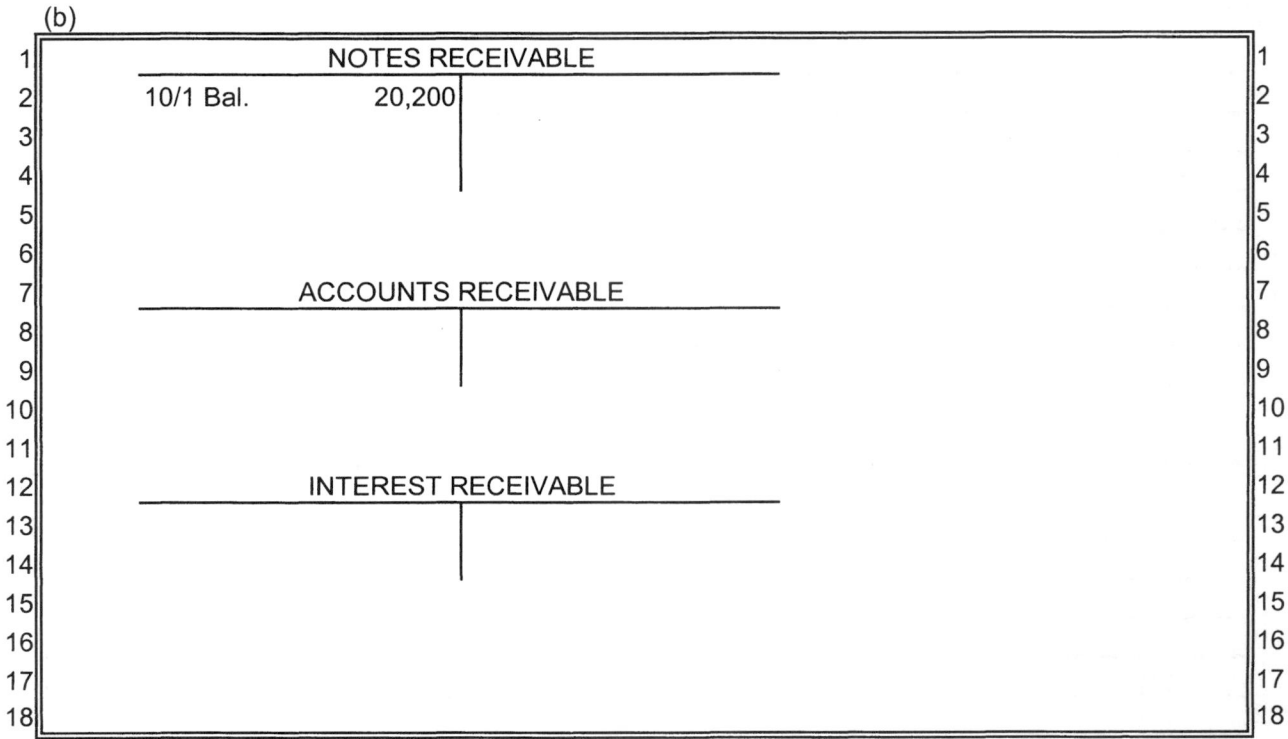

NOTES RECEIVABLE

10/1 Bal.   20,200

ACCOUNTS RECEIVABLE

INTEREST RECEIVABLE

(c)

	BROWN COMPANY	
	Balance Sheet (Partial)	
	October 31, XXXX	

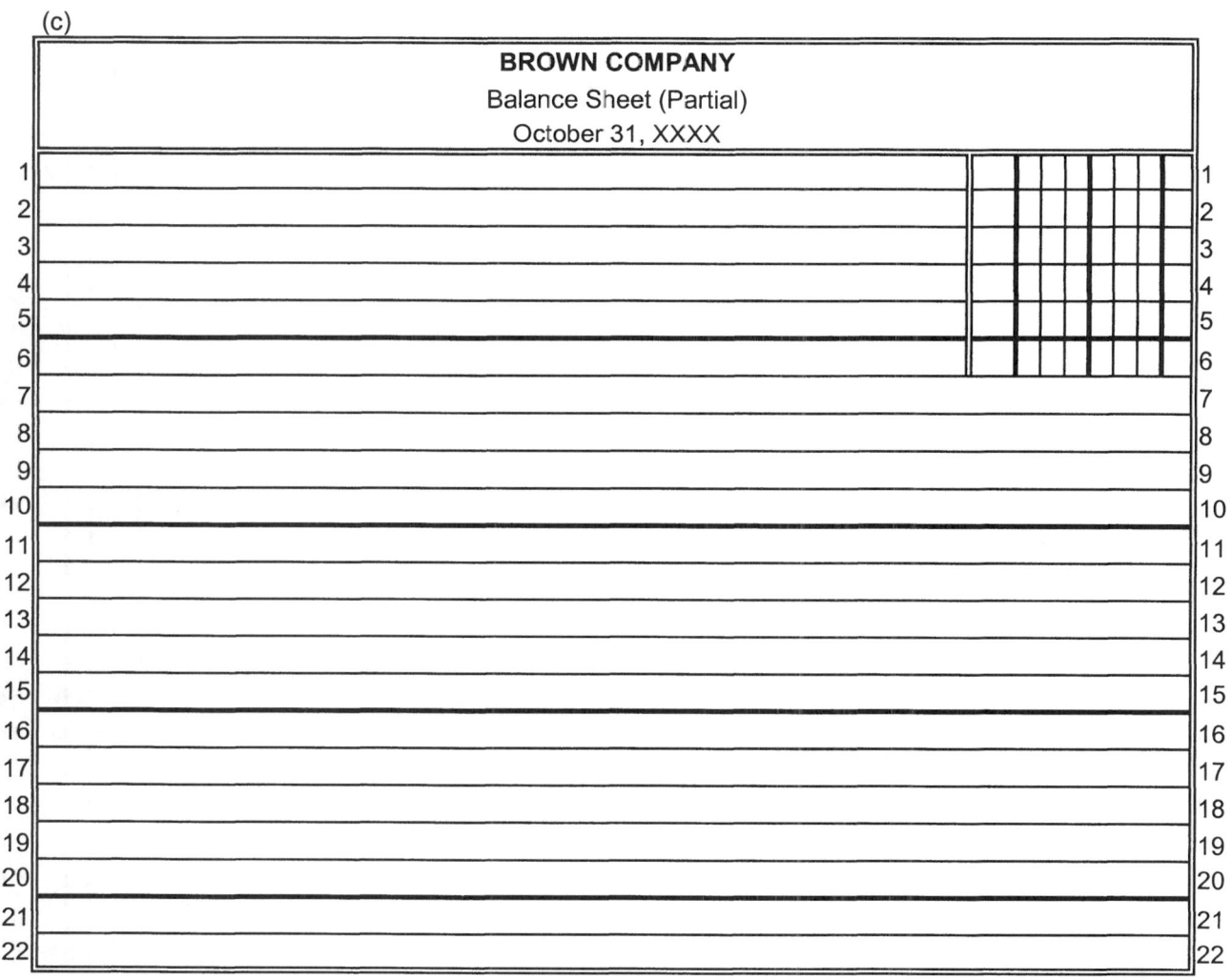

Name

Section

Date

(a)

	Date	Account Titles	Debit	Credit	
1	Jan. 1				1
2					2
3					3
4	3				4
5					5
6					6
7	8				7
8					8
9					9
10	11				10
11					11
12					12
13					13
14					14
15					15
16	15				16
17					17
18					18
19					19
20					20
21					21
22					22
23	17				23
24					24
25					25
26	21				26
27					27
28					28
29	24				29
30					30
31					31
32					32
33					33
34					34
35	27				35
36					36
37					37
38	31				38
39					39
40					40

(a)   (Continued)

	Date	Account Titles	Debit	Credit	
1		Adjusting Entries			1
2	Jan 31				2
3					3
4					4
5	31				5
6					6
7					7
8	31				8
9					9
10					10
11	31				11
12					12
13					13
14					14
15					15

(b)

	POSADA CORPORATION Adjusted Trial Balance January 31, 2010	Debit	Credit	
1				1
2				2
3				3
4				4
5				5
6				6
7				7
8				8
9				9
10				10
11				11
12				12
13				13
14				14
15				15
16				16
17				17
18				18
19				19
20				20
21				21

(b)   Optional T-accounts (for accounts with multiple transactions)

CASH			MERCHANDISE INVENTORY	
1/1 Bal.	13,100		1/1 Bal. 9,400	

ACCOUNTS RECEIVABLE		ADVERTISING SUPPLIES
1/1 Bal.	19,780	

	ACCOUNTS PAYABLE	
	1/1 Bal.	8,750

ALLOWANCE FOR DOUBTFUL ACCOUNTS		SALES
	1/1 Bal. 1,000	

COST OF GOODS SOLD

(c)

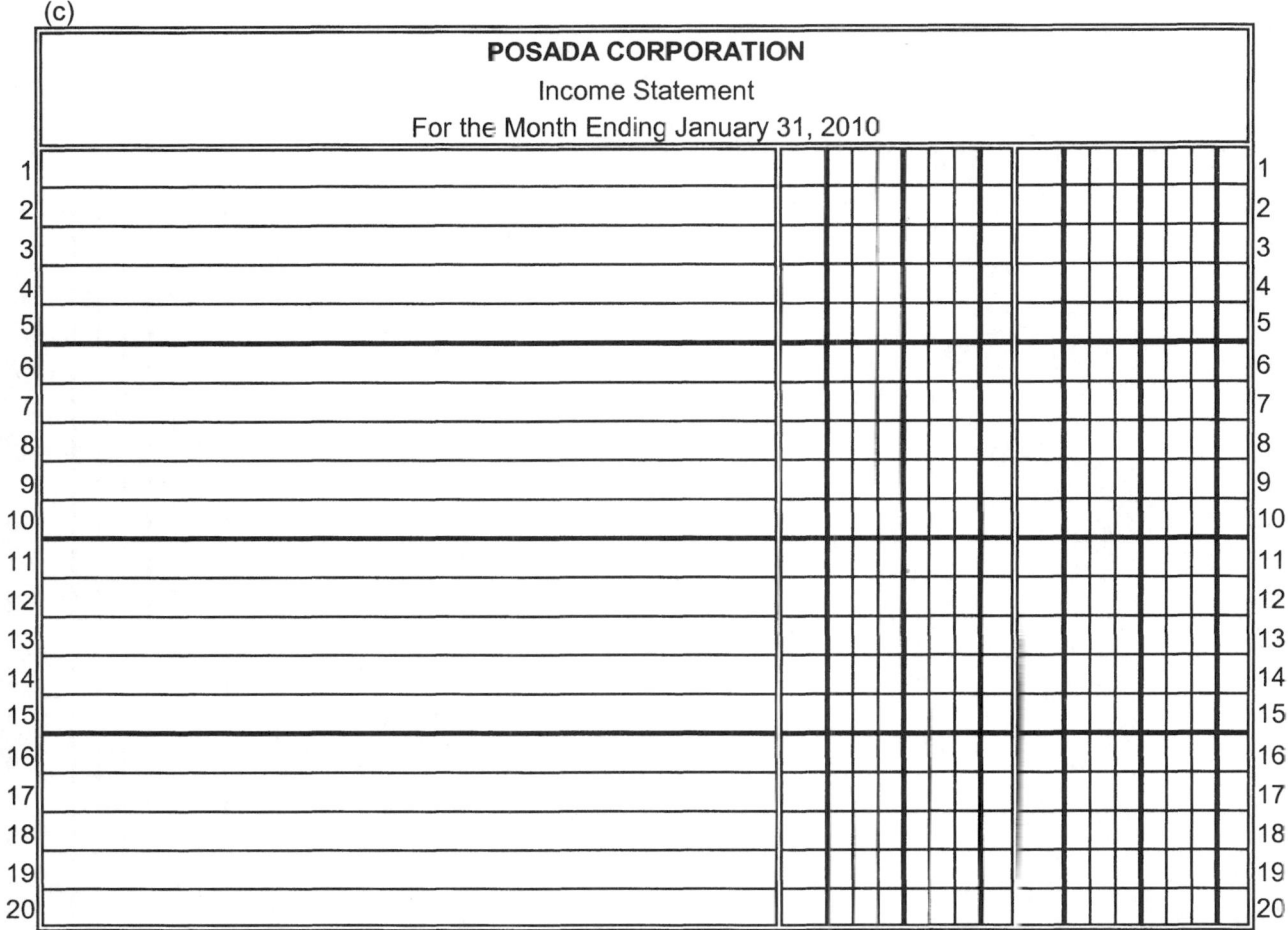

POSADA CORPORATION

Income Statement

For the Month Ending January 31, 2010

POSADA CORPORATION

Retained Earnings Statement

For the Month Ending January 31, 2010

(c)   (Continued)

POSADA CORPORATION

Balance Sheet

January 31, 2010

	Assets		
1			
2			
3			
4			
5			
6			
7			
8			
9			
10			
11			
12			
13	Liabilities and Stockholders' Equity		
14			
15			
16			
17			
18			
19			
20			
21			
22			
23			
24			
25			
26			
27			
28			
29			
30			
31			
32			
33			
34			
35			
36			
37			
38			
39			
40			

(a)	2010	2009	2008
1 Net credit sales			
2			
3 Credit and collection expenses:			
4			
5			
6			
7			
8			
9			
10			
11 Total expenses as a percentage of net			
12 credit sales			
13			
14 (b)			
15 Average accounts receivable			
16			
17 Investment earnings			
18 Total credit and collection expense			
19 per above.			
20 Add: Investment earnings			
21 Net credit and collection expense			
22			
23 Net expenses as a percentage of			
24 net sales			
25			
26			
27			
28 (c)			
29			
30			
31			
32			
33			
34			
35			
36			
37			
38			
39			
40			

BE9-5

	1
1	
2	
3	
4	
5	
6	
7	
8	
9	

BE9-6

	Account Titles	Debit	Credit
(a)			
(b)			

BE9-7

	Account Titles	Debit	Credit
(a)			
(b)			

Calculation of gain/loss incurred for part (b) above:

BE9-8

	Account Titles	Debit	Credit	
1	(a)			1
2				2
3				3
4	(b)			4
5				5
6				6
7				7
8				8
9	Calculation of gain/loss incurred for part (b) above:			9
10				10
11				11
12				12
13				13
14				14
15				15
16				16
17				17

BE9-10

	Account Titles	Debit	Credit	
19				19
20	(a)			20
21				21
22				22
23	(b)			23
24				24
25				25
26				26
27				27
28				28
29				29
30				30

BE9-11

	NIKE, INC. Partial Balance Sheet May 31, 2007 (in millions)		
1	Property, plant, and equipment:			1
2				2
3				3
4				4
5				5
6				6
7				7
8				8
9				9
10	Intangible assets:			10
11				11
12				12
13				13
14				14
15				15
16				16

BE9-12

Net cash provided by operating activities:

*BE9-13

	Book Value	Rate	Depreciation
Year 1			
Year 2			

DO IT! 9-1

1	Cost of the truck:		
2			
3			
4			
5			
6			
7			
8	Other costs:		
9			
10			
11			
12			

DO IT! 9-2

Depreciation expense calculation:

	Account Titles	Debit	Credit
18			
19			
20			
21			

DO IT! 9-3

	Account Titles	Debit	Credit
(a)	Sale of truck for cash at a gain:		
(b)	Sale of truck for cash at a loss:		

E9-3

(a) Cost of land:

1		
2		
3		
4		
5		
6		

(b)

7
8
9
10

E9-6

(a)

	Type of Asset	
	Building	Warehouse
11		
12		
13		
14		
15		
16		
17		
18		
19		
20		

(b)

Date	Account Titles	Debit	Credit
Dec 31			

E9-7

	Account Titles	Debit	Credit
(a)			
(b)			
(c)			

E9-8

	Date	Account Titles	Debit	Credit	
1	Jan 1				1
2					2
3					3
4	June 30				4
5					5
6					6
7	30				7
8					8
9					9
10					10
11					11
12	Dec 31				12
13					13
14					14
15	31				15
16					16
17					17
18					18
19					19
20					20
21					21
22					22
23					23
24					24
25					25
26					26
27					27
28					28
29					29
30					30

E9-13

	Date	Account Titles	Debit	Credit	
1	Dec. 31				1
2					2
3					3
4					4
5	31				5
6					6
7					7
8					8
9					9

10	**E9-14**				10
11	Date	Account Titles	Debit	Credit	11
12	(a)				12
13	1/2/10				13
14					14
15					15
16	4/1/10				16
17					17
18					18
19	7/1/10				19
20					20
21					21
22	9/1/10				22
23					23
24					24
25	(b)				25
26					26
27					27
28					28
29					29
30	(c) Ending balances for intangibles:				30
31					31
32					32
33					33
34					34
35					35
36					36
37					37
38					38
39					39
40					40

	10-year life	15-year life
1		
2 Net income		
3		
4		
5 Net cash from operating activities:		
6		
7		
8		
9		
10		
11 Evaluation:		
12		
13		
14		
15		
16		
17		
18		
19		
20		
21		
22		
23		
24		
25		
26		
27		
28		
29		
30		
31		
32		
33		
34		
35		
36		
37		
38		
39		
40		

	(a) Depreciation rate per unit calculations:						
1							
2							
3							
4							
5							

(b)		Computation			End of Year		
	Years	Units of Activity	Depr. Cost/Unit	Annual Depreciation Expense	Accumulated Depreciation	Book Value
	2010	40,000				
	2011	52,000				
	2012	41,000				
	2013	27,000				

Item	Land	Building	Other Accounts	
			Amount	Account Titles
1				
2 1.				
3				
4 2.				
5				
6 3.				
7				
8 4.				
9				
10 5.				
11				
12 6.				
13				
14 7.				
15				
16 8.				
17				
18 9.				
19				
20 10.				
21				
22				
23				
24				
25				

(a)

	Date	Account Titles	Debit	Credit	
1	Apr 1				1
2					2
3					3
4	May 1				4
5					5
6					6
7	1				7
8					8
9					9
10					10
11					11
12		Computation of gain/loss on disposal:			12
13					13
14					14
15					15
16					16
17					17
18					18
19	June 1				19
20					20
21					21
22					22
23	July 1				23
24					24
25					25
26	Dec 31				26
27					27
28					28
29	31				29
30					30
31					31
32		Computation of book value:			32
33					33
34					34
35					35
36					36
37					37
38					38
39					39
40					40

(b)

	Date	Account Titles	Debit	Credit	
1	Dec 31				1
2					2
3					3
4	31				4
5					5
6					6
7					7
8					8
9					9
10					10
11					11
12					12
13					13
14					14
15					15
16					16
17					17
18					18
19					19
20					20

(c)

RIJO CORPORATION
Balance Sheet (Partial)
December 31, 2011

1				1
2				2
3				3
4				4
5				5
6				6
7				7
8				8
9				9
10				10
11				11
12				12
13				13
14				14
15				15

(a) (Continued)

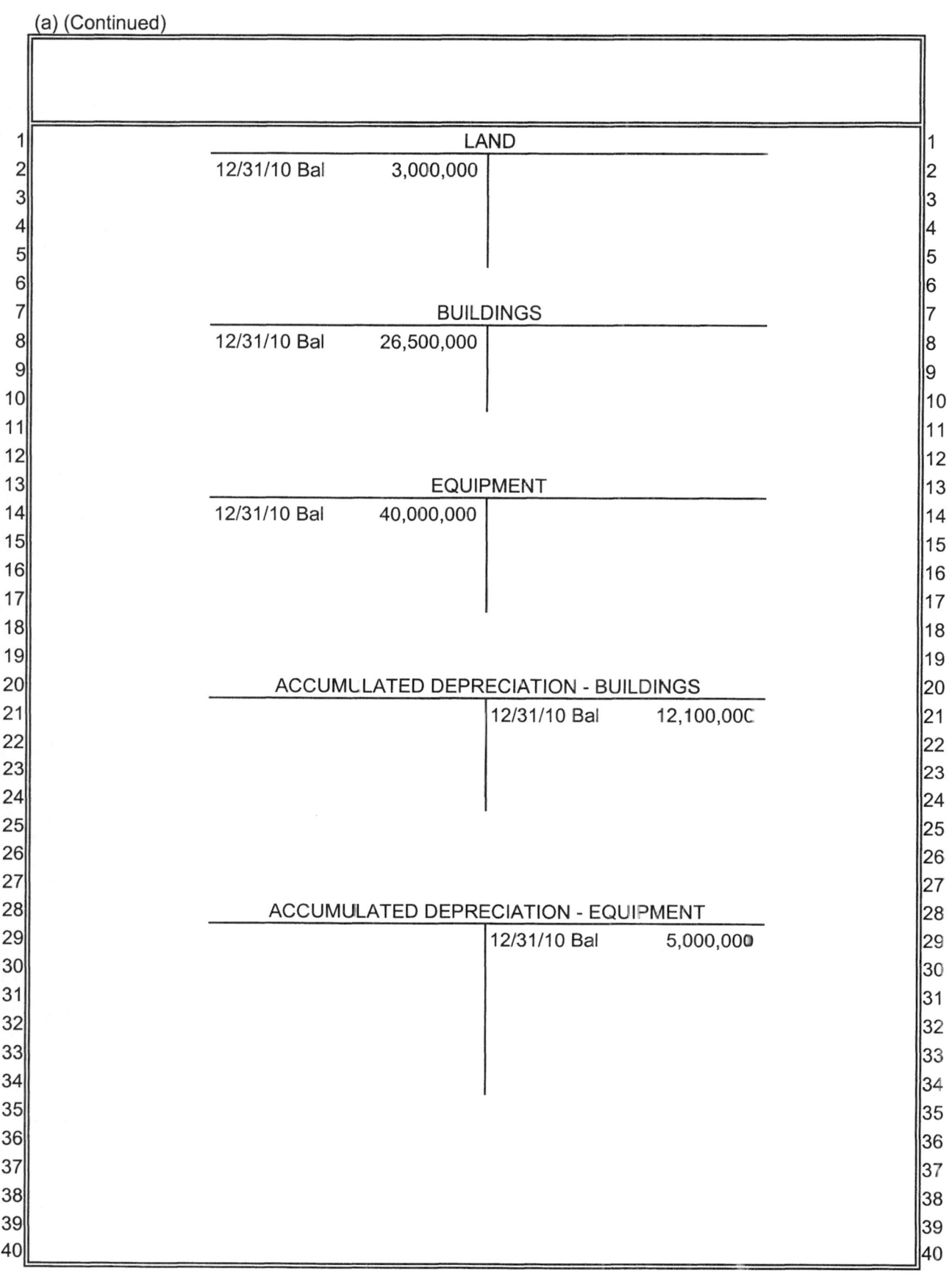

LAND

12/31/10 Bal	3,000,000		

BUILDINGS

12/31/10 Bal	26,500,000		

EQUIPMENT

12/31/10 Bal	40,000,000		

ACCUMULATED DEPRECIATION - BUILDINGS

		12/31/10 Bal	12,100,000

ACCUMULATED DEPRECIATION - EQUIPMENT

		12/31/10 Bal	5,000,000

	Date	Account Titles	Debit	Credit	
1	Jan 1				1
2					2
3					3
4	June 30				4
5					5
6					6
7	30				7
8					8
9					9
10					10
11					11
12		Computation of gain/loss on disposal:			12
13					13
14					14
15					15
16					16
17					17
18					18
19	12/31				19
20					20
21					21
22	31				22
23					23
24					24
25					25
26		Computation of gain/loss on disposal:			26
27					27
28					28
29					29
30					30
31					31
32					32
33					33
34					34
35					35
36					36
37					37
38					38
39					39
40					40

(a)

	Date	Account Titles	Debit	Credit	
1	Jan 2				1
2					2
3					3
4	Jan -				4
5	June				5
6					6
7	July 1				7
8					8
9					9
10	Sept 1				10
11					11
12					12
13	Oct 1				13
14					14
15					15
16 (b)					16
17	Dec 31				17
18					18
19					19
20	31				20
21					21
22					22

(c)

SALMIENTO CORPORATION

Balance Sheet (Partial)

December 31, 2011

1	Intangible assets:	1
2		2
3		3
4		4
5		5
6		6
7		7
8	(d)	8
9		9
10		10
11		11
12		12
13		13
14		14

	Date	Account Titles	Debit	Credit	
1	1.				1
2					2
3					3
4					4
5					5
6					6
7					7
8					8
9					9
10					10
11	2.				11
12					12
13					13
14					14
15					15
16					16
17					17
18					18
19					19
20					20

	Year	Computation	Accumulated Depreciation 12/31	
1	(a)	MACHINE 1		1
2				2
3	2008			3
4				4
5	2009			5
6				6
7	2010			7
8				8
9	2011			9
10				10
11				11
12		MACHINE 2		12
13				13
14	2009			14
15				15
16	2010			16
17				17
18	2011			18
19				19
20				20
21		MACHINE 3		21
22				22
23	2009			23
24				24
25	2010			25
26				26
27	2011			27
28				28
29				29
30	(b)	Computation	Depr. Expense	30
31		MACHINE 2		31
32	(1) 2009			32
33				33
34	(2) 2010			34
35				35
36				36
37				37
38				38
39				39

(a)

		STRAIGHT - LINE DEPRECIATION				
		Computation			End of Year	
	Years	Depreciable Cost	Depr. Rate	Annual Depreciation Expense	Accumulated Depreciation	Book Value
6	2010					
7	2011					
8	2012					
9	2013					

		DOUBLE - DECLINING - BALANCE DEPRECIATION				
		Computation			End of Year	
	Years	Book Value Beginning of Year	Depr. Rate	Annual Depreciation Expense	Accumulated Depreciation	Book Value
19	2010					
20	2011					
21	2012					
22	2013					

(b)

(c)

	Item	Land	Building	Amount	Other Accounts — Account Titles	
1						1
2	1.					2
3						3
4	2.					4
5						5
6	3.					6
7						7
8	4.					8
9						9
10	5.					10
11						11
12	6.					12
13						13
14	7.					14
15						15
16	8.					16
17						17
18	9.					18
19						19
20	10.					20
21						21
22						22
23						23
24						24
25						25

(a)

	Date	Account Titles	Debit	Credit	
1	Apr 1				1
2					2
3					3
4	May 1				4
5					5
6					6
7	1				7
8					8
9					9
10					10
11					11
12		Computation of gain/loss on disposal:			12
13					13
14					14
15					15
16					16
17					17
18					18
19	June 1				19
20					20
21					21
22					22
23	July 1				23
24					24
25					25
26	Dec 31				26
27					27
28					28
29	31				29
30					30
31					31
32		Computation of book value:			32
33					33
34					34
35					35
36					36
37					37
38					38
39					39
40					40

(b)

	Date	Account Titles	Debit	Credit	
1	Dec 31				1
2					2
3					3
4	31				4
5					5
6					6
7					7
8					8
9					9
10					10
11					11
12					12
13					13
14					14
15					15
16					16
17					17
18					18
19					19
20					20

(c)

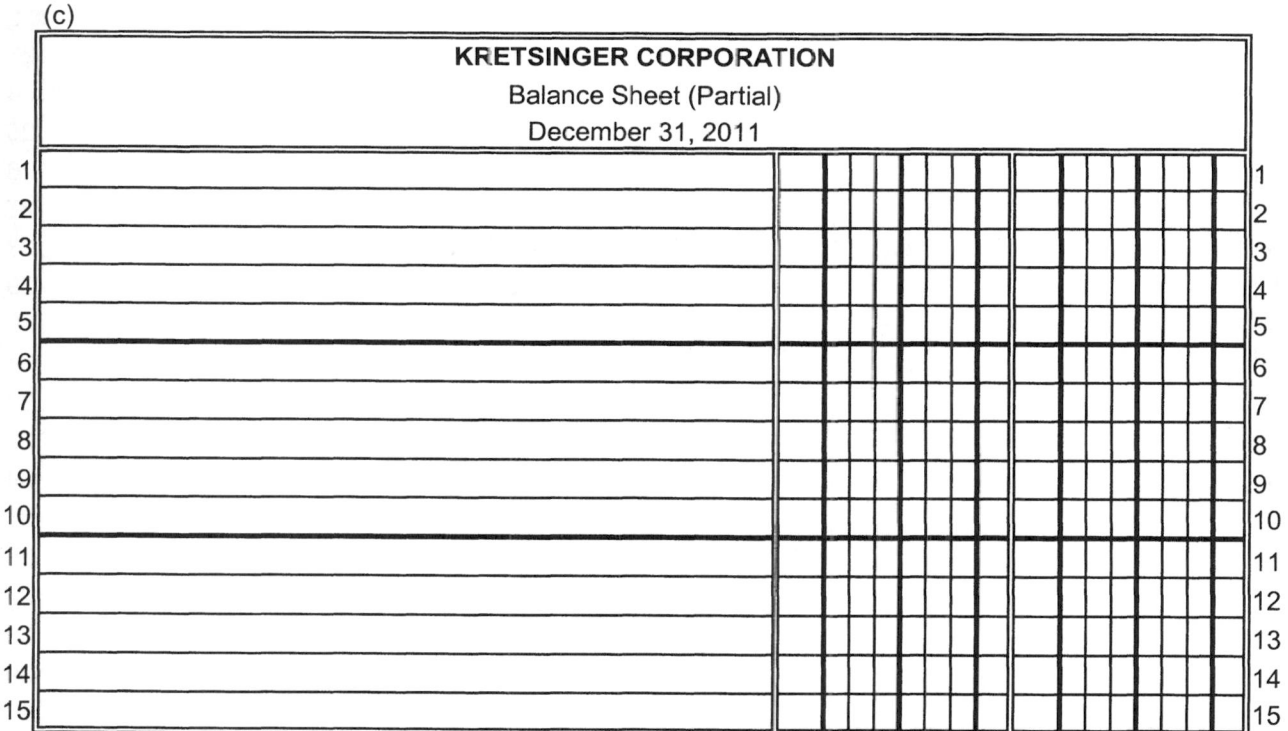

	KRETSINGER CORPORATION Balance Sheet (Partial) December 31, 2011			
1				1
2				2
3				3
4				4
5				5
6				6
7				7
8				8
9				9
10				10
11				11
12				12
13				13
14				14
15				15

(a) (Continued)

	LAND	
12/31/10 Bal	4,000,000	

	BUILDINGS	
12/31/10 Bal	28,500,000	

	EQUIPMENT	
12/31/10 Bal	48,000,000	

	ACCUMULATED DEPRECIATION - BUILDINGS	
	12/31/10 Bal	12,100,000

	ACCUMULATED DEPRECIATION - EQUIPMENT	
	12/31/10 Bal	5,000,000

	Date	Account Titles	Debit	Credit	
1	Jan 1				1
2					2
3					3
4	June 30				4
5					5
6					6
7	30				7
8					8
9					9
10					10
11					11
12		Computation of gain/loss on disposal:			12
13					13
14					14
15					15
16					16
17					17
18					18
19	Dec 31				19
20					20
21					21
22	31				22
23					23
24					24
25					25
26		Computation of gain/loss on disposal:			26
27					27
28					28
29					29
30					30
31					31
32					32
33					33
34					34
35					35
36					36
37					37
38					38
39					39
40					40

(a)

	Date	Account Titles	Debit	Credit	
1	Jan 2				1
2					2
3					3
4	Jan -				4
5	June				5
6					6
7	July 1				7
8					8
9					9
10	Sept 1				10
11					11
12					12
13	Oct 1				13
14					14
15					15
16	(b)				16
17	Dec 31				17
18					18
19					19
20	31				20
21					21
22					22

(c)

GORE COMPANY

Balance Sheet (Partial)

December 31, 2011

1	Intangible assets:	1
2		2
3		3
4		4
5		5
6		6
7		7
8	(d)	8
9		9
10		10
11		11
12		12
13		13
14		14

	Date	Account Titles	Debit	Credit	
1	1.				1
2					2
3					3
4					4
5					5
6					6
7					7
8					8
9					9
10	2.				10
11					11
12					12
13					13
14					14
15					15
16					16
17					17
18					18
19					19
20					20

	Year	Computation	Accumulated Depreciation 12/31
(a)		BUS 1	
	2009		
	2010		
	2011		
		BUS 2	
	2009		
	2010		
	2011		
		BUS 3	
	2009		
	2010		
	2011		
(b)		Computation	Depr. Expense
		BUS 2	
	(1) 2009		
	(2) 2010		

(a)

	STRAIGHT - LINE DEPRECIATION					
	Computation				End of Year	
		Depreciable	Depr.	Annual Depreciation	Accumulated	Book
Years		Cost	Rate	Expense	Depreciation	Value
2010						
2011						
2012						
2013						
2014						

	DOUBLE - DECLINING - BALANCE DEPRECIATION					
	Computation				End of Year	
		Book Value Beginning of Year	Depr. Rate	Annual Depreciation Expense	Accumulated Depreciation	Book Value
Years						
2010						
2011						
2012						
2013						
2014						

(b)

(c)

(a)

	Date	Account Titles	Debit	Credit	
1	1.				1
2					2
3					3
4	2.				4
5					5
6					6
7					7
8					8
9					9
10					10
11					11
12	3.				12
13					13
14					14
15					15
16					16
17					17
18	4.				18
19					19
20					20
21	5.				21
22					22
23					23
24	6.				24
25					25
26					26
27	7.				27
28					28
29					29
30	8.				30
31					31
32					32
33	9.				33
34					34
35					35
36	10.				36
37					37
38					38
39					39
40					40

(a) (Continued)

	Date	Account Titles	Debit	Credit	
1	11.				1
2					2
3					3
4	12.				4
5					5
6					6
7	13.				7
8					8
9					9
10	14.				10
11					11
12					12
13					13
14					14
15					15
16					16
17					17
18					18
19					19
20					20
21					21
22					22
23					23
24					24
25					25
26					26
27					27
28					28
29					29
30					30
31					31
32					32
33					33
34					34
35					35
36					36
37					37
38					38
39					39
40					40

(b)

PINKERTON CORPORATION
Trial Balance
December 31, 2010

	Debit	Credit
1		
2		
3		
4		
5		
6		
7		
8		
9		
10		
11		
12		
13		
14		
15		
16		
17		
18		
19		
20		
21		
22		
23		
24		
25		
26		
27		
28		
29		
30		
31		
32		
33		
34		
35		
36		
37		
38		
39		
40		

(c)

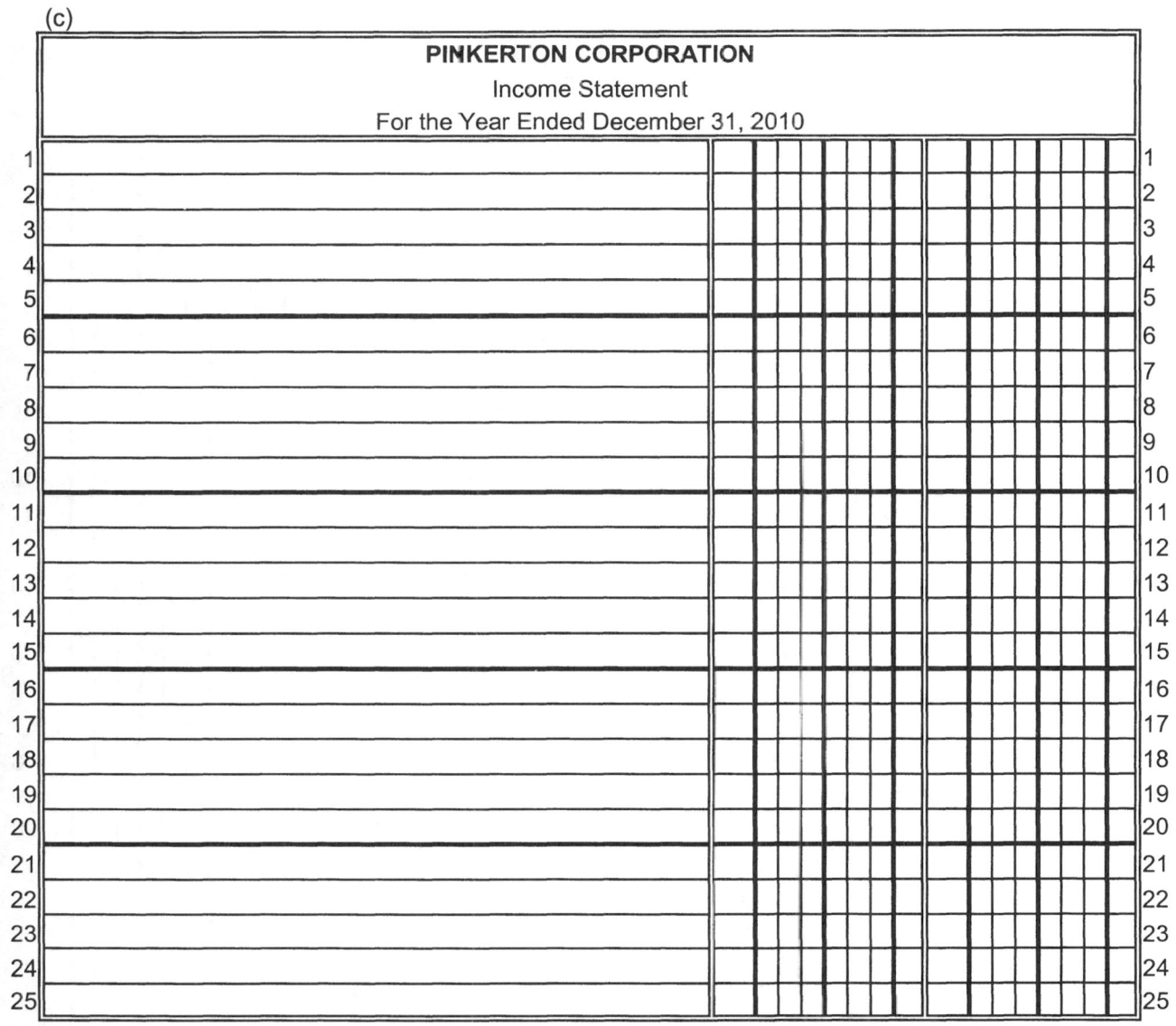

PINKERTON CORPORATION

Income Statement

For the Year Ended December 31, 2010

PINKERTON CORPORATION

Retained Earnings Statement

For the Year Ended December 31, 2010

(d)

	PINKERTON CORPORATION
	Balance Sheet
	December 31, 2010

Assets

Liabilities and Stockholders' Equity

1	(a)		1
2			2
3			3
4			4
5			5
6	(b)		6
7			7
8			8
9			9
10			10
11			11
12			12
13			13
14			14
15			15
16			16
17			17
18			18
19			19
20			20
21	(c)		21
22			22
23		Old Estimates	23
24			24
25			25
26			26
27			27
28			28
29			29
30		Revised	30
31		Estimates	31
32			32
33			33
34			34
35			35
36			36
37			37
38			38
39			39
40			40

BE10-2

	Date	Account Titles	Debit	Credit	
1	(a)				1
2	July 1				2
3					3
4	(b)				4
5	Dec 31				5
6					6
7					7
8					8

9	**BE10-3** Sales tax payable:				9
10					10
11					11
12					12
13					13
14					14

	Date	Account Titles	Debit	Credit	
15					15
16	Mar 16				16
17					17
18					18
19					19
20					20
21					21
22					22
23					23
24					24
25					25

BE10-4

	Account Titles	Debit	Credit
(a)			
(b)			

BE10-5

	Issue Stock	Issue Bonds
Income before interest and taxes	$150000	$150000
Interest expense		
Income before income taxes		
Income tax expense		
Net income		
Outstanding shares		70000
Earnings per share		

BE10-6

Date	Account Titles	Debit	Credit
(a)			
Jan 1			
(b)			
Dec 31			
(c)			
Jan 1			

BE10-7

	Account Titles	Debit	Credit

BE10-8

FELKNER, INC.		
Balance Sheet (Partial)		
December 31, 2010		
1 Long-term liabilities:		
2		
3		
4		
5		
6		
7		

BE10-9

SHEELY INC.		
Balance Sheet (Partial)		
December 31, 2010		

*BE10-12

	Date	Account Titles	Debit	Credit	
1	(a)				1
2	Jan 1				2
3					3
4					4
5	(b)				5
6	Dec 31				6
7					7
8					8
9					9

*BE10-13

		Account Titles	Debit	Credit	
11	(a)				11
12	Jan 1				12
13					13
14					14
15					15
16	(b)				16
17	Dec 31				17
18					18
19					19
20					20
21					21

*BE10-14

	#14	Account Titles	Debit	Credit	
24	(a)				24
25					25
26					26
27					27
28					28
29	(b)				29
30					30
31					31
32					32
33					33
34					34
35	(c)				35
36					36
37					37
38					38
39					39
40					40

DO IT! 10-1

	Account Titles	Debit	Credit	
1	(a)			1
2	Feb 28			2
3				3
4				4
5				5
6				6
7				7
8	(b)			8
9	Feb 28			9
10				10
11				11
12				12
13				13
14				14

DO IT! 10-4

	Account Titles	Debit	Credit	
16				16
17	(a)			17
18				18
19				19
20				20
21				21
22	(b)			22
23				23
24				24
25				25
26				26

DO IT! 10-5

	Account Titles	Debit	Credit	
28				28
29				29
30				30
31				31
32				32
33				33
34				34
35				35
36				36
37				37
38				38
39				39
40				40

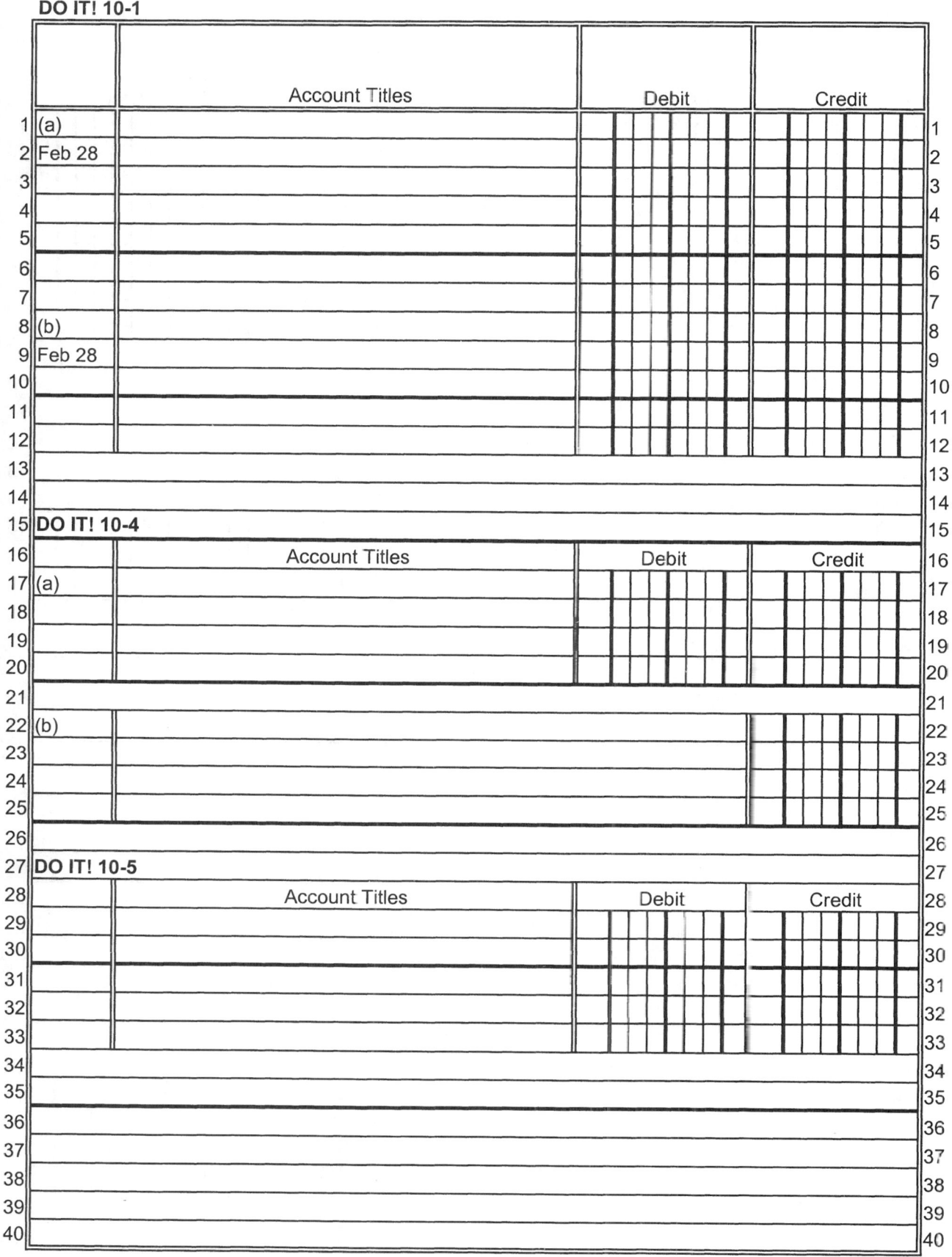

E10-1

Date	Account Titles	Debit	Credit	
(a)				1
June 1				2
				3
				4
(b)				5
30				6
				7
				8
(c)				9
				10
				11
				12
(d)				13

Date	Account Titles	Debit	Credit	
Jan 1				15
				16
				17

E10-2

(a)		1
		2
		3
		4
		5
(b)		6
		7
		8
		9
		10
(c)		11

Date	Account Titles	Debit	Credit	
May 15				13
				14
				15
Sept 15				16
				17
				18

E10-3

	Date	Account Titles	Debit	Credit	
1	(a)				1
2	June 1				2
3					3
4					4
5	(b)				5
6	30				6
7					7
8					8
9	(c)				9
10	Dec 1				10
11					11
12					12
13					13
14	(d)				14
15					15
16					16
17					17
18					18
19					19
20					20

E10-4

	Date	Account Titles	Debit	Credit	
1		Grainger Company			1
2	Apr 10				2
3					3
4					4
5					5
6					6
7		Darby Company			7
8	15				8
9					9
10					10
11					11
12					12
13					13
14					14
15					15

E10-5

	Date	Account Titles	Debit	Credit	
1	(a)				1
2	Mar 31				2
3					3
4					4
5					5
6					6
7					7
8					8
9	(b)				9
10	Mar 31				10
11					11
12					12
13					13
14					14
15					15

E10-6

		Account Titles	Debit	Credit	
1	(a)				1
2					2
3					3
4	(b)				4
5					5
6					6
7					7
8					8
9	(c)				9
10					10
11					11
12					12
13	(d)				13
14					14
15					15
16					16
17					17
18					18
19					19
20					20

E10-7

	Date	Account Titles	Debit	Credit	
1	(a)	2010			1
2	Nov				2
3					3
4					4
5	(b)				5
6	Dec 31				6
7					7
8					8
9	(c)	2011			9
10	Mar 31				10
11					11
12					12
13					13
14					14
15					15

E10-8

	Date	Account Titles	Debit	Credit	
1	(a)				1
2	2010				2
3	Sept 1				3
4					4
5					5
6	(b)				6
7	Dec 31				7
8					8
9					9
10					10
11	(c)				11
12	2011				12
13	Sept 1				13
14					14
15					15
16					16
17					17
18					18
19					19
20					20

E10-9

	Date	Account Titles	Debit	Credit	
1	(a)				1
2	Jan 1				2
3					3
4					4
5	(b)				5
6	Dec 31				6
7					7
8					8
9	(c)				9
10	Jan 1				10
11					11
12					12

E10-10

1	(a)	1
2		2
3		3
4	(b)	4
5		5
6		6
7		7
8		8
9		9
10		10

	Date	Account Titles	Debit	Credit	
11					11
12	(c)				12
13					13
14					14
15					15
16					16
17					17
18					18
19					19
20					20

E10-11

	Date	Account Titles	Debit	Credit	
1	(a)				1
2	2010				2
3	Jan 1				3
4					4
5					5
6	(b)				6
7	Dec 31				7
8					8
9					9
10	(c)				10
11	2011				11
12	Jan 1				12
13					13
14					14
15	(d)				15
16	2030				16
17	Jan 1				17
18					18
19					19
20					20

E10-12

	Date	Account Titles	Debit	Credit	
1	(a)				1
2	June 30				2
3					3
4					4
5					5
6					6
7	(b)				7
8	June 30				8
9					9
10					10
11					11
12					12
13					13
14					14
15					15

(a)

	Account	Classification	Reason
1			
2			
3			
4			
5			
6			
7			
8			
9			
10			
11			
12			
13			
14			
15			
16			
17			
18			
19			
20			
21			
22			
23			
24			
25			
26			
27			
28			
29			
30			
31			
32			
33			
34			
35			
36			
37			
38			
39			
40			

(b)

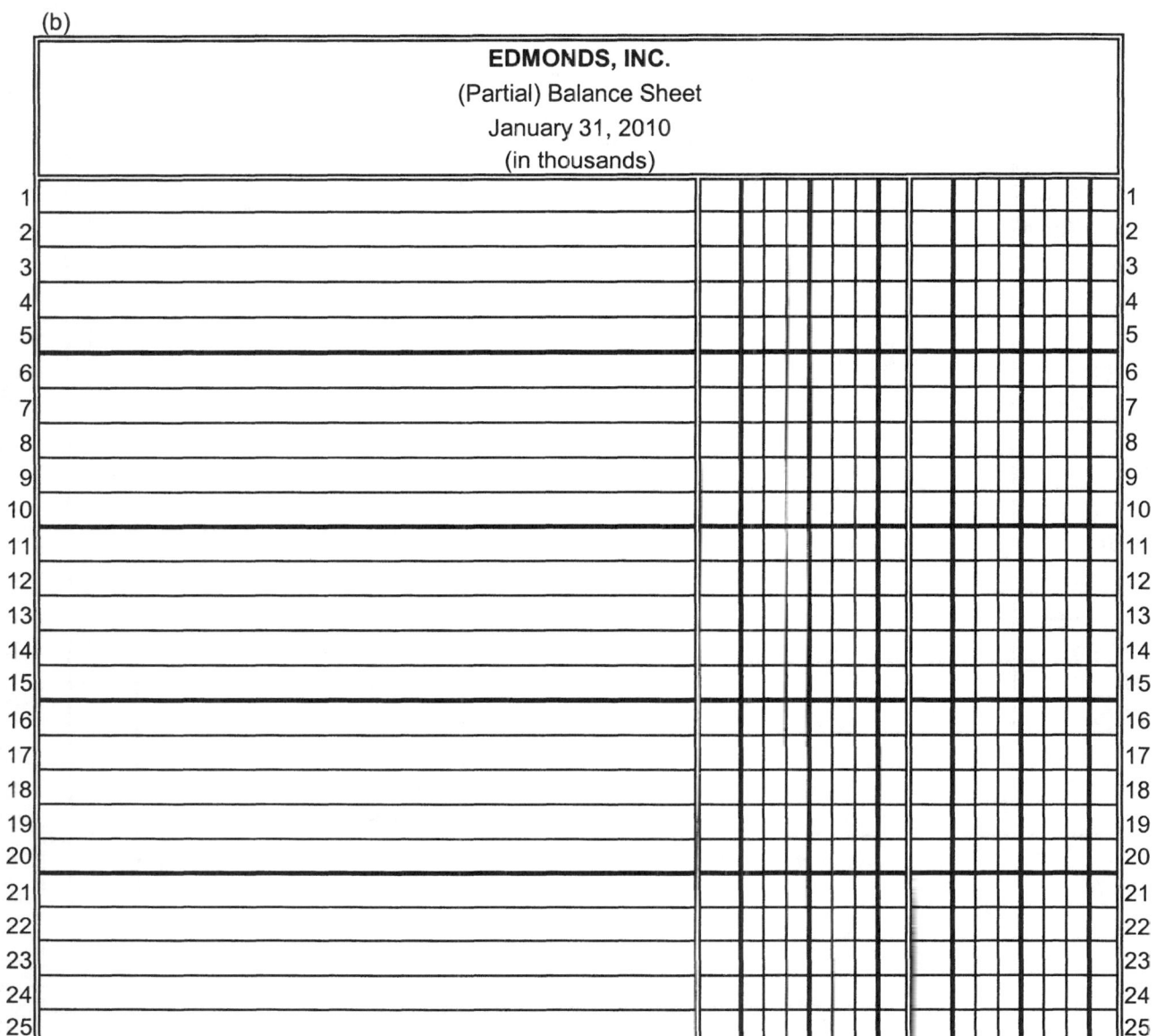

EDMONDS, INC.
(Partial) Balance Sheet
January 31, 2010
(in thousands)

	Date	Account Titles	Debit	Credit	
1	(a)				1
2	2010				2
3	Jan 1				3
4					4
5					5
6					6
7	(b)				7
8	Dec 31				8
9					9
10					10
11					11
12	(c)				12
13	2011				13
14	Jan 1				14
15					15
16					16
17	(d)				17
18	2030				18
19	Jan 1				19
20					20
21					21
22					22
23					23
24					24
25					25

*E10-19

	Date	Account Titles	Debit	Credit	
1	(a)	2009			1
2	Dec 31				2
3					3
4					4
5					5
6	(b)	2010			6
7	Dec 31				7
8					8
9					9
10					10
11	(c)	2019			11
12	Dec 31				12
13					13
14					14
15					15
16					16
17					17

*E10-20

	Date	Account Titles	Debit	Credit	
1	(a)	2010			1
2	Jan 1				2
3					3
4					4
5					5
6	(b)				6
7	Dec 31				7
8					8
9					9
10					10
11	(c)	2011			11
12	Jan 1				12
13					13
14					14
15					15
16	See following table for calculations				16
17					17
18					18

*Exercise 10-20 Concluded

Osage Corporation

(b) and (c) Continued

Interest Period	(A) Interest to Be Paid (in Cash) (7% x $600,000)	(B) Interest Expense to Be Recorded [(E) x .08]	(C) Discount Amortization (A) - (B)	(D) Unamortized Discount (D) - (C)	(E) Carrying Value of the Bonds [$600,000 - (D)]
Issue date					
1					
2					
3					
4					

*E10-21

	Date	Account Titles	Debit	Credit	
1	(a)	2010			1
2	Jan 1				2
3					3
4					4
5					5
6	(b)				6
7	Dec 31				7
8					8
9					9
10					10
11	(c)	2011			11
12	Jan 1				12
13					13
14					14
15					15
16	See next page for supporting calculat ons.				16

*E10-22

	Date	Account Titles	Debit	Credit	
1	2010	Issuance of note			1
2	Dec 31				2
3					3
4					4
5	2011	First Installment Payment			5
6	June 30				6
7					7
8					8
9					9
10		Second Installment Payment			10
11	Dec 31				11
12					12
13					13
14					14
15					15
16	See next page for installment payment schedule.				16
17					17
18					18
19					19

*E10-21

(b) Continued

Interest Period	(A) Interest to Be Paid (in Cash) (7% x $450,000)	(B) Interest Expense to Be Recorded [(E) x .06]	(C) Discount Amortization (B) - (A)	(D) Unamortized Discount (D) - (C)	(E) Carrying Value of the Bonds [$450,000 + (D)]	
Issue date						
1						1
2						2
3						3
4						4

*E10-22

Semiannual Interest Period	(A) Cash Payment	(B) Interest Expense (D x 4%)	(C) Reduction of Principal (A) - (B)	(D) Principal Balance (D) - (C)
Issue date				
6/30/11				
12/31/11				

Date	Account Titles	Debit	Credit
(a)			
Jan 1			
5			
12			
14			
20			
(b)			
Jan 31			
31			
31			

(c)

GLENNON COMPANY				
Balance Sheet (Partial)				
January 31, 2010				
Current liabilities:				

(a)

	Date	Account Titles	Debit	Credit	
1	Sept 1				1
2					2
3					3
4	30				4
5					5
6					6
7	Oct 1				7
8					8
9					9
10	31				10
11					11
12					12
13	Nov 1				13
14					14
15					15
16					16
17	30				17
18					18
19					19
20	Dec 1				20
21					21
22					22
23					23
24	31				24
25					25
26					26
27					27
28					28
29					29
30					30

(c)

MCCULLOUGH CORPORATION

Balance Sheet (Partial)

December 31, 2010

1	Current liabilities:		1
2			2
3			3
4			4
5			5

(b)

NOTES PAYABLE

INTEREST PAYABLE

INTEREST EXPENSE

(d)

	Date	Account Titles	Debit	Credit	
1	(a)				1
2	Jan 1				2
3					3
4					4
5					5
6	(b)				6
7	Jan 1				7
8					8
9					9
10					10
11					11
12	(c)				12
13	Dec 31				13
14					14
15					15
16					16
17					17
18					18
19					19
20					20
21					21
22					22
23					23
24					24
25					25
26					26
27					27
28					28
29					29
30					30

	Date	Account Titles	Debit	Credit	
1	(a)				1
2	2009				2
3	Oct 1				3
4					4
5					5
6	(b)				6
7	Dec 31				7
8					8
9					9
10					10
11	(d)				11
12	2010				12
13	Oct 1				13
14					14
15					15
16					16
17	(e)				17
18	Dec 31				18
19					19
20					20
21	(f)				21
22	2011				22
23	Jan 1				23
24					24
25					25
26	1				26
27					27
28					28
29					29
30					30

(c)

	HAVENHILL CORP. Balance Sheet (Partial) December 31, 2009		
1	Current liabilities:		1
2			2
3			3
4	Long-term liabilities:		4
5			5

	Date	Account Titles	Debit	Credit	
1	(a)	2010			1
2	Jan 1				2
3					3
4					4
5					5
6					6
7	(c)	2011			7
8	Dec 31				8
9					9
10					10
11					11
12					12
13					13
14					14
15					15

(b)

PETTIGREW COMPANY
Balance Sheet (Partial)
December 31, 2010

1	Long-term liabilities:			1
2				2
3				3
4				4
5				5

(a) (dollars in millions)

	2006	2005
1. Current ratio:		
2. Free cash flow:		
3. Debt to total assets ratio:		
4. Times interest earned ratio:		

(b)

(c)

General Journal

	Date	Account Titles	Debit	Credit	
1	(a)	2010			1
2	Jan 1				2
3					3
4					4
5					5
6	(b)				6
7	Dec 31				7
8					8
9					9
10					10
11	(c)	2011			11
12	Jan 1				12
13					13
14					14
15					15
16					16
17	(d)				17
18	Dec 31				18
19					19
20					20
21					21
22					22
23					23
24					24
25					25
26					26
27					27
28					28
29					29
30					30

	Date	Account Titles	Debit	Credit	
1	(a)				1
2	Jan 1				2
3					3
4					4
5					5
6	Dec 31				6
7					7
8					8
9					9
10	(b)				10
11	Jan 1				11
12					12
13					13
14					14
15	Dec 31				15
16					16
17					17
18					18

(c)

LORE CORPORATION

Balance Sheet (Partial)

December 31, 2010

1	(1) Premium:			1
2				2
3				3
4				4
5				5
6				6
7				7
8				8
9	(2) Discount:			9
10				10
11				11
12				12
13				13
14				14
15				15
16				16
17				17

(a) & (c)

	Date	Account Titles	Debit	Credit	
1	(a)				1
2	(1)				2
3	1/1/10				3
4					4
5					5
6					6
7	(2)				7
8	1/1/10				8
9					9
10					10
11					11
12	(b)	See amortization table on following page			12
13					13
14	(c)				14
15	(1)				15
16	12/31/10				16
17					17
18					18
19					19
20	(2)				20
21	12/31/10				21
22					22
23					23
24					24
25					25
26					26
27					27
28					28
29					29
30					30

(b)

(1)

Annual Interest Periods	(A) Interest to Be Paid (in Cash) (9% x $3,000,000)	(B) Interest Expense to Be Recorded (A) - (C)	(C) Premium Amortization ($30,000 /5)	(D) Unamortized Premium (D) - (C)	(E) Carrying Value of the Bonds [$3,000,000 + (D)]
Issue date					
1					
2					
3					

(2)

Annual Interest Periods	(A) Interest to Be Paid (in Cash) (9% x $3,000,000)	(B) Interest Expense to Be Recorded (A) + (C)	(C) Discount Amortization ($90,000 /5)	(D) Unamortized Discount (D) - (C)	(E) Carrying Value of the Bonds [$3,000,000 - (D)]
Issue date					
1					
2					
3					

(d)

KINZIE CO.		
Balance Sheet (Partial)		
December 31, 2010		
(1) Long-term liabilities:		
(2) Long-term liabilities:		

	Date	Account Titles	Debit	Credit	
1	(a)	2010			1
2	Jan 1				2
3					3
4					4
5					5
6	(b)	See next page for amortization table			6
7					7
8	(c)				8
9	Dec 31				9
10					10
11					11
12					12
13	(d)	2011			13
14	Jan 1				14
15					15
16					16
17	(e)				17
18	Dec 31				18
19					19
20					20
21					21
22					22
23					23
24					24
25					25
26					26
27					27
28					28
29					29
30					30
31					31
32					32
33					33
34					34
35					35

(b)

IRIK CORPORATION
Bond Discount Amortization
Effective-Interest Method - Annual Interest Payments
7% Bonds Issued at 8%

Annual Interest Periods	(A) Interest to Be Paid (in Cash)	(B) Interest Expense to Be Recorded	(C) Discount Amortization (B) - (A)	(D) Unamortized Discount (D) - (C)	(E) Carrying Value of the Bonds ($1,800,000 - D)
Issue date					
1					
2					
3					

(a)

	Date	Account Titles	Debit	Credit	
1	(1)	2010			1
2	Jan 1				2
3					3
4					4
5					5
6	(2)				6
7	Dec 31				7
8					8
9					9
10					10
11	(3)	2011			11
12	Jan 1				12
13					13
14					14
15	(4)				15
16	Dec 31				16
17					17
18					18

(b)

	FAIR COMPANY Balance Sheet (Partial) December 31, 2011			
1	Long-term liabilities:			1
2				2
3				3
4				4

(c)

1	(1)	1
2		2
3		3
4	(2)	4
5		5
6		6
7		7
8		8

(a)

	Quarterly Interest Period	(A) Cash Payment	(B) Interest Expense (D) x 2%	(C) Reduction of Principal (A) - (B)	(D) Principal Balance (D) - (C)	
1	Issue Date					1
2	1					2
3	2					3
4	3					4
5	4					5
6	5					6
7						7

(b)   General Journal

	Date	Account Titles	Debit	Credit	
1	2010				1
2	Dec 31				2
3					3
4					4
5					5

(c)

	DAMBRO Balance Sheet (Partial) December 31, 2010			
1	Current liabilities:			1
2				2
3				3
4				4
5				5
6	Long-term liabilities:			6
7				7
8				8
9				9
10				10

(a)

	Period	Cash Payment (A)	Interest Expense (B) = (D) x 7%	Principal Reduction (C) = (A) - (B)	Balance (D) = (D) - (C)	
1	Jul 1, '09					1
2	Jun 30, '10					2
3	Jun 30, '11					3
4	Jun 30, '12					4
5	Jun 30, '13					5
6	Jun 30, '14					6
7	Total					7
8						8

(b)

	Date	Account Titles	Debit	Credit	
1	2009				1
2	July 1				2
3					3
4					4
5	2010				5
6	June 30				6
7					7
8					8
9					9
10	2011				10
11	June 30				11
12					12
13					13
14					14
15					15

(c)

STACY BUTTON

Balance Sheet (Partial)

June 30, 2011

1	Current liabilities:	1
2		2
3		3
4		4
5	Long-term liabilities:	5
6		6
7		7

	Date	Account Titles	Debit	Credit	
1	(a)				1
2	Jan 1				2
3					3
4					4
5	5				5
6					6
7					7
8					8
9	12				9
10					10
11					11
12	14				12
13					13
14					14
15	20				15
16					16
17					17
18					18
19	(b)				19
20	Jan 31				20
21					21
22					22
23	31				23
24					24
25					25
26					26
27					27
28					28
29	31				29
30					30
31					31
32					32
33					33
34					34
35					35
36					36
37					37

(c)

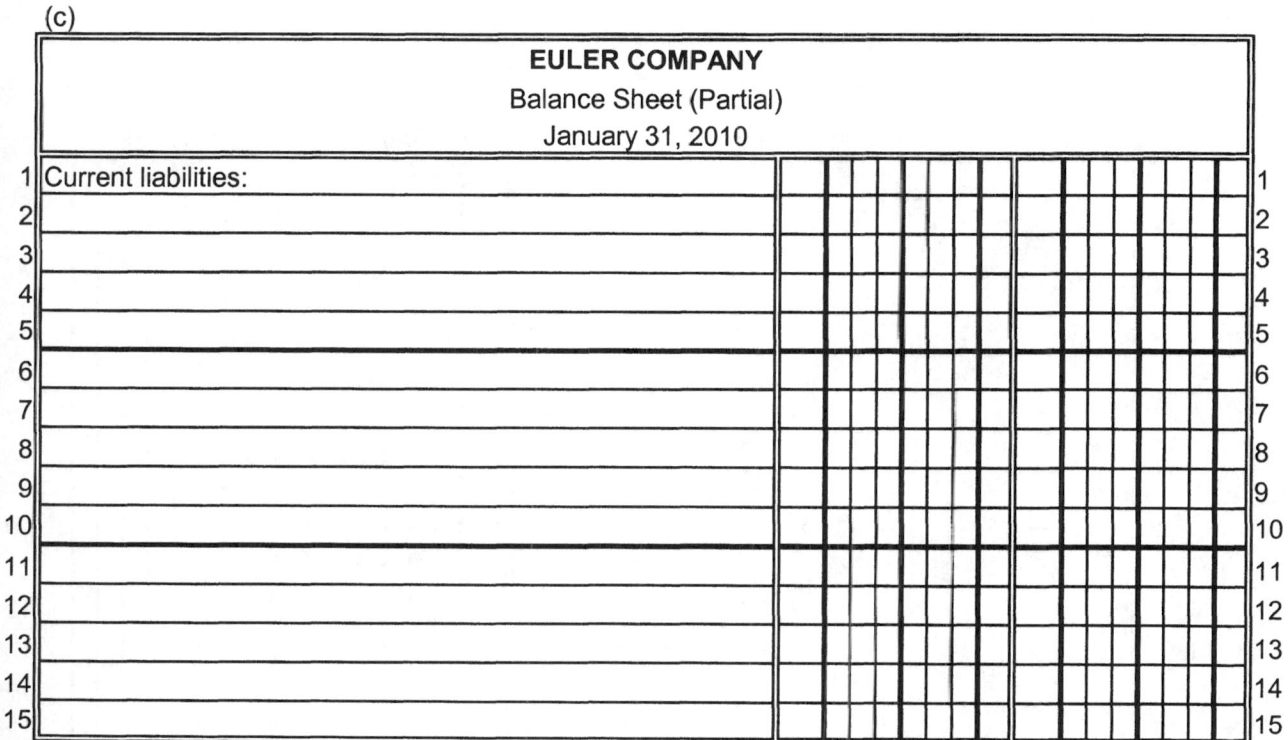

EULER COMPANY
Balance Sheet (Partial)
January 31, 2010

Current liabilities:		

(a)

	Date	Account Titles	Debit	Credit	
1	Mar 1				1
2					2
3					3
4	31				4
5					5
6					6
7	Apr 1				7
8					8
9					9
10	30				10
11					11
12					12
13	May 1				13
14					14
15					15
16	31				16
17					17
18					18
19	June 1				19
20					20
21					21
22					22
23	30				23
24					24
25					25

(c)

ROCKIE MOUNTAIN BIKES

Balance Sheet (Partial)

June 30, 2010

1	Current liabilities:	1
2		2
5		5

(d)

(b)

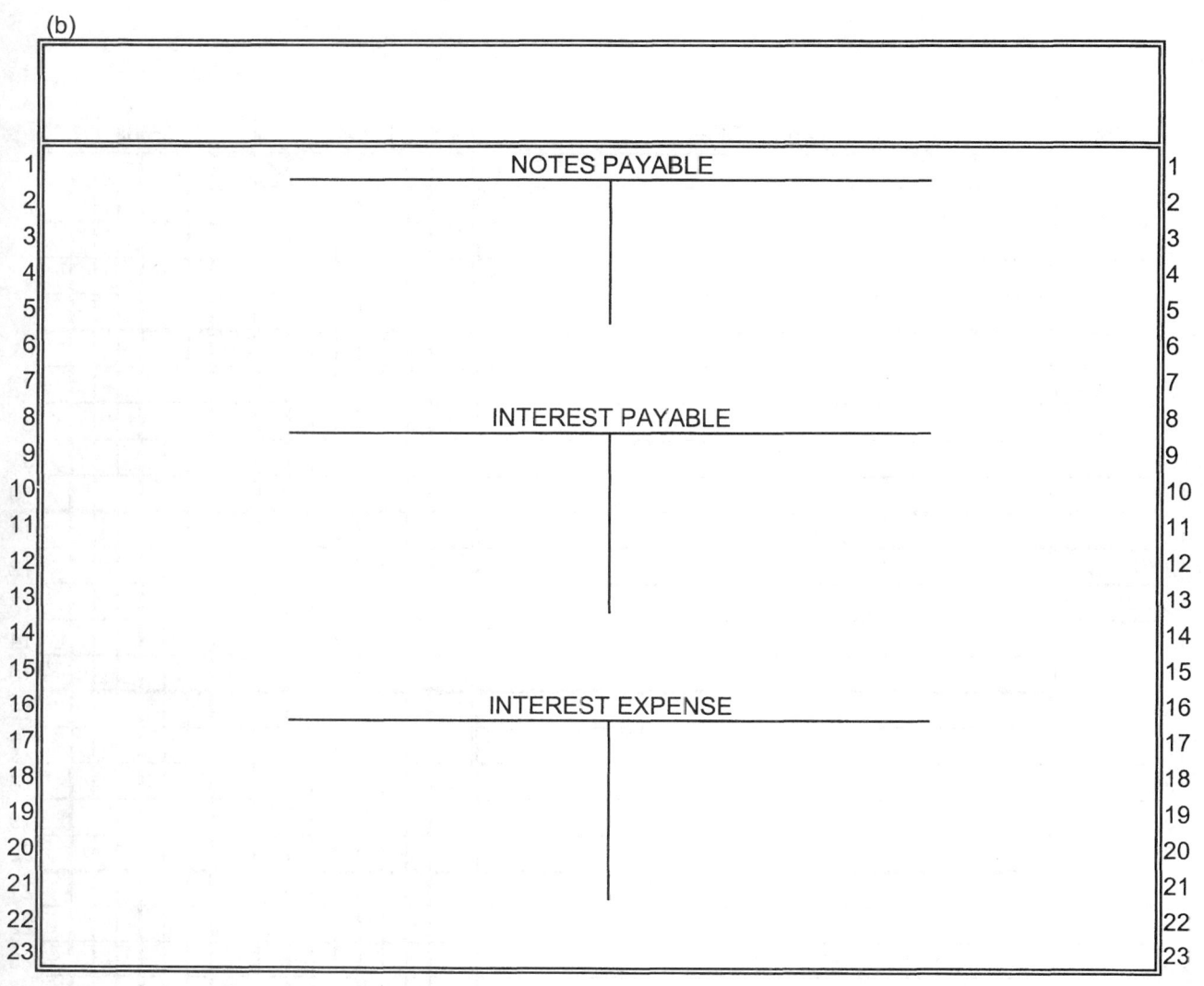

NOTES PAYABLE

INTEREST PAYABLE

INTEREST EXPENSE

	Date	Account Titles	Debit	Credit	
1	(a)				1
2	Jan 1				2
3					3
4					4
5					5
6	(b)				6
7	Jan 1				7
8					8
9					9
10					10
11					11
12	(c)				12
13	Dec 31				13
14					14
15					15
16					16
17					17
18					18
19					19
20					20
21					21
22					22
23					23
24					24
25					25
26					26
27					27
28					28
29					29
30					30

	Date	Account Titles	Debit	Credit	
1	(a)				1
2	2009				2
3	Apr 1				3
4					4
5					5
6	(b)				6
7	Dec 31				7
8					8
9					9
10					10
11	(d)				11
12	2010				12
13	Apr 1				13
14					14
15					15
16					16
17	(e)				17
18	Dec 31				18
19					19
20					20
21	(f)				21
22	2011				22
23	Jan 1				23
24					24
25					25
26	1				26
27					27
28					28
29					29

(c)

	LRF CORP. Balance Sheet (Partial) December 31, 2009			
1	Current liabilities:			1
2				2
3				3
4	Long-term liabilities:			4
5				5
6				6

	Date	Account Titles	Debit	Credit	
1	(a)	2010			1
2	Jan 1				2
3					3
4					4
5					5
6					6
7	(c)	2011			7
8	Dec 31				8
9					9
10					10
11					11
12					12
13					13
14					14
15					15

(b)

	STAR ELECTRIC		
	Balance Sheet (Partial)		
	December 31, 2010		
1	Long-term liabilities:			1
2				2
3				3
4				4
5				5

(a)

	2007	2006	
1. Current ratio:			
2. Free cash flow:			
3. Debt to total assets ratio:			
4. Times interest earned ratio:			

(b)

(c)

	Date	Account Titles	Debit	Credit	
1	(a)	2010			1
2	Jan 1				2
3					3
4					4
5					5
6	(b)				6
7	Dec 31				7
8					8
9					9
10					10
11	(c)	2011			11
12	Jan 1				12
13					13
14					14
15					15
16					16
17	(d)				17
18	Dec 31				18
19					19
20					20
21					21
22					22
23					23
24					24
25					25
26					26
27					27
28					28
29					29
30					30

	Date	Account Titles	Debit	Credit	
1	(a)	2010			1
2	Jan 1				2
3					3
4					4
5					5
6	Dec 31				6
7					7
8					8
9					9
10	(b)	2010			10
11	Jan 1				11
12					12
13					13
14					14
15	Dec 31				15
16					16
17					17
18					18

(c)

	LESTER COMPANY Balance Sheet (Partial) December 31, 2010			
1	(1) Premium:			1
2				2
3				3
4				4
5				5
6				6
7				7
8				8
9	(2) Discount:			9
10				10
11				11
12				12
13				13
14				14
15				15
16				16
17				17

(a) & (c)

	Date	Account Titles	Debit	Credit	
1	(a)				1
2	(1)				2
3	12/31/09				3
4					4
5					5
6					6
7	(2)				7
8	12/31/09				8
9					9
10					10
11					11
12	(b)	See amortization table on following page			12
13					13
14	(c)				14
15	(1)				15
16	12/31/10				16
17					17
18					18
19					19
20	12/31/11				20
21					21
22					22
23					23
24	(2)				24
25	12/31/10				25
26					26
27					27
28					28
29	12/31/11				29
30					30
31					31
32					32
33					33
34					34
35					35

(b)

(1)

Annual Interest Periods	(A) Interest to Be Paid (in Cash) (7% × $2,500,000)	(B) Interest Expense to Be Recorded (A) + (C)	(C) Discount Amortization ($50,000 /20)	(D) Unamortized Premium (D) - (C)	(E) Carrying Value of the Bonds [$2,500,000 - (D)]
Issue date					
1					
2					
3					

(2)

Annual Interest Periods	(A) Interest to Be Paid (in Cash) (7% × $2,500,000)	(B) Interest Expense to Be Recorded (A) - (C)	(C) Discount Amortization ($100,000/20)	(D) Unamortized Discount (D) - (C)	(E) Carrying Value of the Bonds [$2,500,000 + (D)]
Issue date					
1					
2					
3					

(d)

WYLIE CORPORATION Balance Sheet (Partial) December 31, 2010				
(1) Long-term liabilities:				
(2) Long-term liabilities:				

	Date	Account Titles	Debit	Credit	
1	(a)	2010			1
2	Jan 1				2
3					3
4					4
5					5
6	(b)	See next page for amortization table			6
7					7
8	(c)				8
9	Dec 31				9
10					10
11					11
12					12
13	(d)	2011			13
14	Jan 1				14
15					15
16					16
17	(e)				17
18	Dec 31				18
19					19
20					20
21					21
22					22
23					23
24					24
25					25
26					26
27					27
28					28
29					29
30					30
31					31
32					32
33					33
34					34
35					35

(b)

VINEYARD CORPORATION
Bond Premium Amortization
Effective-Interest Method - Annual Interest Payments
12% Bonds Issued at 10%

Annual Interest Periods	(A) Interest to Be Paid (in Cash)	(B) Interest Expense to Be Recorded	(C) Premium Amortization (A) - (B)	(D) Unamortized Discount (D) - (C)	(E) Carrying Value of the Bonds ($2,0o00,000 + D)
Issue date					
1					
2					
3					

(a)

	Date	Account Titles	Debit	Credit	
1	(1)	2010			1
2	Jan 1				2
3					3
4					4
5					5
6	(2)				6
7	Dec 31				7
8					8
9					9
10					10
11	(3)	2011			11
12	Jan 1				12
13					13
14					14
15	(4)				15
16	Dec 31				16
17					17
18					18
19					19

(b)

JAGARD COMPANY		
Balance Sheet (Partial)		
December 31, 2011		
1 Long-term liabilities:			1
2			2
3			3
4			4
5			5

(c)

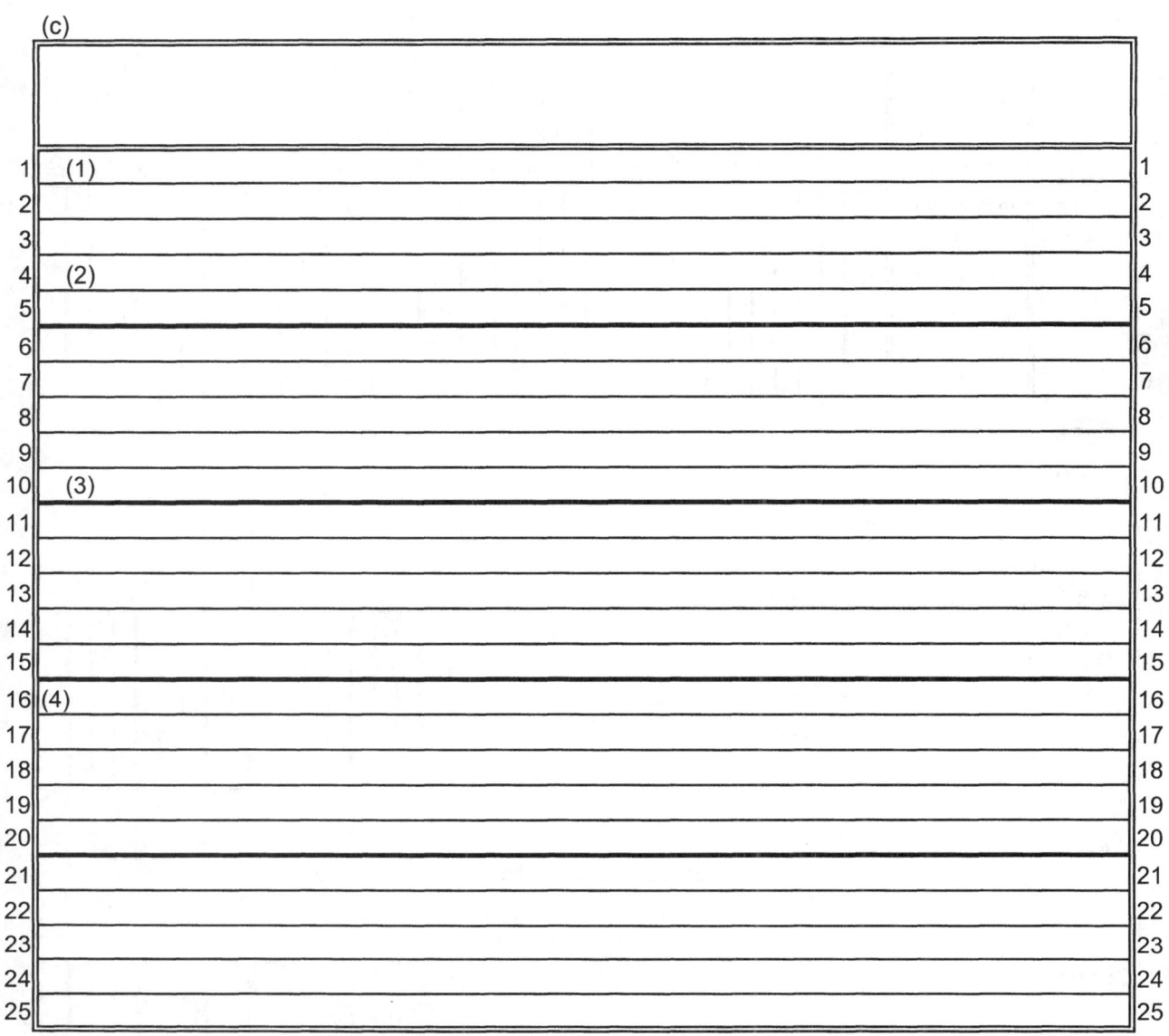

1	(1)
2	
3	
4	(2)
5	
6	
7	
8	
9	
10	(3)
11	
12	
13	
14	
15	
16	(4)
17	
18	
19	
20	
21	
22	
23	
24	
25	

(a)

	Quarterly Interest Period	(A) Cash Payment	(B) Interest Expense (D) x 2%	(C) Reduction of Principal (A) - (B)	(D) Principal Balance (D) - (C)	
1	Issue Date					1
2	1					2
3	2					3
4	3					4
5	4					5
6	5					6
7						7

(b)

	Date	Account Titles	Debit	Credit	
1	2010				1
2	Dec 31				2
3					3
4					4
5					5

(c)

DONALD CORPORATION
Balance Sheet (Partial)
December 31, 2010

1	Current liabilities:		1
2			2
3			3
4			4
5			5
6	Long-term liabilities:		6
7			7
8			8
9			9
10			10

(a)

	Period	Cash Payment (A)	Interest Expense (B) = (D) x 2%	Principal Reduction (C) = (A) - (B)	Balance (D) = (D) - (C)	
1	May 1, '10					1
2	May 31, '10					2
3	Jun 30, '10					3
4	Jul 31, '10					4
5	Aug 31, '10					5
6	Total					6
7						7
8						8

(b)

	Date	Account Titles	Debit	Credit	
1	2010				1
2	May 1				2
3					3
4					4
5	31				5
6					6
7					7
8					8
9	June 30				9
10					10
11					11
12					12
13	July 31				13
14					14
15					15
16					16

(a)

	Date	Account Titles	Debit	Credit	
1	1.				1
2					2
3					3
4	2.				4
5					5
6					6
7	3.				7
8					8
9					9
10					10
11					11
12					12
13					13
14	4.				14
15					15
16					16
17	5.				17
18					18
19					19
20	6.				20
21					21
22					22
23	7.				23
24					24
25					25
26	8.				26
27					27
28					28
29	9.				29
30					30
31					31
32	10.				32
33					33
34					34
35					35
36					36
37					37
38					38
39					39
40					40

	Date	Account Titles	Debit	Credit	
1	11.				1
2					2
3					3
4					4
5		Adjusting Entries			5
6	1.				6
7					7
8					8
9	2.				9
10					10
11					11
12	3.				12
13					13
14					14
15					15
16					16
17					17
18					18
19					19
20					20
21					21
22					22
23					23
24					24
25					25
26					26
27					27
28					28
29					29
30					30
31					31
32					32
33					33
34					34
35					35
36					36
37					37

(b)

ABER CORPORATION		
Trial Balance		
12/31/2010		
Account	Debit	Credit

(a) & (b) Optional T-accounts

	CASH		BOND INTEREST PAYABLE	
1				1
2	Bal. 30,500		Bal. 3,000	2
3				3
4				4
5				5
6		SALES TAX PAYABLE		6
7				7
8				8
9				9
10				10
11		INCOME TAX PAYABLE		11
12				12
13	MERCHANDISE INVENTORY			13
14	Bal. 25,750			14
15		BONDS PAYABLE		15
16			Bal. 50,000	16
17				17
18				18
19	PREPAID INSURANCE			19
20	Bal. 5,600			20
21		PREMIUM ON BONDS PAYABLE		21
22				22
23				23
24				24
25	EQUIPMENT	COMMON STOCK		25
26	Bal. 38,000		Bal. 20,000	26
27				27
28				28
29	ACCUMULATED DEPRECIATION	RETAINED EARNINGS		29
30			Bal. 13,100	30
31				31
32				32
33	ACCOUNTS PAYABLE	SALES		33
34	Bal. 13,750			34
35				35
36				36
37				37
38				38
39				39
40				40

(a) & (b) Optional T-accounts   (Continued)

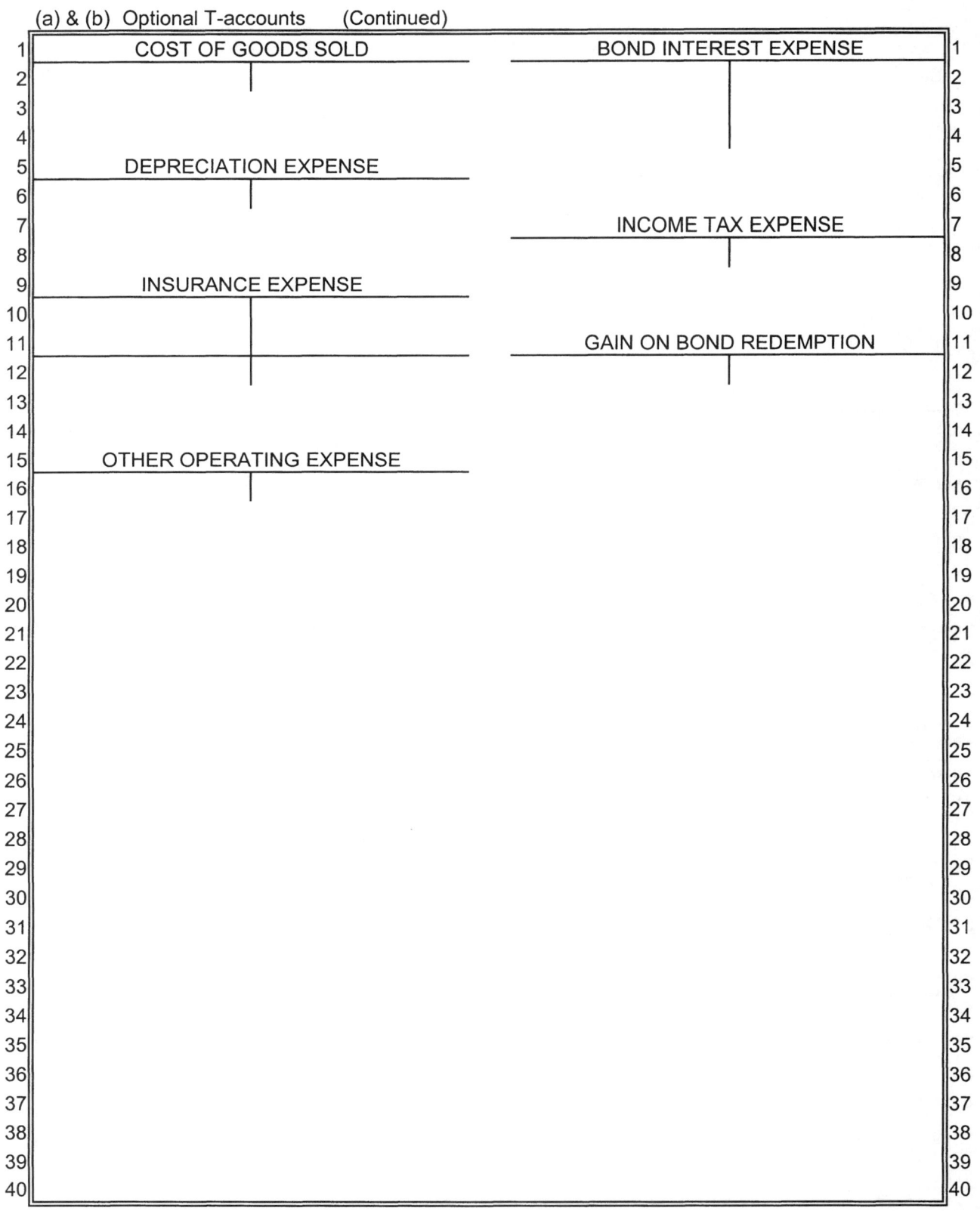

	COST OF GOODS SOLD	BOND INTEREST EXPENSE	
1			1
2			2
3			3
4			4
5	DEPRECIATION EXPENSE		5
6			6
7		INCOME TAX EXPENSE	7
8			8
9	INSURANCE EXPENSE		9
10			10
11		GAIN ON BOND REDEMPTION	11
12			12
13			13
14			14
15	OTHER OPERATING EXPENSE		15

(c)

ABER CORPORATION		
Income Statement		
For the Year Ending 12/31/10		

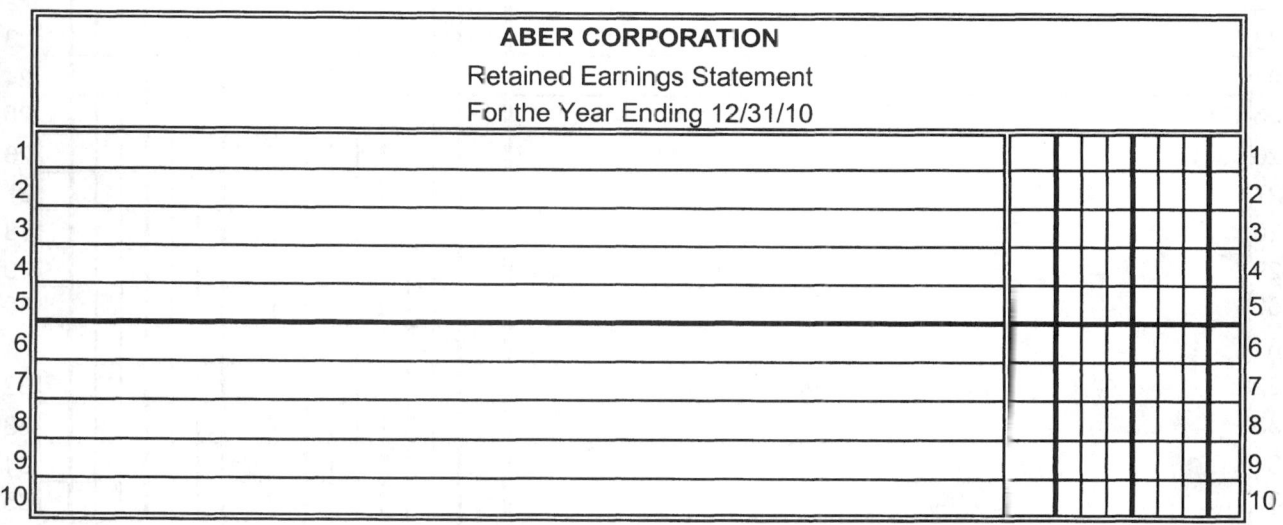

ABER CORPORATION	
Retained Earnings Statement	
For the Year Ending 12/31/10	

(c) (Continued)

ABER CORPORATION

Balance Sheet

12/31/2010

	Assets						
1	Assets						1
2							2
3							3
4							4
5							5
6							6
7							7
8							8
9							9
10							10
11							11
12							12
13							13
14							14
15	Liabilities and Stockholders' Equity						15
16							16
17							17
18							18
19							19
20							20
21							21
22							22
23							23
24							24
25							25
26							26
27							27
28							28
29							29
30							30
31							31
32							32
33							33
34							34
35							35
36							36
37							37

(a)

		Account Titles	Debit	Credit
1	1.			
2				
3				
4				
5				
6				
7	2.			
8				
9				
10				

(b)

	1		1
2			2
3			3
4			4
5			5
6			6
7			7
8			8
9			9
10			10
11			11
12			12
13			13
14			14
15			15
16			16
17			17
18			18
19			19
20			20
21			21
22			22
23			23
24			24
25			25
26			26
27			27
28			28
29			29
30			30
31			31
32			32
33			33
34			34
35			35
36			36
37			37
38			38
39			39
40			40

BE11-2

	Date	Account Titles	Debit	Credit	
1	May 10				1
2					2
3					3
4					4
5					5

BE11-3

	Date	Account Titles	Debit	Credit	
6					6
7	June 1				7
8					8
9					9
10					10

BE11-4

	Date	Account Titles	Debit	Credit	
11					11
12					12
13					13
14					14
15					15
16					16

BE11-5

	Date	Account Titles	Debit	Credit	
17					17
18	Nov. 1				18
19					19
20					20
21	Dec 31				21
22					22
23					23
24					24

BE11-6

			Before Dividend	After Dividend	
25					25
26					26
27					27
28	(a)				28
29					29
30					30
31					31
32					32
33					33
34					34
35					35
36	(b)				36
37					37
38					38
39					39
40					40

BE11-8

1						1
2						2
3						3
4						4
5						5
6						6
7						7
8						8
9						9
10						10
11						11
12						12
13						13
14						14
15						15
16						16
17						17
18						18
19						19
20						20
21						21

BE11-11

	Date	Account Titles	Debit	Credit	
23					23
24					24
25					25
26					26
27					27
28					28
29					29
30					30
31					31
32					32
33					33
34					34
35					35
36					36
37					37
38					38
39					39
40					40

DO IT! 11-2

	Date	Account Titles	Debit	Credit	
1	Apr 1				1
2					2
3					3
4					4

DO IT! 11-3

	Date	Account Titles	Debit	Credit	
5					5
6	Date	Account Titles	Debit	Credit	6
7	Aug 1				7
8					8
9					9

DO IT! 11-5

10				10
11	(a) 1. The stock dividend amount is:			11
12				12
13	The new balance in retained earnings is:			13
14				14
15				15
16	2. Retained earnings after the stock split is:			16
17				17

	(b)	Original Balance	After Dividend	After Split	
18					18
19					19
20					20
21					21
22					22
23					23
24					24
25					25
26					26
27					27
28					28
29					29
30					30
31					31
32					32
33					33
34					34
35					35
36					36
37					37
38					38
39					39
40					40

DO IT! 11-6

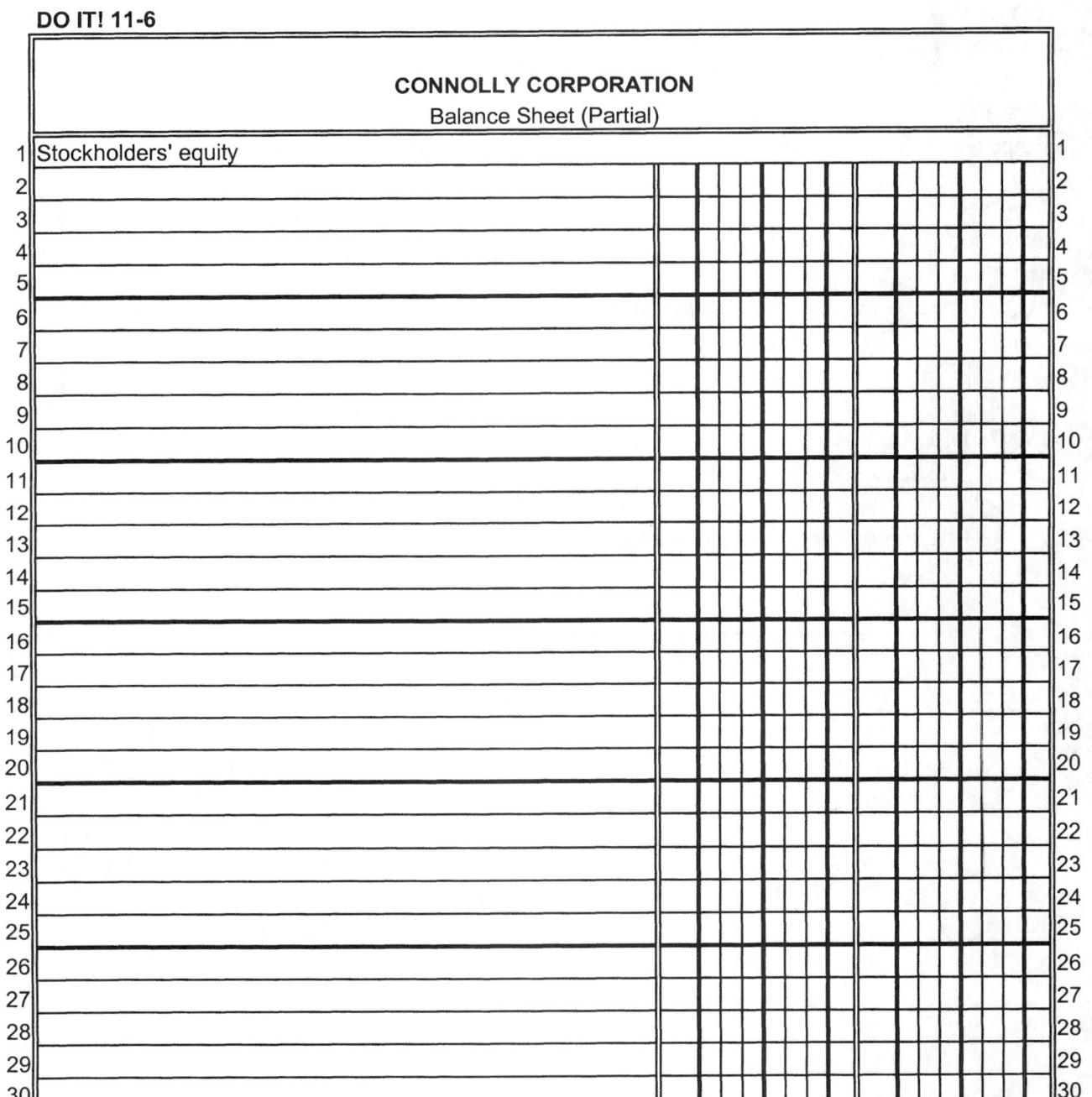

	CONNOLLY CORPORATION Balance Sheet (Partial)						
1	Stockholders' equity						1
2							2
3							3
4							4
5							5
6							6
7							7
8							8
9							9
10							10
11							11
12							12
13							13
14							14
15							15
16							16
17							17
18							18
19							19
20							20
21							21
22							22
23							23
24							24
25							25
26							26
27							27
28							28
29							29
30							30

E11-1

	Date	Account Titles	Debit	Credit	
1	(a)				1
2	Jan 10				2
3					3
4					4
5					5
6	July 1				6
7					7
8					8
9					9
10	(b)				10
11	Jan 10				11
12					12
13					13
14					14
15					15
16	July 1				16
17					17
18					18
19					19
20					20
21	**E11-2**				21
22	June 12				22
23					23
24					24
25					25
26	July 11				26
27					27
28					28
29					29
30					30
31	Nov 28				31
32					32
33					33
34					34
35					35
36					36
37					37
38					38
39					39
40					40

(a)

	Date	Account Titles	Debit	Credit	
1	Feb 1				1
2					2
3					3
4					4
5					5
6					6
7	July 1				7
8					8
9					9
10					10
11					11
12					12
13					13
14					14
15					15

(b)

PREFERRED STOCK

PAID-IN CAPITAL IN EXCESS OF PAR VALUE -
PREFERRED STOCK

(c)

	Date	Account Titles	Debit	Credit	
1	May 2				1
2					2
3					3
4					4
5					5
6					6
7	10				7
8					8
9					9
10					10
11					11
12					12
13	15				13
14					14
15					15
16					16
17					17
18					18
19					19
20					20

E11-6

	(a) Date	Account Titles	Debit	Credit	
1	June 15				1
2					2
3					3
4					4
5	July 10				5
6					6
7					7
8					8
9					9
10	Dec 15				10
11					11
12					12
13					13
14	(b)				14
15					15
16					16
17					17
18					18
19					19

	E11-7	Before Action	After Stock Dividend	After Stock Split	
20					20
21	Effect on total stockholders' equity and				21
22	No. of shares outstanding:				22
23					23
24					24
25					25
26					26
27					27
28					28
29					29
30					30
31					31
32					32
33					33
34					34
35					35

WELLS FARGO & COMPANY Balance Sheet (Partial) December 31, 2006 (in millions)		
1		
2		
3		
4		
5		
6		
7		
8		
9		
10		
11		
12		
13		
14		
15		
16		
17		
18		
19		
20		

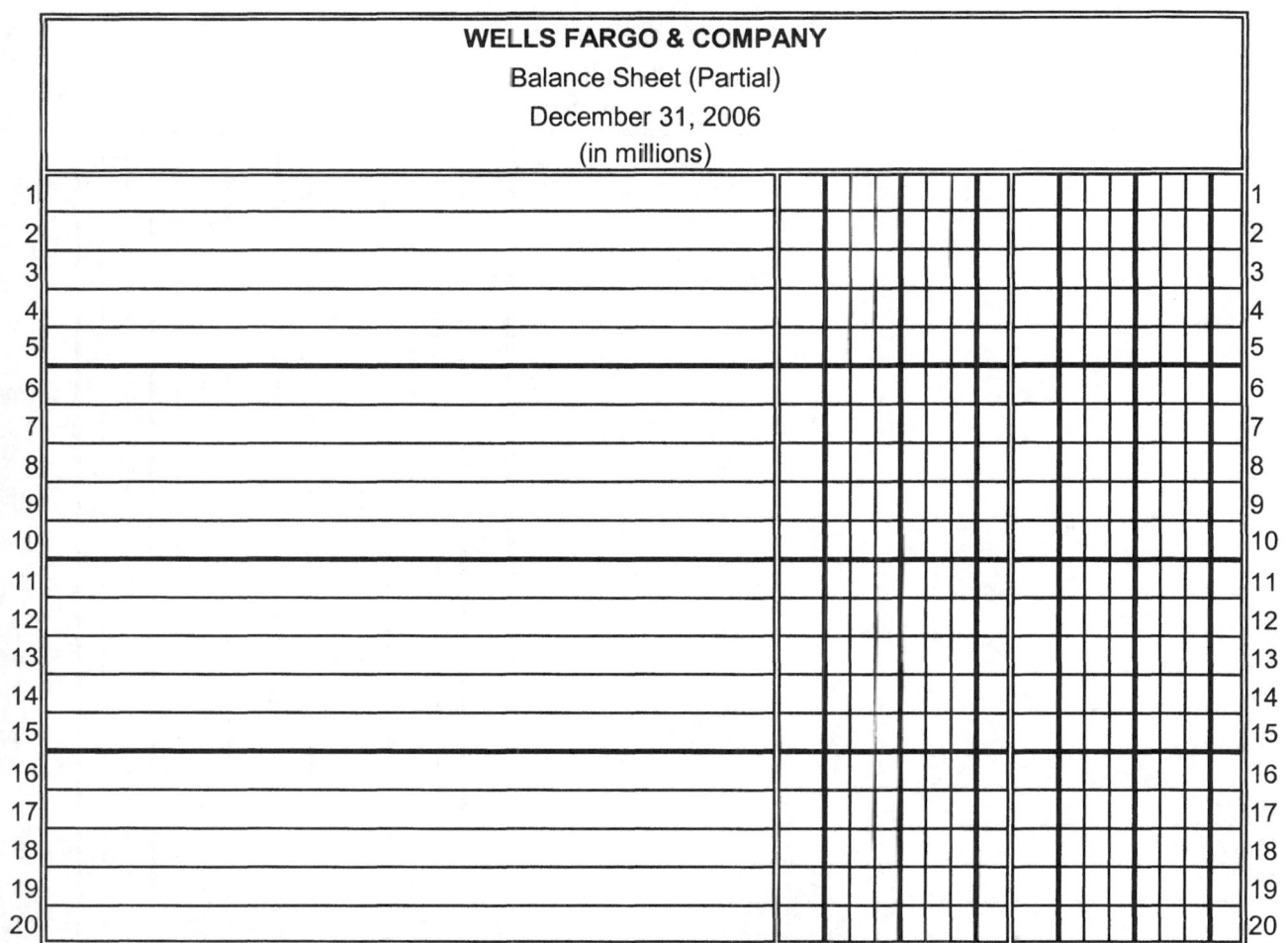

KENTON CORPORATION
Balance Sheet (Partial)
December 31, 2010

1				1
2				2
3				3
4				4
5				5
6				6
7				7
8				8
9				9
10				10
11				11
12				12
13				13
14				14
15				15
16				16
17				17
18				18
19				19
20				20
21				21
22				22
23				23
24				24
25				25
26				26
27				27
28				28
29				29
30				30
31				31
32				32
33				33
34				34
35				35
36				36
37				37
38				38
39				39
40				40

	ROSSWELL INC. Partial Balance Sheet December 31, 2010		
1			1
2			2
3			3
4			4
5			5
6			6
7			7
8			8
9			9
10			10
11			11
12			12
13			13
14			14
15			15
16			16
17			17
18			18
19			19
20			20
21			21
22			22
23			23
24			24
25			25
26			26
27			27
28			28
29			29
30			30
31			31
32			32
33			33
34			34
35			35
36			36
37			37
38			38
39			39
40			40

E11-14

	(a) Plan One Issue Stock	(b) Plan Two Issue Bonds
1		
2		
3		
4		
5		
6		
7		
8		
9		
10		

*E11-16

		Account Titles	Debit	Credit
1	(a)			
2				
3				
4				
5				
6				
7				
8	(b)			
9				
10				
11				
12				
13				
14				
15				

(a)		2009	2010
1			
2			
3			
4			
5			
6			
7			
8			

(b)			
Return on common stocholders' equity		2009	20 0

(c)			
Debt to asset ratio			

(d)

(a)

	Date	Account Titles	Debit	Credit	
1	Jan 10				1
2					2
3					3
4					4
5					5
6	Mar 1				6
7					7
8					8
9					9
10					10
11	May 1				11
12					12
13					13
14					14
15					15
16	Sept 1				16
17					17
18					18
19					19
20					20
21	Nov 1				21
22					22
23					23
24					24
25					25
26					26
27					27
28					28
29					29
30					30

(b)

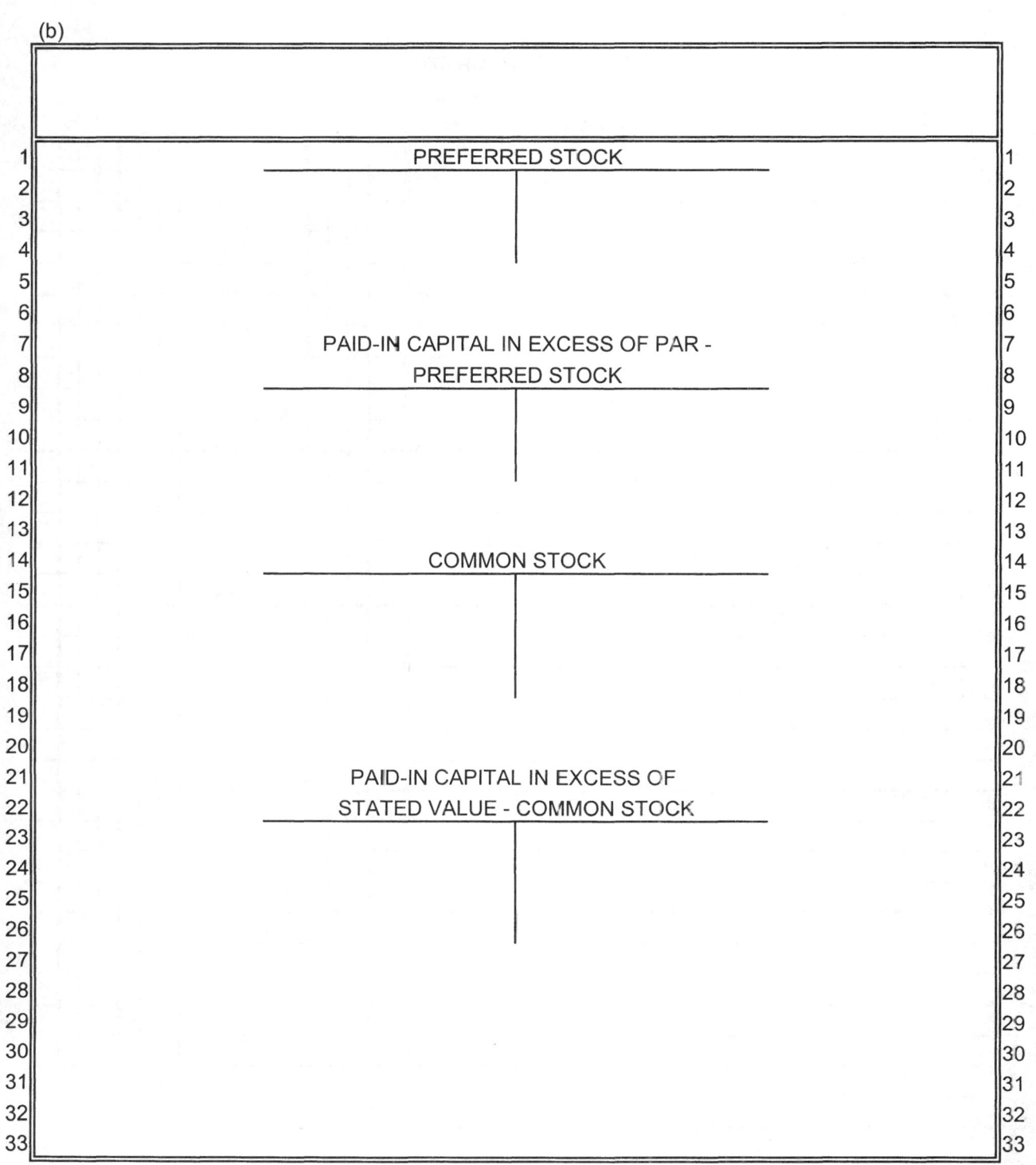

	PREFERRED STOCK	
1		1
2		2
3		3
4		4
5		5
6		6
7	PAID-IN CAPITAL IN EXCESS OF PAR -	7
8	PREFERRED STOCK	8
9		9
10		10
11		11
12		12
13		13
14	COMMON STOCK	14
15		15
16		16
17		17
18		18
19		19
20		20
21	PAID-IN CAPITAL IN EXCESS OF	21
22	STATED VALUE - COMMON STOCK	22
23		23
24		24
25		25
26		26
27		27
28		28
29		29
30		30
31		31
32		32
33		33

(c)

	PINSON CORPORATION								
	Partial Balance Sheet								
	December 31, 2010								

(a)

	Date	Account T tles	Debit	Credit	
1	Feb 1				1
2					2
3					3
4					4
5					5
6					6
7	Mar 20				7
8					8
9					9
10	Oct 1				10
11					11
12					12
13	Nov 1				13
14					14
15					15
16	Dec 1				16
17					17
18					18
19	Dec 31				19
20					20
21					21
22	31				22
23					23
24					24
25					25
26					26
27					27
28					28
29					29
30					30
31					31
32					32
33					33
34					34
35					35
36					36
37					37
38					38
39					39
40					40

(b)

PREFERRED STOCK

	1/1 Bal	300,000

PAID-IN CAPITAL IN EXCESS OF PAR VALUE - PREFERRED STOCK

	1/1 Bal	15,000

COMMON STOCK

	1/1 Bal	1,000,000

PAID-IN CAPITAL IN EXCESS OF STATED VALUE - COMMON STOCK

	1/1 Bal	480,000

RETAINED EARNINGS

	1/1 Bal	688,000

TREASURY STOCK - COMMON

1/1 Bal	40,000	

CASH DIVIDENDS

(c)

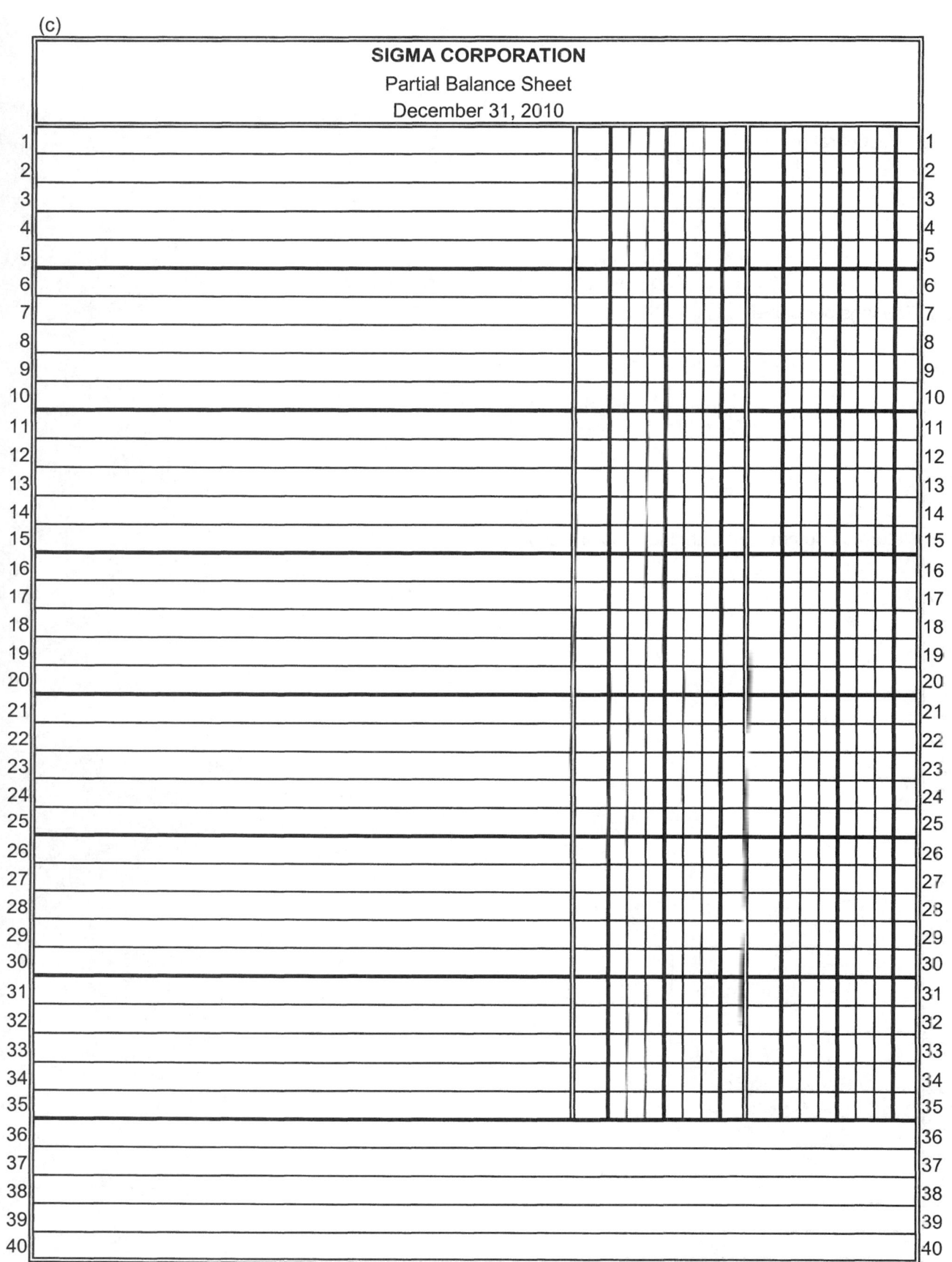

SIGMA CORPORATION
Partial Balance Sheet
December 31, 2010

(d)

1	Payout ratio:
2	
3	
4	
5	
6	
7	Earnings per share:
8	
9	
10	
11	
12	
13	
14	
15	Return on common stockholders' equity ratio:
16	
17	
18	
19	
20	
21	
22	
23	
24	
25	
26	
27	
28	
29	
30	
31	
32	
33	
34	
35	
36	
37	
38	
39	
40	

MILO COMPANY
Partial Balance Sheet
December 31, 2010

1								1
2								2
3								3
4								4
5								5
6								6
7								7
8								8
9								9
10								10
11								11
12								12
13								13
14								14
15								15
16								16
17								17
18								18
19								19
20								20
21								21
22								22
23								23
24								24
25								25
26								26
27								27
28								28
29								29
30								30
31								31
32								32
33								33
34								34
35								35
36								36
37								37
38								38
39								39
40								40

(a)

	Retained Earnings	
1		1
2		2
3		3
4		4
5		5
7		7

(b)

GAMMA CORPORATION
Partial Balance Sheet
December 31, 2010

1		1
2		2
3		3
4		4
5		5
6		6
7		7
8		8
9		9
10		10
11		11
12		12
13		13
14		14
15		15
16		16
17		17
18		18
19		19
20		20
21		21
22		22
23		23
24		24
25		25
26		26
27		27
28		28
29		29

(a)

	Date	Account Titles	Debit	Credit	
1	(1)				1
2					2
3					3
4					4
5					5
6					6
7	(2)				7
8					8
9					9
10					10
11					11
12					12
13	(3)				13
14					14
15					15
16					16
17					17
18					18
19					19
20					20
21					21
22					22
23					23
24					24
25					25
26					26
27					27
28					28
29					29
30					30
31					31
32					32
33					33
34					34
35					35
36					36
37					37
38					38
39					39
40					40

(b)

BODLEY CORPORATION		
Partial Balance Sheet		
December 31, 2010		

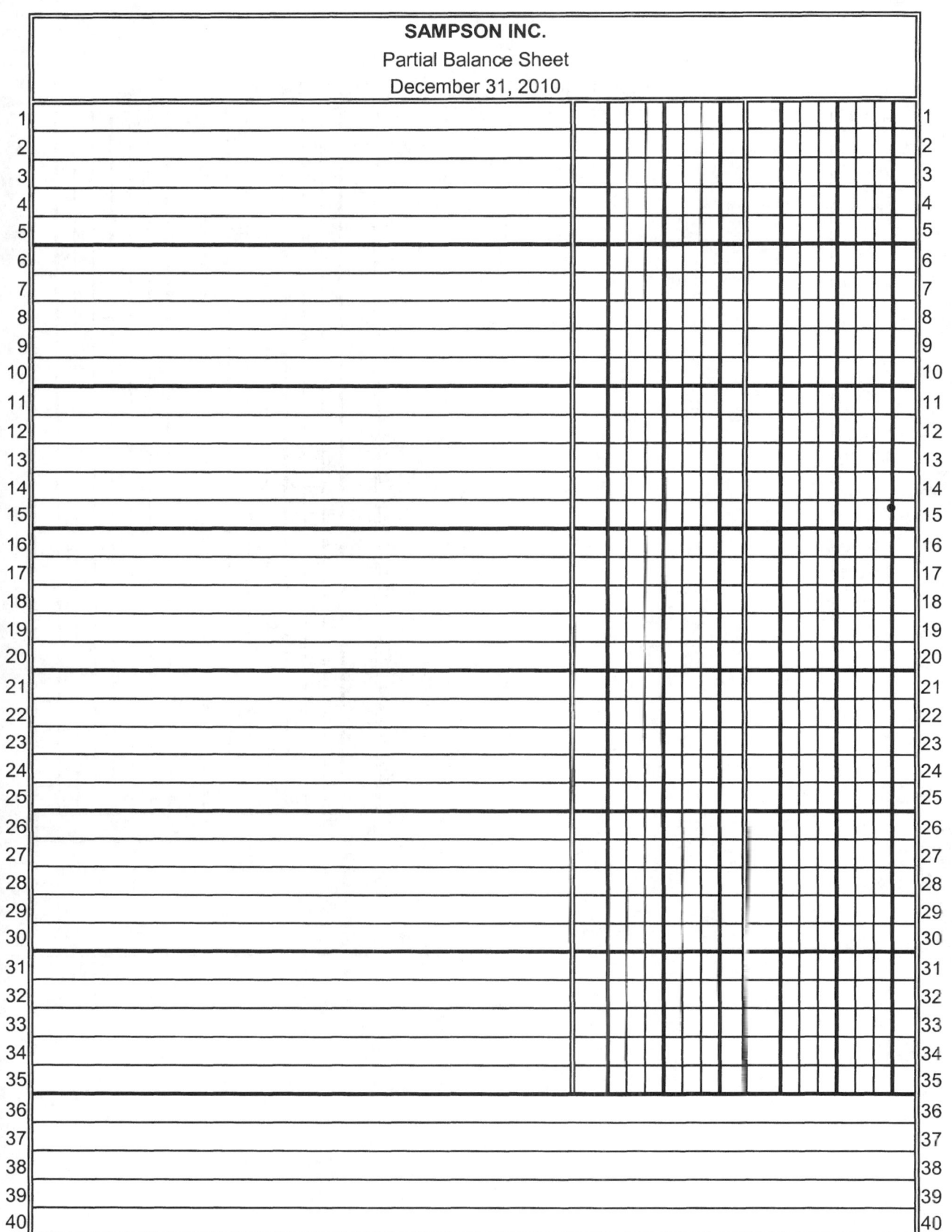

SAMPSON INC.
Partial Balance Sheet
December 31, 2010

(a)

	Date	Account Titles	Debit	Credit	
1	Jan 15				1
2					2
3					3
4	Feb 15				4
5					5
6					6
7	Apr 15				7
8					8
9					9
10					10
11					11
12					12
13	May 15				13
14					14
15					15
16					16
17	Dec 1				17
18					18
19					19
20	31				20
21					21
22					22
23					23
24					24
25					25
26					26
27					27
28					28
29					29
30					30

(b)

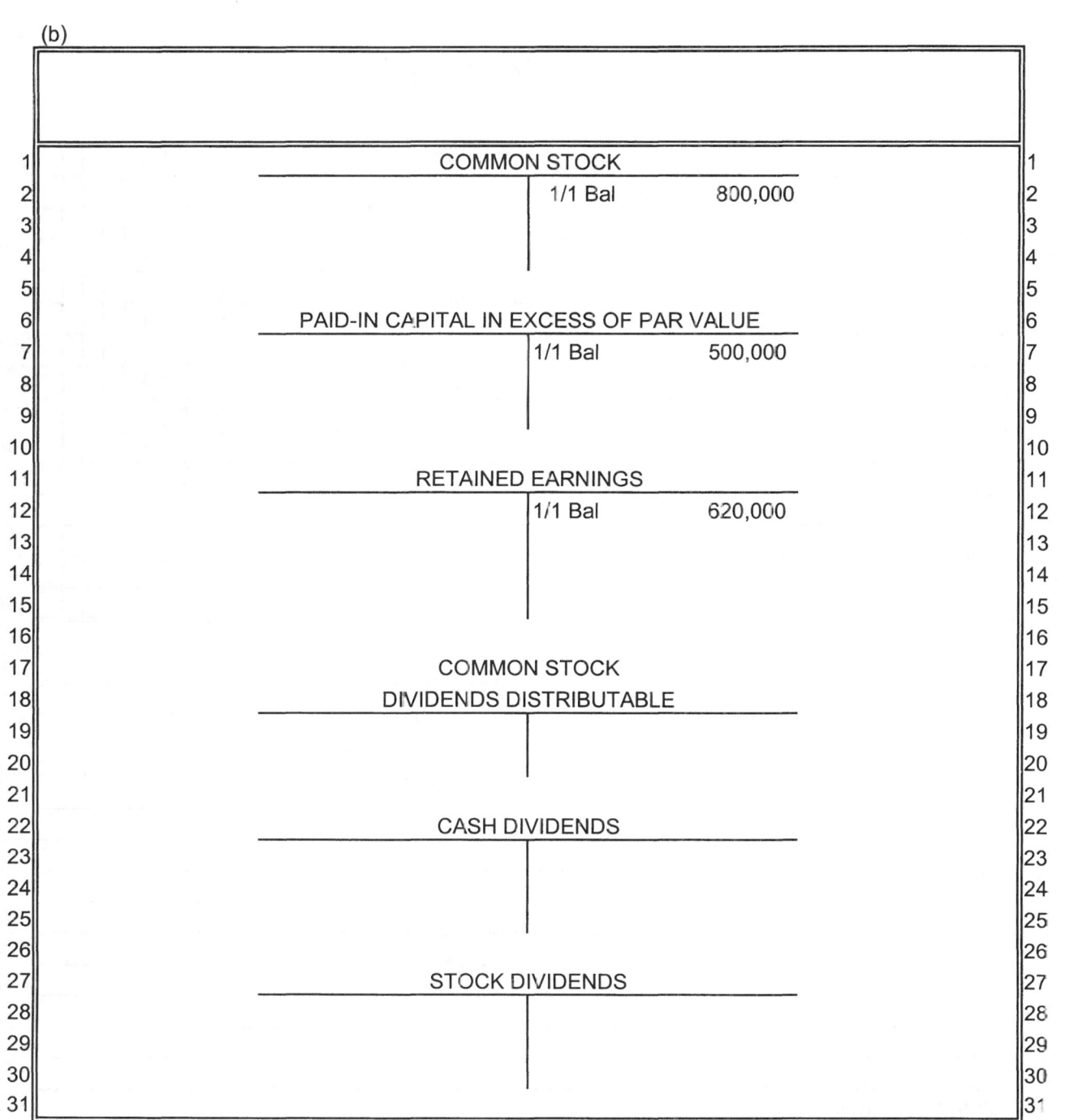

COMMON STOCK	
	1/1 Bal 800,000
PAID-IN CAPITAL IN EXCESS OF PAR VALUE	
	1/1 Bal 500,000
RETAINED EARNINGS	
	1/1 Bal 620,000
COMMON STOCK DIVIDENDS DISTRIBUTABLE	
CASH DIVIDENDS	
STOCK DIVIDENDS	

(c)

WERTH CORPORATION		
Partial Balance Sheet		
December 31, 2010		
1		
2		
3		
4		
5		
6		
7		
8		
9		
10		
11		
12		
13		
14		
15		

(d)

1 Payout ratio:	
2	
3	
4	
5	
6	
7	
8	
9	
10	
11 Return on common	
12 stockholders' equity ratio:	
13	
14	
15	
16	
17	
18	
19	
20	

(a)

	Date	Account Titles	Debit	Credit	
1	Jan 10				1
2					2
3					3
4					4
5					5
6	Mar 1				6
7					7
8					8
9					9
10					10
11	May 1				11
12					12
13					13
14					14
15					15
16					16
17	Sept 1				17
18					18
19					19
20					20
21					21
22					22
23	Nov 1				23
24					24
25					25
26					26
27					27
28					28
29					29
30					30

(b)

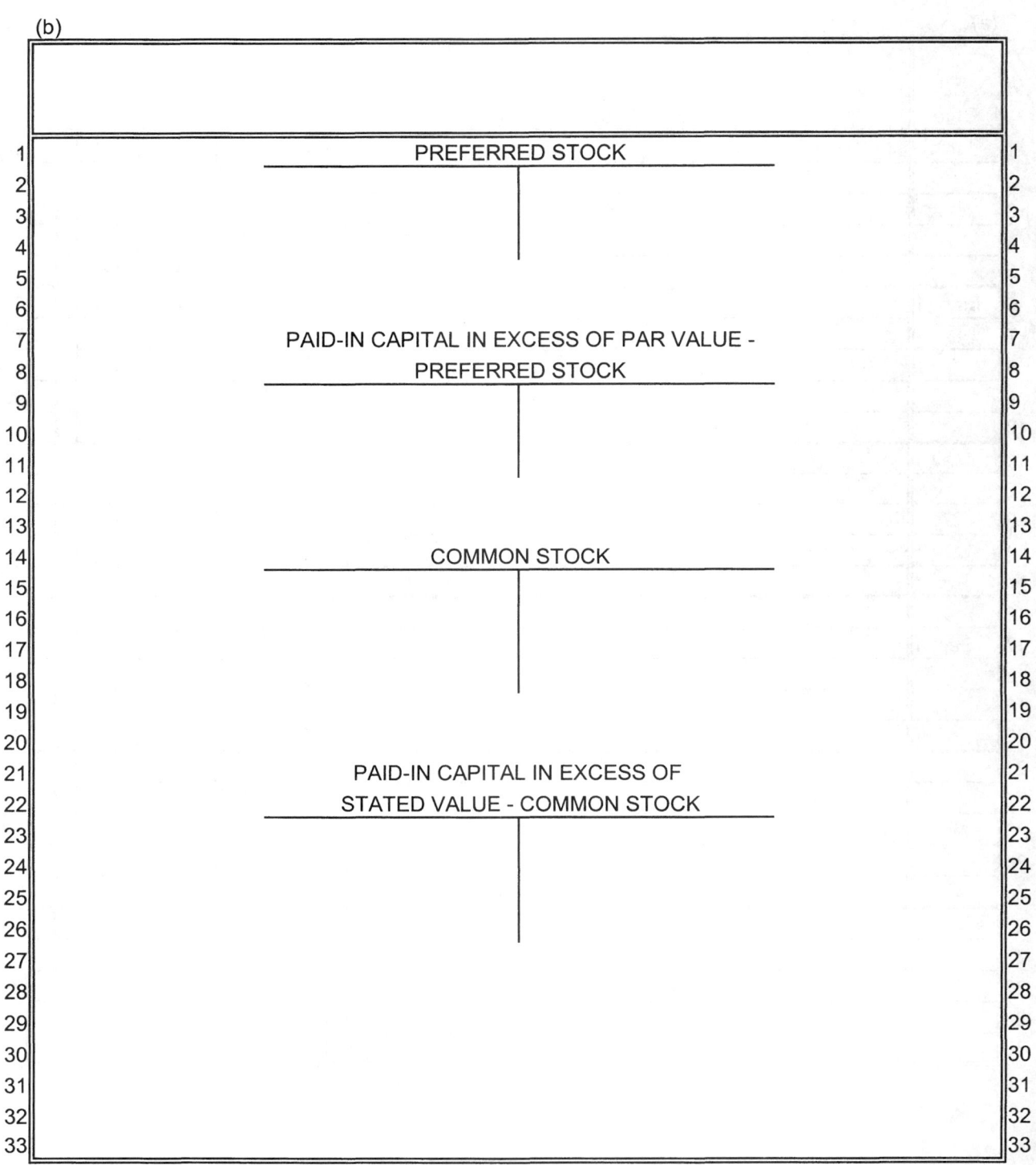

	PREFERRED STOCK
	PAID-IN CAPITAL IN EXCESS OF PAR VALUE - PREFERRED STOCK
	COMMON STOCK
	PAID-IN CAPITAL IN EXCESS OF STATED VALUE - COMMON STOCK

(c)

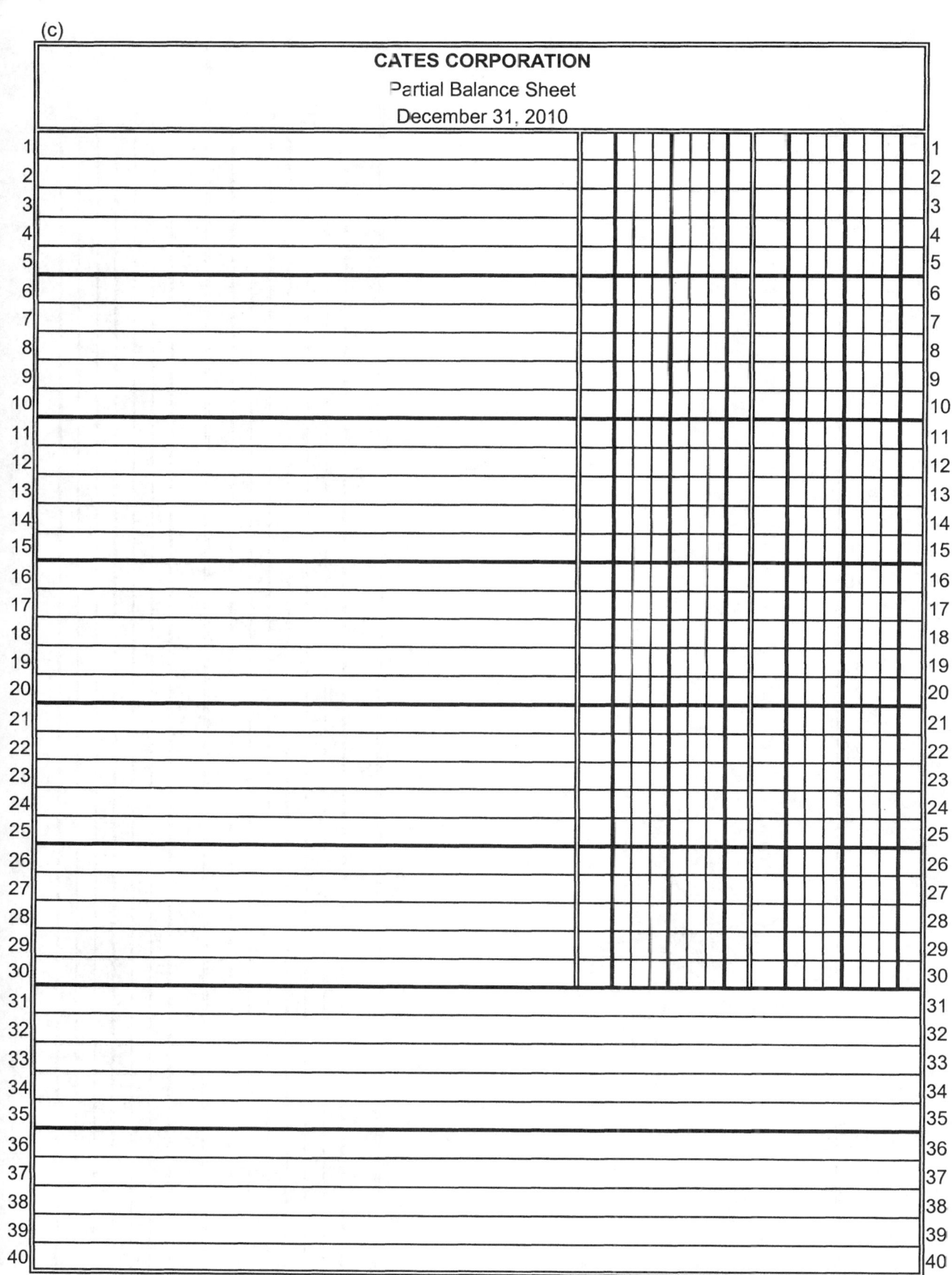

CATES CORPORATION
Partial Balance Sheet
December 31, 2010

(a)

	Date	Account Titles	Debit	Credit	
1	Feb 1				1
2					2
3					3
4					4
5					5
6					6
7	Nov 10				7
8					8
9					9
10	15				10
11					11
12					12
13	Dec 1				13
14					14
15					15
16	15				16
17					17
18					18
19	31				19
20					20
21					21
22	31				22
23					23
24					24
25					25
26					26
27					27
28					28
29					29
30					30
31					31
32					32
33					33
34					34
35					35
36					36
37					37
38					38
39					39
40					40

(b)

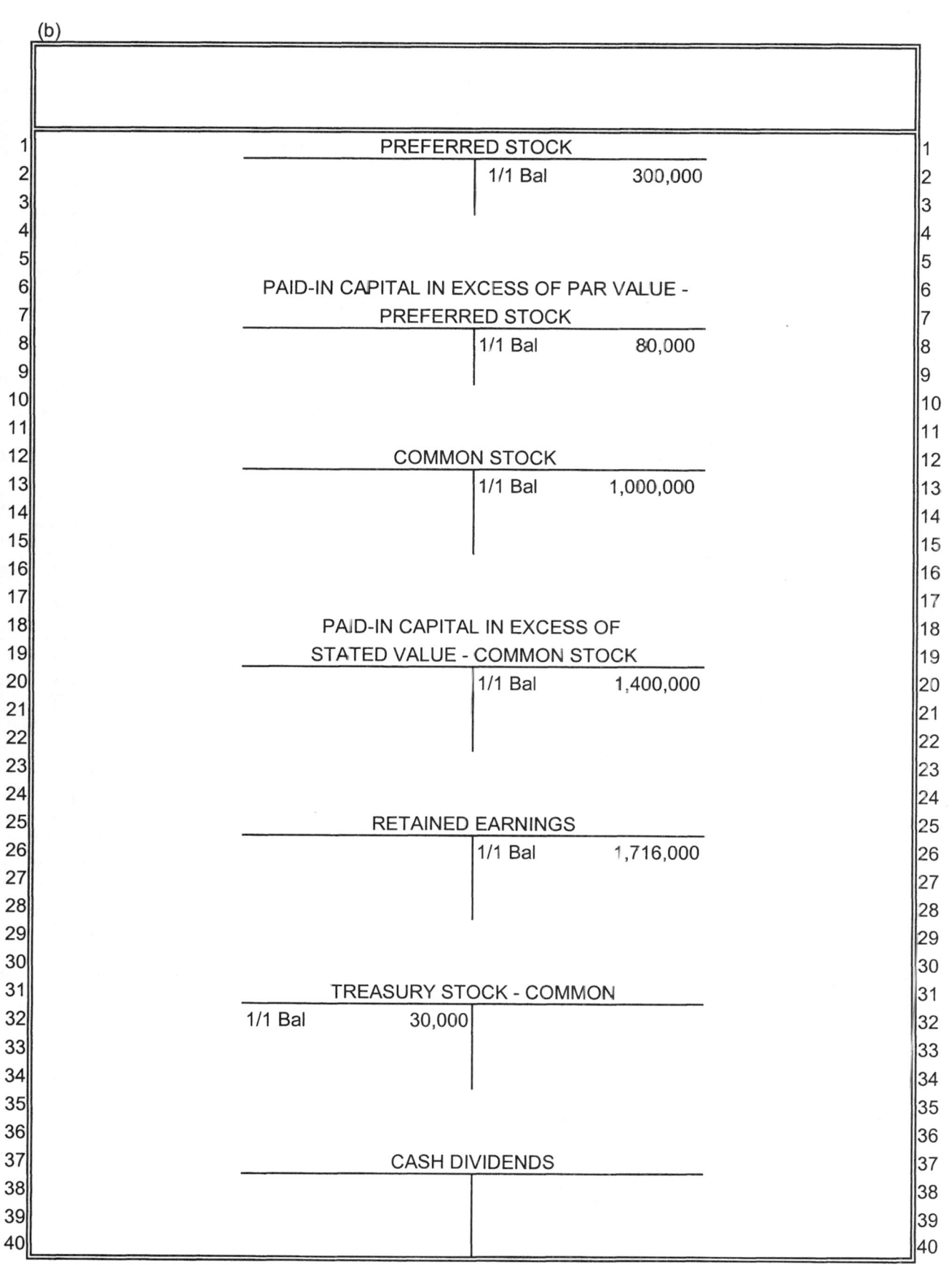

1	PREFERRED STOCK		1
2		1/1 Bal	300,000	2
3			3
4			4
5			5
6	PAID-IN CAPITAL IN EXCESS OF PAR VALUE -		6
7	PREFERRED STOCK		7
8		1/1 Bal	80,000	8
9			9
10			10
11			11
12	COMMON STOCK		12
13		1/1 Bal	1,000,000	13
14			14
15			15
16			16
17			17
18	PAID-IN CAPITAL IN EXCESS OF		18
19	STATED VALUE - COMMON STOCK		19
20		1/1 Bal	1,400,000	20
21			21
22			22
23			23
24			24
25	RETAINED EARNINGS		25
26		1/1 Bal	1,716,000	26
27			27
28			28
29			29
30			30
31	TREASURY STOCK - COMMON		31
32	1/1 Bal	30,000		32
33			33
34			34
35			35
36			36
37	CASH DIVIDENDS		37
38			38
39			39
40			40

(c)

MOTA CORPORATION

Partial Balance Sheet

December 31, 2010

(d)

1	Payout ratio:
2	
3	
4	
5	
6	
7	Earnings per share:
8	
9	
10	
11	
12	
13	
14	
15	
16	
17	
18	
19	
20	
21	Return on common stockholders' equity ratio:
22	
23	
24	
25	
26	
27	
28	
29	
30	
31	
32	
33	
34	
35	
36	
37	
38	
39	
40	

BRANT COMPANY

Partial Balance Sheet

December 31, 2010

1		
2		
3		
4		
5		
6		
7		
8		
9		
10		
11		
12		
13		
14		
15		
16		
17		
18		
19		
20		
21		
22		
23		
24		
25		
26		
27		
28		
29		
30		
31		
32		
33		
34		
35		
36		
37		
38		
39		
40		

(a)

	Retained Earnings	
1		1
2		2
3		3
4		4
5		5
7		7

(b)

FERNETTI CORPORATION
Partial Balance Sheet
December 31, 2010

1			1
2			2
3			3
4			4
5			5
6			6
7			7
8			8
9			9
10			10
11			11
12			12
13			13
14			14
15			15
16			16
17			17
18			18
19			19
20			20
21			21
22			22
23			23
24			24
25			25
26			26
27			27
28			28
29			29

Name Problem 11-5B

Section

Date Selig Corporation

SELIG CORPORATION

Partial Balance Sheet

December 31, 2010

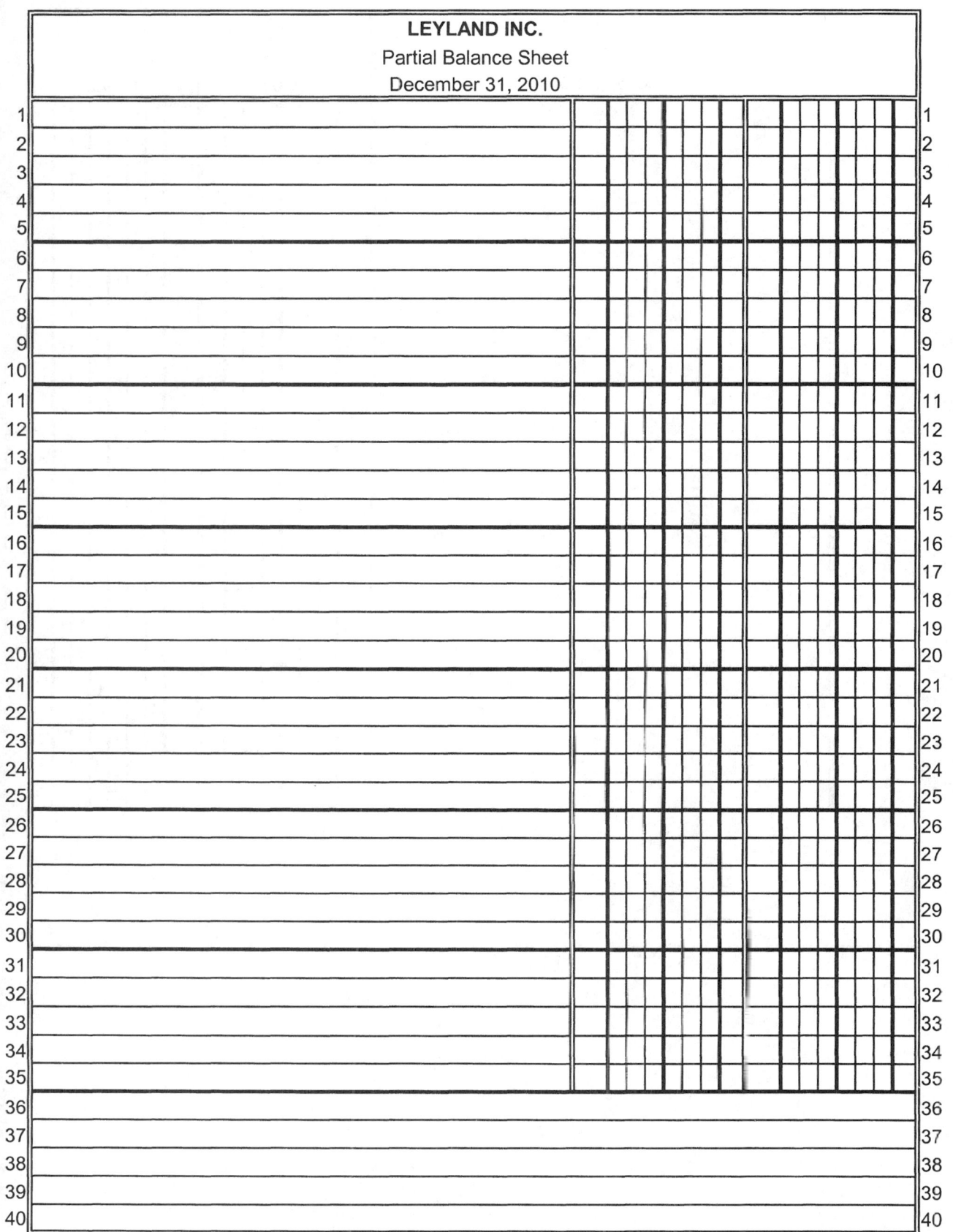

LEYLAND INC.

Partial Balance Sheet

December 31, 2010

(a)

	Date	Account Titles	Debit	Credit	
1	Feb 1				1
2					2
3					3
4	Mar 1				4
5					5
6					6
7	July 1				7
8					8
9					9
10					10
11					11
12					12
13	31				13
14					14
15					15
16					16
17	Dec 1				17
18					18
19					19
20	31				20
21					21
22					22
23					23
24					24
25					25
26					26
27					27
28					28
29					29
30					30

(b)

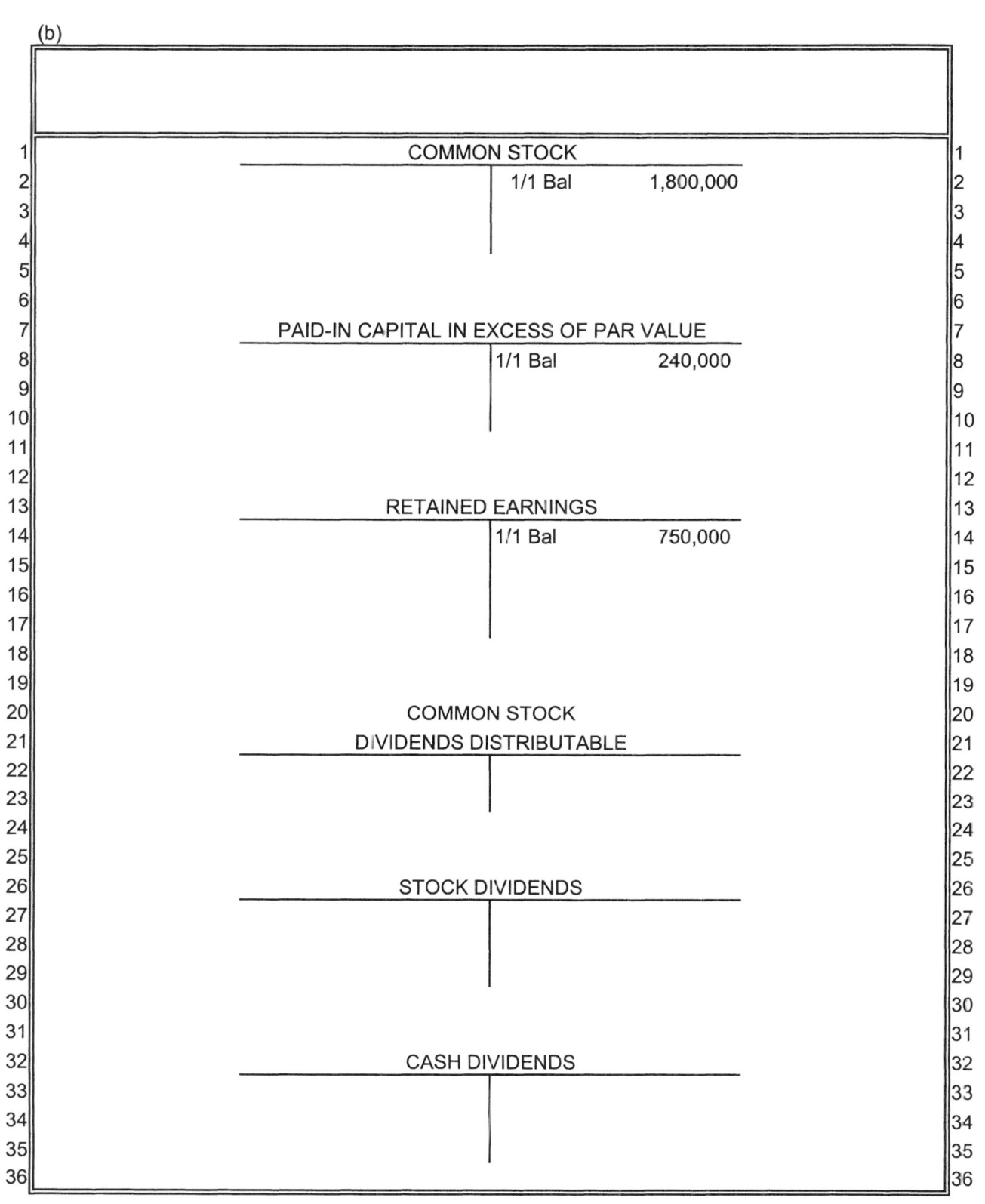

	COMMON STOCK	
	1/1 Bal	1,800,000

	PAID-IN CAPITAL IN EXCESS OF PAR VALUE	
	1/1 Bal	240,000

	RETAINED EARNINGS	
	1/1 Bal	750,000

COMMON STOCK
DIVIDENDS DISTRIBUTABLE

STOCK DIVIDENDS

CASH DIVIDENDS

(c)

DOLEN CORPORATION		
Partial Balance Sheet		
December 31, 2010		

1	
2	
3	
4	
5	
6	
7	
8	
9	
10	
11	
12	
13	
14	
15	

(d)

1	Payout ratio:
2	
3	
4	
5	
6	
7	
8	
9	
10	
11	Return on common
12	stockholders' equity ratio:
13	
14	
15	
16	
17	
18	
19	
20	

(a)

	Date	Account Titles	Debit	Credit	
1	1.				1
2					2
3					3
4					4
5					5
6	2.				6
7					7
8					8
9					9
10					10
11	3.				11
12					12
13					13
14	4.				14
15					15
16					16
17	5.				17
18					18
19					19
20	6.				20
21					21
22					22
23	7.				23
24					24
25					25
26	8.				26
27					27
28					28
29	9.				29
30					30
31					31
32	10				32
33					33
34					34
35	11.				35
36					36
37					37
38					38
39					39
40					40

(a) (Continued)

	Date	Account Titles	Debit	Credit	
1		Adjusting Entries			1
2	1.				2
3					3
4					4
5	2.				5
6					6
7					7
8	3.				8
9					9
10					10
11	4.				11
12					12
13					13
14	5.				14
15					15
16					16
17					17
18					18
19					19
20					20
21					21
22					22
23					23
24					24
25					25
26					26
27					27
28					28
29					29
30					30
31					31
32					32
33					33
34					34
35					35
36					36
37					37
38					38
39					39
40					40

HIATT CORPORATION
Adjusted Trial Balance
December 31, 2010

	Accounts	Debit	Credit	
1				1
2				2
3				3
4				4
5				5
6				6
7				7
8				8
9				9
10				10
11				11
12				12
13				13
14				14
15				15
16				16
17				17
18				18
19				19
20				20
21				21
22				22
23				23
24				24
25				25
26				26
27				27
28				28
29				29
30				30
31				31
32				32
33				33
34				34
35				35
36				36
37				37
38				38
39				39
40				40

(a)   Optional T-accounts

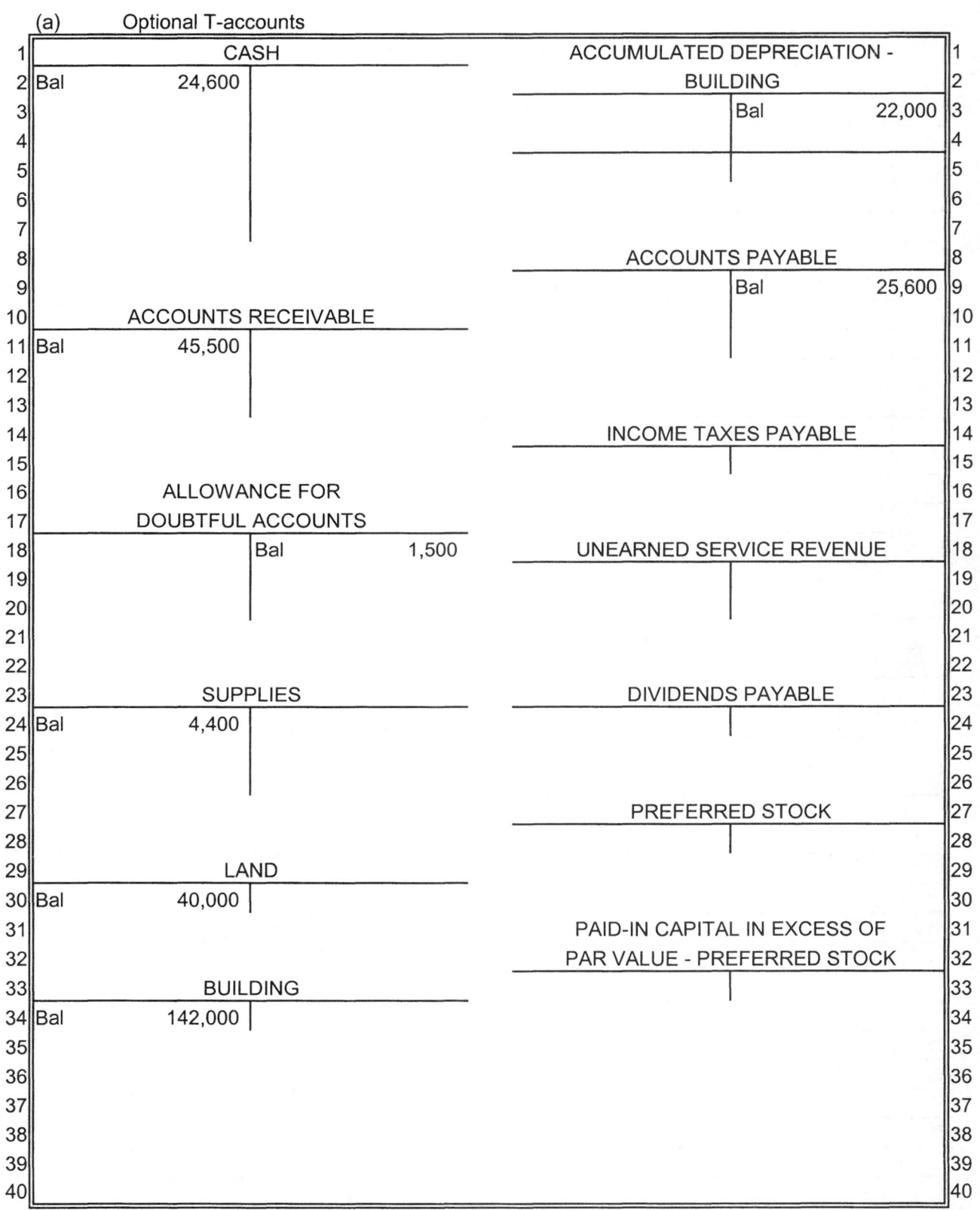

1	**CASH**		**ACCUMULATED DEPRECIATION -**	1
2	Bal	24,600	**BUILDING**	2
3			Bal	22,000	3
4				4
5				5
6				6
7				7
8			**ACCOUNTS PAYABLE**	8
9			Bal	25,600	9
10	**ACCOUNTS RECEIVABLE**			10
11	Bal	45,500		11
12				12
13				13
14			**INCOME TAXES PAYABLE**	14
15				15
16	**ALLOWANCE FOR**			16
17	**DOUBTFUL ACCOUNTS**			17
18		Bal 1,500	**UNEARNED SERVICE REVENUE**	18
19				19
20				20
21				21
22				22
23	**SUPPLIES**		**DIVIDENDS PAYABLE**	23
24	Bal	4,400		24
25				25
26				26
27			**PREFERRED STOCK**	27
28				28
29	**LAND**			29
30	Bal	40,000		30
31			**PAID-IN CAPITAL IN EXCESS OF**	31
32			**PAR VALUE - PREFERRED STOCK**	32
33	**BUILDING**			33
34	Bal	142,000		34
35				35
36				36
37				37
38				38
39				39
40				40

(a) (Continued)

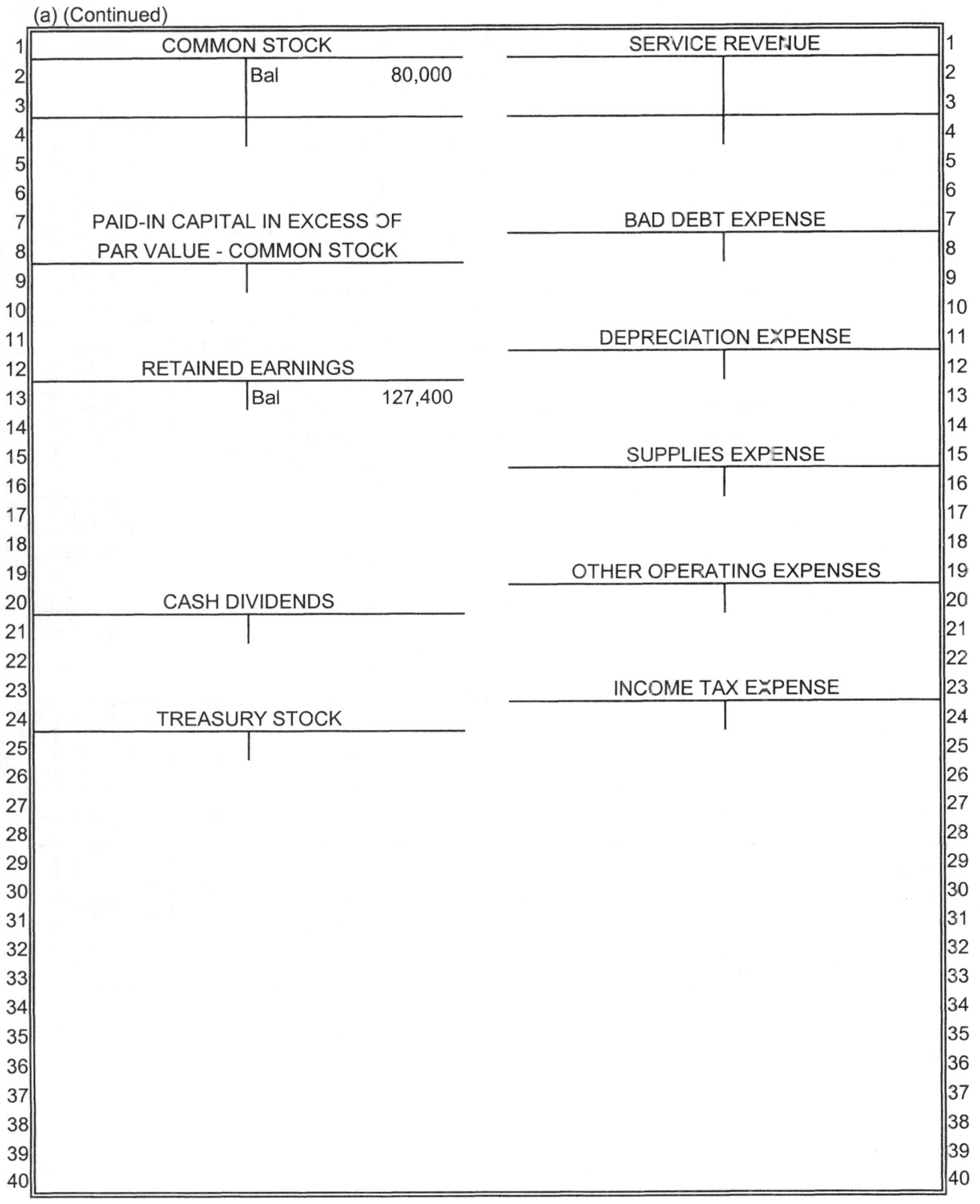

	COMMON STOCK				SERVICE REVENUE			
1								1
2		Bal	80,000					2
3								3
4								4
5								5
6								6
7	PAID-IN CAPITAL IN EXCESS OF				BAD DEBT EXPENSE			7
8	PAR VALUE - COMMON STOCK							8
9								9
10								10
11					DEPRECIATION EXPENSE			11
12	RETAINED EARNINGS							12
13		Bal	127,400					13
14								14
15					SUPPLIES EXPENSE			15
16								16
17								17
18								18
19					OTHER OPERATING EXPENSES			19
20	CASH DIVIDENDS							20
21								21
22								22
23					INCOME TAX EXPENSE			23
24	TREASURY STOCK							24
25								25
26								26
27								27
28								28
29								29
30								30
31								31
32								32
33								33
34								34
35								35
36								36
37								37
38								38
39								39
40								40

(c)

HIATT CORPORATION		
Income Statement		
For the Year Ending 12/31/010		

1			1
2			2
3			3
4			4
5			5
6			6
7			7
8			8
9			9
10			10
11			11
12			12
13			13
14			14
15			15

HIATT CORPORATION	
Retained Earnings Statement	
For the Year Ending 12/31/10	

1		1
2		2
3		3
4		4
5		5
6		6
7		7
8		8
9		9
10		10

(c) (Continued)

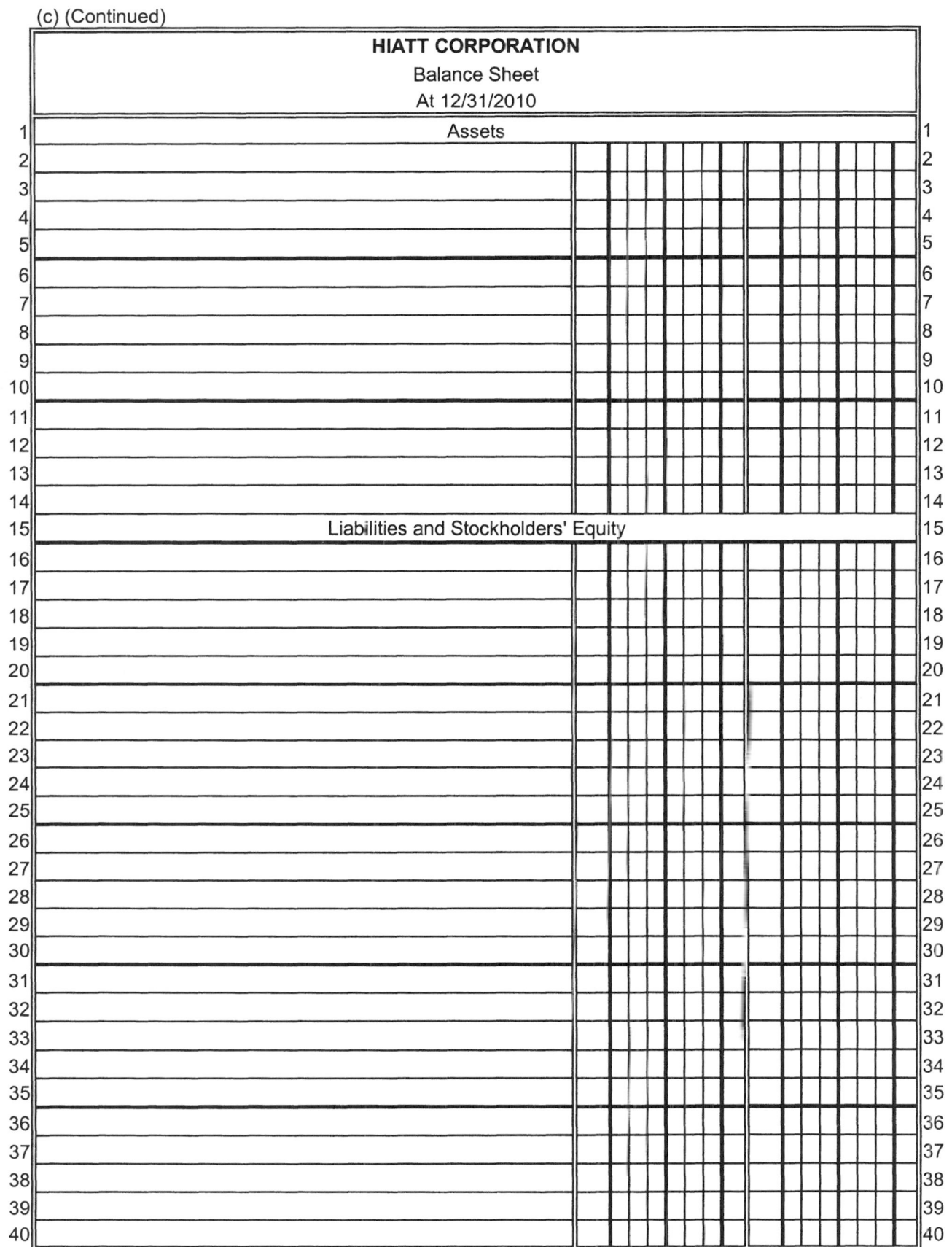

HIATT CORPORATION
Balance Sheet
At 12/31/2010

		Assets				
1	Assets					1
2						2
3						3
4						4
5						5
6						6
7						7
8						8
9						9
10						10
11						11
12						12
13						13
14						14
15	Liabilities and Stockholders' Equity					15
16						16
17						17
18						18
19						19
20						20
21						21
22						22
23						23
24						24
25						25
26						26
27						27
28						28
29						29
30						30
31						31
32						32
33						33
34						34
35						35
36						36
37						37
38						38
39						39
40						40

BE12-3

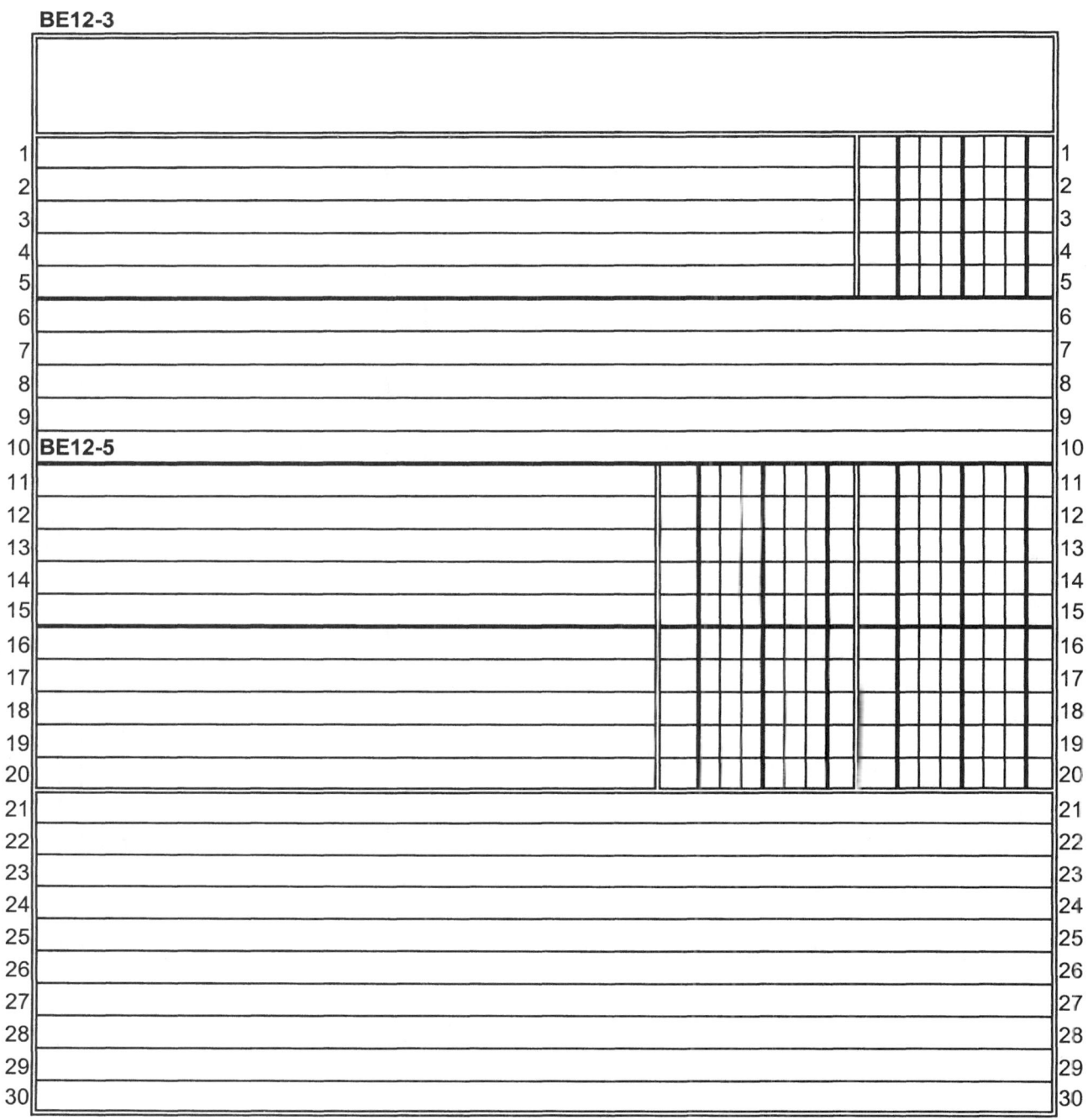

BE12-5

BE12-6

1		1
2		2
3		3
4		4
5		5
6		6
7		7
8		8
9		9
10		10
11		11

BE12-7

12		12
13		13
14		14
15		15
16		16
17		17
18		18
19		19
20		20
21		21
22		22
23		23

BE12-8

24		24
25		25
26		26
27		27
28		28
29		29
30		30

BE12-9

31			31
32	(a)		32
33			33
34		Free cash flow	34
35			35
36	(b)	Current cash debt	36
37		coverage ratio =	37
38			38
39	(c)	Cash debt coverage	39
40		ratio =	40

BE12-10

1	(a)	
2		
3	Free cash flow	
4		
5	(b) Current cash debt	
6	coverage ratio =	
7		
8	(c) Current debt coverage	
9	ratio =	
10		

BE12-11

12		
13		
14	Free cash flow	
15		

BE12-12

17		
18		
19		
20	Free cash flow	
21		

BE12-13

BE12-14

BE12-15

1											1
2											2
3											3
4											4
5											5
6											6
7											7
8											8
9											9
10											10
11											11
12											12
13											13
14											14
15											15
16											16
17											17
18											18
19											19
20											20
21											21
22											22
23											23
24											24
25											25
26											26
27											27
28											28
29											29
30											30
31											31
32											32
33											33
34											34
35											35
36											36
37											37
38											38
39											39
40											40

DO IT! 12-1

1	(1)	1
2	(2)	2
3	(3)	3
4	(4)	4
5	(5)	5
6		6
7	**DO IT! 12-2**	7
8		8
9		9
10		10
11		11
12		12
13		13
14		14
15		15
16		16
17		17
18		18
19		19
20	**DO IT! 12-3**	20
21	(a)	21
22		22
23		23
24		24
25	Free cash flow	25
26		26
27	(b)	27
28		28
29		29
30		30
31		31
32		32
33		33
34		34
35		35
36		36
37		37
38		38
39		39
40		40

Indirect Method

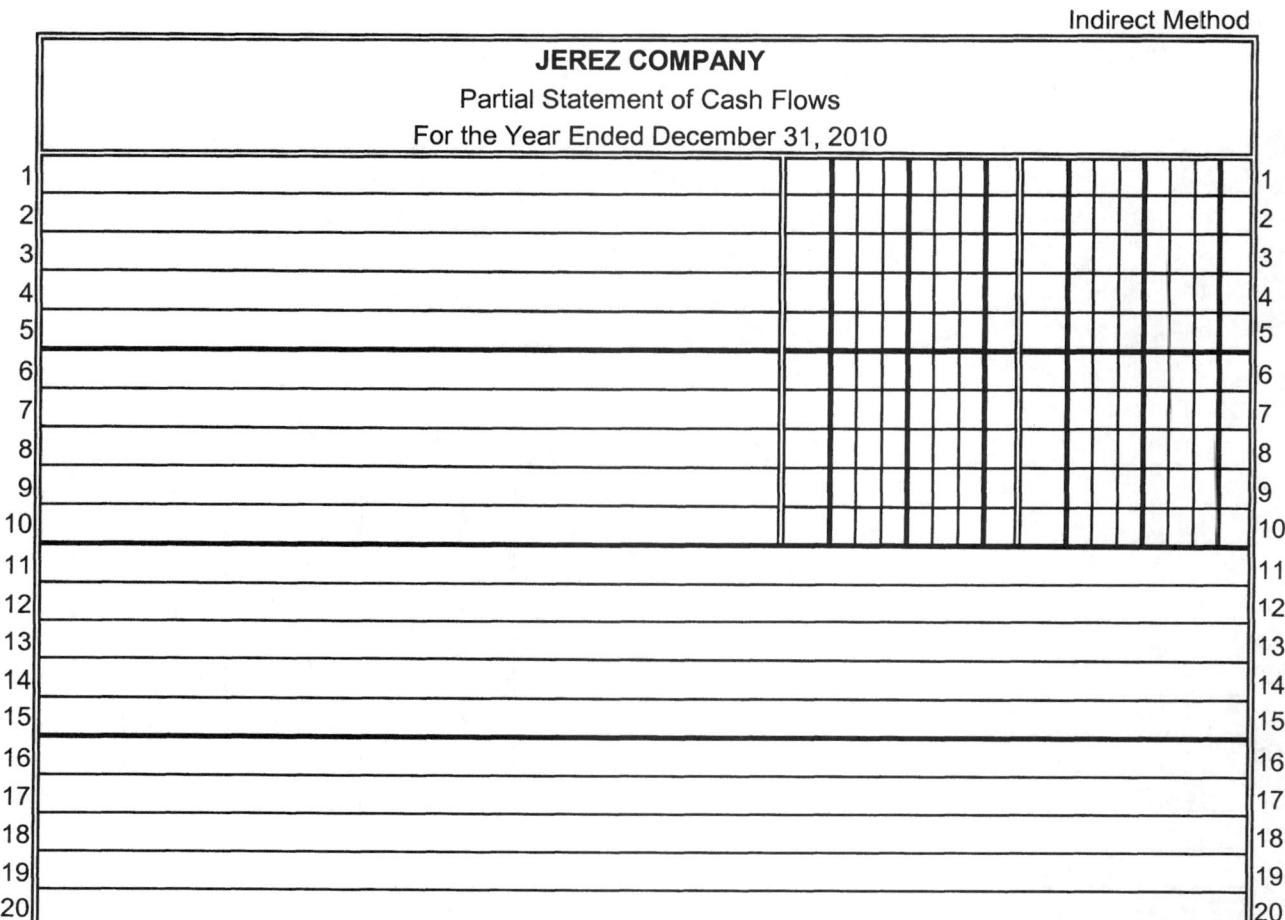

JEREZ COMPANY
Partial Statement of Cash Flows
For the Year Ended December 31, 2010

E12-5   Indirect Method

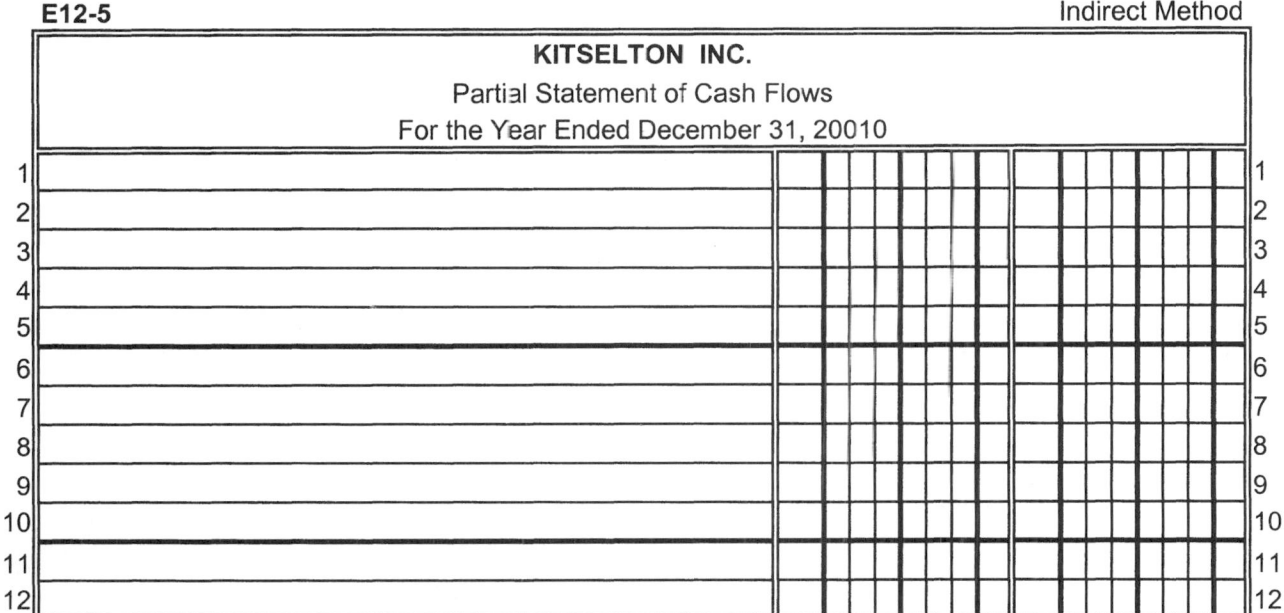

KITSELTON INC.

Partial Statement of Cash Flows

For the Year Ended December 31, 20010

E12-6   Indirect Method

FELIX CORPORATION

Statement of Cash Flows

For the Year Ended December 31, 2010

Indirect Method

TOVAR CORP.

Partial Statement of Cash Flows

For the Year Ended December 31, 2010

1		
2		
3		
4		
5		
6		
7		
8		
9		
10		
11		
12		
13		
14		
15		
16		
17		
18		
19		
20		
21		
22	Cash proceeds from equipment sale:	
23		
24		
25		
26		
27		
28		
29		
30		
31		
32		
33		
34		
35		
36		
37		
38		
39		
40		

(a)   Indirect Method

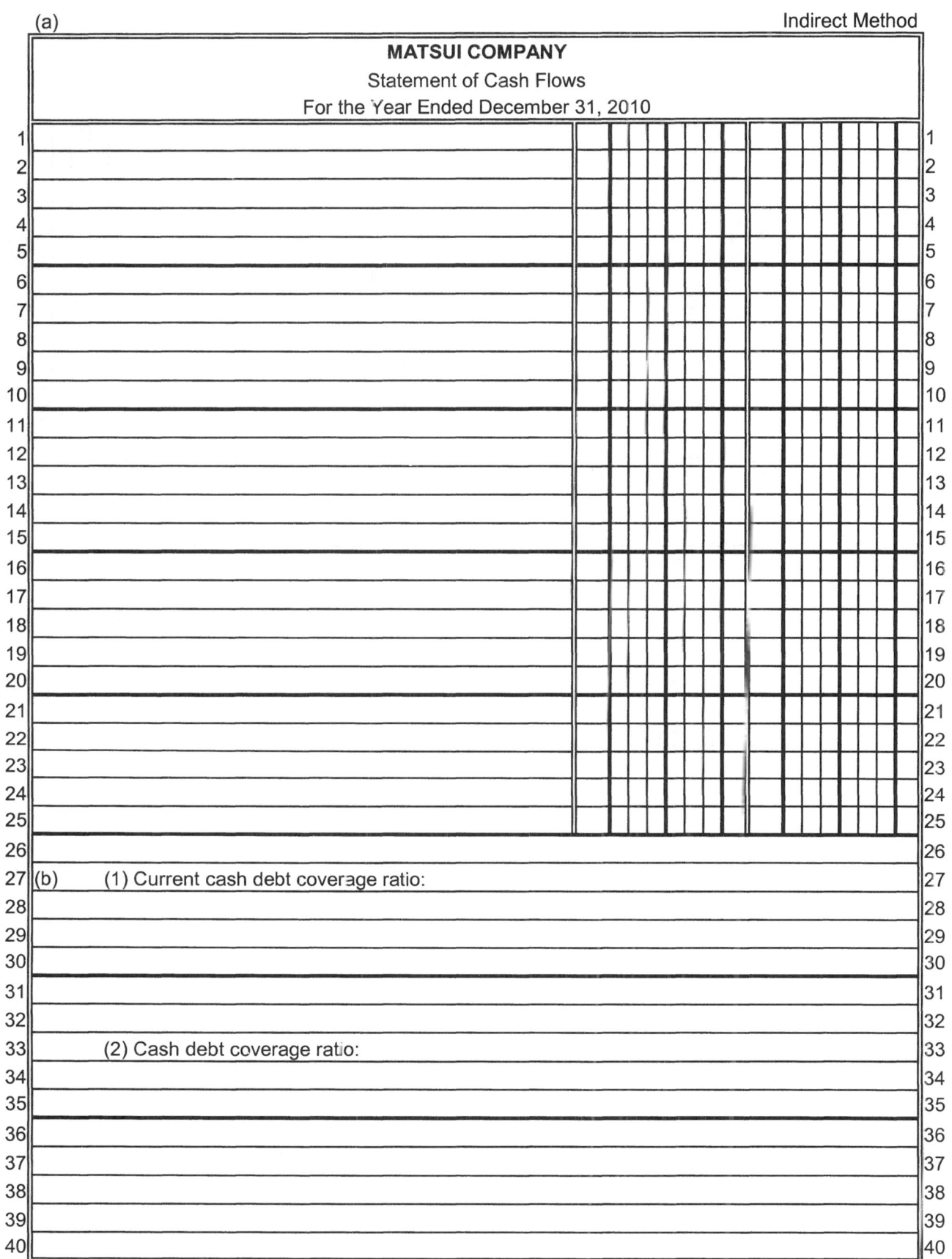

MATSUI COMPANY
Statement of Cash Flows
For the Year Ended December 31, 2010

(b)   (1) Current cash debt coverage ratio:

             (2) Cash debt coverage ratio:

Direct method

1					1
2					2
3					3
4					4
5					5
6					6
7					7
8					8
9					9
10					10

ACCOUNTS RECEIVABLE

ACCOUNTS PAYABLE

*E12-12

	(a)		
1	Cash payments to suppliers:		1
2			2
3			3
4			4
5			5
6			6
7			7
8			8
9	(b)		9
10	Cash payments for operating expenses:		10
11			11
12			12
13			13
14			14
15			15
16			16
17			17
18			18
19			19
20			20

*E12-13   Direct Method

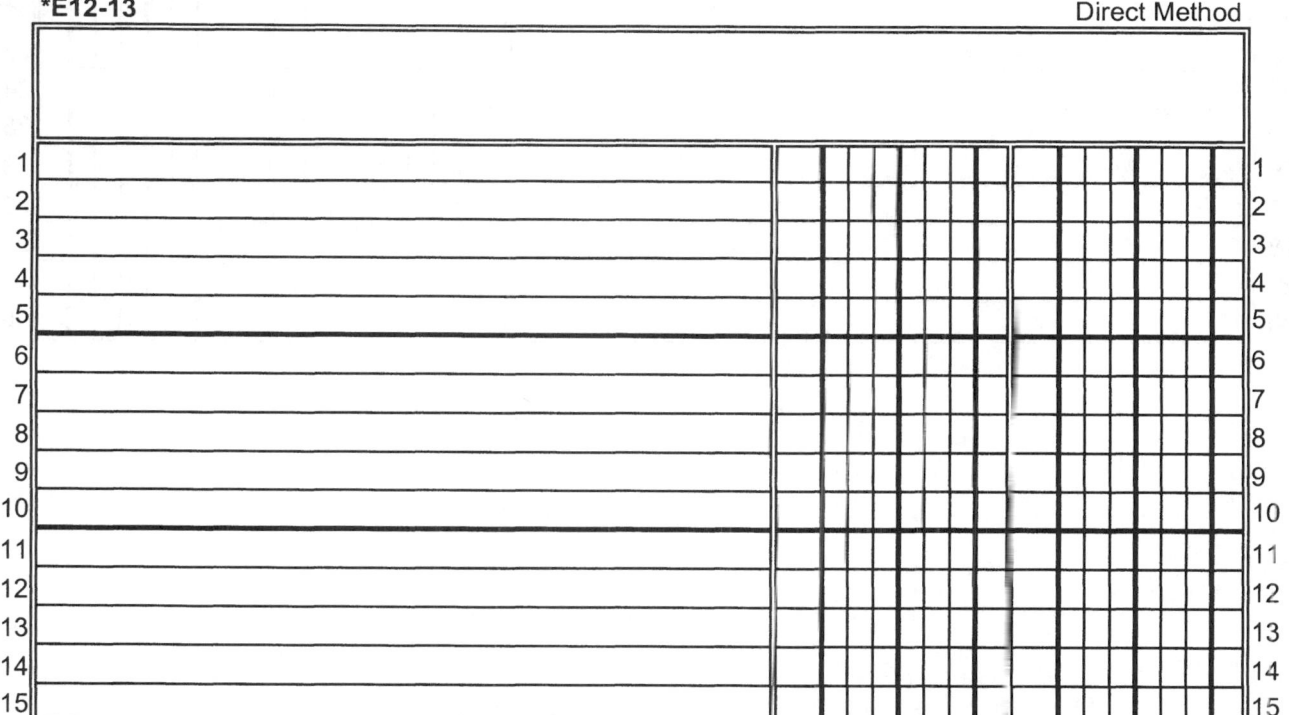

Direct Method

MOSQUITO HOLLOW CORP.		
Statement of Cash Flows		
For the Year Ended December 31, 2010		

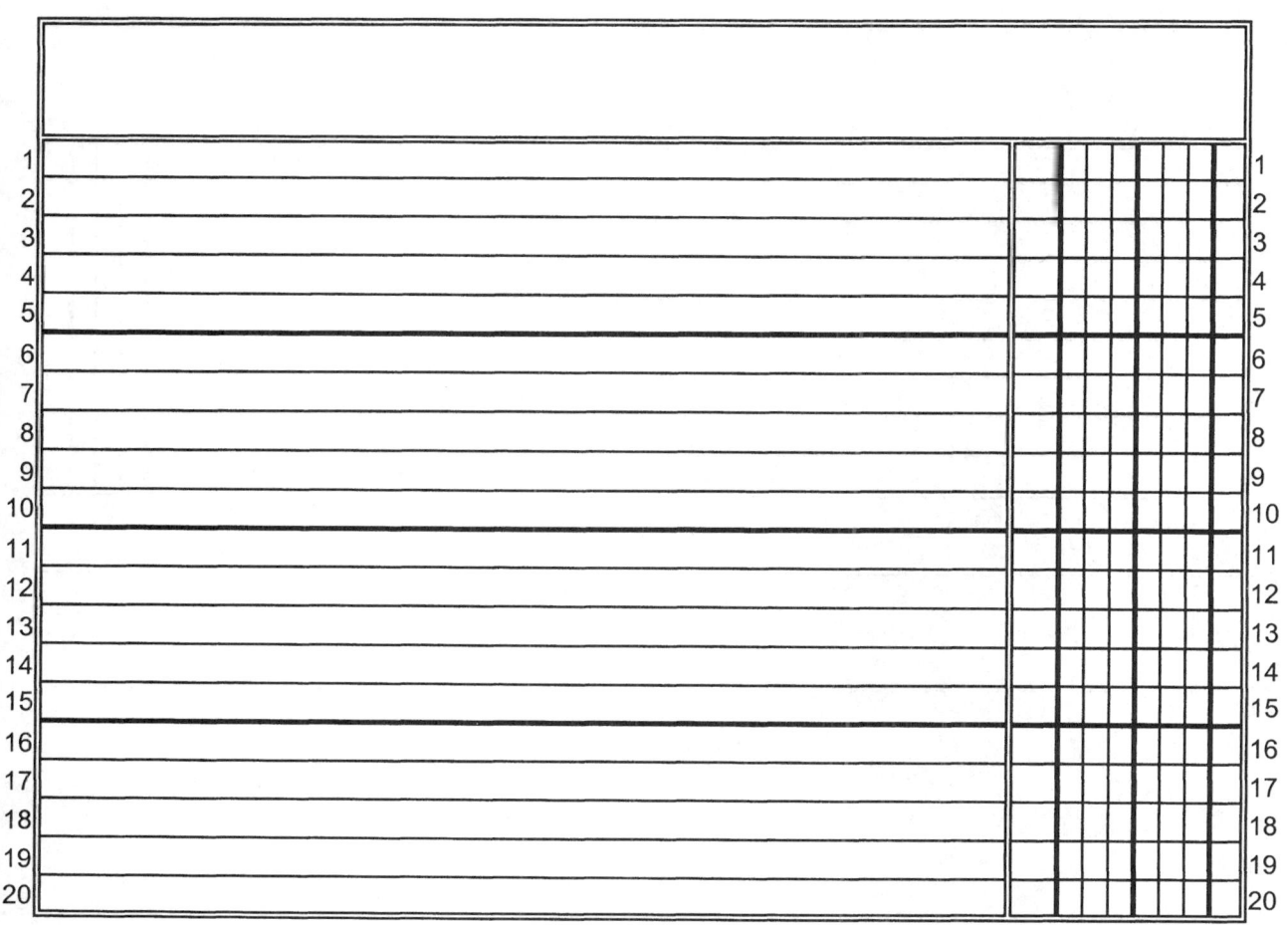

(a)

1			1
2			2
3			3
4			4
5			5
6			6
7			7
8			8
9			9

(b)

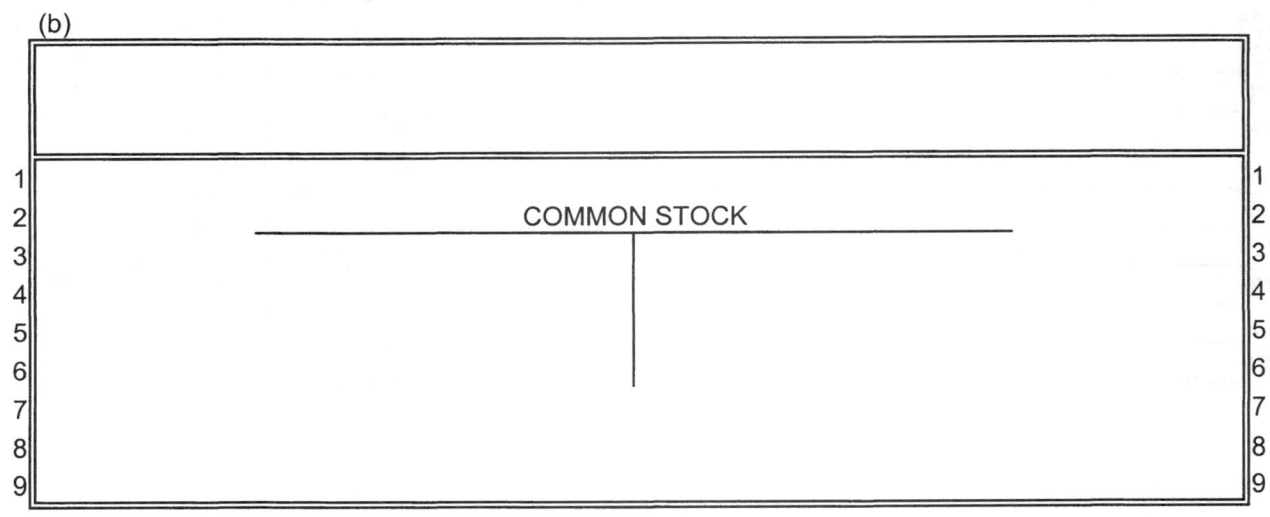

COMMON STOCK

(c)

1		1
2		2
3		3
4		4
5		5
6		6
7		7

Indirect Method

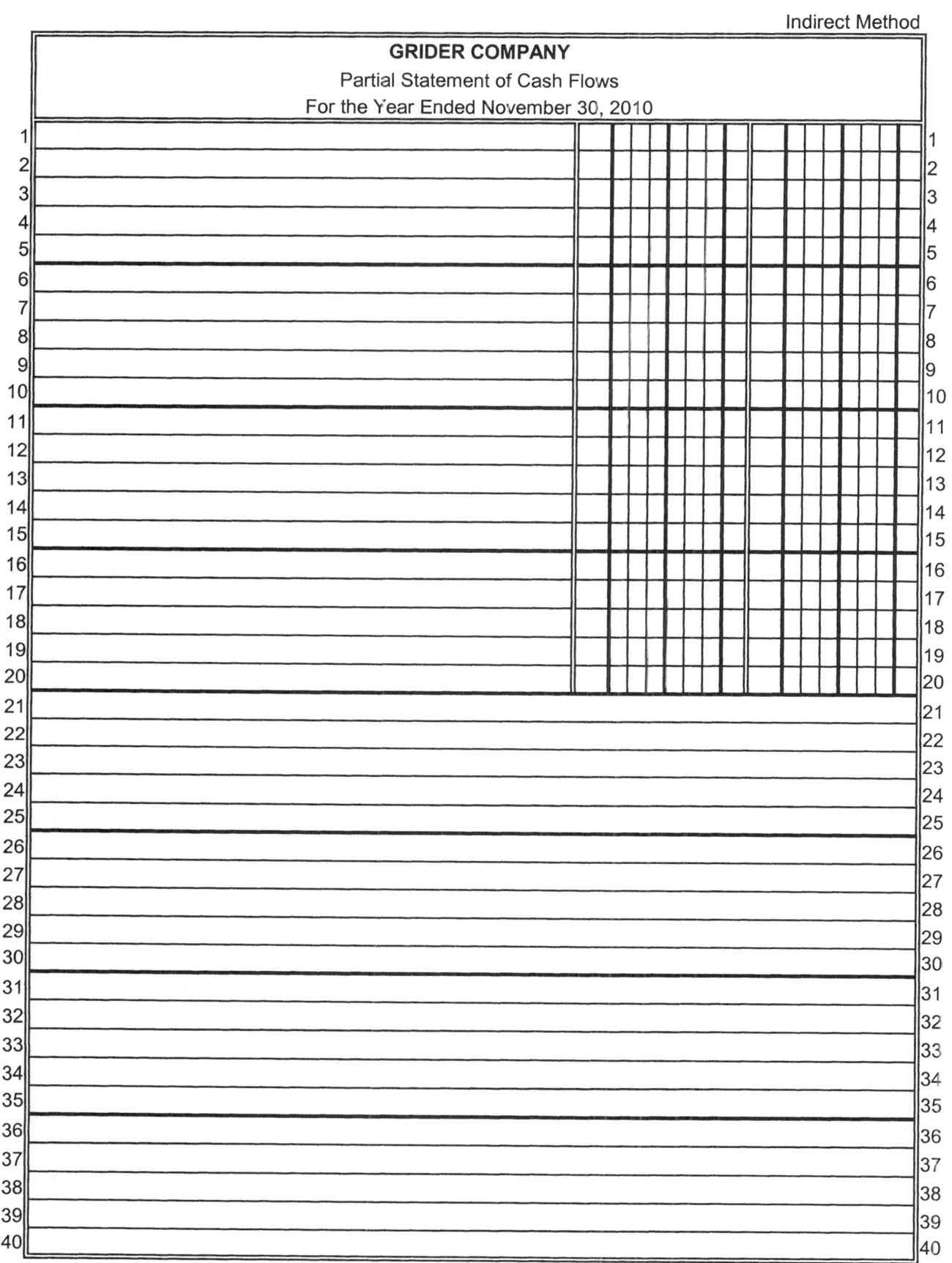

GRIDER COMPANY

Partial Statement of Cash Flows

For the Year Ended November 30, 2010

Direct Method

GRIDER COMPANY				
Partial Statement of Cash Flows				
For the Year Ended November 30, 2010				

1		
2		
3		
4		
5		
6		
7		
8		
9		
10		
11		
12 Computations:		
13		
14		
15		
16		
17		
18		
19		
20		
21		
22		
23		
24		
25		
26		
27		
28		
29		
30		
31		
32		
33		
34		
35		
36		
37		
38		
39		
40		

Indirect Method

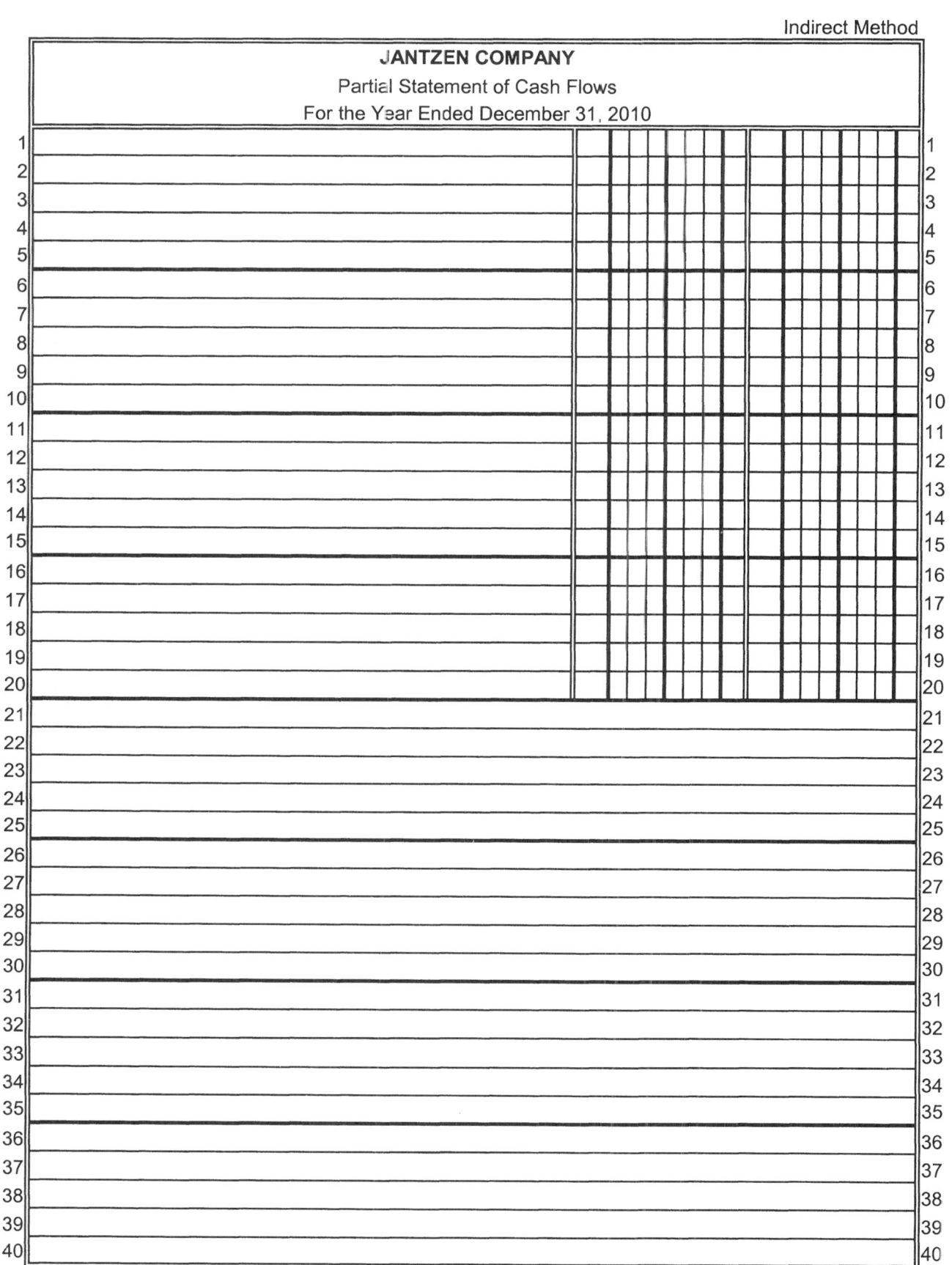

JANTZEN COMPANY

Partial Statement of Cash Flows

For the Year Ended December 31, 2010

Direct Method

JANTZEN COMPANY		
Partial Statement of Cash Flows		
For the Year Ended December 31, 2010		

1			
2			
3			
4			
5			
6			
7			
8			
9			
10			
11			
12			
13			
14			
15			
16			
17 Computations:			
18			
19			
20			
21			
22			
23			
24			
25			
26			
27			
28			
29			
30			
31			
32			
33			
34			
35			
36			
37			
38			
39			
40			

(a)   Indirect Method

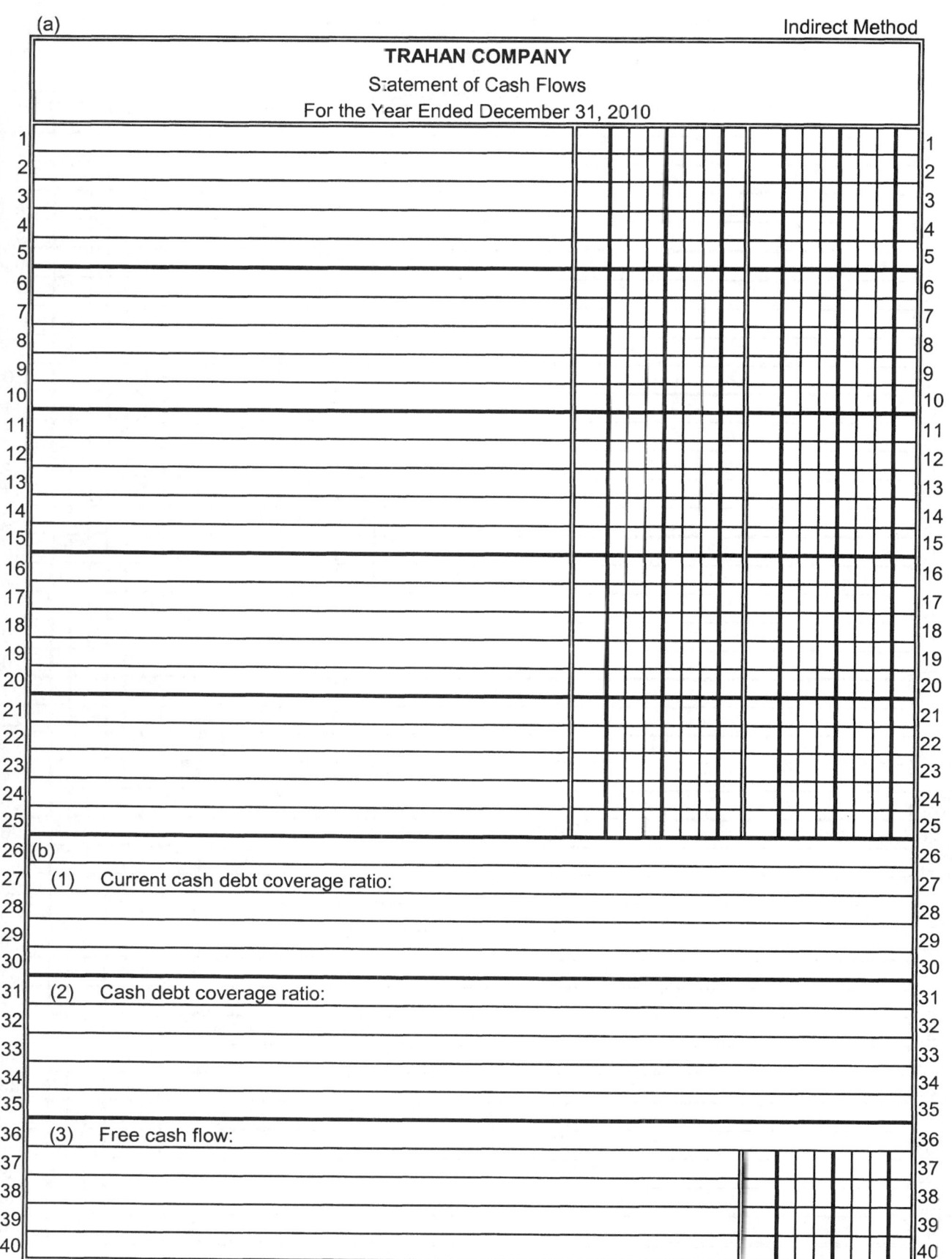

TRAHAN COMPANY
Statement of Cash Flows
For the Year Ended December 31, 2010

(b)

(1)   Current cash debt coverage ratio:

(2)   Cash debt coverage ratio:

(3)   Free cash flow:

(a)   Direct Method

TRAHAN COMPANY
Statement of Cash Flows
For the Year Ended December 31, 2010

1			
2			
3			
4			
5			
6			
7			
8			
9			
10			
11			
12			
13			
14			
15			
16			
17			
18			
19			
20			
21			
22			
23			
24			
25			

Computations:

27		
28		
29		
30		
31		
32		
33		
34		
35		
36		
37		
38		
39		
40		

(a) (Continued)   Direct Method

1	Computations:					1
2						2
3						3
4						4
5						5
6						6
7						7
8						8
9						9
10						10
11						11
12						12
13						13
14						14
15	(b)					15
16	(1) Current cash debt coverage ratio:					16
17						17
18						18
19						19
20						20
21						21
22	(2) Cash debt coverage ratio:					22
23						23
24						24
25						25
26						26
27						27
28	(3) Free cash flow:					28
29						29
30						30
31						31
32						32
33						33
34						34
35						35
36						36
37						37
38						38
39						39
40						40

Indirect Method

CIPRA INC. Statement of Cash Flows For the Year Ended December 31, 2010					
1					1
2					2
3					3
4					4
5					5
6					6
7					7
8					8
9					9
10					10
11					11
12					12
13					13
14					14
15					15
16					16
17					17
18					18
19					19
20					20
21					21
22					22
23					23
24					24
25					25
26					26
27					27
28					28
29					29
30					30
31					31
32					32
33					33
34					34
35					35
36					36
37					37
38					38
39					39
40					40

Direct Method

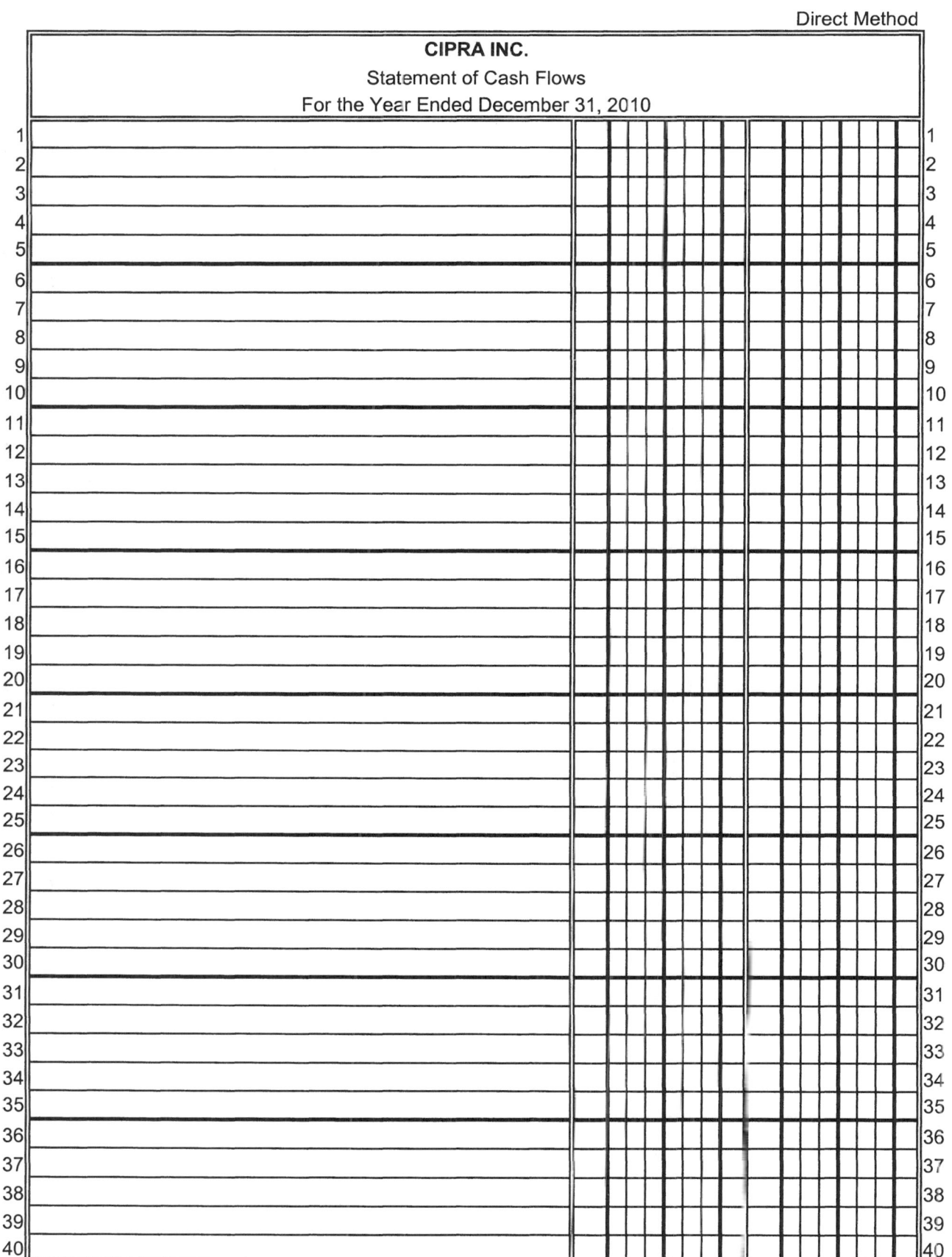

CIPRA INC.
Statement of Cash Flows
For the Year Ended December 31, 2010

Direct Method

Computations:

	1	2	3	4	5	6	7	8	9	10	11	12	13	14	15	16	17	18	19	20	21	22	23	24	25	26	27	28	29	30	31	32	33	34	35	36	37	38	39	40

Indirect Method

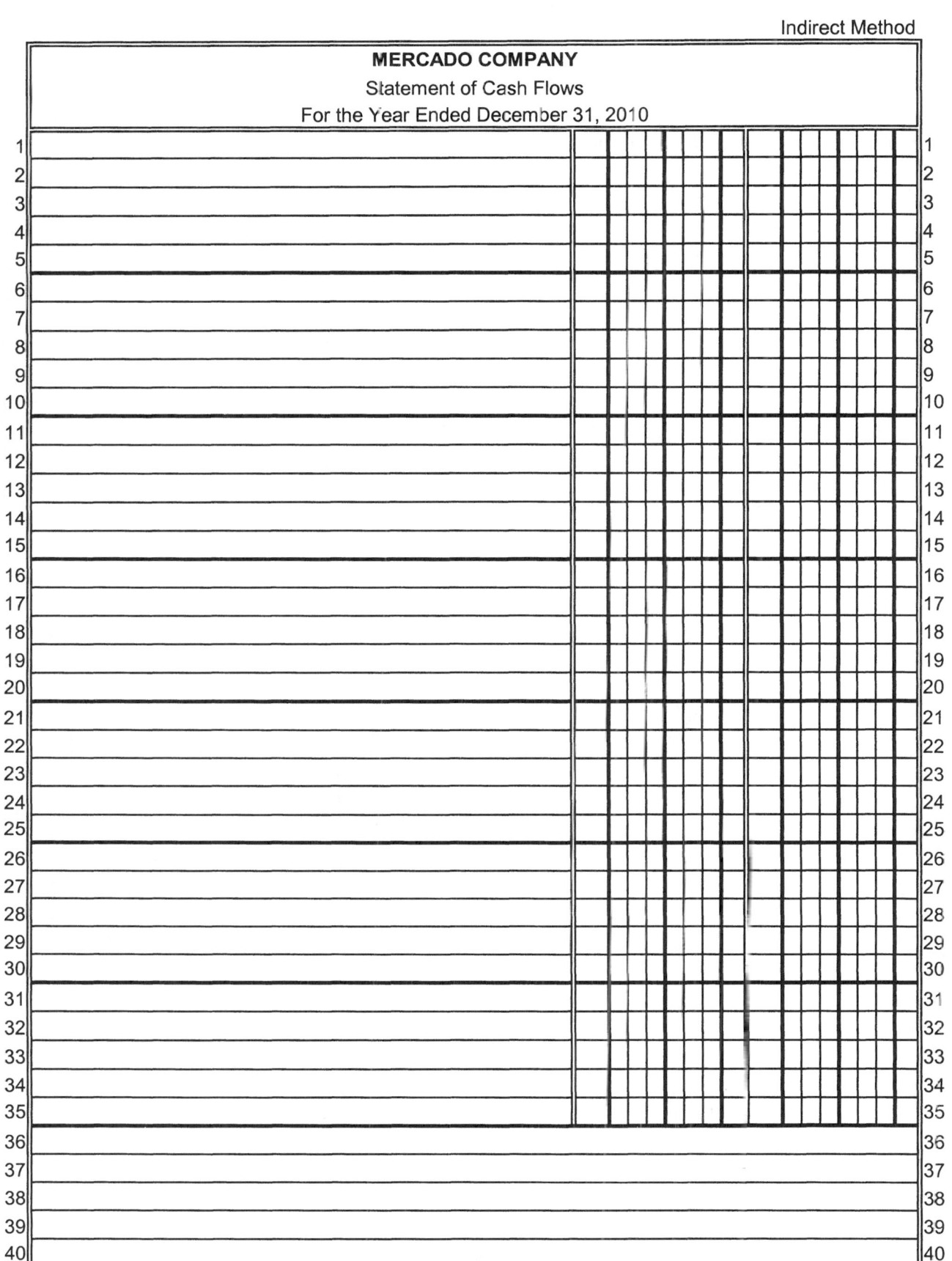

MERCADO COMPANY
Statement of Cash Flows
For the Year Ended December 31, 2010

1	(a) Cash inflows (outflows) related to plant assets in 2010:	1
2		2
3		3
4		4
5		5
6		6
7		7
8		8
9		9
10		10
11	ACCUMULATED DEPRECIATION -	11
12	EQUIPMENT	12
13		13
14		14
15		15
16		16
17		17
18		18
19		19
20		20

	Account Titles	Debit	Credit	
21				21
22				22
23				23
24				24
25				25
26				26
27				27
28				28
29				29
30				30
31				31
32				32
33				33
34				34

	Cash Flows	Classification	
35	(b)		35
36			36
37			37
38			38
39			39
40			40

Indirect Method

PERCIVAL COMPANY

Partial Statement of Cash Flows

For the Year Ended December 31, 2010

Direct Method

	PERCIVAL COMPANY				
	Partial Statement of Cash Flows				
	For the Year Ended December 31, 2010				
1					
2					
3					
4					
5					
6					
7					
8					
9					
10					
11					
12	Computations:				
13					
14					
15					
16					
17					
18					
19					
20					
21					
22					
23					
24					
25					
26					
27					
28					
29					
30					
31					
32					
33					
34					
35					
36					
37					
38					
39					
40					

Indirect Method

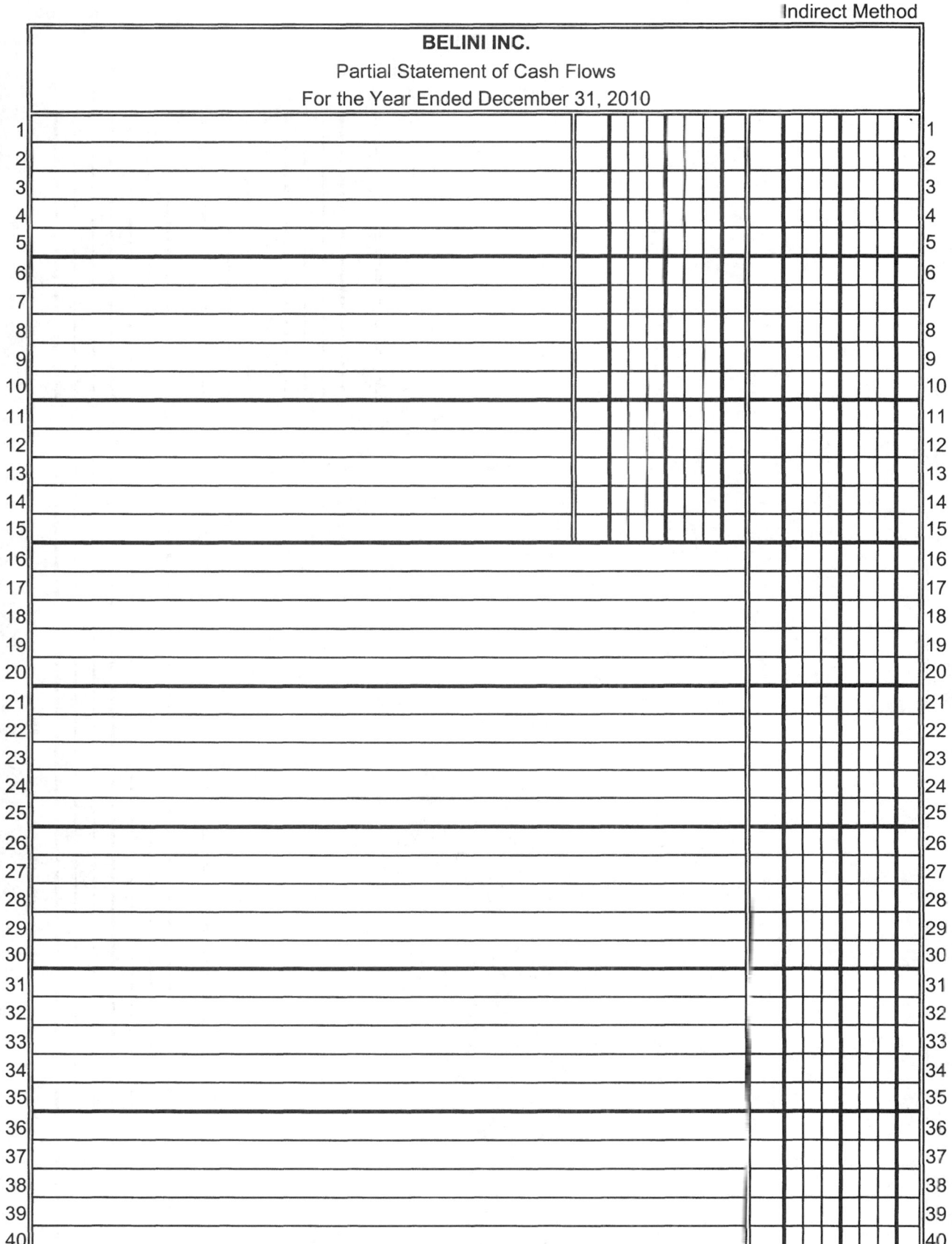

BELINI INC.

Partial Statement of Cash Flows

For the Year Ended December 31, 2010

Direct Method

BELINI INC. Partial Statement of Cash Flows For the Year Ended December 31, 2010		
1		
2		
3		
4		
5		
6		
7		
8		
9		
10		
11		
12 Computations:		
13		
14		
15		
16		
17		
18		
19		
20		
21		
22		
23		
24		
25		
26		
27		
28		
29		
30		
31		
32		
33		
34		
35		
36		
37		
38		
39		
40		

(a)   Indirect Method

RIVERA COMPANY
Statement of Cash Flows
For the Year Ended December 31, 2010

1	
2	
3	
4	
5	
6	
7	
8	
9	
10	
11	
12	
13	
14	
15	
16	
17	
18	
19	
20	
21	
22	
23	
24	
25	

(b)

(1)   Current cash debt coverage ratio:

(2)   Cash debt coverage ratio:

(3)   Free cash flow:

(a)   Direct Method

RIVERA COMPANY

Statement of Cash Flows

For the Year Ended December 31, 2010

1		1
2		2
3		3
4		4
5		5
6		6
7		7
8		8
9		9
10		10
11		11
12		12
13		13
14		14
15		15
16		16
17		17
18		18
19		19
20		20
21		21
22		22
23		23
24		24
25		25
26	Computations:	26
27		27
28		28
29		29
30		30
31		31
32		32
33		33
34		34
35		35
36		36
37		37
38		38
39		39
40		40

(a) (Continued)   Direct Method

1	Computations:	1
2		2
3		3
4		4
5		5
6		6
7		7
8		8
9		9
10	(b)	10
11	(1) Current cash debt coverage ratio:	11
12		12
13		13
14		14
15		15
16		16
17	(2) Cash debt coverage ratio:	17
18		18
19		19
20		20
21		21
22		22
23	(3) Free cash flow:	23
24		24
25		25
26		26
27		27
28		28
29		29
30		30
31		31
32		32
33		33
34		34
35		35
36		36
37		37
38		38
39		39
40		40

Indirect Method

	ULRICH COMPANY					
	Statement of Cash Flows					
	For the Year Ended December 31, 2010					

1				1
2				2
3				3
4				4
5				5
6				6
7				7
8				8
9				9
10				10
11				11
12				12
13				13
14				14
15				15
16				16
17				17
18				18
19				19
20				20
21				21
22				22
23				23
24				24
25				25
26				26
27				27
28				28
29				29
30				30
31				31
32				32
33				33
34				34
35				35
36				36
37				37
38				38
39				39
40				40

Direct Method

ULRICH COMPANY Statement of Cash Flows For the Year Ended December 31, 2010		
1		
2		
3		
4		
5		
6		
7		
8		
9		
10		
11		
12		
13		
14		
15		
16		
17		
18		
19		
20		
21		
22		
23		
24		
25		
26		
27		
28		
29		
30		
31		
Computations:		

Direct Method

Computations:								

Indirect Method

NUNEZ COMPANY

Statement of Cash Flows

For the Year Ended December 31, 2010

1		
2		
3		
4		
5		
6		
7		
8		
9		
10		
11		
12		
13		
14		
15		
16		
17		
18		
19		
20		
21		
22		
23		
24		
25		
26		
27		
28		
29		
30		
31		
32		
33		
34		
35		
36		
37		
38		
39		
40		

(a)   Indirect Method

DEVITO COMPANY

Statement of Cash Flows

For the Year Ended January 31, 2010

(a) (Continued)

Computation of net income (loss):

(b)

BE13-1

GOMEZ CORPORATION		
Partial Income Statement		
For the Year Ended December 31, 200X		
1		1
2		2
3		3
4		4
5		5

BE13-2

OSBORN CORPORATION		
Partial Income Statement		
For the Year Ended December 31, 2010		
1		1
2		2
3		3
4		4
5		5
6		6
7		7
8		8
9		9
10		10

BE13-4

	Dec. 31, 2010	Dec. 31, 2009	Increase or (Decrease) Amount	Percentage
1 Accounts receivable				
2 Inventory				
3 Total assets				
4				

E13-5

	Dec. 31, 2010 Amount	Percentage	Dec. 31, 2009 Amount	Percentage
13 Accounts receivable				
14 Inventory				
15 Total assets				

E13-6

	2010	2009	2008
25 Net income			

	Increase or (Decrease) Amount	Percentage	
31 (a) 2008 - 2009			
32 (b) 2009 - 2010			

BE13-7

	2010	2009	Increase
1			
2			
3			
4			
5			
6			
7			
8			
9			
10			

BE13-8	2010	2009	2008
Sales	100.0	100.0	100.0
Cost of goods sold	60.5	62.4	64.5
Expenses	26.0	26.6	28.5
Net income			

BE13-15

1	(a)　　Current cash debt coverage ratio:
2	
3	
4	
5	
6	
7	
8	
9	
10	
11	(b)　　Cash debt coverage ratio:
12	
13	
14	
15	
16	
17	
18	
19	
20	
21	
22	(c)　　Free cash flow:　　　　　　　　　　　2007
23	
24	
25	
26	
27	
28	
29	
30	
31	
32	
33	
34	
35	
36	
37	
38	
39	
40	

DO IT! 13-1

SUPPLY CORPORATION
Income Statement (Partial)

1	
2	
3	
4	
5	
6	
7	
8	
9	
10	
11	

DO IT! 13-2

	Dec 31, 2011	Dec 31, 2010	Amount	Percent
Current assets	$ 199000	$ 220000		
Plant assets	821000	780000		
Total assets	$1020000	$1000000		

DO IT! 13-3

	2010	2009
(a) Current ratio:		
(b) Inventory turnover:		

OKLAHOMA COMPANY						
Partial Income Statement						
For The Year Ended December 31, 2010						

E13-3 Horizontal Analysis

				Increase or (Decrease)		
				GALENTI INC.		
				Condensed Balance Sheets		
				December 31,		
1						1
2	Assets	2010	2009	Amount	Percent	2
3	Current assets	$ 1 0 6 0 0 0	$ 8 0 0 0 0			3
4	Plant assets (net)	5 0 6 0 0 0	3 6 0 0 0 0			4
5	Total assets					5
6						6
7	Liabilities					7
8	Current liabilities	9 1 0 0 0	6 5 0 0 0			8
9	Long-term liabilities	1 2 2 0 0 0	9 0 0 0 0			9
10	Total liabilities					10
11						11
12	Stockholders' Equity					12
13	Common stock, $1 par	1 3 8 0 0 0	1 1 5 0 0 0			13
14	Retained earnings	1 5 5 0 0 0	1 7 0 0 0 0			14
15	Total stockholders' equity					15
16	Total liabilities and					16
17	stockholders' equity					17
18						18

E13-4 Vertical Analysis

		ROBINSON CORPORATION				
		Condensed Income Statements				
		For the Years Ended December 31,				
1		2010		2009		1
2		Amount	Percent	Amount	Percent	2
3	Sales	$ 8 0 0 0 0 0		$ 6 0 0 0 0 0		3
4	Cost of goods sold	5 2 0 0 0 0		4 0 8 0 0 0		4
5	Gross profit					5
6	Selling expenses	1 2 0 0 0 0		7 2 0 0 0		6
7	Administrative expenses	7 2 0 0 0		4 8 0 0 0		7
8	Total operating expenses					8
9	Income before income taxes					9
10	Income tax expense	3 2 0 0 0		2 1 6 0 0		10
11	Net income	$ 5 6 0 0 0		$ 5 0 4 0 0		11
12						12
13						13
14						14
15						15

(a)   Horizontal Analysis

NIKE, INC.
Comparative Balance Sheets
December 31,
($ in millions)

		2007	2006	Increase or (Decrease)		
	Assets			Amount	Percent	
3	Current assets	$ 8 0 7 6	$ 7 3 4 6			3
4	Property, plant, & equip. (net)	1 6 7 8	1 6 5 8			4
5	Other assets	9 3 4	8 6 6			5
6	Total assets	$ 1 0 6 8 8	$ 9 8 7 0			6
7						7
8	Liabilities & Stockholders'					8
9	Equity					9
10	Current liabilities	$ 2 5 8 4	$ 2 6 1 2			10
11	Long-term liabilities	1 0 7 9	9 7 3			11
12	Stockholders' equity	7 0 2 5	6 2 8 5			12
13	Total liabilities and					13
14	stockholders' equity	$ 1 0 6 8 8	$ 9 8 7 0			14

(b)   Vertical Analysis

NIKE, INC.
Condensed Balance Sheet
December 31, 2007

	Assets	$ (in millions)	Percent	
2	Current assets	$ 8 0 7 6		2
3	Property, plant, and equipment (net)	1 6 7 8		3
4	Other assets	9 3 4		4
5	Total assets	$ 1 0 6 8 8		5
6				6
7	Liabilities and Stockholders' Equity			7
8	Current liabilities	$ 2 5 8 4		8
9	Long-term liabilities	1 0 7 9		9
10	Stockholders' equity	7 0 2 5		10
11	Total liabilities and Stockholders' equity	$ 1 0 6 8 8		11

E13-6 (a)   Horizontal Analysis

	2010	2009	Increase or (Decrease)	
			Amount	Percent
Net sales	$ 598 000	$ 520 000		
Cost of goods sold	477 000	450 000		
Gross profit	121 000	70 000		
Operating expenses	80 000	45 000		
Net income	$ 41 000	$ 25 000		

WINFREY CORPORATION
Comparative Condensed Income Statements
For the Years Ended December 31,

(b)   Vertical Analysis

WINFREY CORPORATION
Comparative Condensed Income Statements
For the Years Ended December 31,

	2010		2009	
	Amount	Percent	Amount	Percent
Net sales	$ 598 000		$ 520 000	
Cost of goods sold	477 000		450 000	
Gross profit	121 000		70 000	
Operating expenses	80 000		45 000	
Net income	$ 41 000		$ 25 000	

1	(a)	Current ratio:
2		
3		
4		
5	(b)	Receivables turnover ratio:
6		
7		
8		
9		
10		
11		
12	(c)	Average collection period:
13		
14		
15	(d)	Inventory turnover ratio:
16		
17		
18		
19		
20		
21		
22	(e)	Days in inventory:
23		
24		
25	(f)	Cash debt coverage ratio:
26		
27		
28		
29		
30	(g)	Current cash debt
31		coverage ratio:
32		
33		
34		
35		
36	(h)	Free cash flow:
37		
38		
39		
40		

(a)

	COMPARATIVE VERTICAL ANALYSIS Condensed Income Statements For the Year Ended December 31, 2010					
	Blue Company		Gray Company			
	Dollars	Percent	Dollars	Percent		
1 Net sales	$1 8 4 9 0 3 5		$5 4 6 0 0 0		1
2 Cost of goods sold	1 0 8 0 4 9 0		2 7 8 0 0 0		2
3 Gross profit					3
4 Operating expenses	2 5 0 0 0 0		8 2 0 0 0		4
5 Income from operations					5
6 Other expenses and losses					6
7 Interest expense	6 8 0 0		1 6 0 0		7
8 Income before income taxes					8
9 Income tax expense	6 2 0 3 0		3 1 0 0 0		9
10 Net income					10
11					11

(b)

1	1
2	2
3	3
4	4
5	5
6	6
7	7
8	8
9	9
10	10
11	11
12	12
13	13
14	14
15	15
16	16
17	17
18	18
19	19
20	20
21	21

(b) (Continued)

1		1
2		2
3		3
4		4
5		5
6		6
7		7
8		8
9		9
10		10
11		11
12		12
13		13
14		14
15		15
16		16
17		17
18		18
19		19
20		20
21		21
22		22
23		23
24		24
25		25
26		26
27		27
28		28
29		29
30		30
31		31
32		32
33		33
34		34
35		35
36		36
37		37
38		38
39		39
40		40

(a)	Earnings per share:
(b)	Return on common stockholders' equity ratio:
(c)	Return on assets ratio:
(d)	Current ratio:
(e)	Receivables turnover ratio:
(f)	Average collection period:
(g)	Inventory turnover ratio:
(h)	Days in inventory:
(i)	Times interest earned ratio:

1	(j)	Asset turnover ratio:		1
2				2
3				3
4				4
5				5
6	(k)	Debt to total assets ratio:		6
7				7
8				8
9				9
10	(l)	Current cash debt		10
11		coverage ratio:		11
12				12
13				13
14				14
15				15
16	(m)	Cash debt coverage ratio:		16
17				17
18				18
19				19
20				20
21				21
22				22
23				23
24	(n)	Free cash flow:		24
25				25
26				26
27				27
28				28
29				29
30				30
31				31
32				32
33				33
34				34
35				35
36				36
37				37
38				38
39				39
40				40

(a)

(All dollars are in millions) Target Corporation	Wal-Mart Stores, Inc.
(1) Current ratio:	
(2) Receivables turnover ratio:	
(3) Average collection period:	
(4) Inventory turnover ratio:	
(5) Days in inventory:	
(6) Profit margin ratio:	
(7) Asset turnover ratio:	
(8) Return on assets ratio:	
(9) Return on common stockholders' equity ratio:	
(10) Debt to total assets ratio:	

(a) (Continued)

	Target Corporation	Wal-Mart Stores, Inc.	
1	(11) Times interest earned ratio:		1
2			2
3			3
4			4
5	(12) Current cash debt coverage ratio:		5
6			6
7			7
8			8
9	(13) Cash debt coverage ratio:		9
10			10
11			11
12			12
13	(14) Free cash flow		13
14			14
15			15
16			16
17			17
18			18
19	Computations:		19
20			20
21			21
22			22
23			23
24			24
25			25
26			26
27	(b)		27
28			28
29			29
30			30
31			31
32			32
33			33
34			34
35			35
36			36
37			37
38			38
39			39
40			40

(a)

COMPARATIVE VERTICAL ANALYSIS Condensed Income Statements For the Year Ended December 31, 2007					
	Clark Company		Kent Company		
	Dollars	Percent	Dollars	Percent	
1 Net sales	$350000		$1200000		1
2 Cost of goods sold	180000		624000		2
3 Gross profit					3
4 Operating expenses	66000		266000		4
5 Income from operations					5
6 Other expenses and losses					6
7 Interest expense	3000		10000		7
8 Income before income taxes					8
9 Income tax expense	17000		54000		9
10 Net income					10
11					11

(b)

1	1
2	2
3	3
4	4
5	5
6	6
7	7
8	8
9	9
10	10
11	11
12	12
13	13
14	14
15	15
16	16
17	17
18	18
19	19
20	20
21	21

(b) (Continued)

1		1
2		2
3		3
4		4
5		5
6		6
7		7
8		8
9		9
10		10
11		11
12		12
13		13
14		14
15		15
16		16
17		17
18		18
19		19
20		20
21		21
22		22
23		23
24		24
25		25
26		26
27		27
28		28
29		29
30		30
31		31
32		32
33		33
34		34
35		35
36		36
37		37
38		38
39		39
40		40

1	(a)	Earnings per share:	1
2			2
3			3
4			4
5	(b)	Return on common	5
6		stockholders' equity ratio:	6
7			7
8			8
9			9
10			10
11	(c)	Return on assets ratio:	11
12			12
13			13
14			14
15			15
16	(d)	Current ratio:	16
17			17
18			18
19			19
20	(e)	Receivables turnover ratio:	20
21			21
22			22
23			23
24			24
25	(f)	Average collection period:	25
26			26
27			27
28			28
29	(g)	Inventory turnover ratio:	29
30			30
31			31
32			32
33			33
34	(h)	Days in inventory:	34
35			35
36			36
37	(i)	Times interest earned ratio:	37
38			38
39			39
40			40

1	(j)	Asset turnover ratio:
2		
3		
4		
5		
6	(k)	Debt to total assets ratio:
7		
8		
9		
10	(l)	Current cash debt
11		coverage ratio:
12		
13		
14		
15		
16	(m)	Cash debt coverage ratio:
17		
18		
19		
20		
21		
22		
23		
24	(n)	Free cash flow:
25		
26		
27		
28		
29		
30		
31		
32		
33		
34		
35		
36		
37		
38		
39		
40		

(a)   (dollars in millions)

	Black & Decker	Snap-On Tools	
1	(1) Current ratio:		1
2			2
3			3
4			4
5	(2) Receivables turnover ratio:		5
6			6
7			7
8			8
9	(3) Average collection period:		9
10			10
11			11
12			12
13	(4) Inventory turnover ratio:		13
14			14
15			15
16			16
17	(5) Days in inventory:		17
18			18
19			19
20			20
21	(6) Profit margin ratio:		21
22			22
23			23
24			24
25	(7) Asset turnover ratio:		25
26			26
27			27
28			28
29	(8) Return on assets ratio:		29
30			30
31			31
32			32
33	(9) Return on common stockholders' equity ratio:		33
34			34
35			35
36			36
37	(10) Debt to total assets ratio:		37
38			38
39			39
40			40

(a) (Continued)

	Black & Decker	Snap-On Tools	
1	(11) Times interest earned ratio:		1
2			2
3			3
4			4
5	(12) Current cash debt coverage ratio:		5
6			6
7			7
8			8
9	(13) Cash debt coverage ratio:		9
10			10
11			11
12			12
13	(14) Free cash flow		13
14			14
15			15
16			16
17			17
18			18
19	Computations:		19
20			20
21			21
22			22
23			23
24			24
25			25
26			26
27	(b)		27
28			28
29			29
30			30
31			31
32			32
33			33
34			34
35			35
36			36
37			37
38			38
39			39
40			40

	Coca-Cola Company	PepsiCo, Inc.	
1	(a) Liquidity Ratios		1
2			2
3	(1) Current ratio		3
4			4
5			5
6			6
7	(2) Receivables turnover		7
8			8
9			9
10			10
11	(3) Average collection period		11
12			12
13			13
14			14
15	(4) Inventory turnover		15
16			16
17			17
18			18
19	(5) Days in inventory		19
20			20
21			21
22			22
23	(6) Current cash debt coverage ratio		23
24			24
25			25
26			26
27			27
28			28
29			29
30			30
31	(b) Solvency Ratios		31
32			32
33	(1) Debt to total assets		33
34			34
35			35
36			36
37	(2) Times interest earned		37
38			38
39			39
40			40

(b) (Continued)

	Coca-Cola Company	PepsiCo, Inc.	
1	Liquidity Ratios		1
2	(3) Cash debt coverage ratio:		2
3			3
4			4
5			5
6	(4) Free cash flow:		6
7			7
8			8
9			9
10			10
11			11
12			12
13			13
14			14
15	(c) Profitability Ratios		15
16			16
17	(1) Profit margin ratio:		17
18			18
19			19
20			20
21	(2) Asset turnover ratio:		21
22			22
23			23
24			24
25			25
26	(3) Return on assets ratio:		26
27			27
28			28
29			29
30			30
31	(4) Return on common stockholders' equity ratio		31
32			32
33			33
34			34
35			35
36			36
37			37
38			38
39			39
40			40

BEC-11

	1
	2
	3
	4
	5
	6
	7
	8
	9

BEC-12

	10
	11
	12
	13
	14
	15
	16
	17
	18
	19
	20

BEC-13

	21
	22
	23
	24
	25
	26
	27
	28
	29
	30
	31
	32
	33
	34
	35
	36
	37
	38
	39
	40

BEC-14

BEC-15

BEC-16

BEC-17

1		1
2		2
3		3
4		4
5		5
6		6
7		7
8		8
9		9

BEC-18

10		10
11		11
12		12
13		13
14		14
15		15
16		16
17		17
18		18
19		19

BEC-19

20		20
21		21
22		22
23		23
24		24
25		25
26		26
27		27
28		28
29		29
30		30
31		31
32		32
33		33

BEC-20

34		34
35		35
36		36
37		37
38		38
39		39
40		40

BED-1

	Date	Account Titles	Debit	Credit	
1	Date	Account Titles	Debit	Credit	1
2	Jan 1				2
3					3
4					4
5	July 1				5
6					6
7					7
8	**BED-2**				8
9	Aug 1				9
10					10
11					11
12	Dec 1				12
13					13
14					14
15					15
16	**BED-3**				16
17	Dec 31				17
18					18
19					19
20	31				20
21					21
22					22
23	**BED-4**				23
24	Dec 31				24
25					25
26					26
27					27
28	**BED-5**	Balance Sheet			28
29					29
30					30
31					31
32		Income Statement			32
33					33
34					34
35					35
36	**BED-6**				36
37	Date	Account Titles	Debit	Credit	37
38	Dec 31				38
39					39
40					40

BED-7

Balance Sheet

BED-8

Balance Sheet

ED-1

Date	Account Titles	Debit	Credit	
(a)				1
Jan 1				2
				3
				4
July 1				5
				6
				7
1				8
				9
				10
				11
(b)				12
Dec 31				13
				14
				15

ED-2

Date	Account Titles	Debit	Credit	
(a)				1
Feb 1				2
				3
				4
July 1				5
				6
				7
Sept 1				8
				9
				10
				11
				12
Dec 1				13
				14
				15
(b)				16
				17
				18
				19
				20

ED-3

	Date	Account Titles	Debit	Credit	
1	Jan 1				1
2					2
3					3
4	July 1				4
5					5
6					6
7	Dec 1				7
8					8
9					9
10					10
11					11
12	31				12
13					13
14					14
15					15

ED-4

	Date	Account Titles	Debit	Credit	
1	(a)				1
2	Jan 1				2
3					3
4					4
5	Dec 31				5
6					6
7					7
8	31				8
9					9
10					10
11					11
12	(b)				12
13					13
14					14
15					15
16					16
17					17
18					18
19					19
20					20

ED-5

	Date	Account Titles	Debit	Credit	
1	(a)	Milton Cosmetics			1
2	Mar 18				2
3					3
4					4
5	June 30				5
6					6
7					7
8	Dec 31				8
9					9
10					10
11					11
12	(b)	Isringhausen Inc.			12
13	Jan 1				13
14					14
15					15
16	June 15				16
17					17
18					18
19	Dec 31				19
20					20
21					21
22					22

ED-6

	Date	Account Titles	Debit	Credit	
1	(a)				1
2	Dec 31				2
3					3
4					4
5					5
6	(b)	Balance Sheet			6
7					7
8					8
9					9
10		Income Statement			10
11					11
12					12
13					13

Name — Appendix D Exercise 7

Section

Date — Linger, Inc.

(a)

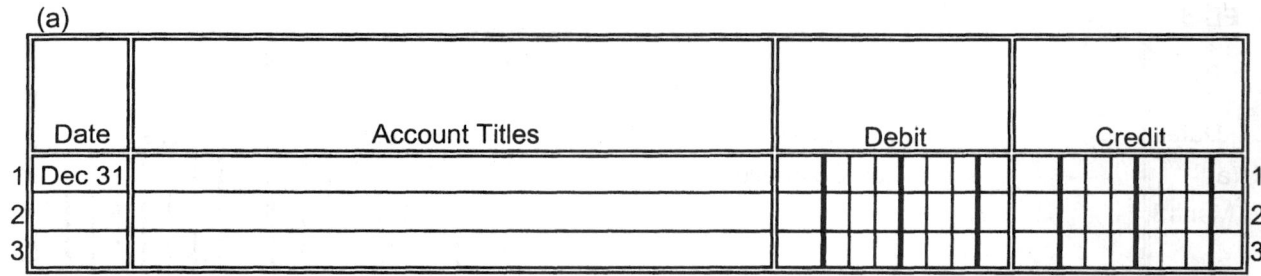

	Date	Account Titles	Debit	Credit	
1	Dec 31				1
2					2
3					3

(b)

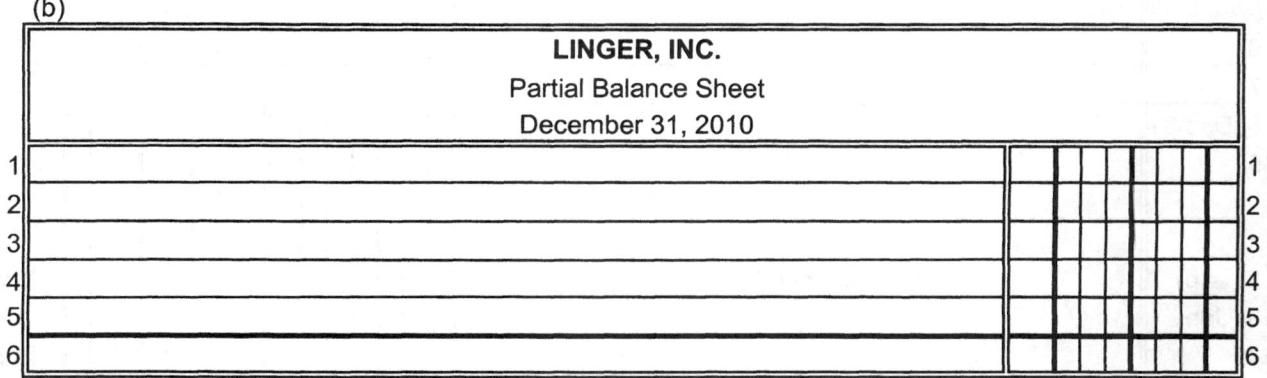

LINGER, INC.

Partial Balance Sheet

December 31, 2010

1			1
2			2
3			3
4			4
5			5
6			6

(c)

1		1
2		2
3		3
4		4
5		5
6		6
7		7
8		8
9		9
10		10
11		11
12		12
13		13
14		14
15		15
16		16
17		17
18		18
19		19
20		20
21		21

(a)

	Date	Account Titles	Debit	Credit	
1	Dec 31	Trading Securities			1
2					2
3					3
4					4
5	Dec 31	Available for Sale Securities			5
6					6
7					7
8					8

(b)

JAMISON COMPANY
Partial Balance Sheet
December 31, 2010

1		1
2		2
3		3
4		4
5		5
6		6
7		7
8		8
9		9
10		10

MARKOWITZ COMPANY
Income Statement (Partial)
For the Year Ended December 31, 2007

1		1
2		2
3		3
4		4
5		5

(a) & (b)

	Date	Account Titles	Debit	Credit	
1	2010				1
2	Jan 1				2
3					3
4					4
5	July 1				5
6					6
7					7
8	Dec 31				8
9					9
10					10
11	2013				11
12	Jan 1				12
13					13
14					14
15	1				15
16					16
17					17
18					18
19	July 1				19
20					20
21					21
22	Dec 31				22
23					23
24	(b)	2010			24
25	Dec 31				25
26					26
27					27

(c)

SCHUMAKER FARMS

Partial Balance Sheet

December 31, 2010

1			1
2			2
3			3
4			4
5			5
6			6
7			7
8			8

(a)

	Date	Account Titles	Debit	Credit	
1	Feb 1				1
2					2
3					3
4	Mar 1				4
5					5
6					6
7	Apr 1				7
8					8
9					9
10	July 1				10
11					11
12					12
13	Aug 1				13
14					14
15					15
16					16
17	Sept 1				17
18					18
19					19
20	Oct 1				20
21					21
22					22
23	1				23
24					24
25					25
26					26

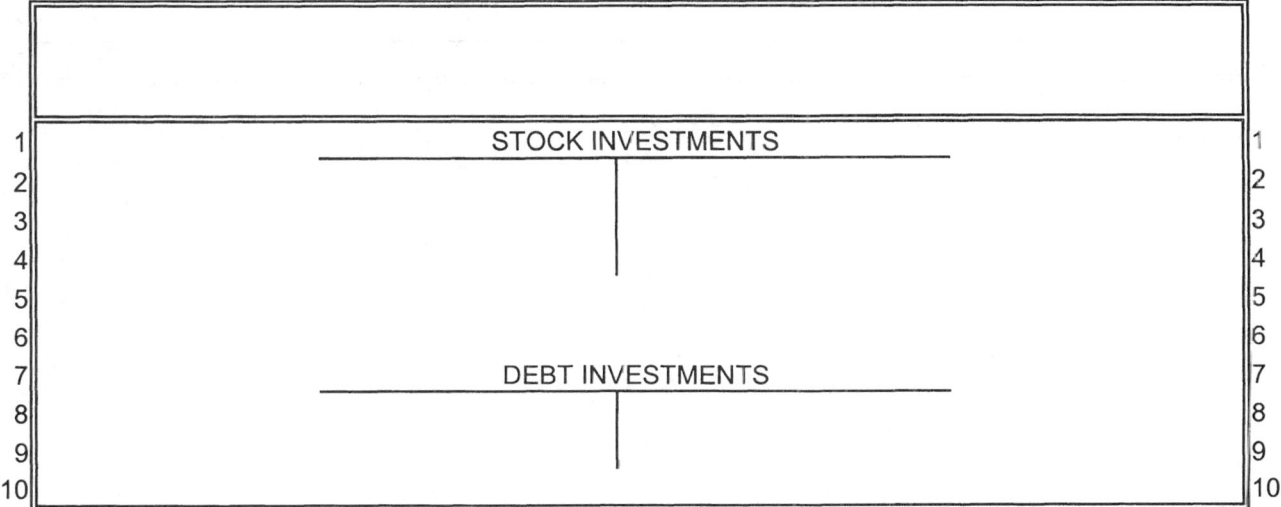

STOCK INVESTMENTS

DEBT INVESTMENTS

(b)

	Security	Cost	Fair Value	
1				1
2				2
3				3
4				4
5				5
6	Adjusting Entry			6
7	Dec 31			7
8				8
9				9
10				10

(c)

WOOD COMPANY
Partial Balance Sheet
December 31, 2010

1		1
2		2
3		3
4		4
5		5

(d)

1		1
2		2
3		3
4		4
5		5

(a)

	Date	Account Titles	Debit	Credit	
1	2010				1
2	July 1				2
3					3
4					4
5	Aug 1				5
6					6
7					7
8	Sept 1				8
9					9
10					10
11					11
12					12
13	Oct 1				13
14					14
15					15
16					16
17					17
18	Nov 1				18
19					19
20					20
21	Dec 15				21
22					22
23					23
24	31				24
25					25
26					26

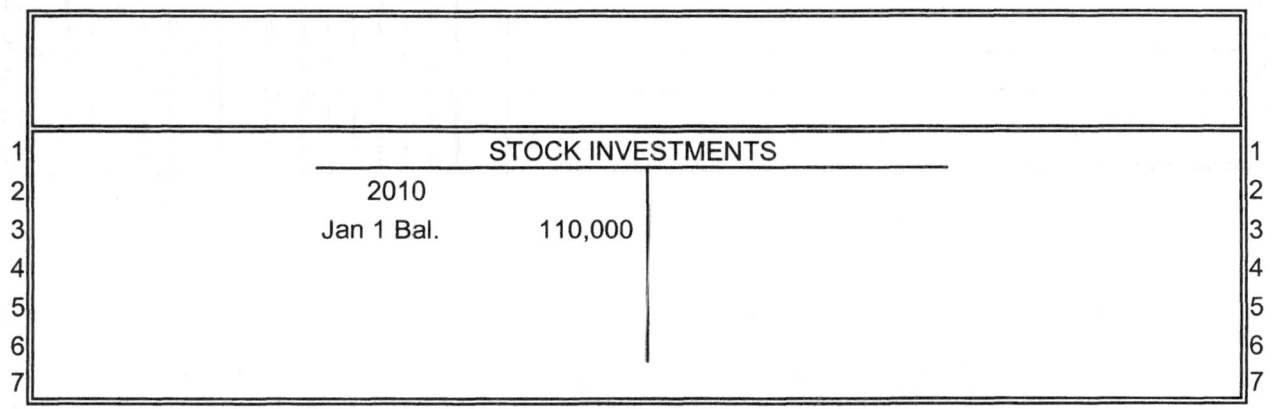

STOCK INVESTMENTS

2010	
Jan 1 Bal.	110,000

(b)

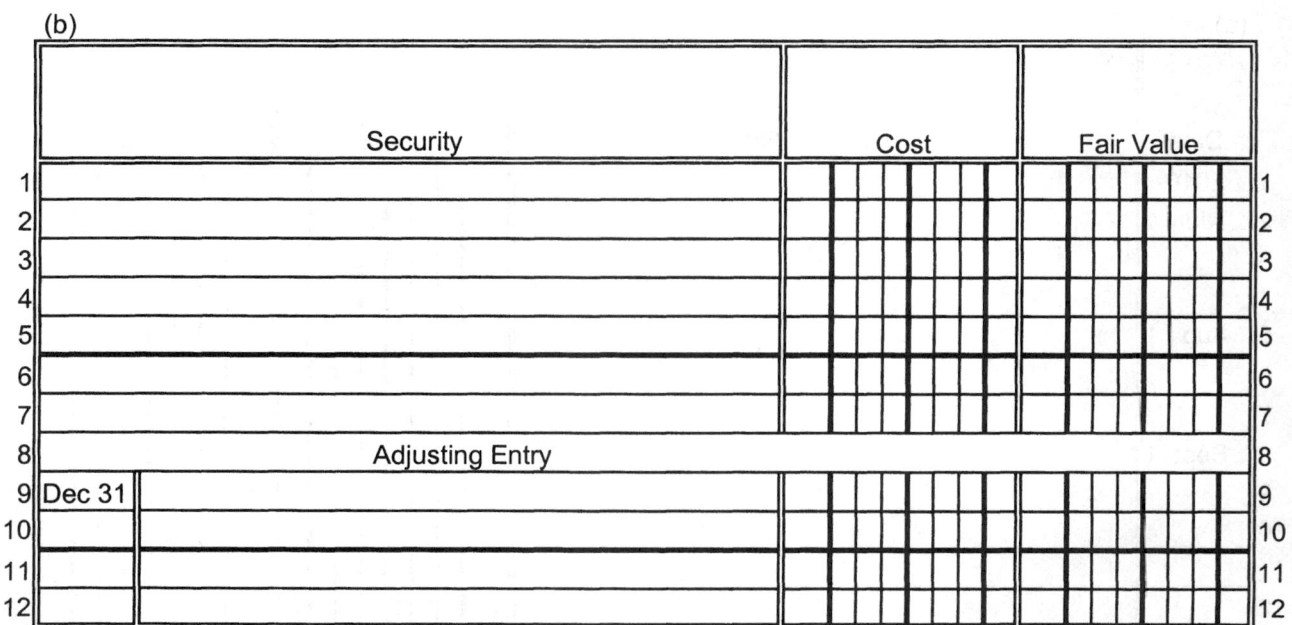

Security	Cost	Fair Value
1		
2		
3		
4		
5		
6		
7		

	Adjusting Entry		
Dec 31			

(c)

RICH ASSOCIATES
Partial Balance Sheet
December 31, 2010

Assets		
1		
2		
3		
4		
5		
6		
Liabilities and Stockholders' Equity		
8		
9		
10		
11		
12		
13		
14		
15		

Cost Method

	Date	Account Titles	Debit	Credit	
1	(a)	2010			1
2	Jan 1				2
3					3
4					4
5	June 30				5
6					6
7					7
8	Dec 31				8
9					9
10					10
11					11
12					12
13					13
14					14

Equity Method

	Date	Account Titles	Debit	Credit	
1	(b)	2010			1
2	Jan 1				2
3					3
4					4
5	June 30				5
6					6
7					7
8	Dec 31				8
9					9
10					10
11	31				11
12					12
13					13
14					14
15					15
16					16
17					17
18					18
19					19
20					20
21					21

(c)

		Cost Method	Equity Method
21			
22			

(a)

	Date	Account Titles	Debit	Credit	
1	Jan 20				1
2					2
3					3
4					4
5	28				5
6					6
7					7
8	30				8
9					9
10					10
11	Feb 8				11
12					12
13					13
14	18				14
15					15
16					16
17					17
18	July 30				18
19					19
20					20
21	Sept 6				21
22					22
23					23
24					24
25	Dec 1				25
26					26
27					27

(b)

1	INVESTMENT IN LUDWICK INC.			1
2	COMMON STOCK			2
3	1/1 Bal.	52,000		3
4				4
5				5
6				6
7	INVESTMENT IN B. HUNT			7
8	COMMON STOCK			8
9	1/1 Bal.	84,000		9
10				10
11				11

(b) (Continued)

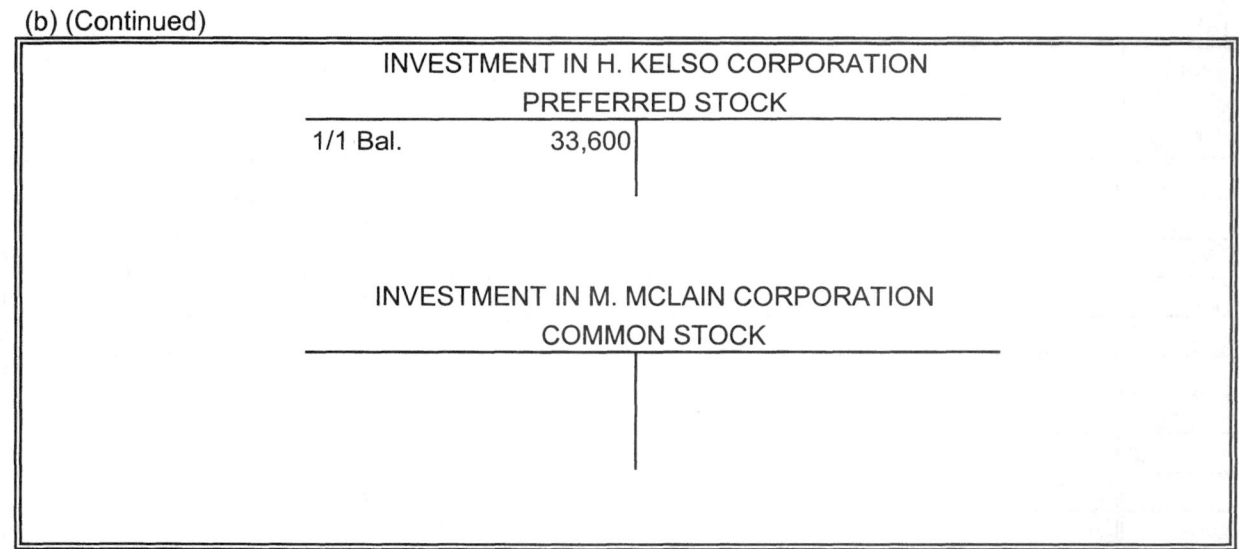

INVESTMENT IN H. KELSO CORPORATION
PREFERRED STOCK

1/1 Bal.   33,600

INVESTMENT IN M. MCLAIN CORPORATION
COMMON STOCK

(c)

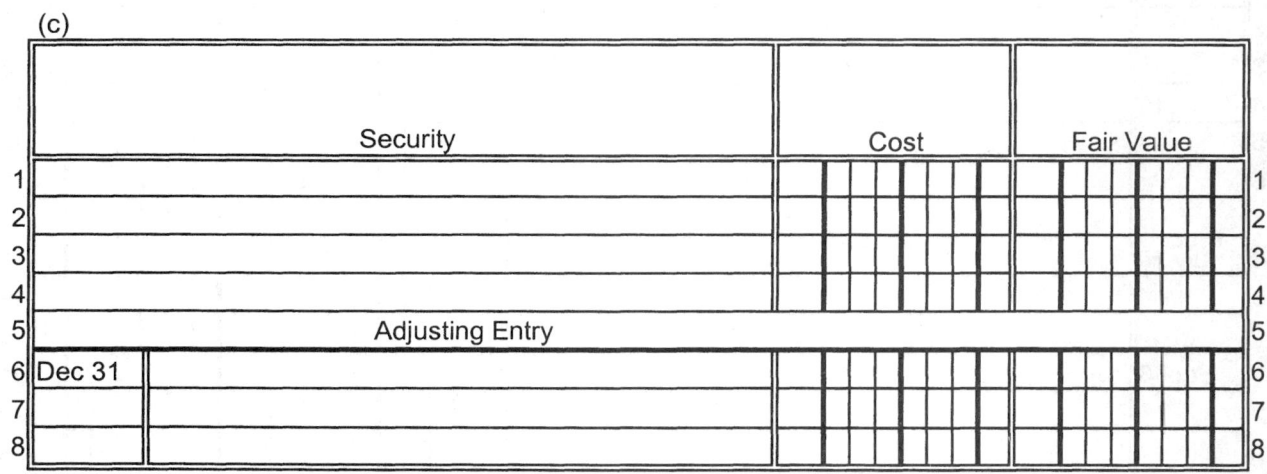

	Security	Cost	Fair Value	
1				1
2				2
3				3
4				4
5	Adjusting Entry			5
6	Dec 31			6
7				7
8				8

(d)

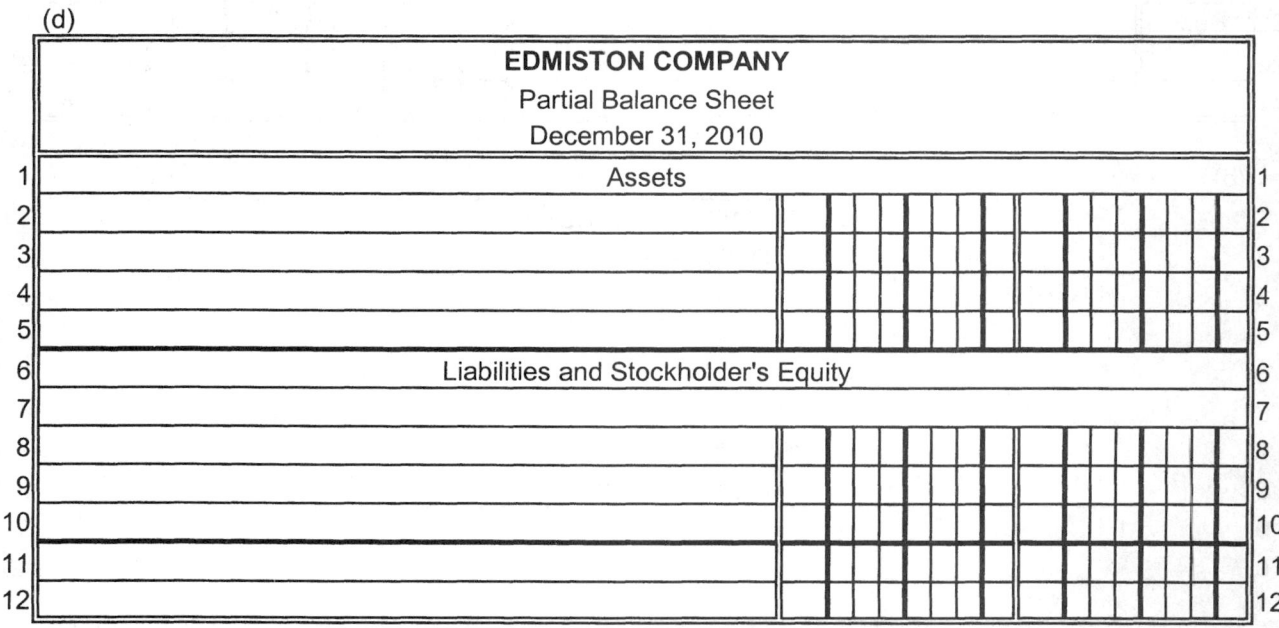

EDMISTON COMPANY
Partial Balance Sheet
December 31, 2010

1	Assets		1
2			2
3			3
4			4
5			5
6	Liabilities and Stockholder's Equity		6
7			7
8			8
9			9
10			10
11			11
12			12

RITTER CORPORATION
Balance Sheet
December 31, 2010

	Assets																
1																	1
2																	2
3																	3
4																	4
5																	5
6																	6
7																	7
8																	8
9																	9
10																	10
11																	11
12																	12
13																	13
14																	14
15																	15
16																	16
17																	17
18																	18
19																	19
20																	20
21																	21
22																	22
23																	23
24																	24
25																	25
26																	26
27																	27
28																	28
29																	29
30																	30
31																	31
32																	32
33																	33
34																	34
35																	35
36																	36
37																	37
38																	38
39																	39
40																	40

RITTER CORPORATION								
Balance Sheet (continued)								
December 31, 2010								
Liabilities and Stockholders' Equity